The Quiet Hand of God

The Quiet Hand of God

Faith-Based Activism and the
Public Role of Mainline Protestantism

Edited by

ROBERT WUTHNOW *and* JOHN H. EVANS

University of California Press

BERKELEY   LOS ANGELES   LONDON

University of California Press
Berkeley and Los Angeles, California

University of California Press, Ltd.
London, England

Portions of chapter 5 were published in *Doing Good in American Communities* (Hartford: Hartford Institute for Religious Research, 2001), available at www.hirr.hartsem.edu; other portions of this chapter were published in "Still Gathering after All These Years: Congregations in U.S. Cities," in *Religion's Role in American Urban Life* (Andrew Walsh, ed., Hartford: Greenburg Center for the Study of Religion in Public Life, 2001).

Library of Congress Cataloging-in-Publication Data

The quiet hand of God : faith-based activism and the public role of
mainline Protestantism / edited by Robert Wuthnow and John H. Evans.
   p. cm.
  Includes bibliographical references and index.
  ISBN 0-520-23312-3 (cloth : alk. paper). —
ISBN 0-520-233313-1 (paper : alk. paper)
    1. Church and state—United States. 2. Protestantism—United States.
3. Religion and politics—United States. I. Wuthnow, Robert. II.
Evans, John Hyde, 1965–.
BR516.Q4 2002
261.8'0973—dc21   2002000713

Manufactured in the United States of America
10 09 08 07 06 05 04 03
10 9 8 7 6 5 4 3 2 1

The paper used in this publication meets the minimum requirements of
ANSI/NISO Z39.48–1992 (R 1997) *(Permanence of Paper).*

Contents

Tables and Figures

Tables

Figures

Acknowledgments

In 1998 the Religion Division of the Pew Charitable Trusts of Philadelphia, under the guidance of Director Luis E. Lugo, initiated a series of projects called Religious Communities and the Public Square, the aim of which was to further both the understanding and the effectiveness of religion's role in strengthening and preserving civic life in America. The Public Role of Mainline Protestantism project was one of seven three-year projects funded under this initiative; the others focused on African American Protestantism, American Judaism, evangelical Protestantism, Roman Catholicism, Muslims in America, and Hispanic Christians. Administered by Princeton University's Center for the Study of Religion, the Public Role of Mainline Protestantism project sought to examine the ways in which the six largest mainline denominations (American Baptist Churches in the USA, Episcopal Church, Evangelical Lutheran Church in America, Presbyterian Church USA, United Church of Christ, and United Methodist Church) had been active since 1970 in attempting to influence public discussion of collective values and involvement in social issues.

The chapters for this volume were commissioned in fall 1998 in consultation with a Liaison and Advisory Committee, which consisted of Thom White Wolf Fassett, general secretary of the General Board of Church and Society, United Methodist Church; Thomas Hart, interim director of Government Relations, Episcopal Church; Elenora Giddings Ivory, director of the Washington Office, Presbyterian Church (USA); Curtis Ramsey Lewis, director of Legislative Advocacy, Office of Government Relations, American Baptist Churches; Steve Miller, Just Peace coordinator and Hunger Action director, United Church of Christ; Jay Lintner, director, Washington Office, United Church of Christ; James Nash, Churches' Center for Theology and Public Policy, Wesley Theological Seminary; Albert

Pennybacker, director, Washington Office, National Council of the Churches of Christ in the USA; Russell O. Siler, director, Lutheran Office of Government Affairs; and James Wind, president of the Alban Institute. Two kinds of chapters were commissioned: chapters that provided information about the various traditions, organizations, and activities of mainline churches, and chapters that examined specific issues in which mainline denominations have been actively engaged. We thought of the two kinds of chapters as complementing each other, the one providing a broad view of who the mainline is and what it tries to do, the other focusing on how these resources were deployed. Among the former, we were able to draw on other studies then under way to learn more about mainline congregations and their partnerships with community agencies, in addition to conducting original research of our own. Over the next year and a half, we interviewed denominational staff members in Washington and elsewhere, interviewed approximately 150 clergy and laity, and collected a large amount of material from denominational archives, the National Council of Churches, and several other organizations. We commissioned a survey of Presbyterian clergy, elders, and laity, which was conducted by the Research Office of the Presbyterian Church (USA) as part of its ongoing survey, the Presbyterian Panel. We also conducted a nationally representative survey of the U.S. population through Princeton University's Survey Research Center.

During the research process, the researchers at Princeton University met regularly to discuss methodology, common issues, preliminary findings, and outlines of chapters. Drafts of some of the chapters were presented at the Religion and Culture Workshop and at meetings of several academic societies. All of the researchers met for a conference at Princeton University in June 2000 to discuss first drafts of chapters and strategies for integrating the chapters. Each chapter received commentary by two discussants, and each chapter was reviewed by two anonymous peer reviewers. Representatives of the research team also met periodically with the Liaison and Advisory Committee. One meeting of the Liaison and Advisory Committee included religion writers for the nation's leading newspapers and news periodicals who contributed insights about the mainline's efforts to gain publicity for its programs; another meeting included policymakers and representatives of research organizations who provided advice on the mainline's programs.

In cooperation with the Aspen Institute, a national leadership conference was held in March 2001 at which selected church leaders, clergy, and laity discussed the results of the research project and focused on ways to develop and implement recommendations based on the research. James Wind of the Alban Institute prepared a summary of the research findings that was presented at the conference and distributed as a separate report.

Special thanks go to the members of the Liaison and Advisory Committee, both for their assistance in guiding the project and for their willingness to be interviewed on more than one occasion about their activities and work. David Devlin-Foltz of the Aspen Institute, with the assistance of Anni Taussig-Gilliam and Tracey Totten, directed all the Washington-based aspects of the project, including the Liaison and Advisory Committee meetings and the national leadership conference. At Princeton, Anita Kline handled all the administrative tasks associated with the project, including budgetary matters, conference planning, and coordination of schedules. At the Pew Charitable Trusts, Luis E. Lugo and Kimon Sargeant gave generously of their time to attend meetings and provide constructive advice on the project at critical steps in its development. Marilyn Marks of Princeton's Office of Communication and Barbara Beck of the Pew Charitable Trusts assisted in publicizing results of the survey. Natalie Searl assisted with the transcription of interviews, and Conrad Hackett helped with library research. The editors also gratefully acknowledge the support provided by the Pew Charitable Trusts through its grant to Princeton University and its contribution toward the production costs of this book.

So many others contributed at various points that to mention some is to risk overlooking others; nevertheless, grateful acknowledgment is especially due to Kenneth Briggs, Diane Winston, Audrey Chapman, Mike Cromartie, Cynthia Eller, David Saperstein, and John Dart.

It was a particular privilege to work collaboratively with the scholars who contributed chapters to the volume. The Princeton-based researchers, who dubbed themselves PROMPT (Public Role of Mainline Protestantism Team), included Wendy Cadge, John Evans, Marie Griffith, Michael Moody, Laura Olson, Lynn Robinson, Brian Steensland, Brad Verter, Brad Wilcox, and Robert Wuthnow. Their efforts to keep the project on track and to offer assistance to one another represent contributions well beyond those evident in their individual chapters. Robert Wuthnow was the project director, and John Evans the assistant director. Peter Thuesen, Mark Chaves, Nancy Ammerman, Jeff Manza, Clem Brooks, Derek Davis, and Lester Kurtz all proved to be wonderful colleagues whose insights and careful research contributed immensely to the project.

Introduction

Since 1970, the United States has experienced a large number of social developments that have brought religion face to face with government and with the wider community in often unanticipated and sometimes conflictive ways. These developments include the mobilization of religious forces on the abortion issue following *Roe v. Wade* in 1973; Jimmy Carter's successful bid for the presidency as an avowed, born-again, evangelical Christian in 1976; the escalation of tensions between the United States and Iran following the rise to power of militant Islamic leader Ayatollah Khomeni in 1978; the emergence of the Moral Majority under the leadership of the Reverend Jerry Falwell in 1980; Pat Robertson's 1988 bid for the presidency and subsequent formation of the Christian Coalition; the 1993 conflict between the Department of Justice and the Branch Davidian compound near Waco, Texas; and new legislation and White House initiatives that permit churches and other faith-based organizations to play a more active role in public welfare and social service provision. All of these developments make it abundantly clear that religion is here to stay—not only in the hearts and minds of individual Americans but in the public life of our nation and world.[1]

But the juxtaposition of religion and public life poses difficult questions, not the least of which concern changing understandings of separation between church and state. Forged from two centuries of religious conflict in Europe, the U.S. Constitution guarantees freedom to practice religion without fear of reprisal or repression by the agents of government, but in return promises government autonomy from direct intervention by religion as well. Recent efforts on the part of religious groups to influence the electoral process or to gain the passage of legislation favorable to their own views of morality have thus been regarded with concern by many in re-

1

ligion and politics alike. At the same time, religion is also regarded as a source of personal and public morality that is essential to the preservation of democracy. Not only is there a close relationship in American culture between conceptions of conscience and understandings of citizenship; there is also a well-established tradition of grassroots participation in public life through the activities of local churches and synagogues. Thus, while concerns are evident about the appropriate uses of religious belief and practice in the public life of the nation, most leaders are reluctant to argue that religion should be less publicly involved than it is; indeed, evidence of weakening in institutional religion is more likely to be regarded as an indication of possible decline in the strength of civil society itself.[2]

Discussions of the public role of religion invariably emphasize the divisions among religious groups. Protestant evangelicals receive a great deal of attention in the media and among scholars of religion because of the national influence of some of their leaders. In comparison, mainline Protestantism is discussed far less often. Despite the large numbers of Americans who still affiliate with mainline churches, and despite the historic importance of these churches, their activities and the ways in which they seek to influence public policy are poorly understood.

This volume aims to enhance our understanding of the public role of mainline Protestantism and to encourage reflection among mainline Protestant leaders, academics, and concerned members of the wider public about how to engage more effectively in the important challenges that face our nation at the start of the twenty-first century. Our focus is the period from 1970 to the present (although we also provide a longer historical view of the activities leading up to this period). We begin with the 1970s because a considerable amount has already been written about the political role of mainline Protestantism in the 1960s, including the civil rights movement and the so-called new breed of activist clergy. That work provides a valuable background for the present volume. Beginning in 1970 means taking a relative high point of mainline activity as a starting point: clergy activism was still prominent, especially in the protests against the Vietnam War and to some extent in the black power movement. The question is: What happened after that? And what potential does mainline Protestantism hold for being more effective in the future?

WHAT WE MEAN BY *PUBLIC*

Nearly everything churches do is public: their worship services are open to the public, their buildings are usually marked by distinctive architecture and insignia that make them a public witness, and even the religious behavior of church members is often public (e.g., when neighbors see people leaving for church or hear them talking about church activities).[3] But these ways of being public are typically unintended—the by-products of being embedded in the surrounding society. We are more interested in this volume in what mainline churches do intentionally to shape the society, its values, and its behavior. Intentionality involves planning, coordination, activity, and an expenditure of resources; it means trying to influence how people vote, or what corporations do, or how well needy families are served.

To speak of churches playing a public role is thus broader than to talk about religion and politics. Sometimes church leaders run for public office or launch movements that threaten to unseat incumbents unless they vote differently. Mainline churches certainly have tried to influence public life in these ways. But public influence is often channeled through other means than the political process. It takes such forms as holding meetings at which controversial social issues are discussed, working cooperatively with non-profit organizations in one's community, formulating shareholder resolutions to be presented to corporation boards, and challenging members to keep informed about important current events.

We are especially interested in activities that are directed toward audiences or groups external to local congregations, such as the wider community and policymakers. The internal and external publics of churches sometimes overlap: discussions of social issues that take place among church members may then influence how they think, vote, and behave toward others; family programs benefit members as well as neighbors and church visitors; food banks welcome both needy members and nonmembers alike. We consider these activities, but our main concern is with the ways in which mainline churches influence the wider society.

When we say "churches," we include the several levels at which church life in the United States is organized. At one level, churches consist of individual members who act on their own behalf, but whose behavior may reflect the fact that they belong to churches and hold certain religious beliefs. At another level, churches consist of local congregations that function as corporate entities. Congregations sponsor programs for the wider community and bring people together to hear sermons or listen to guest speakers talk about social issues. At yet another level, churches are represented by offices and agencies that span several congregations, a region, or the entire nation. These offices and agencies include local clergy councils, regional judicatories (such as presbyteries and dioceses), and special offices sponsored by whole denominations. One kind of agency that is of particular interest in the present context are the Washington offices that mainline denominations sponsor to make their positions known to national policymakers.

MAINLINE PROTESTANTISM

We have chosen to concentrate most of our attention on the six largest mainline Protestant denominations. These are the United Methodist Church (UMC), which currently numbers approximately 8.5 million members; the Evangelical Lutheran Church in America (ELCA), with approximately 5.2 million members; the Presbyterian Church (USA), or PCUSA, with 2.6 million members; the Episcopal Church, with 2.5 million members; the American Baptist Churches in the USA, with 1.5 million members; and the United Church of Christ (UCC), also with approximately 1.5 million members. Our choice of these six was determined largely by the need to be able to work with a limited number of denominational leaders and to conduct research intensively in several denominational archives. The 22 million members of these denominations make up the vast majority of American mainline Protestants. What we leave out of consideration are smaller denominations such as the Disciples of Christ and Reformed Church in America, although in several of the chapters that draw on survey data members of these denominations are also included.

While the six denominations have distinct theological traditions and governmental structures (and thus provide for some interesting comparisons), they have much in common as well. As Peter Thuesen's historical chapter shows, they followed somewhat similar trajectories during the last half of the nineteenth century and early years of the twentieth century, developing national denominational structures and identifying increasingly with progressive social issues. During the last half of the twentieth century, these denominations took an active part in ecumenical discussions that resulted in mergers within several of the confessional traditions represented (especially among Lutherans and to a lesser extent among Presbyterians and Methodists) and pastoral or conciliar agreements permitting closer cooperation across major traditions. These denominations were active supporters of the Federal Council of Churches and later of the National Council of Churches, earning a reputation as public- or civic-minded churches because of their emphasis on social action, and sometimes being opposed by other organizations (such as the National Association of Evangelicals) who regarded them as too progressive or liberal.

We recognize that "mainline" includes a certain irony, given the fact that these denominations comprise less than a tenth of the American population and that even among Protestants, more than half belong to other denominations. The justification for this rubric is sufficiently precarious to avoid taking it too seriously. "Historically old-line Protestant" is perhaps better in some respects, although the backward-looking connotation of this phrase is unfortunate. And, while some scholars prefer "mainstream" to "mainline," the subtlety of this distinction has escaped us.[4] In the end, we believe it is clear enough to talk about a well-defined set of denominations as having certain public elements in common, while recognizing that considerable diversity exists even among these denominations.

THE QUESTION OF DECLINE

So much has been written about the declining membership of mainline denominations that it was virtually impossible to avoid framing the present volume in relation to this literature. But we sought to avoid formulating our research as a quest to find out why the mainline's influence was waning. Indeed, there are several reasons to be skeptical toward the declensionist view of mainline Protestantism. One is that our impressions are now shaped by the mass media to such an extent that we need to be cautious of nearly all generalizations about American religion. Journalists try hard to write accurately and objectively, but necessarily focus on conflict, contention, and novelty. They find evangelicalism flashy and assume it is growing, leaving the impression (if only by default) that mainline influence is declining. Another is that allegations of decline serve polemical functions in religious circles, just as stories of growth do. That which declines must be wrong, while that which grows must be right. Yet it is necessary to separate polemics from reality. Still another reason is simply that decline is by no means the whole story: even where resources are diminishing, they may be considerable, and decline itself does not happen evenly in all organizations or at all times.

Table Int.1 presents selected membership figures for the six mainline denominations under consideration.[5] We include figures from 1947 to indicate the considerable growth these denominations (except for American Baptists) experienced through the 1950s and early 1960s. The peak year for most of these denominations was 1965, after which membership declined steadily (especially during the 1970s) until at least 1990. During this twenty-five-year period, the Episcopal Church, Presbyterian Church

Table Int.1. Inclusive Membership of Six Mainline Denominations

	1947	1965	1990	1998	Annual Change (%) 1965–1990	Annual Change (%) 1990–1998
American Baptist Churches	1,592,349	1,559,103	1,535,971	1,503,267	−.059	−.266
Episcopal Church	2,155,514	3,429,153	2,446,050	2,505,000	−1.147	+.301
Evangelical Lutheran Church in America	3,607,473	5,684,298	5,240,739	5,190,489	−.312	−.119
Presbyterian Church (USA)	2,969,382	4,254,460	2,847,437	2,609,191	−1.323	−1.046
United Church of Christ	1,835,853	2,070,413	1,599,212	1,472,213	−.910	−.993
United Methodist Church	9,135,248	11,067,497	8,904,824	8,456,986	−.782	−.629
Total mainline membership	21,295,819	28,064,924	22,574,233	21,737,146	−.783	−.463

(USA), and United Church of Christ lost approximately a quarter of their members, while the other denominations suffered smaller losses. The trouble was mostly a demographic problem to which members of mainline denominations were particularly susceptible: being better educated and more upscale economically, mainline members married later, had fewer children, and waited longer to have them.[6] As a result, there were simply fewer young people to populate the pews as time went on. In addition, mainline churches sometimes did a poor job of keeping their youth because these young people had opportunities to explore spiritual alternatives and were encouraged to do so. But the table also shows that mainline decline in the 1990s was considerably more gradual than during the previous quarter century. In four of the six denominations, the annualized rate of change during the 1990s showed less decline than during the earlier period.

Of course the population of the United States grew significantly during the last half of the twentieth century, and if this growth is taken into account, mainline churches clearly commanded the loyalties of a shrinking proportion of the population. But it is also important to consider how mainline members *perceive* their churches. Indeed, perceptions may be more important than reality. If people *feel* their churches are declining, they may sense their influence in the society slipping away. But when we asked mainline members nationally if their churches were declining, we found that perceptions were more optimistic than pessimistic. Nearly half (48 percent) said membership at their own church had been increasing in the past few years, while only 14 percent said it had been decreasing (34 percent said it was holding steady). Moreover, most of those who did sense their church declining were concentrated in small congregations. For instance, among mainliners attending churches with fewer than two hundred members, 22 percent thought their congregations were declining, whereas among those in churches with five hundred to a thousand members, 59 percent said their congregations were growing.[7]

In short, many more mainliners think their churches are growing than think they are declining—a perception that does not exactly correspond with the fact that mainline memberships nationally (according to denominational reports) are *not* growing. One explanation for this discrepancy may be that *attendance* is growing (leading people to think their churches are expanding), a trend that does seem to characterize many mainline congregations. The more likely explanation is probably that churches make more to do about people joining than leaving—giving the impression that things may be better than they really are.

Whatever the reasons, the notion that mainliners suffer from self-doubt inspired by the lack of growth in their numbers seems unwarranted. It is equally unwarranted to say that mainliners think their *public influence* is diminishing. When asked to compare the public influence of their denomination now with its influence in the 1960s, only a quarter (24 percent) thought it was weaker now. A third (33 percent) thought it was stronger now, and another third (30 percent) thought it was about the same now as then.

THE QUESTION OF CONFLICT

Another issue that seems synonymous with the mainline in journalistic and academic writing is internal conflict over social issues. While the highly democratic nature of mainline denominations seems to ensure conflict, thus giving perceptions of conflict a factual basis, it also appears that conflict may be the only mainline phenomena noticed by journalists, who require a dramatic story. The arrest of delegates to the annual meeting of the Presbyterian Church (USA) while protesting the stance of the denomination on homosexuality fits journalistic standards of news better than a story of the Presbyterian congregation in the same town that might be feeding the hungry.[8]

It is true that the mainline is polarized at a national policy level over a number of social issues such as homosexuality and abortion. For example, studies have shown that the mainline has become increasingly polarized over abortion since 1972, which has limited its ability to maintain a publicly unified voice on this issue.[9] The chapter by Wendy Cadge in this volume describes conflict over policies toward homosexuals in great detail. While conflict remains a primary theme in academic and journalistic accounts of the mainline, we have attempted to steer clear of this formulation as well. What has become lost from view in the writing about polarized issues are the myriad issues that the mainline is nearly in total consensus about—such as helping the poor—which are central components of mainline activity in the public sphere. While polarization and conflict inevitably are raised in many of the chapters, we treat them as a part of the reality of pluralistic, democratic Protestant denominations.

MAINLINE BELIEF

The members of mainline churches overwhelmingly ascribe to the basic beliefs of Christianity. More than nine in ten (92 percent) believe the Bible is the inspired word of God, almost this many (88 percent) believe that

God has been fully revealed to humans in Jesus Christ, and about eight in ten (79 percent) agree that Christianity is the best way to understand God (table Int.2).

At the same time, mainliners largely reject some of the tenets that came to be emphasized by Protestant fundamentalists early in the twentieth century; for instance, only about a quarter of mainline members (28 percent) think everything in the Bible should be taken literally, word for word; in contrast, nearly two-thirds (63 percent) say the Bible may contain historical or scientific errors.

Mainline denominations have encouraged members to respect historic church teachings, as well as the Bible, but also to use reason and personal experience to interpret these teachings. These multiple ways of knowing God are evident in the way mainline members respond to survey questions. Approximately eight members in ten (79 percent) agree that church teachings are the best way we have of relating to God. But a majority (55 percent) also agree that religious doctrines get in the way of truly relating to God—a view that may reflect concerns emphasized in mainline ecumenical efforts about the divisiveness of specific doctrines. Like many other Americans, a large minority of mainline members also appears to favor experiential as opposed to intellectual religious approaches (agreeing that people must empty their minds and look inside themselves to know God).

What Peter Thuesen refers to in his chapter on the history of mainline Protestantism as its emphasis on "universalism" is also evident in members' current beliefs. While strongly affirming the distinctiveness and value of Christianity, mainline members are largely open to the idea that truth can be found in other religions. Indeed, eight in ten (81 percent) think all religions contain some truth about God, and seven in ten (70 percent) agree that all religions are equally good ways of knowing about God. Thuesen's argument that mainline teachings emphasize the universal relevance and availability of divine grace is helpful for interpreting these responses. In talking at greater length about their beliefs, mainline members often emphasize both the value of proclaiming the good news of the gospel and the need to avoid trying to convert members of other religions. Mainline members sometimes argue that God calls all people to the love and hope that is most clearly revealed in the life and teachings of Jesus.

But mainline members characteristically understand that their congregations and denominations are places in which people with quite different theological views can come together for worship and service. When asked to describe their own religious views, about a quarter (22 percent) of mainline members classify themselves as religious conservatives, another quar-

Table Int.2. Religious Beliefs of Mainline Members

Belief	Response (%)
The Bible is the inspired word of God (true).	92
Everything in the Bible should be taken literally, word for word (true).	28
The Bible may contain historical or scientific errors (true).	63
God has been fully revealed to humans in Jesus Christ (agree).	88
Christianity is the best way to understand God (agree).	79
Church teachings are the best way we have of relating to God (agree).	79
All religions contain some truth about God (agree).	81
All religions are equally good ways of knowing about God (agree).	70
God can only be known as people empty their minds and look inside themselves (agree).	67
Religious doctrines get in the way of truly relating to God (agree).	55
God is a mystery and can never be understood by humans (agree).	44
Where would you place yourself in terms of your religious views?	
Conservative	22
Moderate	51
Liberal	26
How important has it been to you as an adult to grow in your spiritual life?	
Extremely important or very important	79

ter (26 percent) say they are religious liberals, and the majority (51 percent) place themselves in the middle. What unites them is the nearly universal belief that spiritual growth is important. Indeed, approximately eight members in ten (79 percent) say that growth in their spiritual life is extremely important or very important.

SOCIAL PROFILE OF MAINLINE MEMBERS

In many respects, the members of mainline denominations do not differ in social composition from other Americans. They are spread across all regions of the United States, include people of all ages and races, and are quite diverse in levels of education and occupations. When mainline clergy are asked to give a social profile of their congregations, this diversity comes immediately to their minds. They are reluctant to reinforce popular stereotypes of mainline churches as bastions of WASP (white Anglo-Saxon Protestant) respectability or privilege. Yet research on mainline members suggests that these stereotypes are not altogether false and that the social characteristics of mainline members are indeed relevant for understanding the public role of mainline Protestantism.

Mainline members are, in the first place, distributed across all age groups, but are older than a random cross section of the population. Only one mainline member in eight is in his or her late teens or twenties, and fewer than a third of mainline adults are under the age of forty (see table Int.3). In comparison, one in five is in his or her seventies or eighties, and a third are past the age of 60. Thus, the average age of adult mainline members is 52, compared to 46 in the adult population at large.

Because they are older on average, mainline members are more likely to be married or widowed and less likely than in the general population to have never been married (factors that become important in understanding mainline policies toward family issues, as Brad Wilcox shows in his chapter). Mainline members are more likely to be women than one would expect if they simply reflected the gender distribution in the wider population, a pattern that is evident in other religious traditions as well. But the percentage of mainline members who are, as stereotypes suggest, white Anglos is greater than in the general population or in other religious traditions. Because racial minorities tend to be concentrated in large cities, it is also not surprising that mainline members are underrepresented in these cities, while they are overrepresented in small towns and rural areas.

What is most distinctive about mainline members is the extent to which they are drawn from better-educated segments of the middle class. It is important to remember that not all mainline members are college educated; indeed, nearly four in ten have never attended college. Yet, 35 percent of mainline members have either graduated from college or attained a postgraduate degree, compared to only 24 percent of the general population. Moreover, among those who are currently employed, nearly half (49 percent) of mainline members are professionals, managers, or owners of businesses, compared to only 26 percent of the labor force in the general population.

The higher levels of educational attainment and upscale occupations of mainline members are relevant to any consideration of the ways in which

Table Int.3. Social Profile of Mainline Members

Characteristic	Mainline Members in Specified Category (%)
Age	
18–29	12
30–39	17
40–49	19
50–59	17
60–69	13
70 and over	19
Marital status	
Married	62
Never married	16
Separated/divorced	10
Widowed	12
Gender	
Male	42
Female	58
Ethnicity	
White	91
Black	7
Other	2
Residential Context	
Large city	16
Suburb	20
Small town	37
Rural	26
Education	
Grade school only	10
High school diploma	29
Some college	26
College degree	21
Postgraduate degree	14
Occupation	
Professional/managerial	49
Other white collar	33
Laborer	18
Social connections	
Have elite friends[a]	66
Do not have elite friends	34

[a]Public officials, corporate executives, scientists, or wealthy friends.

mainline Protestants exercise influence in the wider society. Some of this influence occurs simply through the networks to which mainline members are connected. For instance, when asked if they had any close personal friends who were public officials, corporation executives, scientists, or wealthy individuals, two-thirds of mainline members (66 percent) said they did, compared with only 42 percent in the general population. The other potential resource that mainline Protestants have at their disposal is lay leaders with high levels of education or positions of influence in the wider community. Thus, among the quarter (28 percent) of mainline members who said they currently occupied a leadership position in their congregations, 59 percent of those with jobs were employed as professionals or managers, 72 percent had at least some college education, and 72 percent claimed to be close personal friends with a public official, corporation executive, scientist, or wealthy individual.

MAINLINE RESOURCES

Although their declining memberships have undoubtedly made it harder for some mainline churches to exercise influence in their communities, the resources at the disposal of mainline denominations are considerable. Most significant of these resources are the 75,000 local congregations that are formally affiliated with the six largest mainline denominations. Each year, approximately 4 million sermons are preached by the 72,000 clergy assigned to these congregations and, on occasion, by some of the additional 50,000 mainline clergy who serve in more specialized capacities.[10] In addition, the 53 seminaries affiliated with the six mainline denominations have 1,120 faculty training 16,236 students.[11] The United Methodist Church, which accounts for more than a third of all mainline membership, is an instructive case. On an average Sunday, approximately 3.4 million Americans attend some 36,000 Methodist churches. About 1.7 million people attend a Sunday school class at these churches or are among the half million church school leaders. And they will be ministered to by nearly 37,000 pastors serving these congregations.

Besides its members and pastors, one of the mainline's most important resources is the amount of money it receives through pledges, offerings, and other donations. In 1997 the congregations of the six mainline denominations raised and spent over $11 billion, more than the annual expenditures of the state of Colorado and substantially more than the $6.6 billion Americans spent on admissions to movie theaters in the same year.[12] While most of this money went to the support of clergy and the maintenance of church buildings, it contributed in a larger sense to the mainline's capacity to influence the values and lives of its members and the society in which they live. Thus, it is interesting to compare this amount with the $500 million spent by political action committees during the two-year 1997–98 election cycle—a mere 2 percent of what Americans were contributing to mainline churches during the same period.[13]

Apart from cash donations, mainline churches also benefit from having accumulated sizable assets ranging from buildings and land to investments and pension funds. Currently, the property of the congregations in the six mainline denominations is valued at roughly $63.5 billion.[14] Many churches, of course, struggle to maintain their buildings and pay off mortgages, yet the mainline denominations have historically included large churches located in the hearts of major cities—churches that have sometimes acquired substantial holdings. For instance, Trinity Episcopal Church in New York, once the owner of much of what is today lower Manhattan, currently owns twenty-seven commercial buildings with space totaling approximately six million square feet, making it one of the largest commercial landlords in New York City.[15] In addition to such relatively nonliquid assets, mainline congregations hold roughly $7.6 billion in cash, securities, and other properties.[16] Mainline seminaries have a combined endowment of over $2.7 billion.[17] And the six mainline denominations have approximately $32 billion in pension funds.[18]

The financial status of mainline denominations, like their membership, has diminished in recent years, leaving members and clergy open to concerns about how well they will be able to support programs in the future. Per capita giving in mainline churches is generally smaller than in evangelical denominations and has declined as a percentage of personal income in recent years. Recommendations about larger budgets for national offices, denominational lobbyists, or expanded social programs generally find little support, especially at a time when mainline congregations expend a declining share of local budgets for the support of denomination-wide activities. Nevertheless, the potential for mainline denominations to use their financial base to influence public life remains considerable.

This influence depends in no small measure on the *cultural* resources of the mainline churches, not just their assets and donations. These resources consist above all of the depth of understanding and commitment to the Christian gospel that is evident in mainline beliefs and teachings. While mainline churches are often criticized by fundamentalists who deplore the apparent relativism of mainline teachings, mainline congregations provide a haven for American Christians who value striving for balance between faith and reason, creeds and experience, and intellect and emotion.

THE PUBLIC ACTIVITIES OF MAINLINE CHURCHES

Popular impressions of the ways in which religion influences public life often focus on highly visible leaders, such as the Reverend Jerry Falwell, Pat Robertson, Billy Graham, or the pope. Alternatively, it is easy to assume that religion's influence takes place mostly through the work of local clergy or the informal activities of church members. One of the main conclusions from the research presented here is that neither of these images is adequate. Mainline Protestants are well organized through their denominations, including countless committees, presbyteries and other judicatories, clergy councils, and bureaus. Yet this kind of formal organization also fails to capture the complexity of the ways in which mainline influence is exercised.

At the top, the most active efforts to influence public policy are organized by the denominations' Washington offices. None of the six is amply staffed (and all function on meager budgets), but they maintain a vocal presence on Capitol Hill, meeting with Congressional leaders and executive branch representatives to bring church positions to bear on such varied topics as environmental legislation, First Amendment issues, and international debt relief. The Washington offices operate under the mandate of their denominations' nationally elected bodies, addressing issues that have been approved by these bodies, but also working with communication directors and church educators to keep clergy and laity informed of impending legislation. As Laura Olson's chapter shows, the effectiveness of the Washington offices depends partly on cultivating networks of interested clergy who can be mobilized on appropriate occasions. The Washington offices often work closely with each other and with other pressure groups and nonprofit organizations.

At the local level, congregations are the front lines of mainline efforts to live out the gospel in their communities. Much of this work is performed by clergy who act both as private citizens and on behalf of their churches. Mainline clergy overwhelmingly feel it is appropriate to engage directly in political activities, such as showing up at planning board meetings or lobbying town councils for better youth programs. They also address social issues from the pulpit, although endorsing political candidates clearly strikes them as inappropriate. Besides delivering sermons, clergy frequently help to arrange special forums, Sunday School classes, or seminars at which social issues are discussed. Congregations are thus places in which civic gatherings take place, often in ways that bring religious values to bear on public issues.

Congregations also routinely engage in activities that go well beyond discussing public issues. Most mainline congregations mobilize volunteers to help at soup kitchens, homeless shelters, day care centers, and tutoring programs. As Mark Chaves and his coauthors show from their National Congregations Study (chapter 4), mainline congregations are more likely than other Protestant congregations or Catholic parishes to sponsor service programs and to make space available for community organizations, cultural events, and self-help groups. Increasingly, mainline congregations also work cooperatively with other organizations. As Nancy Ammerman's research demonstrates (chapter 5), mainline congregations are closely tied to complex networks of secular and faith-based nonprofit organizations.

Both historically and at present, women's organizations have played a critical role in linking the local activities of congregations with regional, national, and international concerns. Marie Griffith's chapter discusses how these organizations have developed alongside clergy structures, how they have mobilized lay women, and how their focus has shifted with the ordination of women and expanding opportunities for women to serve through careers in the professions. At present, mainline women's organizations face significant challenges, partly because of ambiguous roles in relation to feminism and partly because of limitations imposed by denominational hierarchies.

The linkages from local congregations to Washington offices or other national-level church bodies are often weak, perhaps reflecting a larger tendency in the society to focus on local issues and to retreat from national politics. Members of mainline churches typically do not know that their denominations have offices in the nation's capital, and many doubt that it is important to exercise influence at this level. In between, church efforts at the state or metropolitan level are often weak as well, especially in relation to the growing importance of governmental decisions at these levels.

Nevertheless, mainline churches have found ways to have a significant and continuing influence on a number of issues. Racial justice has been emphasized by most mainline leaders, many of whom look back with nostalgia on the ways in which mainline clergy became actively involved in the civil rights movement; some of this memory is, as Brad Verter's chapter shows, little more than nostalgia, resulting in few serious efforts by mainline churches in more recent decades to listen to and work alongside the leaders of African American churches. Yet mainline commitment to racial justice provides the principles around which such cooperation might still be developed. Social welfare policy is another area in which mainline churches have tried to be advocates on behalf of the disadvantaged and, as Brian Steensland discusses (chapter 8), has led mainline leaders in recent years to seek more creative ways in which to work with government and private agencies. Other issues provide interesting comparisons: environmental justice has been an issue in which mainline churches have played a notable role, although few in the wider public are aware of it; the same is true of efforts to pressure corporations into taking their social roles more seriously. In contrast, debates about homosexuality show how mainline churches sometimes contribute to public discussion by providing places for genuine disagreements to be voiced, while support for marriage and children has been an instance where mainline action has been better than its rhetoric.

How effective mainline churches have been on these issues is difficult to assess, just as it is difficult to assess how much of an impact watching television or reading the *New York Times* has on people's approach to broad public issues. Unlike the leaders of conservative, evangelical Protestant movements, mainline churches seldom take an absolute stand on single issues (such as abortion) that become a kind of litmus test for being or not being a legitimate Christian; instead, mainline churches focus on keeping a number of issues on the front burner (and a number of others simmering on back burners), fostering debate even when members and the wider public disagree on specific strategies and programs.

SUSTAINING AND ENLARGING MAINLINE INFLUENCE

Mainline Protestants can no longer speak for America in the way they sought to do throughout much of the nation's history. Their voice is now one of many—a voice that often blends quietly with those of other religions and confessional traditions, rather than speaking from a distinctive or unique perspective. Those who decry the weakness of mainline Protestantism can point to its diminished membership and finances, its failure to mount effective media campaigns on behalf of its programs, and the relative absence of nationally visible mainline clergy who can promote issues or run for public office. Yet the strength of mainline influence is less appropriately measured in these ways than in the less showy, behind-the-scenes activities that take place in congregations, faith-based service agencies, clergy councils, special-purpose groups, and denominational offices.

At present, there is widespread public interest in many of the issues that mainline leaders have been trying to facilitate. A large majority of the American public claims to be interested in social policies to help the poor, in legislation to protect the environment, and in achieving racial reconciliation and racial justice. Americans are justifiably leery of religious leaders who become too actively involved in partisan politics. Yet the public is more interested in bringing the resources of religious communities to bear on social needs than previous studies have sometimes suggested. Most Americans would like religious groups to play a more active role in alleviating such problems as poverty, pollution, discrimination, and indifference.

But if mainline Protestants are going to sustain or enlarge their efforts to promote racial justice, environmental protection, human rights, and the dozens of other activities in which they wish to be involved, they must do some serious reflecting on how best to make use of limited resources. Bureaucracies have a way of ossifying, resulting in inefficiency and ineffectiveness. Mainline churches are sometimes hindered by their bureaucracies and by the very traditions these bureaucracies represent. Reflection and evaluation must take place both in the national offices of the mainline denominations and among the leaders of local congregations.

One of the first orders of business for such reflection and evaluation is to recognize the distinctive strengths of mainline Protestantism. It is a diverse tradition that includes denominational structures and teachings that have stood the tests of time. Its members are committed to the principles of Christianity but have largely learned to live in a pluralistic world that requires respect for other faiths and other religions. Although its members tend to be among the more privileged segments of American society, their faith encourages them to respond with compassion to the injustices that so visibly characterize the human condition.

Reflection and evaluation should take into account that mainline memberships and finances have declined, rather than dwelling only on the signs of vitality that may be apparent in scattered locations. But mainline leaders, as well as the public at large, should acknowledge the considerable resources that are still available within mainline churches. These resources are sufficient to draw millions of Americans into lives of service to their churches and to the wider community. Mainline clergy account for hundreds of thousands of hours devoted each year to community programs, and the agencies and offices operated by mainline denominations function actively at all levels of American public life. Mainline members are mostly optimistic about their churches' ability to play a positive role in the spiritual and material well-being of our society. Some leaders suggest that mainline churches might do well to celebrate the many areas of social life in which effective contributions have been made—a suggestion that corresponds well with the liturgical and commemorative roles that are so much a part of what it means to be the church.

At the local level, mainline congregations are as varied as American society itself, including struggling parishes, richly endowed churches, meeting houses populated by the elderly, those bursting at the seams with young families, and virtually everything in between. Mainline churches have adapted well to the more complex environments in which they now exist, especially to the greater roles in local communities of government agencies, nonprofit organizations, and faith-based coalitions. During the next two decades, many smaller congregations may cease to exist, while larger churches will take an even more prominent place in the religious landscape. These larger congregations will be able to mount a wider variety of social programs than smaller churches have sponsored in the past. The so-called megachurch will follow models developed by independent evangelical churches, emphasizing pastoral entrepreneurship and functions for the entire family. But mainline churches will probably benefit by continuing to work in cooperation with other community organizations. Increasingly, the model of church life becomes that of a network, or referral system, where exchanging ideas and information works to the advantage of all.

With the clergy and laity focusing so much attention at the local level, it is difficult to imagine that national offices will continue as important sources of mainline influence in public affairs. Yet the evidence presented in this volume suggests that these offices do play an important role—one that can probably be strengthened if denominational leaders are willing to acknowledge it and support it. Consider the fact that the United Methodist Church devotes only seventeen one-hundredths of 1 percent of the funds it receives through individual donations to the support of its General Board of Church and Society.[19] Or consider the fact that the Evangelical Lutheran Church in America spends approximately two-tenths of 1 percent of its revenues on its entire Church and Society operation.[20] The Washington office gets a smaller fraction of this small fraction—little wonder, then, that the staff of these offices believe the main limitation on their effectiveness is lack of support.

Were more funding provided to Washington offices and other church-wide agencies, denominational officials would also be encouraged to undertake a thorough evaluation of these offices and agencies. Our research was not oriented toward making such an evaluation; yet it was evident that denominational offices (not unlike many administrative structures) have been governed by precedent, by piecemeal innovations, and often by adjusting to the pressing demands of the moment. With new technology for communicating electronically and with (in many cases) sparser budgets and smaller staffs, a review of what has been effective and what needs to be deleted or restructured would be of enormous value.

One of the ways in which mainline denominations can contribute to the well-being of civil society more broadly is through the wisdom their leaders have accumulated about running organizations (in the Presbyterian phrase) "decently and in order." Reverend Eugene Rivers, pastor of Azuza Community Church and founder of Boston's highly successful Ten Point Program, which uses faith communities to combat violence and drugs among inner-city youth, suggests that African American churches too often falter by depending too much on charismatic leaders and that they could benefit by sitting down with mainline leaders to learn about governance structures, democratic procedures, and methods of delegating responsibility.[21] The same might be suggested about white evangelical churches, some of which have grown rapidly in recent years as a result of entrepreneurial leadership, yet face longer-term problems because these leaders exercise almost dictatorial control over church decisions and budgets.[22] The administrative procedures of the mainline churches have evolved in most cases over a period of more than three hundred years and account for much of their stability as well as episodes of significant growth (such as that experienced by Methodism in the nineteenth century). While mainline leaders sometimes complain that their administrative structures are top-heavy and burdensome, these same structures are used by many of the nation's major corporations and often resemble the legislative systems of democratic governments. They function well to draw people into decision-making capacities, to give voice to and resolve significant controversial issues, and to coordinate activities that extend beyond the local level.

Whether or not mainline Protestants can maintain and enlarge their influence in partisan electoral politics seems at best doubtful. But the evidence presented here corrects several popular misperceptions—and candidates' handlers and party leaders risk perpetuating these misperceptions at their own peril. Mainline Protestants have not, on the whole, moved from the political center to the political left; instead, they have moved from the political right to the political center. This shift has two important consequences: evangelical Protestants who continue to support the causes of the far right and the conservative wing of the Republican party are increasingly marginalizing themselves from the mainstream of American Christianity. The Religious Right has been able, with the help of well-meaning journalists, to capture a significant share of the spotlight in Republican politics in recent elections; however, it is not clear that the Republican party has benefited from this involvement, nor is it evident that Republican leaders have actively pursued many of the Religious Right's interests. Meanwhile, mainline Protestants make up a substantial share of Republican voters: even though their numbers have declined since the 1960s, they continue to vote Republican as often as (if not more than) Democratic. They represent an important and involved constituency for moderate Republicans, especially pro-choice Republicans. At the same time, mainline Protestants also make up a large minority of Democratic voters and, compared to earlier decades when Catholics and southern Protestants could ensure Democratic victories, Democratic candidates can scarcely ignore the interests of mainline Protestants. None of this suggests that mainline influence is likely to increase, but it does indicate the continuing importance of mainline voters.

The continuing influence of mainline Protestants is also evident when hotly contested political issues are considered. In the electorate as a whole, support for strict pro-life legislation has diminished, support for gay and lesbian civil rights has increased, and widespread support exists for policies that promote environmental protection, efforts to reduce racial inequality, and programs to help the poor. All of these are issues that a majority of mainline Protestants have supported. It seems unlikely that this support will erode in the near future.

But mainline Protestants cannot retain a distinctive voice in public life if they merely follow popular sentiments that happen to be moving in a liberal or progressive direction. The mainline churches are, after all, *churches*, not political interest groups, or think tanks, or science advisory panels. To the extent that they can work cooperatively with other organizations, they are likely to expand their influence. Yet their leaders also underscore the importance of speaking in Christian language and with Christian conviction. For mainliners, this does not mean proclaiming themselves to be the exclusive mouthpieces of God or selectively citing Bible verses to show why one manifestation of evil is so much worse than others. It means tapping into the deeper truths about love, redemption, reconciliation, and justice that are recurrent themes in biblical tradition. Understanding these truths and finding ways to put them into practice requires the church above all to function as a church—preaching and teaching, gathering for worship, praying, and serving. When that happens, influencing public values for the good does not always or necessarily follow. But without it, public influence is destined to falter.

NOTES

1. José Casanova, *Public Religion in the Modern World* (Chicago: University of Chicago Press, 1994).

2. Robert D. Putnam, *Bowling Alone: The Collapse and Revival of American Community* (New York: Simon & Schuster, 2000).

3. Robert Wuthnow, *Producing the Sacred: An Essay on Public Religion* (Urbana: University of Illinois Press, 1994).

4. Martin Marty, personal communication.

5. The figures in table I.1 are from Milton J. Coalter, John M. Mulder, and Louis B. Weeks, *Vital Signs: The Promise of Mainstream Protestantism* (Grand Rapids, MI: Eerdmans, 1996), p. 21; and from http://www.adherents.com.

6. Michael Hout, Andrew Greeley, and Melissa J. Wilde, "The Demographic Imperative in Religious Change in the United States," *American Journal of Sociology* 107 (2001): 468–500.

7. These survey figures and those reported in subsequent sections are from the Religion and Politics Survey, a national study conducted for the research project on which this volume is based; for further details, see chapter 15, note 1.

8. Larry B. Stammer, "Pro-Gay Activists Arrested at Presbyterian Convention," *Los Angeles Times*, June 26, 2000, p. B1.

9. On polarization among mainliners, see John H. Evans, "Polarization in Abortion Attitudes in U.S. Religious Traditions, 1972–1998," forthcoming, *Sociological Forum*. On the effect of this polarization on political activity, see John H. Evans, "Multi-Organizational Fields and Social Movement Organization Frame Content: The Religious Pro-Choice Movement," *Sociological Inquiry* 67, no. 4 (1997): 451–69.

10. Eileen W. Lindner, *Yearbook of American and Canadian Churches* (Nashville, TN: Abingdon Press, 1998).

11. Figures compiled from Matthew Zyniewicz and Daniel Aleshire, *Fact Book on Theological Education* (Pittsburgh, PA: Association of Theological Schools, 1999). Faculty are full-time equivalent positions. The actual number of full-time faculty is less. Adding inter-denominational and independent seminaries that generally train mainliners, such as Union Theological in New York City, would significantly increase these figures.

12. Of this amount, $9.4 billion was given for congregational finances and $1.5 billion to benevolences; see Lindner, *Yearbook of American and Canadian Churches*. For example, the UMC spent $3.99 billion in 1997 (*General Minutes of the Annual Conferences of the United Methodist Church* [Evanston, IL: Section of Records and Statistics, United Methodist Church, 1998], p. 29; hereafter cited as *General Minutes*). The Colorado figure is from *The World Almanac and Book of Facts* (New York: World Almanac Books, 1999), p. 114. Additionally, the fifty-three seminaries affiliated with the six mainline denominations spent $344 million

in 1998 training the next generation of leaders for the mainline; see Zyniewicz and Aleshire, *Fact Book on Theological Education*. Adding inter-denominational and independent seminaries that generally train mainliners, such as Union Theological in New York City, would significantly increase these figures.

13. Data on political action committees from the Federal Election Commission. See "PAC Financial Activity" at the following website: www.fec.gov/press/pacsum98.htm.

14. The UMC has $28.2 billion in church land, buildings, and equipment, and another $2.7 billion in parsonages, less $1.7 billion in indebtedness (*General Minutes*, 1998, p. 29). The ELCA has $10.3 billion in similar holdings (Evangelical Lutheran Church in America, *1999 Yearbook* [Minneapolis, MN: Publishing House of the Evangelical Lutheran Church in America], p. 81). The estimate for the entire mainline was made by creating a property per congregation figure for these two denominations and extrapolating it to the rest of the mainline. If anything, this would be an underestimate because, of the six denominations, the UMC and the ELCA are among the most heavily represented in rural areas where values would be low, while denominations for which we lack measures (such as the Episcopal Church and the UCC) tend to have congregations in more urban areas where values would be high.

15. Information about Trinity Church is from http://www.trinitywallstreet.org/looking.html.

16. The congregations in the UMC have $2.9 billion in cash, securities, and other property (*General Minutes*, 1998, p. 29). The congregations in the ELCA have $1.7 billion in other real estate, endowments, cash, and other assets (*1999 Yearbook*, p. 81). We use these two figures to create a per congregation asset figure and then extrapolate it to the remainder of the six denominations, assuming a similar asset level across the denominations. Once again, we expect this to produce a low estimate because the denominations largely thought to have the least massed wealth are used to make the estimate. Other denominations do not collect these figures. One hint of investments in other denominations is that in 1997 the congregations of the PCUSA earned $186 million from their investments (*General Assembly Minutes*, 1997, part 2, "Statistics" [Louisville, KY: Office of General Assembly, PCUSA]).

17. Figures were compiled from Zyniewicz and Aleshire, *Fact Book on Theological Education*. Adding inter-denominational and independent seminaries that generally train mainliners, such as Union Theological in New York City, would significantly increase this figure.

18. In 1998, the UMC Board of Pensions had $12.2 billion in its pension fund. The PCUSA board of pensions has approximately $6 billion in pension funds (interview with Mark Amstutz at the Presbyterian Board of Pensions, July 29, 1999). The Episcopal Church retirement fund has $4.3 billion in assets (*1999 Annual Report* [New York: Church Pension Group, 2000], p. 15). The ABC retirement plan had $2.16 billion in assets in 1998 (*1998 Annual Report* [New York: Ministers and Missionaries Benefit Board of the American Baptist Churches, 1999], p. 6). The United Church of Christ had $2.4 billion in assets in 1998 (*Annual Report, 1998* [New York: Pension Boards of the United Church of Christ], p. 4). The ELCA had $4.8 billion in assets in 1998 (*Annual Report, 1998* [Minneapolis, MN: Board of Pensions of the Evangelical Lutheran Church in America], p. 12.

19. "Some frequently asked questions concerning the general board of church and society," at http://www.umc-gbcs.org/faqgbcs.htm.

20. ELCA, *1999 Yearbook*, p. 21; figures exclude the budget for the world hunger program.

21. Personal communication during a visit to Princeton University, April 25, 2000.

22. Donald E. Miller, *Reinventing American Protestantism: Christianity in the New Millennium* (Berkeley and Los Angeles: University of California Press, 1997); Miller's analysis of Calvary Chapel, Vineyard, and Hope Chapel points to some of these concerns.

Part I

HISTORY, ORGANIZATION, AND ACTIVITIES

1 The Logic of Mainline Churchliness

Historical Background since the Reformation

Peter J. Thuesen

In his classic study, *The Social Sources of Denominationalism* (1929), H. Richard Niebuhr denounced the "denominational self-consciousness and inertia" that had frustrated a united ethical witness in American Christianity. The theological differences among Christian groups, he believed, tended to obscure the social origins of denominationalism in modern prejudices of race, class, politics, and nation. Denominationalism thwarted the churches' public role as heralds of God's kingdom, preoccupying Christians instead with the "spurious differences of provincial loyalties." Niebuhr gave voice to the deep-seated Protestant fear that religious institutions inevitably cool the fires of evangelical zeal, extinguishing the impulse to reform the larger society by succumbing to the "self-interest and the machinery of denominationalism."[1]

Yet one of the great paradoxes of American religious history is the perennial confidence among Protestants, especially mainline church leaders, in the reforming power of denominational institutions. This recurring faith in institutional structures runs contrary to Protestantism's genetic code, which tends to elevate the individual and Scripture as the primary loci of reform. Despite their ideological inheritance from the Reformation, mainline Protestants over the course of American history have adopted an increasingly institutional model of social activism—what I shall call the logic of mainline churchliness—characterized by three main features: a reasonable tolerance of ethical differences, a thoroughgoing commitment to ecumenical cooperation, and an all-embracing conception of the church's public role. This logic, which resembles secular progressivism while also sharing a Catholic commitment to universality, evolved in the course of successive historical transformations, including the Reformation, the Enlightenment, the American Revolution, the American Civil War, and the advent of modern bureaucratic capitalism. In this chapter, I shall provide a broad historical overview of how these successive events contributed to the liberal institutional logic so familiar to the mainline churches' supporters and critics today.

THE REFORMATION BACKGROUND

In sixteenth-century Europe, the modern notion of the church's "public" role (as distinguished from its "private" spiritual functions) had little or no meaning. Ever since the time of Constantine, politics and religion had been virtually indistinguishable, and the leading sixteenth-century reformers did not seek to destroy the Constantinian synthesis. In this respect, the Reformation was a premodern event. Significantly, the Reformation was also premodern in its readings of Scripture: the biblical narrative was generally assumed to be continuous with the drama of late-medieval daily life as one seamless web of truth. Religious skepticism, though present to some degree in all ages, lacked the modern scientific valences familiar in discourse today.

In its practical effects, however, the Reformation began the irreversible transition to modernity. Three closely interrelated effects are particularly important for later American life. First, the Reformation led to an enduring Protestant suspicion of ecclesiastical authority. Although Luther, and in the next generation Calvin, retained an emphasis on the special functions of ministers, the reformers' theologies provided new justification for the exercise of lay authority. Luther, in particular, spoke of the "priesthood of all believers" and rejected the notion that clergy belonged to a hierarchical caste with an indelible priestly character.

Second, and closely related, the Reformation enthroned the individual as the final judge of religious authenticity. Despite Protestantism's emphasis on "Scripture alone" (sola scriptura) as the new rule of faith and practice, the Bible never exerted its authority in sociological isolation. Because Scripture still had to be read and interpreted, the individual Protestant—and individual Protestant sects—always occupied a place of primacy over Holy Writ. The advent of printing and the introduction of new vernacular versions of Scripture lessened the importance of ecclesiastical intermediaries between the individual and God's Word, thus granting the individual unprecedented autonomy in the quest for authentic religious experience. Although a more modern notion of the self would not emerge until the seventeenth and eighteenth centuries, the Protestant sola scriptura, reinforced by the idea of the priesthood of all believers, would contribute a great deal to the proverbial individualism of later American religion.[2]

Third, the Reformation contributed to the modern emphasis on textual evidence in religion. The Reformation's *sola scriptura* drew much of its impetus from another slogan, *ad fontes* (to the sources), which was the byword of Renaissance humanism. Humanists placed great value on classical antiquity—the Greek and Latin sources of Western culture—and brought new sophistication to the study of these texts. When appropriated by Protestants, the humanist emphasis on authentic documents from antiquity encouraged the rise of iconoclasm, especially among Calvinists. The words of Scripture became the only source of religious truth, while images, music, and drama (most notably, the Eucharistic drama of transubstantiation) were rejected as idolatrous. This preoccupation with the Word would not only profoundly shape American Protestant culture but would also contribute to serious division among Protestants over the Bible's implications for ethical and social questions.

The Reformation's effects, then, were far-reaching in the New World. The most influential bearers of the magisterial Reformation tradition in colonial America were the New England Puritans, but other groups also made their mark, including Dutch Calvinists and Lutherans in New Netherland (later New York), Scottish Presbyterians in New Jersey and Pennsylvania, and Anglicans in Virginia and the Carolinas. Though all of these original settlers shared a sixteenth-century heritage, one should not assume a monolithic picture of colonial Protestantism. Like their European forebears, the various colonial Protestants often differed sharply on questions of theology and ritual. Moreover, "orthodox" piety always coexisted with both widespread religious indifference and a variety of "unorthodox" beliefs and practices.[3]

This popular religious diversity, which thrived on the notion of a priesthood of all believers, periodically provoked the coercive authority of the clerical elite, who attempted to bring the churches in line with their own conceptions of orthodoxy. Since the civil and religious arms were united or closely linked in many of the colonies, the clergy possessed considerable power to legislate both morality and theology. The Puritan "city upon a hill" had been founded on a strict covenantal Calvinism, a system based on the Old Testament idea of a contract between God and the nation. As interpreted by the clergy, this contract demanded genuine conversion as evidenced by good works. Yet such legalism sometimes prompted challenges from the laity, as in the celebrated "Antinomian" crisis of 1636–38, when Anne Hutchinson was banished from Massachusetts Bay for accusing leading ministers of preaching a "covenant of works." Periodic revivals also prompted debate among clergy and lay people over the problem of authority in the churches and in the wider civic realm. In New England, at least, this debate over authority would eventually come to a head in the period known as the Great Awakening.

THE EIGHTEENTH CENTURY:
REASON, REVIVAL, AND REVOLUTION

Meanwhile in Europe, the traditions of the Reformation were feeling the effects of the Enlightenment, a diffuse intellectual movement that shared with Protestant iconoclasm a suspicion of ecclesiastical authority. Developing simultaneously on the Continent and in England, the Enlightenment elevated human reason over the dictates of inherited orthodoxy. Taken to its logical conclusion, this led to deism, but in its more moderate forms, the Enlightenment produced a "reasonable" style of Christianity that enjoyed great popularity among clergy in the Church of England after the Restoration in 1660. By the eighteenth century, many American divines had also been converted to its tenets, which included an "Arminian" confidence in human freedom, a distaste for conflicts over polity and doctrine, and an emphasis on morality as religion's chief end. This broad-minded, ecumenical spirit—called "catholick" by its contemporaries—won converts even among some New England Congregationalists, who joined their Anglican brethren in speaking of God as the "Supreme Architect," of the visible universe as "stupendous" and "sublime," and of religion as a matter of "essential truths."[4]

This cultural milieu is important for understanding the outbreak of the Great Awakening in the 1730s and 1740s. Though the revivals have often been viewed as the seedbed of republican ideology during the later American Revolution, their origin, at least, was theologically conservative: an effort to recover traditional Calvinism in an age of enlightened rationalism.[5] The most famous revivalist, George Whitefield, differed from old-style Calvinists in preaching the necessity of immediate conversion, but he was a traditionalist in hammering home the themes of human depravity and predestination. Whitefield's more intellectual contemporary, Jonathan Edwards, also emphasized traditional Calvinist themes, as in his dramatic debut in Boston in 1731, when he preached a sermon on God's absolute sovereignty and humanity's complete dependence. Within a few years of this opening salvo against the "Arminians," Edwards was leading his

Northampton, Massachusetts, congregation in the revivals that would constitute a prelude to Whitefield's preaching tour in 1739–41.

As pro-revival and anti-revival ministers battled for the upper hand, the revivals were awakening among the laity a new spiritual self-reliance that would become one of the hallmarks of modern American evangelicalism and would contribute to the proliferation of Protestant denominations. Already by 1760, as one scholar has estimated, the pluralism of American religion had no equal in any single European society.[6] The revivals also reignited old debates over church and state as conservatives in the colonial assemblies enacted laws designed to restore ecclesiastical order. In Connecticut, for example, the assembly passed the Act for Regulating Abuses and Correcting Disorders in Ecclesiastical Affairs (1742), which banned itinerant evangelism. Ironically, opponents of the measure drew on Enlightenment thought, particularly the natural rights theories of Locke, in a plea for liberty of conscience and religious tolerance. "Conscience" thus began to rival the old Puritan "covenant" as a central theme in both religion and politics.[7] This rhetoric of freedom of conscience increasingly united both pro-revival and anti-revival ministers as they preached against the "tyranny" of kings, popes, and priests during the French and Indian War, and soon thereafter, during the war for American independence from the British crown.[8]

The paradox of Protestant ministers—the elites of institutional religion—preaching against the tyranny of elites underscores the ambiguities of the American Revolution for the churches. On the one hand, the war with England seemed to bode ill for institutional Protestantism by hastening the demise of the state church system, which had subsidized the churches through taxation. Never uniform throughout British America, the system had provided at one time for a single establishment (the Church of England) in five southern colonies: Virginia, Maryland, North Carolina, South Carolina, and Georgia. Four colonies (New York, Massachusetts, Connecticut, and New Hampshire) had multiple establishments in the eighteenth century, though the Congregational "standing order" operated as a powerful de facto establishment in all but New York. Meanwhile, four colonies with greater religious diversity (Rhode Island, Pennsylvania, Delaware, and New Jersey) had no establishments.[9] At the federal level, the original Constitution of 1787 was silent on the issue, but the First Amendment (ratified as part of the Bill of Rights in 1791) stipulated that "Congress shall make no law respecting an establishment of religion, or prohibiting the free exercise thereof." The amendment did not require the immediate abolition of existing state establishments, though in the South this had already proven a political necessity for the discredited Church of England after 1776. Full disestablishment elsewhere would occur in the coming decades, with Massachusetts being the last to disengage state and church in 1833.

Yet the official disestablishment of religion did not weaken the "establishment" mentality of many Protestants, nor did it lead to the replacement of institutional forms of Protestantism with a thousand warring sects. Though religious bodies in the new republic were more like voluntary associations than the all-encompassing church of the medieval past, these voluntary associations soon became powerful institutions in their own right through skillful communication and organization. The "standing orders" of America's founding era relinquished little of their former role as guardians of the commonweal; their authority was now simply mediated through private institutions. And many of these institutions were built through large-scale private benevolence, which was uncommon before 1800.[10] From inside and outside the denominations emerged a variety of new religious entities, including reform societies, colleges, seminaries, and newspapers. The dominant Protestant groups, especially Methodists, Baptists, Presbyterians, and Congregationalists, exercised cultural authority through these institutions, but also through time-tested methods such as revivalism. This great flurry of voluntary activity effectively made evangelicalism—a movement with different social and political concerns than its twentieth-century successor—the official religion of the antebellum republic. Within the evangelical empire, individual denominations were, as Martin Marty has observed, like price-fixers who united to protect themselves from outsiders.[11] The identity of these "outsiders" would vary over time, and the encounter with them would reshape evangelicalism itself in important ways.

THE BENEVOLENT EMPIRE AND ANTEBELLUM REFORM

The first "outsiders" to challenge evangelical Protestantism in the new nation were a familiar foe: the deists. Through most of the eighteenth century, outright deism had threatened mainly from the pages of arid philosophical treatises imported from England. Then in 1789, two years after the signing of the U.S. Constitution, deism (and its more radical cousin, atheism) burst anew onto the world stage in the French Revolution. In the ironic political developments of the previous two decades, France, America's onetime enemy, had become an ally against the British. Consequently, Americans at first looked with favor upon the rise of republicanism in France and the overthrow of the "papist" clergy. American clergymen praised the French cause from their pulpits—until deism and anticlericalism began to threaten at home. The specter of "French" infidelity was most evident in Thomas Paine's *Age of Reason* (1794–95), penned while he was imprisoned in Paris, which broke publishing records on both sides of the Atlantic. Written in the engaging style of a popular tract, this work declared Paine's belief in "one God, and no more" and mocked the absurdity of such biblical stories as the Resurrection, which had "every mark of fraud and imposition stamped upon the face of it."[12] Deism of a more decorous sort was common among the framers of the American republic, but their most unorthodox views were not widely discussed until religion became a political issue in the 1800 presidential election, when opponents of Thomas Jefferson branded him an "atheist."[13] Jefferson survived politically, but radical deism, save for a brief revival in the Jacksonian era, was successfully banished by evangelicals from the public sphere.[14]

The widespread public association of deism with immorality was ironic, since for Jefferson and other deists, morality was the very essence of enlightened religion. Yet in the wake of the evangelical battle with deism, moral reflection grounded chiefly in human reason was rejected in favor of moral reflection grounded chiefly in divine revelation. Or so the evangelicals thought. In reality, evangelicalism during the past century had gradually internalized the vocabulary of the eighteenth-century Age of Reason. Whereas faith for premodern Protestants had tended to be a matter of assenting to a creed, stressing belief rather than actual knowledge, faith in the wake of the Enlightenment tended to be grounded on rock-hard epistemological certainties about the unambiguity and historical accuracy of the biblical account. Both premodern and modern Protestants justified their dogmatic and ethical assertions with Scripture, but by the early nineteenth century, Holy Writ operated less as a set of narrative and linguistic parameters than as a sourcebook of religious "facts."[15]

This marriage of reason and evangelicalism had significant consequences for the public role of the churches. Ethical reflection and practice were increasingly grounded in an optimistic religious positivism, which posited that regeneration was simply a matter of biblical evidence and common sense.[16] From this ideology emerged a vast network of reform societies, including the American Bible Society, founded in 1816, which repeatedly conducted "General Supply" campaigns designed to place a copy of Holy Writ in every American home.[17] In the following decade, other large reform societies were founded in rapid succession, including the American Sunday School Union (1824), the American Tract Society (1825), and the American Home Missionary Society (1826).[18] This "benevolent empire" unleashed a deluge of printed literature: Bibles, to be sure, but also tracts devoted to the elimination of such sins as cursing, drinking, dueling, gambling, and profaning the Sabbath. Though these vices were often associated with the deists, the religiously indifferent (whose ranks had always been far more numerous) became the new targets of moral reform.[19]

The battle against everyday vices was fueled by a great sense of postmillennial expectation—a feeling that God's kingdom really would be realized through human effort in the course of American destiny. Earlier evangelicals, imbued with a Calvinist sense of the inscrutability of God's designs, had been more cautious about America's millennial role. As historian Henry F. May has put it, "Destiny, for [Jonathan] Edwards, was never really Manifest."[20] But by the early nineteenth century, evangelicals were seeking—as well as finding—assurance of both personal and national salvation. "Arminianism," the old bugbear of Puritans, increasingly eclipsed old Calvinism during the nineteenth century as many Americans confidently proclaimed the possibility of Christian perfection.[21]

Millennial and perfectionist fervor were closely tied to an antebellum resurgence of revivalism. The first great wave of revivals in the new republic, enveloping all regions of the country between the 1780s and 1830s, would be dubbed by historians the "Second Great Awakening." In this crucible, Methodism, especially in the South, grew exponentially from its modest formal beginnings in 1784. Baptists adopted many of the Methodists' techniques, especially the rapid organization of small societies, and by the 1830s, the two denominations had taken center stage among American Protestants.[22] Revivalism also occurred among the New England Congregationalists, who now were commonly espousing an "Arminianized Calvinism" that closely resembled the voluntaristic theology of the Methodists and Baptists.[23] The most dramatic success for Arminianized Calvinism came in 1830–31, when Charles Grandison Finney preached for six months in Rochester, New York, converting a largely unchurched middle class to evangelicalism.[24]

Meanwhile, the Second Great Awakening also helped give birth to "outsider" traditions such as Mormonism, which threatened establishment Protestants' visions of an evangelical America. But the outsiders who would pose the greatest threat by far to evangelical Protestant hegemony were the Catholics. In 1776, Catholics had constituted roughly 1 percent of the American population, but by 1850, an influx of Irish and other European immigrants had made the Catholic Church the largest single American denomination.[25] Besides igniting nativist violence, Catholicism's meteoric rise proved a major impetus to ecumenical cooperation among Protestants, who sought a united front against Rome. Representatives from more than fifty Protestant groups met in London in 1846 to found the Evangelical Alliance, which prefigured in some respects twentieth-century ecumenical entities such as the National Council of Churches. Though the original organization eventually faltered amid internal divisions, a reincarnated Evangelical Alliance was formed in the United States in 1866. Along with smaller ecumenical ventures, the alliance would contribute a great deal to the emergence of a pan-denominational evangelical identity, while also reasserting the claim that Protestantism was the only true religion of the republic.[26]

The formation of the Evangelical Alliance bespoke a subtle but important transformation in mainline Protestant thought. Though the axioms of the Reformation—suspicion of ecclesiastical authority, elevation of the individual, and an emphasis on textual evidence in religion—were still operative in the alliance's vigorous anti-Catholicism, the existence of such organizations revealed Protestants' increasing faith in reform through large-scale institutions. Moreover, the alliance's ecumenism, though not as liberal as twentieth-century church-unity movements, clearly foreshadowed later Protestant conciliarism. We therefore see in mid-nineteenth-century evangelicalism—its institutional, ecumenical agenda coupled with a millennialistic optimism about realizing God's kingdom in this world—an embryonic version of the modern logic of mainline churchliness. What remained to develop was a more modern ethical progressivism; this would gradually emerge in debates over specific social questions as Protestants wrestled with the old problem of biblical interpretation.

DISINTEGRATION OF EMPIRE: EVANGELICAL FRACTURES

In the years leading up to the Civil War, the most salient social questions concerned race and gender. On both issues, the biblical testimony, which was all-important to evangelicals, admitted of conflicting readings, and the resulting rifts over interpretation cut across the spectrum of denominations both inside and outside mainline Protestantism. Behind the conflicts lurked the specter of cultural conformity: that Christianity would cease to be a prophetic voice for justice and reform. Indeed, both nineteenth-century debates had similar overtones of enslavement and emancipation that would reverberate within the mainline churches well into the twentieth century.

The ravages of the color line in modern America, including religious denominations organized by race, stemmed from a slave trade established before the full dawning of modernity. Between the sixteenth and nineteenth centuries, ten to fifteen million enslaved Africans were brought to the Americas by traders from the principal European powers.[27] In the American South, the economic benefits of slavery for the landed aristocracy gave rise to biblical interpretations supporting slaveholding: Noah's prophetic declarations to his sons Shem, Japheth, and Ham in Genesis 9 became an outline of all human history, with Ham's descendants representing the Africans, who had been condemned to perpetual servitude. Many northern Protestants at first proved reluctant to challenge this logic, instead holding out hope for a united evangelical front. Similarly, the status quo in the realm of gender relations exerted a powerful hold over most antebellum Protestants. The flourishing of republican political ideology during the Jeffersonian and Jacksonian eras, with all the emphasis on natural rights and popular sovereignty, did little to ameliorate the legal status of women, who, somewhat like slaves, were propertyless and disenfranchised. Moreover, evangelical Christian notions about a providential hierarchy of sexes and races, when grafted to republicanism, tended to produce a political ideology that centered on the inalienable rights of white males.[28]

The social consequences of evangelicalism, however, were not inevitably conservative. Biblically informed notions about the equality of all people in Christ, along with African Americans' own use of the Exodus motif in challenging slavery, contributed to the birth of a radical reform movement in the 1820s and 30s.[29] The movement's white leaders included journalist William Lloyd Garrison, businessmen Arthur and Lewis Tappan, and revivalist Theodore Dwight Weld, who all hailed from deeply evangelical backgrounds and had begun their reformist careers attacking such lesser social problems as intemperance. Garrison's case is particularly instructive. Influenced early on by prominent preacher Lyman Beecher's preoccupation with irreligion, whiskey, and associated vices, Garrison eventually rejected Beecher's gradualism on slavery—that it was a problem to be solved in God's own time. Garrison concluded that slavery was not only a national sin but *the* national sin—"a gangrene preying upon our vitals"—that would bring death and destruction if not immediately abolished. Though Garrison himself was a pacifist, many evangelicals blamed him for bloody slave revolts such as Nat Turner's rebellion (1831), which further deepened

the fracture between the advocates of immediate and gradual emancipation.[30]

The issue of women's rights was intimately linked to antislavery debates. Women had always been a mainstay of evangelical reform movements, serving both in unofficial capacities and in their own female reform
societies. But when women, including the Quaker sisters Angelina and
Sarah Grimké, began speaking against slavery to "promiscuous" assemblies of both men and women, this upset many evangelicals' sensibilities
regarding proper gender roles in society. Catharine Beecher (daughter of
Lyman) vigorously attacked Angelina Grimké in print for overstepping
the bounds of woman's proper sphere. To Beecher, women were providen-
tially suited to influence society through loving persuasion in the home
rather than through forceful debate in public. The rift over the "woman
question" stymied the abolition movement in the 1830s and 40s, eventually causing a formal schism within the American Anti-Slavery Society.
It also helped engender a more radical women's rights movement symbolized by the 1848 convention at Seneca Falls, New York, convened by
Elizabeth Cady Stanton and Lucretia Mott.[31]

Yet other political exigencies would soon eclipse women's rights for at
least a generation as America careened toward military conflict over slavery. The institutional consequence of the Civil War for American religion
was an unprecedented series of denominational schisms. The first split
occurred in the Presbyterian Church in 1837, when the predominately
southern "Old School" faction (which included the traditionalist theologians at Princeton Seminary) separated from the predominately northern
"New School" (which included a vocal abolitionist wing). A further split
occurred in 1861 when the outbreak of the war forced the Old School's
northern constituency to secede. Schism among the Methodists occurred
in 1844 when the southern conferences withdrew to form the Methodist
Episcopal Church, South. Meanwhile, Baptists, though strictly congregational in polity, participated in the quasi-denominational Baptist Missionary Convention, which split in 1845 into northern and southern organizations. All three of these major denominational schisms would prove
long-lasting. The Methodists were the first to reunite, though nearly a
century later, in 1939. The Presbyterians did not reunite until 1983, and
the Baptist rift persists to this day in the existence of the Southern Baptist
Convention and the American Baptist Churches in the USA.[32]

The Episcopalians and Lutherans avoided full-scale schisms for a variety
of reasons, including a tendency to value sacramentalism over social activism. For the Episcopalians, social status was also a factor, since their ranks

included many prominent and widely respected southerners such as Jefferson Davis and Robert E. Lee. The onset of war did force territorial divisions within the two traditions, but reunions occurred soon after the war. (The Lutheran case was complicated by the persistence of numerous ethnic and regional synods.) Other groups avoided schism for geographic reasons: the Congregationalists and Disciples of Christ as yet lacked truly national church structures, and in addition, the Disciples followed their founder Alexander Campbell in relegating the slavery question to the realm of private conscience.

The Civil War also affected American religion in ways that transcended denominational boundaries. First, the war represented a new chapter in the complex history of Protestant reflection on the millennium and America's national destiny. On the one hand, it seemed to complicate the optimistic "Arminian" evangelicalism of the early republic, as preachers and other public figures reiterated old Puritan themes of divine sovereignty and judgment. President Lincoln, for example, though eschewing belief in a personal God or the incarnation, articulated an essentially Calvinistic civil religion centered on the inscrutable will of an omnipotent Creator. In more conservative Protestant circles, the themes of divine sovereignty and judgment melded naturally with the language of the apocalypse, prompting new speculations, especially during the postwar social and economic upheaval, about an imminent, cataclysmic end to history. At the same time, paradoxically, the death and destruction wrought by the war helped preserve among more liberal Protestants a confidence in the gradual but steady march of human progress. Of symbolic significance was Lincoln himself, who was hailed as a Christlike figure after his assassination on Good Friday, April 15, 1865. The following Sunday, dubbed "Black Easter," he was eulogized across the North as the redeemer president who saved the nation from the sin of slavery. To liberal Protestant observers, Lincoln's own death and the deaths of thousands of soldiers on the fields of battle were not in vain but were part of the orderly march to a millennium of peace and prosperity. Far from being passive observers of an arbitrary divine will, Americans—even through their wars—were playing a central role in inaugurating God's kingdom.[33]

Finally, the Civil War laid bare as never before the instability of the dominant strain of American biblicism: the literal, "commonsense," Reformed hermeneutic, from which Protestants drew such radically opposing conclusions. President Lincoln at his second inaugural gave proverbial expression to the resulting North-South division over slavery: "Both read the same Bible and pray to the same God, and each invokes His aid against the other." The long-term results of this schism in American Protestantism could not have been more momentous. On the one hand, it hastened the rise of twentieth-century-style Protestant liberalism, which tended to relativize biblical texts (such as those supporting slavery) that were not amenable to a progressive ethic. On the other hand, the schism increased anxieties among Protestant conservatives about the waning of biblical authority. This in turn helped give rise to a twentieth-century form of evangelicalism that, quite apart from the slavery question, was intent on proving the "inerrancy" and "infallibility" of the whole Bible and its applicability at all times and in all places.[34]

Liberals, including the nationally known Congregational preacher Henry Ward Beecher, strenuously opposed the notion of an inerrant Bible. In 1871, Beecher delivered the inaugural Lyman Beecher Lectures (named for his father) at Yale, but he went far beyond his father in articulating a liberal view of Scripture. "All that has been evolved in human existence you may find as germ-forms in the Bible," Beecher explained, "but you must not shut yourselves up to those germ-forms, with stupid reverence merely for the literal text of the gospel." Similarly, the Presbyterian Charles Augustus Briggs, professor at Union Theological Seminary in New York, denounced the traditional Protestant assumption that the Bible decides all questions of doctrine and morality. Theology and ethics, he believed, must be "constructed by the induction of divine truth from all spheres of information."[35]

Such ideas did not sit well with the more traditional clergy and laity in the mainline churches. Both Beecher and Briggs were accused of heresy by members of their denominations; Briggs was formally suspended, while Beecher resigned his affiliation under pressure. Meanwhile, prominent conservatives at mainline institutions like Princeton Seminary were taking up their pens to defend Scripture against the liberal assault. Yet in the battle for the soul of the mainline churches, time was on the side of the liberals, whose victory was foreshadowed by developments in a different realm: the world of American higher education.

During the late Victorian era, many Protestant colleges originally founded as nurseries of piety were reconceiving themselves as research universities devoted to the impartial pursuit of knowledge. Meanwhile the nondenominational divinity school, introduced when Harvard Divinity School severed its Unitarian ties in 1880, was emerging as a new center of scholarship in religion. A particularly dramatic split occurred in 1892 when the Presbyterian bastion Union Seminary severed its denominational ties in solidarity with assailed professor Charles Briggs; the school became fully nondenominational twelve years later. Elsewhere many divinity schools and seminaries, though retaining formal denominational ties, were becoming more ecumenical and adopting the scholarly and bureaucratic conventions of secular universities. Both inside and outside the academy, what historian Gerald Graff has called the "cult of expertise" was elevating professional over lay authority and enthroning university professors as arbiters of debates over scriptural exegesis as much as organic chemistry.[36]

Meanwhile, Darwinism, Comtean positivism, and other intellectual currents were contributing to a general reappraisal of traditional teleological accounts of human history. Some of this scholarship was popularized in venues such as the *Woman's Bible* (1895–98), edited by the erstwhile Seneca Falls reformer Elizabeth Cady Stanton and more than two dozen female collaborators. This scriptural commentary went through seven printings in the first six months and prompted a division in the women's movement between evangelicals and those such as Stanton who were willing to dispense with traditional Christianity altogether. Despite this rift, the *Woman's Bible* bespoke a widespread Victorian consensus regarding the ameliorative power of scientific inquiry to reform society. Reinterpreting the biblical parable of the wise and foolish virgins, Stanton praised those wise young women who would fill their lamps with the oil of human knowledge and thus be permitted to celebrate the "marriage feast of science and religion."[37] Though rejecting Stanton's radicalism, many mainline Protestants shared her positive view of science and embraced Darwinian evolution and other modern theories as eminently compatible with Christianity. Indeed, a liberal acceptance of evolution would become one of the hallmarks of mainline Protestantism—especially its leadership—and would go hand in hand with liberal theories of social progress.

Optimism about the advance of American civilization was temporarily interrupted by a nationwide economic depression in 1893. Widespread labor unrest came on the heels of three decades of rapid postbellum industrialization and urbanization. These economic and demographic changes in turn prompted political restructuring, as discontented farmers, fearing that they were being left behind in the new, large-scale, capitalist economy, rallied behind the populist Democrat William Jennings Bryan in the presidential election of 1896. Bryan, who would later represent the anti-evolution forces in the infamous Scopes trial (1925), came to symbolize the fundamentalist Protestant solution to social upheaval: a dogged defense of an inerrant Bible. But it was Republican William McKinley who emerged victorious in the 1896 election. As the historian Henry Adams put it, Americans had for a century vacillated "between two forces, one simply industrial, the other capitalistic, centralizing, and mechanical," and in the 1890s, "the majority at last declared itself, once and for all, in favor of the capitalistic system, with all its necessary machinery."[38]

THE BUREAUCRATIZED MAINLINE, 1900–1960

The transition to a fully modern, centralized, large-scale economy had a paradoxical effect on the mainline churches. The tumult of the 1890s had convinced many liberal Protestants that Christianity's chief end was to reform the present social order, and out of this emerged a new "Social Gospel" bent on curbing capitalism's excesses. Yet the Social Gospel also partook deeply of the bureaucratic ethos of big business and the scientific ethos of the university. As the unofficial theology of mainline church executives, the Social Gospel was thoroughly establishmentarian: its rise paralleled the emergence of religious denominations in their modern form, and its tenets reflected the predilections and prejudices of an emerging managerial class.

The Social Gospel was a diverse movement. Its more conservative wing supported the cause of Prohibition during the 1910s and 1920s (thus harking back to the antebellum Protestant campaigns against vice), while its better-known liberal wing led the fight for reforms such as antitrust legislation and laws against child labor. Apart from the specific reforms it promoted, however, the Social Gospel exhibited certain cultural characteristics that are important for understanding the public role of the mainline churches in the Progressive era—the years spanning the presidencies of Theodore Roosevelt, William Howard Taft, and Woodrow Wilson (1901–1920)—and beyond.

First, the Social Gospel was a gendered phenomenon. Though its proponents included prominent female reformers such as the Unitarian Caroline Bartlett Crane, its theology tended to eschew Victorian sentimentalism in favor of more masculine idiom and imagery. Jesus in this milieu was transformed from a gentle, even effeminate, figure into what the influential theologian Walter Rauschenbusch called "a man's man." Like the weary laborers of America's urban economy, Jesus was a carpenter-reformer who worked with his hands while agitating for justice. Other Social Gospelers such as Shailer Mathews, dean of the University of Chicago Divinity School, borrowed imagery from athletics. Jesus was a team player who worked well with others, as well as a team leader who helped people recognize their common interests and act in concert.[39]

Second, the Social Gospel was a bureaucratic phenomenon. For all their identification with the victims of big business, Social Gospelers were clearly enamored of corporate, bureaucratic models for realizing God's kingdom. In this they reflected a much wider cultural obsession with efficiency during the Progressive era. In 1911, for example, the engineer Frederick W. Taylor published the widely influential *Principles of Scientific Management*, which outlined efficient strategies of time management, task specialization, and authority delegation. Taylor's manifesto was followed in 1912 by Shailer Mathews's *Scientific Management in the Churches*, which embodied trends toward ecclesiastical bureaucratization that had been under way for several decades. Already by the 1870s, many of the reform and mission agencies of antebellum Protestantism had consolidated into larger denominational bureaucracies; by the turn of the century, these structures were being staffed by increasingly specialized personnel working within elaborate tiers of church commissions, including offices dedicated to social reform. The typical executive working in these church offices was more cosmopolitan than the average parish pastor: he had several advanced degrees, had authored at least one book, had traveled a great deal, and was much better paid. Executives spent a great deal of time on education and publicity campaigns, which were premised on Progressive ideas about the infinite educability of the people.[40]

Third, the Social Gospel was an ecumenical phenomenon. Though cooperation with Catholics was still beyond the pale, mainline Protestants forged an important new alliance in 1908 when thirty-three denominations joined in establishing the Federal Council of Churches. At its constituting convention in Philadelphia, the council adopted unanimously the first version of what would be known as the "Social Creed of the Churches," which laid out a broad program of social reforms and effectively made the Social Gospel the official theology of the ecumenical movement. As in the past, the continued growth of Catholicism was a major spur to Protestant ecumenism. Mainline leaders contrasted their own ecumenical openness with Rome's supposed designs on American democratic institutions.

Fourth and finally, the Social Gospel was a political phenomenon. Washington Gladden put it most memorably when he wrote in 1905 that "if the kingdom of heaven ever comes to your city, it will come in and through the City Hall." Similarly, the Chicago settlement-house worker Mary Eliza McDowell spoke of the necessary blending of Christianity and democracy and saw the state as the principal instrument of morality. Yet the Social Gospel's emphasis on political action, as historian Susan Curtis has argued, inadvertently marginalized the churches as agents of reform. As the size of the government's own bureaucracy increased, activities such as ministering to the poor, relegated primarily to the churches and other voluntary associations throughout the nineteenth century, became the concern of federal and local agencies.[41]

The administration of Woodrow Wilson, a devout Presbyterian and political idealist, did not reverse the trend of an expanding, reform-minded federal bureaucracy, though the entry of America into World War I sounded the death knell of Progressivism as a political movement and ushered in a new age of uncertainty. The era's most unsettling event for Americans, irrespective of gender or race, was the onset of the Great Depression in 1929. Within the churches, the 1930s brought sober reassessments of the Social Gospel's optimism and heralded a new theological movement, neo-orthodoxy. The movement's harbinger had been the Swiss theologian Karl Barth, whose commentary on the Book of Romans (1919–1922), in the oft-quoted words of Catholic systematician Karl Adam, "fell like a bomb on the playground of the theologians." Somewhat like Jonathan Edwards in his inaugural public lecture in 1731, Barth in his debut reiterated the old themes of divine sovereignty and human depravity. In America a decade later, the brothers Reinhold and H. Richard Niebuhr forcefully expressed similar themes. Reinhold's latter-day jeremiad, *Moral Man and Immoral Society* (1932), dismissed as unrealistic the liberal ideal of perpetual peace and brotherhood, arguing that the churches must learn to work within a perpetual state of war. Richard's *Kingdom of God in America* (1935) criticized the liberal attempt to establish God's kingdom on earth and instead invoked Edwards on God's absolute sovereignty. The ghost of Edwards would soon loom even larger amid the rise of fascism in Europe, the outbreak of World War II, the revelation of Nazi genocide, and the emergence of the atomic age. As Richard would recall in 1958 at an event marking the two-hundredth anniversary of Edwards's death, "We have seen evil somewhat as he saw it, not because we desired to see it, but because it thrust itself upon us."[42]

Yet the image of a bomb shattering the theological playground does not do justice to the significant continuities between the earlier Social Gospel and neo-orthodoxy. The Niebuhr brothers, after all, were no less socially conscious or politically engaged than the crusading liberals of the Progressive era and were themselves children of the Social Gospel. And Richard's protestations in *The Social Sources of Denominationalism* notwithstanding, mainline Protestants during the interwar and immediate postwar years were no less committed to the Social Gospel's central themes, especially the bureaucratic denominational ideal. So pervasive was this denominational model that by the 1950s, American Lutherans, once atomized in an array of ethnic synods, had consolidated into several large church bodies and, with the exception of the conservative Missouri Synod, had become full partners in the mainline. Their new mainstream status was symbolized by the appearance of Franklin Clark Fry, president of the United Lutheran Church in America, on the cover of *Time* magazine on April 7, 1958. Similarly, the Disciples of Christ, once a decentralized frontier tradition, by mid-century resembled the older mainline churches in structure and social outlook. The chief symbol of the denomination's new status was the Disciples minister Charles Clayton Morrison, who served from 1908 to 1947 as editor of the *Christian Century*, the ecumenical weekly and leading voice of liberal Protestantism.

The bureaucratic, establishment mentality of mainline Protestants in the years immediately following World War II was clearly evident in the founding of the National Council of the Churches of Christ in the United States of America in 1950. As successor to the Federal Council of Churches, the National Council of Churches (NCC) represented twenty-nine Protestant and Eastern Orthodox denominations with a combined membership of thirty-three million. The National Council also served as an umbrella organization for councils of churches in forty states and 875 communities. Under its newly elected president, Henry Knox Sherrill, presiding bishop of the Episcopal Church, the NCC consisted of a vast bureaucracy with offices scattered throughout seven buildings in New York and one in Chicago. As Union Seminary president and veteran ecumenist Henry Pitney Van Dusen put it, the National Council was "the most complex and intricate piece of ecclesiastical machinery this planet has ever witnessed."[43]

The National Council expended considerable resources in its first decade on public relations—and with a notable degree of success. Both Sherrill and Van Dusen joined Franklin Clark Fry in the elite assemblage of mainline executives to grace covers of *Time* magazine. In 1952 the NCC, in cooperation with Thomas Nelson Publishers, issued the Revised Standard Version (RSV) of the Bible, touted by the council as a new authorized translation for all the churches. When RSV committee chairman Luther Weigle sought an invitation to the White House to present a copy to the president, Harry Truman readily complied; indeed, church executives of the era often had the ear of secular politicians.[44]

THE BELEAGUERED MAINLINE, 1960 TO THE PRESENT

Yet the world of secular politics was all the while drawing more and more public attention away from the churches. In the new age of television, political events increasingly superseded religious events in the competition for valuable air time. Meanwhile the federal government bureaucracy, which had expanded exponentially in Roosevelt's New Deal and later in Johnson's Great Society, offered the promise of social salvation through welfare and related programs. By the 1960s, the churches' role in providing social services, already diminished by the expansion of government programs in the Progressive era, was even further reduced. The loss was not altogether lamentable to many observers because of the government's superior resources. After all, the churches had long ago lost direct state support. Only the government could compel Americans to give up a portion of their income to support programs for the poor, the elderly, and others in need. Through the modern welfare state, the government had finally become the principal guardian of the commonweal.

Beginning in the 1960s, the mainline churches were further buffeted by a variety of forces from without and within. The primary external force was the burgeoning diversity of American society, along with greater acceptance of religious pluralism. This was most powerfully symbolized by the election in 1960 of America's first Catholic president, John F. Kennedy. During the presidential campaign, fundamentalist Protestants had purveyed some of the same anti-Catholic conspiracy theories once circulated by the Puritans. But when it became clear that the American polis would survive a non-Protestant president, anti-Catholic rhetoric quickly lost much of the acceptance it had long enjoyed among both conservative and liberal Protestants. The worldwide popularity of Pope John XXIII and the reforms of the Second Vatican Council also went a long way toward defusing the centuries-old animus between Protestants and Catholics. Meanwhile Congress in 1965 abolished the national origin quotas that had restricted immigration since the 1920s. This paved the way for a large influx of non-Protestants, thus straining in demographic terms, at least, the historic Protestant denominations' claim to mainline status.

The greater religious pluralism of American society was evident in other ways. As late as 1955, only one American in twenty-five had moved outside his or her childhood faith. Within three decades, the ratio was one in three.[45] At the beginning of the twentieth century, almost half of all American undergraduates attended church-related, mostly mainline colleges. By 1965, two-thirds of undergraduates were attending public institutions.[46] Even within church-related schools, the historic denominational affiliation often was largely eclipsed by ideals of diversity and tolerance. With increasing numbers of Americans attending college, academia was producing a new class of professionals whose attitudes were often markedly more liberal than those of their parents. The liberalism of this new class was frequently refined in the fires of activism over Vietnam and civil rights. Many college students in the 1960s and 1970s were also affected by the women's movement, which was finally achieving substantial progress after enduring more than a century of societal recalcitrance. Women now studied alongside men at most colleges, including the Ivy League bastions of elite male privilege. Meanwhile, the mainline churches were finally ordaining women. The rapid increase of women—and feminist theology—in the seminaries was changing the face of theological education.

These trends toward greater diversity, influenced by civil rights activism and the rise of affirmative action programs, tended to reinforce the acceptance of a social gospel among mainline church bureaucrats, who increasingly turned their attention to the drafting of social statements on a variety of contemporary problems.[47] Though not uniformly liberal on all issues, these statements did reveal something of an ethical consensus that was, as Mark Ellingsen has observed, "uncannily consistent with the values of Western democratic liberalism."[48] These statements also revealed a shared opinion among mainline executives that the churches' primary public role was social advocacy. On the most basic level, they reflected the widespread assumption that certain issues required authoritative public statements by corporate ecclesiastical bodies. This churchly, top-down model—always present within Protestantism but often cloaked in the sixteenth-century rhetoric of dissent—had finally emerged as the mainline's common procedure for addressing social questions.

No sooner had it begun, however, than the tradition of Protestant social statements encountered serious opposition. The old Reformation themes—suspicion of ecclesiastical authority, elevation of the individual, and an emphasis on textual evidence in religion—came back to haunt church leaders. Intensified in the modern democratic context, anti-authoritarianism and individualism among Protestants tended to breed indifference if not hostility to ethical directives handed down from above. This occasionally resulted in stark conflicts at the denominational assemblies charged with ratifying social policy statements. Such conflicts were exacerbated by an enduring rift, confirmed by sociological studies, between a generally liberal, socially conscious clergy and a more politically and socially conservative laity.[49] All the while, the abiding Protestant emphasis on textual—namely, biblical—evidence was proving as divisive as ever in American religious history. In the century since the Civil War, the fracture between Protestant conservatives and liberals over biblical interpretation and other issues had become a gaping chasm cutting across denominational lines.

Social questions such as abortion and sexuality, which—like slavery before them—admitted of conflicting positions when considered from purportedly biblical perspectives, created seemingly irreparable divisions within the mainline churches themselves.

By the closing years of the twentieth century, the conservative-liberal divide had superseded old denominational boundaries in sociological importance.[50] It was now easier in some cases for Catholics and conservative Protestants to find common moral ground than for warring Protestants within the same denomination to achieve consensus. A striking example of the former tendency was "Evangelicals and Catholics Together," a 1994 statement affirming a common conservative stance on abortion and other issues that was signed by a number of prominent Catholic intellectuals as well as evangelically minded Protestants from both inside and outside the mainline churches.[51] Meanwhile, the intractability of intra-Protestant divisions was evident in independent periodicals such as *Lutheran Forum* and *Presbyterian Layman*, which published a steady stream of articles criticizing the liberal social advocacy and alleged doctrinal laxity of their respective denominational administrations. Though many Protestant laypeople resisted unqualified identification as either conservatives or liberals, this two-party fracture persisted on many levels, especially in coverage by the secular media.[52] Reinhold Niebuhr's ruminations about a perpetual state of conflict seemed uncannily prescient as the mainline churches entered the twenty-first century.

CONCLUSIONS AND RECOMMENDATIONS

Amid the efflorescent religious diversity of present-day American society, the mainline churches' attachment to old denominational forms—and bureaucratic ways of doing social ethics—are often regarded by observers as outmoded, stubborn, and even arrogant. Moreover, the seemingly intractable conservative-liberal divisions over ethical questions have contributed to a widespread sense of mainline ineffectiveness. Partisans on the right point to the twentieth-century sociological truism that conservative churches are outpacing mainline churches because the former draw sharp moral and doctrinal boundaries and demand genuine commitment from their members. Partisans on the left excoriate the mainline churches for not providing a genuinely liberal alternative to American evangelicalism or for failing to experiment with new paradigms in worship and ethical-theological reflection. Meanwhile, some secular critics ridicule the term *mainline* altogether, insisting that it suggests a demographic preeminence that never really existed, and that it implicitly relegates all other religious traditions to inferior status.

Whatever the validity of these assertions, their practical effect has been to increase a negative impression of mainline Protestantism among academics and church leaders. This is unfortunate because it ignores the unique contributions of the mainline churches to contemporary American society. These contributions are not necessarily in the realm of specific social questions, since effective nonreligious arguments can be marshaled on most pressing moral issues of the day. Instead, the mainline's unique gifts to the American religious mixture lie in the logic of mainline churchliness. As I have suggested, this logic in its present form was not native to the Protestant traditions first imported from Europe but has evolved over the past few centuries in the American pluralistic context. The three primary tenets of this logic, while not addressing specific ethical debates head-on, offer a distinctive approach to the challenge of the church's public role. I therefore conclude with some final reflections on these three points.

First, the logic of mainline churchliness entails a reasonable tolerance of ethical differences. This may come as a surprise to conservative veterans of contemporary denominational infighting, who rankle at the apparent heavy-handedness of church administrators in spearheading liberal social statements. And yet, the mainline churches still encompass a remarkable diversity of ethical positions. Whether formal schisms will be avoided in the future is another question, but at their best, mainline Christians remain committed to civil and orderly means of addressing ethical differences. This tolerance of ethical diversity, however "lukewarm" it may appear to partisans on both sides, is in fact a virtue in its own right and a necessary characteristic of civil society.

Second, the logic of mainline churchliness is ecumenical. The existence of the National Council of Churches and other organizations committed to identifying points of agreement among seemingly incommensurate doctrinal traditions ought to be cause for rejoicing among American Christians. Some critics have charged that the recent spate of new mainline ecumenical alliances is weakening the doctrinal coherence and diluting the cultural potency of the individual denominations.[53] This is not a criticism to take lightly, and yet the most ecumenically involved church leaders are very often the ones most knowledgeable about their own historic traditions. When it is recognized that ecumenism goes hand in hand with the faithful stewardship of tradition, then the ecumenical movement emerges not as a threat but as an excellent means for negotiating religious pluralism.

Finally, and closely related, the logic of mainline churchliness is all-encompassing. By this, I mean that mainline Christians have grand ideas of the church and its role in the public sphere. Much has been said in this essay about the affinities of the mainline mentality with big business, and it is true that the denominations' centralized administrative structures, with elaborate tiers of authority staffed by specialized professionals, do mimic American corporate models. But it should not be forgotten that the root of "corporate" is *corpus;* that is, body: a unified whole made up of disparate parts. For mainline Christians, the church as the Body of Christ is a universal reality that mystically encompasses the nation, and indeed, the world. Such logic is evident in the mainline's corporate procedure for addressing social ethics. The magisterial practice of addressing social policy statements to a denomination's faithful presupposes a large (usually nationwide) communion and an expansive notion of the scope of the church's ethical responsibility. In other words, mainline Christians at their best set their sights not primarily on the individual person or parish but on the universal church and its work in the world.

This last feature of mainline logic—its all-embracing vision of the church—bears some resemblance to Catholicism, but without the more autocratic dimensions of Catholic polity, especially its notions of papal primacy and infallibility. Protestants, as this essay has shown, have always tended to distrust large ecclesiastical institutions, and this perennial suspicion continues to fuel, among other things, the proliferation of "nondenominational" evangelical churches in contemporary America. More generally, this suspicion has contributed to the widespread popular assumption among religious liberals and conservatives alike that religion is about personal "spirituality" rather than about church affiliation. The logic of mainline churchliness is a check on this ever-present tendency to reduce religion to a quest for personal self-fulfillment, even though religious practice always retains a vital individualistic dimension. Mainline logic instead places primary emphasis on the collective aspects of Christianity—on what it means to be the church in the world. Mainline logic stresses collective action not only by denominational institutions but also by the wider church represented by ecumenical organizations such as the National Council of Churches.

The mainline churches at their best are not the culturally captive institutions once denounced by H. Richard Niebuhr, though it is undeniable that many of the problems he identified—especially racial division—persist to this day. Rather, the mainline churches at their best combine the pan-denominational and postmillennial zeal of nineteenth-century evangelicalism, the tolerance and social concern of modern secular liberalism, and the institutional and universalistic vision of Roman Catholicism. The greatest challenge facing the mainline churches is not, therefore, to devise a coherent logic of churchliness but to find forceful and media-savvy ways to convey this logic to a nation of religious seekers.

NOTES

1. H. Richard Niebuhr, *The Social Sources of Denominationalism* (1929; reprint, New York: Meridian Books, 1957), 3–25, 270, 281–82. For a sociological retrospect on this work, see Wade Clark Roof and William McKinney, *American Mainline Religion: Its Changing Shape and Future* (New Brunswick, N.J.: Rutgers University Press, 1987), chap. 4.

2. On the emergence of the "self" in the American religious context, see Rodger M. Payne, *The Self and the Sacred: Conversion and Autobiography in Early American Protestantism* (Knoxville: University of Tennessee Press, 1998).

3. On the diversity of early American religion, see Jon Butler, *Awash in a Sea of Faith: Christianizing the American People* (Cambridge, Mass.: Harvard University Press, 1990), especially chapter 3. On religious indifference, see Roger Finke and Rodney Stark, *The Churching of America, 1776–1990: Winners and Losers in Our Religious Economy* (New Brunswick, N.J.: Rutgers University Press, 1992), chap. 2.

4. Sydney Ahlstrom summarizes the characteristics of "enlightened" Christianity in *A Religious History of the American People* (New Haven, Conn.: Yale University Press, 1972), 356–59. On the Enlightenment's influence among the New England clergy, see John Corrigan, *The Prism of Piety: Catholick Congregational Clergy at the Beginning of the Enlightenment* (New York: Oxford University Press, 1991). See also Harry S. Stout, *The New England Soul: Preaching and Religious Culture in Colonial New England* (New York: Oxford University Press, 1986), 127–35.

5. The thesis that the Great Awakening led to Revolutionary radicalism received classic expression in Alan Heimert, *Religion and the American Mind from the Great Awakening to the Revolution* (Cambridge, Mass.: Harvard University Press, 1966). On the extensive debate surrounding this text, see Philip Goff, "Revivals and Revolution: Historiographic Turns since Alan Heimert's *Religion and the American Mind*," *Church History* 67 (1998): 695–721.

6. Butler, *Sea of Faith*, 174.

7. Christopher Grasso, *A Speaking Aristocracy: Transforming Public Discourse in Eighteenth-Century Connecticut* (Chapel Hill: University of North Carolina Press, 1999), 48–51.

8. On preaching during this era, see Stout, *New England Soul*, 259–81.

9. Leonard W. Levy, *The Establishment Clause: Religion and the First Amendment*, 2nd ed., rev. (Chapel Hill: University of North Carolina Press, 1994), 1–26.

10. Peter Dobkin Hall, *The Organization of American Culture, 1700–1900: Private Institutions, Elites, and the Origins of American Nationality* (New York: New York University Press, 1982), 109–10.

11. Martin E. Marty, *Protestantism in the United States: Righteous Empire*, 2nd ed. (New York: Scribner's, 1986), 71. On the power of denominationalism in the early republic, see also Butler, *Sea of Faith*, 268–80; and Paul K. Conkin, *The*

Uneasy Center: Reformed Christianity in Antebellum America (Chapel Hill: University of North Carolina Press, 1995), 115–19.

12. Thomas Paine, *The Age of Reason: Being an Investigation of True and Fabulous Theology* (1794–95; reprint, Boston: Josiah P. Mendum, 1875), 6, 11.

13. A. James Reichley, *Religion in American Public Life* (Washington, D.C.: Brookings Institution, 1985), 178–79.

14. Henry F. May, *The Enlightenment in America* (New York: Oxford University Press, 1976), 325–27.

15. Theodore Dwight Bozeman, *Protestants in an Age of Science: The Baconian Ideal and Antebellum Religious Thought* (Chapel Hill: University of North Carolina Press, 1977), especially 138–43.

16. This positivism even entailed the use of the new science of statistics to bolster claims about social reform; see Robert H. Abzug, *Cosmos Crumbling: American Reform and the Religious Imagination* (New York: Oxford University Press, 1994), 93–97.

17. Paul C. Gutjahr, *An American Bible: A History of the Good Book in the United States, 1777–1880* (Stanford, Calif.: Stanford University Press, 1999), 9–11, 19; Peter J. Wosh, *Spreading the Word: The Bible Business in Nineteenth-Century America* (Ithaca, N.Y.: Cornell University Press, 1994), 11–13.

18. For an overview of organizations in the "benevolent empire," see Mary K. Cayton, "Social Reform from the Colonial Period through the Civil War," in *Encyclopedia of the American Religious Experience*, 3 vols., ed. Charles H. Lippy and Peter W. Williams, 3: 1429–40.

19. Christine Leigh Heyrman makes this point in reference to the South in *Southern Cross: The Beginnings of the Bible Belt* (New York: Alfred A. Knopf, 1997), 6–8.

20. Henry F. May, "Jonathan Edwards and America," in *Jonathan Edwards and the American Experience*, ed. Nathan O. Hatch and Harry S. Stout (New York: Oxford University Press, 1988), 30.

21. Timothy L. Smith, *Revivalism and Social Reform in Mid-Nineteenth-Century America* (New York: Abingdon Press, 1957), 80, 92–93, 140–46.

22. Donald G. Mathews, "The Second Great Awakening as an Organizing Process, 1780–1830: An Hypothesis," *American Quarterly* 21 (1969): 23–43.

23. The term "Arminianized Calvinism" is from William G. McLoughlin, *Revivals, Awakenings, and Reform: An Essay on Religion and Social Change in America, 1607–1977* (Chicago: University of Chicago Press, 1978), 138.

24. Paul E. Johnson, *A Shopkeeper's Millennium: Society and Revivals in Rochester, New York, 1815–1837* (New York: Hill and Wang, 1978), 4–5, 8.

25. The claim about Catholic success by 1850 is made by Ahlstrom, *Religious History of the American People*, 527; and Martin E. Marty, *Pilgrims in Their Own Land: Five Hundred Years of Religion in America* (New York: Penguin Books, 1984), 272. Finke and Stark, in *Churching of America*, 110–15, claim a later date of 1890.

26. Philip D. Jordan, *The Evangelical Alliance for the United States of America, 1847–1900: Ecumenism, Identity, and the Religion of the Republic* (New York: Edwin Mellen Press, 1982), especially 22–30 on the role of anti-Catholicism in the alliance's creation.

27. For estimates of numbers, see Philip D. Curtin, *The Atlantic Slave Trade: A Census* (Madison: University of Wisconsin Press, 1969), 3–13.

28. Stephanie McCurry, "The Two Faces of Republicanism: Gender and Proslavery Politics in Antebellum South Carolina," *Journal of American History* 78 (1992): 1245–64.

29. On the Exodus motif, see Albert J. Raboteau, "African-Americans, Exodus, and the American Israel," in *A Fire in the Bones: Reflections on African-American History* (Boston: Beacon Press, 1995), 17–36.

30. Abzug, *Cosmos Crumbling*, 129–62.

31. Ibid., 204–29.

32. C. C. Goen, *Broken Churches, Broken Nation: Denominational Schisms and the Coming of the American Civil War* (Macon, Ga.: Mercer University Press, 1985). On the political implications of denominational schisms, see Richard J. Cardine, *Evangelicals and Politics in Antebellum America* (New Haven, Conn.: Yale University Press, 1993), 133–318.

33. On the Civil War and notions of progress, see James H. Moorhead, *World without End: Mainstream American Protestant Visions of the Last Things, 1880–1925* (Bloomington: Indiana University Press, 1999), 18. On Lincoln, see Allen C. Guelzo, *Abraham Lincoln: Redeemer President* (Grand Rapids, Mich.: Eerdmans, 1999), 150–57, 313–14, 439–42.

34. Much of this paragraph draws on Mark A. Noll, "The Bible and Slavery," in *Religion and the American Civil War*, ed. Randall M. Miller, Harry S. Stout, and Charles Reagan Wilson (New York: Oxford University Press, 1998), 43–73.

35. Beecher and Briggs quotations from William R. Hutchison, ed., *American Protestant Thought in the Liberal Era* (New York: Harper and Row, 1968), 39, 41, 33.

36. Gerald Graff, *Professing Literature: An Institutional History* (Chicago: University of Chicago Press, 1987), 56–64. See also Burton J. Bledstein, *The Culture of Professionalism: The Middle Class and the Development of Higher Education in America* (New York: W. W. Norton, 1976); and Conrad Cherry, *Hurrying toward Zion: Universities, Divinity Schools, and American Protestantism* (Bloomington: Indiana University Press, 1995).

37. Elizabeth Cady Stanton, commentary on Matthew 25:1–12, in *The Woman's Bible*, ed. Stanton et al. (1895–98; reprint, Boston: Northeastern University Press, 1993), 125, New Testament section.

38. Quoted in Hall, *Organization of American Culture*, 274.

39. Susan Curtis, *A Consuming Faith: The Social Gospel and Modern American Culture* (Baltimore: Johns Hopkins University Press, 1991), 48–71, 81–83.

40. Ben Primer, *Protestants and American Business Methods* (Ann Arbor, Mich.: UMI Research Press, 1979), 35, 66–69; cf. James H. Moorhead, "Presbyterians and the Mystique of Organizational Efficiency, 1870–1936," in *Reimagining Denominationalism: Interpretive Essays*, ed. Robert Bruce Mullin and Russell E. Richey (New York: Oxford University Press, 1994), 264–87.

41. Curtis, *Consuming Faith*, 130, 165, 177.

42. H. Richard Niebuhr, "The Anachronism of Jonathan Edwards," in *Theology, History, and Culture: Major Unpublished Writings*, by H. Richard Niebuhr, ed. William Stacy Johnson (New Haven, Conn.: Yale University Press, 1996), 133.

43. Quoted in Samuel McCrea Cavert, *The American Churches in the Ecumenical Movement, 1900–1968* (New York: Association Press, 1968), 210.

44. Peter J. Thuesen, *In Discordance with the Scriptures: American Protestant Battles over Translating the Bible* (New York: Oxford University Press, 1999), 90–91. On church executives and secular media outlets such as *Time*, see Dennis N. Voskuil, "Reaching Out: Mainline Protestantism and the Media," in *Between the Times: The Travail of the Protestant Establishment in America, 1900–1960*, ed. William R. Hutchison (Cambridge: Cambridge University Press, 1989), 72–92.

45. Robert Wuthnow, *The Restructuring of American Religion: Society and Faith since World War II* (Princeton, N.J.: Princeton University Press, 1988), 88.

46. Dorothy C. Bass, "Ministry on the Margin: Protestants and Education," in *Between the Times*, ed. Hutchison, 49.

47. See, e.g., two surveys: Mark Ellingsen, *The Cutting Edge: How Churches Speak on Social Issues* (Geneva, Switzerland, and Grand Rapids, Mich.: WCC Publications and Eerdmans, 1993); and Christa R. Klein with Christian D. von Dehsen, *Politics and Policy: The Genesis and Theology of Social Statements in the Lutheran Church in America* (Minneapolis: Fortress Press, 1989).

48. Ellingsen, *Cutting Edge*, 136.

49. The classic sociological study of clergy-laity differences is Jeffrey K. Hadden, *The Gathering Storm in the Churches* (Garden City, N.Y.: Doubleday, 1969).

50. This is the argument of Wuthnow, *Restructuring of American Religion*.

51. The text is printed in *First Things*, no. 43 (May 1994): 15–22.

52. On popular attitudes toward the conservative and liberal labels, see David Sikkink, " 'I Just Say I'm a Christian': Symbolic Boundaries and Identity Formation among Church-Going Protestants," in *Re-Forming the Center: American Protestantism, 1900 to the Present*, ed. Douglas Jacobsen and William Vance Trollinger Jr. (Grand Rapids, Mich.: Eerdmans, 1998), 49–71.

53. See, e.g., Randall Balmer, "United We Fall," *New York Times*, August 28, 1999, A13.

2 Mainline Protestant Washington Offices and the Political Lives of Clergy

Laura R. Olson

Despite the official separation of church and state in the United States, clergy have always played public roles in American politics. Reverend John Witherspoon of New Jersey signed the Declaration of Independence, and Reverend Abraham Baldwin of Georgia was one of the framers of the United States Constitution. Countless other clergy have shaped the course of American politics by leading, joining, and opposing social movements, and by making statements on almost every conceivable political issue and candidate. Clergy have also played a variety of roles in social service delivery, from nineteenth-century mutual aid societies to today's vast array of nonprofit organizations and public-private partnerships. Even for the most politically involved pastors, though, political action must take a back seat to ministerial duties. There are also plenty of clergy who do not engage the political realm at all because they are not interested, do not have time, or feel intimidated by their congregations. Nevertheless, clergy have the potential to be a political force with which to be reckoned.[1]

More than most other groups of clergy in the United States—with the noteworthy exception of those who serve in African American religious traditions—mainline Protestant clergy have long been interested and involved in politics. Mainline clergy played nationally visible roles in the civil rights movement, the nuclear-freeze movement, and the sanctuary movement.[2] Today, many mainline clergy are particularly concerned about disadvantaged, marginalized members of society. They take action on this concern in part because mainline Protestantism embraces H. Richard Niebuhr's notion of "Christ the transformer of culture"; involvement by the faithful in the broader society is not just tolerated, but encouraged and expected.[3] Not all mainline clergy, however, find it easy—or even possible—to involve themselves in politics. Relatively few mainline laity wholeheartedly endorse the liberal political outlook that often accompanies mainline theology—and which clergy learn in seminary.[4] Consequently, since at least the 1960s, dividing lines have been drawn between many mainline clergy and the moderate-to-conservative people in their pews.

In recent years mainline clergy have been less visible on the national political stage than they were a generation ago. Their political and social outreach increasingly has come to focus on addressing problems on the local level, especially the causes and consequences of poverty.[5] In part this change has been a result of the federal government's devolution of policy authority to the state level, as well as its recent enthusiasm about the work of "faith-based organizations" in addressing social problems at the local level. Several other factors have energized some clergy to engage in local antipoverty work as well, including the decay of cities that followed the middle class's drift to the suburbs and the general disillusionment with the federal government born during the Reagan/Bush years. Meanwhile, many clergy feel a personal sense of calling to work for social justice stemming from their belief that religious people should be actively involved in secular society, addressing the problems of the less fortunate in a Christlike manner.

Even though its clergy are not as visibly involved in national-level politics as in the past, mainline Protestantism retains an *institutional* presence on the national political stage. Each major mainline Protestant denomination in the United States supports an office in Washington, DC.[6] These offices function as interest groups by representing the political interests of the denominations and coordinating their national advocacy efforts.[7] The oldest and largest of the mainline offices, the United Methodist Church's General Board of Church and Society, traces its history to the Prohibition era. Other mainline denominations added Washington offices in the mid-twentieth century. As a group these offices have long advocated liberal political agendas. All except the Lutheran office are housed in the stately United Methodist Building, conveniently located on Capitol Hill beside the United States Supreme Court.

The Washington offices pursue a "peace and justice" agenda by advocating human rights at home and abroad, working to preserve the environment, questioning U.S. use of military force, and above all else fighting for the disadvantaged. The offices lobby members of Congress and executive branch staff, often working in coalition with religious and secular interest groups alike. They also file *amicus curiae* ("friend of the court") briefs in key federal cases. To connect with local congregations, the offices support "action networks" of interested laity and clergy with whom they communicate about policy. These action networks are designed to stimulate grassroots discussion of politics and involvement in lobbying activities.

Mainline Protestant Washington offices continue to operate in an era when religiopolitical action is increasingly carried out at the local level. At times they play important roles in policy debates, particularly about international human rights issues, but they rarely exercise a great deal of political power. The offices themselves do not exist at the apex of the denominations' organizational structures, so they must take direction from denominational officials who rank above them while remaining sensitive to grassroots pressures and demands. And because the mainline Protestant denominations are not headquartered in Washington, DC, the Washington officials are geographically separated from both the top levels of the denominational hierarchy and their grassroots. For the most part the offices are underfunded and understaffed. The offices' staffs must conform to the idiosyncratic and often unwritten rules of the Washington game, because they (unlike their denominations) are part of the capital city's "inside the Beltway" political culture.

The work of the Washington offices is further complicated by the tremendous diversity inherent within mainline Protestant denominations. The specific policy areas in which the mainline Washington offices work are dictated by decisions made at national denominational meetings, where the voices of both the hierarchy and the grassroots influence the outcomes of contentious debates. Mainline Protestantism can count its openness and diversity among its strengths, but these factors present a challenge for finding (much less articulating) a unified political voice. As other chapters in this volume make clear, there is often substantial disagreement within mainline denominations over issues, positions, and strategies.

Moreover, the Washington offices themselves have faced serious challenges from critics within their own denominations about whether they serve a valuable purpose. In 1998 the United Methodist Office came under attack by conservative Methodists who said the office was too liberal and inappropriately partisan.[8] Even more recently, controversy has erupted over the Presbyterian Washington Office. The results of a major survey of Presbyterians revealed very little knowledge of or support for the office, and the conservative *Presbyterian Layman* accused the office of wasting the denomination's money by pandering to liberals.[9]

My purpose in this chapter is to explore the relationship that exists today between mainline Protestant clergy and their denominations' Washington offices. In the past, the offices have successfully mobilized clergy for political action.[10] But are clergy and the Washington offices still relevant to each other's political work? Do the Washington offices facilitate political action by clergy, especially now that much of it is done at the local level? Do the Washington officials think clergy should help them chart and carry out their agendas? Is it reasonable to expect liberal, politically activist mainline clergy to feel comfortable working in conjunction with denominational officials, because the leadership is more likely to agree with them politically (that is, to be more liberal) than their own congregants? On the other hand, clergy's increasingly local focus may make the Washington offices irrelevant to their work. Many clergy are uninformed about the offices and their purpose.[11] Do the Washington offices play legitimate and vital roles in the lives of mainline clergy and, by extension, the operation of denominational business? Perhaps the challenges the Washington offices face—and the controversy they have generated within their denominations—suggest that the time has come to phase the offices out of existence.

To explore these matters, I interviewed the heads of five mainline Washington offices and sixty-two mainline clergy across the United States.[12] Half of the clergy were chosen on the basis of a national random sample. The remaining clergy belong to the action networks of their denominations' Washington offices.[13] Because only a small percentage of all clergy belong to these action networks, "networked" clergy are vastly overrepresented in this study—but for a reason. Comparing these two separate groups of clergy illustrates the extent and nature of the ties between parish clergy and the Washington offices. What characteristics, if any, differentiate "networked" clergy from randomly selected clergy?

I proceed by exploring clergy's attitudes about whether they ought to be involved in politics in the first place and then investigating the types of political issues and actions they favor. Next, the Washington offices enter the mix. How aware are clergy of these offices and their work, and how involved are—and ought—they to be with each other? Finally, I ask whether the offices still play a vital role in mainline Protestant political efforts and consider their future prospects, particularly in conjunction with the work clergy undertake.

DO CLERGY FEEL THEY BELONG IN THE POLITICAL REALM?

Politics is not the primary vocation of clergy, and the principle of church-state separation constrains their ability to engage in political action. Yet as religious professionals and leaders in the powerful social institution that is organized religion, clergy find themselves in a unique position to shape the interplay of religion and politics in the United States. The organization within which they work carries the force of moral suasion. At least once a week, clergy have the opportunity—if they choose to take advantage of it—to provide congregants with political cues. They can also choose to participate directly in politics and the policy process. But if clergy do not believe there is a place for them in the political realm, then the question of whether their denominations' Washington offices are relevant to their work is moot.

I did not impose any particular definition of "politics" on the clergy and officials interviewed for this study. "Political" may be read as "social or political," as many clergy include social action (such as feeding the hungry) in their definitions of the political. There was near unanimity among the ministers I interviewed that clergy should be involved in politics (only four ministers argued otherwise). In fact, almost half of the randomly chosen clergy (45 percent) and more than half of the networked clergy (55 percent) stated resolutely that clergy have an *obligation* to be involved in politics. They were even more likely to say political activity was important to them *personally:* four out of five pastors in both groups felt personally compelled to be involved.

The importance of political activity for these clergy flows from their sense of religious calling and their interpretation of the appropriate role of church in society. Several ministers cited the notion of Christian responsibility in this regard. As one Baptist pastor said, "We're supposed to be light and salt according to the Savior we follow, and I see being involved in these things as a big part of being light and salt." Others stressed the idea that the church must be part of the broader world: "Politics cannot be separated from daily life and from the church . . . they are intricately woven together, politics and the church and the community. Clergy should be engaged at the deepest level, because politics impacts all of our lives." A Methodist pastor provided an even bolder assessment: "I think [clergy] should spend at least a third of their time involved in community work outside the congregation, politically and socially." Even more extreme: "I'm Presbyterian clergy *because* of my political perspective. I went to seminary after working for a congressperson and I wanted to learn more about my faith underpinnings that got me in the political arena."

Moreover, both sets of clergy thought ministers who become involved in politics were effective. Half the pastors in each group expressed strong feelings of political efficacy, particularly because they thought both clergy and organized religion in general enjoyed a good measure of public trust:

We are viewed as representatives of God. There is a certain ethical and moral weight clergy carry when they speak out. The reason we carry that weight is because it's hard to say, "Well, that's just a liberal speaking," or "That's a Democrat or a Republican speaking," because we have to be held to a higher standard. . . . So when we speak, it's not possible as it is in the normal political discourse to write us off and just label us and then dismiss us as softheaded liberals who want to spend government money. . . . We do carry a certain amount of authority as a result.

Other clergy noted that they benefit from having a built-in audience. As an Episcopal priest explained, "I have to be very careful what I say and do, because there are always people watching. . . . They either are doing that to attack me or because they think what I am doing is right and so they just want to copy it. . . . [Clergy] have the stage every week." Several pastors also pointed out that clergy might sometimes be *too* effective: "They can make a difference in either direction. I think if they shoot their minds off . . . they can make either a denomination or the church or the clergy look . . . downright stupid."

Not all of the pastors, though, expressed unqualified feelings of political efficacy. A few argued that some clergy are more effective than others, depending on factors such as geographic area, *Zeitgeist*, and personal credibility. "You know as well as I do there's a lot of nuts out there. I think they destroy their credibility. I think clergy have an influence as long as they are credible members of the community." Only six ministers (all in the random group) said clergy do not make a difference in politics. Four of them argued that clergy enjoy *less* public trust than in the past: "We're not a very trusted profession any more. I think at one point in time clergy packed a real wallop . . . but not so much today. . . . The public has seen that we've betrayed a sacred trust." A Lutheran pastor in a southern state indirectly blamed the Christian Right for making the public think all clergy are conservative: "I think that because of an individual's expectations of where a clergy person is coming from [politically], sometimes clergy are dismissed."

As a group the networked clergy have somewhat stronger feelings of political efficacy than the randomly selected clergy.[14] However, the randomly selected clergy do *not* convey the sense that they feel political action is either inappropriate or a waste of time. Because the differences between the randomly selected and networked clergy on these two matters are small, it would be a mistake to conclude that being networked with the

Washington offices plays a substantial role in shaping clergy's base attitudes about the propriety and effectiveness of political action. It would be reasonable, though, to infer that clergy might constitute a massive yet untapped activist base for mainline Protestantism.

CLERGY'S EVERYDAY POLITICAL LIVES

Generations of mainline Protestants have supported the notion of church-state separation, in part because of perceived threats from Roman Catholics.[15] Yet mainline theology teaches that the church should play an active role in the outside society. Unlike evangelical Protestantism, mainline Protestantism maintains low and permeable barriers between church and society; mainline Protestants are more likely than evangelicals to embrace life in "this world" as opposed to heavenly salvation. In contrast with Catholicism, mainline Protestantism allows for substantial variety in political expression because its hierarchical structures are relatively flexible. This variety characterizes mainline clergy's everyday political lives—both in terms of the political issues they emphasize and the political actions they choose to take.

When asked to identify the issue or set of political issues that concerned them most, the sixty-two clergy mentioned a wide array of policy areas, but the broad rubric of social justice infused most of their comments. Poverty—hunger, the end of welfare, homelessness, and what many pastors identified as "the growing gap between rich and poor in this country"—was by far their greatest concern. Racism also rated high on their collective priority list, along with economic justice, which encompasses fair employment and housing policy. Other tolerance-related issues, particularly gay rights, concerned them as well.[16]

How, if at all, do clergy put these concerns into action? The pastors I interviewed stressed their commitment to ameliorating poverty through involvement in what Nancy Ammerman (in Chapter 5 of this volume) calls "human service" and "public benefit" activities. They reported working in conjunction with food pantries, soup kitchens, and groups such as Bread for the World and Habitat for Humanity, as well as other forms of advocacy for the disadvantaged, such as fighting homelessness, supporting street ministries, mentoring people affected by welfare reform, opposing the "regentrification" of urban areas, working for equal housing and employment opportunity, and providing financial assistance to those unable to pay their utility bills. Twelve reported involvement in community development work, often through clergy caucuses with ties to organizing networks such as the Industrial Areas Foundation (IAF).[17] Some said they actively fought discrimination on the basis of race, ethnicity, and sexual orientation. As a group, these clergy may not be doing things most people think of as "political." Nor were they interested in the sorts of activities their denominations' Washington offices might define as "political." Yet their work carries strong political implications.

Clear differences exist between the everyday political worlds of the two groups of clergy. Most notably, the networked clergy were involved in a wider array of political activities than those in the random group. For some of the networked clergy, it was as if involvement in one area necessarily involved them in other areas. As one pastor whose congregation is deeply involved in antipoverty work explained, "The church has two meal programs that serve here daily and a social service program that also works in conjunction with that. . . . But it's incomplete unless we're also involved in public policy issues related to the poor and the homeless and housing and job services and other things that go along with that. . . . We do get involved in political action around those things." Clergy in the networked group were also likely to express interest in—and act on—controversial, cutting-edge issues such as employment and housing inequities and gay rights. *Only* networked clergy said they worked on crime-related issues, including police brutality, gun control, and peaceful conflict resolution. Such issues require a fair amount of direct action, which may carry substantial risk for ministers by distracting them from their pastoral duties and alienating their congregations. The networked clergy appear to rank ongoing political action "in the trenches" as a higher priority than would the average pastor.

Notice that the issues in which both sets of pastors were most heavily involved, especially poverty, are usually addressed at the local level. Only one of the pastors focused the *bulk* of his political work on nonlocal matters. In recent years, federal devolution and Charitable Choice have afforded clergy enhanced opportunities and incentives to engage in political action at the *local* level.[18] Pastors who feel called to political action may find the best opportunities to heed that call locally. Meanwhile, the Washington offices spend the bulk of their time working on issues with a stronger international component. As cases in point, consider the offices' two most visible recent efforts, both of which are primarily international in focus: their "Jubilee 2000" fight to bring about debt relief for developing countries and their unsuccessful 1999 struggle for Senate consent to the Comprehensive Test Ban Treaty.

ARE CLERGY AWARE OF THE WASHINGTON OFFICES?

Do mainline Protestant Washington offices mobilize clergy to become involved in their work, or do the clergy who wish to become involved seek out the offices on their own? Certainly the Washington offices may play a role in motivating clergy's political activity, even though much of the clergy's work is done locally. In part the mobilizational potential of the Washington offices depends on clergy's levels of awareness about the offices. I asked the clergy to rate their own level of knowledge about the Washington offices on a scale of one to ten. The average level of awareness among the randomly selected clergy was four, whereas the average for the networked group was seven.[19] Only two of the sixty-two clergy admitted to having no awareness at all of the Washington office.

For their part, how do the Washington officials assess ministers' general level of awareness of their offices? Russell Siler of the Evangelical Lutheran Church in America's (ELCA) Lutheran Office of Government Affairs said, "They know we're here. They know the church speaks out on issues. [But] beyond that, it can get very sketchy." Thomas Hart of the Episcopal Church's Office of Government Relations said, "I would say on a scale of one to ten, . . . we are around a three or four." (And he was correct, at least for the random group.) Curtis Ramsey-Lucas of the American Baptist Churches' Office of Government Relations thought "it's mixed. . . . It's hard to say exactly. I got a call last week from a member of our network who was at a meeting with some clergy, and they didn't know at all about the work of the office but were interested." According to Jay Lintner of the United Church of Christ's (UCC) Office for Church in Society, clergy "are reasonably knowledgeable about what we're doing in general, but I think they're reasonably unknowledgeable about the particulars."

The Washington officials cited several reasons for clergy's lack of awareness about their work. Some pastors, they acknowledged, are either uninterested in politics or unwilling to risk the consequences of becoming involved. As Hart of the Episcopal Church put it, "There's a real sense of 'let's not create problems within the congregation where we don't have them.'" Some ministers, according to the ELCA's Siler, lack understanding of the relevance of political work: "We so often miss the connection between direct services and public policy advocacy, changing the conditions that create the need for which we provide direct services." And there is the ever-present constraint of time. Parish clergy have so many responsibilities that they often find it difficult to fulfill their basic obligations, much less find time to network with their denominational offices in Washington, unless they have an innate interest in politics.

I also asked the networked clergy to reflect on whether the average mainline minister is aware of the Washington offices' work. Not a single one felt the average minister was well informed. Instead, 68 percent said most clergy know very little about the offices. As one networked pastor put it, "I think [the Washington office] is one of the best kept secrets in the church." Others attributed pastors' lack of awareness to a more general lack of interest in denominational structures: "The average Lutheran pastor tends not to pay attention to the structures of the organization, and [the Washington office] is embedded in a part of the organization that's pretty far away from a lot of the clergy in the ELCA." Others blamed time constraints and, to an extent, inertia: "Typically in a congregation when the pews are filled, the offering plates are filled, and the Sunday School rooms are filled, [only] then [do] they start thinking about things like social ministry, and only when they're well into the direct service kind of social ministry do they think to go upstream and look at the causes of why there are people in need in this wealthy nation, . . . in [their] own neighborhood."

The remaining 32 percent expressed slightly more hope about their colleagues' levels of awareness. The problem, as they saw it, is that the average pastor possesses skewed or incomplete information: "I think they've been made aware in terms of some persons who don't like what [the Washington office] is doing or stands for." Levels of awareness may also vary by region. As one pastor in the New York City area stated, "New York and the California conferences, [and] Northern Illinois are different. . . . Maybe a little above average in terms of awareness." Several ministers in the Washington, DC area also mentioned that serving in the nation's capital had enhanced their awareness of the office and its activities.

Since so many clergy seem to know so little about the Washington offices, how do the networked clergy first become aware of the offices and their work? A surprising 55 percent of the networked pastors said they could not identify the precise moment when they became aware of the offices. As one UCC pastor said, "That's like asking me how [I] got acquainted with my uncle. . . . It's just part of the whole scene, [especially because] I've always been interested in social justice issues." The remaining 45 percent of the networked pastors, though, shared stories about how they first learned about the offices. An Episcopal priest explained, "When I was in college, I was just a hippie. . . . One of the reasons I even went to the Episcopal Church is because there were priests who didn't think I was weird, unusual, or stupid. . . . What I found in the Episcopal Church [were]

. . . people that were honestly trying to have a voice. . . . [I was thrilled] that there was actually an office in the top part of the organization that [stood against the Vietnam War]."

Specific policy interests led another Episcopal priest to become aware of his denomination's Washington office: "That became more incarnate for me when I . . . began [a] refugee ministry and then was able to see [the office] personally when I made a trip to Washington [for] a refugee conference." And a Methodist pastor relates, "[My] consciousness was raised when I was involved [in] high school [with what was] called then the Methodist Youth Fellowship. . . . We had a seminar to New York and Washington. We went to the UN [Methodist] Church center. . . . And from there we went down to Washington." In at least some cases, it seems that clergy gravitate naturally toward the offices rather than being recruited by them.

Clergy are as diverse as the congregations they serve. Some are simply not interested in politics in any form. Local-level activities appear to keep many of them quite busy, so networking with the denomination's Washington office might not be a high priority. They are often able to do their work at the local level without the assistance of the Washington office. National-level work can even become extraneous:

> We have to deal with so many more immediate issues. . . . Since there's
> so many pressing problems in the immediate community we live in,
> people coming looking for food, looking for a place to live, looking for
> money to get back on their feet, . . . we're much more familiar . . .
> with local political issues. . . . The further you get away from home,
> the more distant and remote and less connected you feel. . . . You feel
> a certain sense of . . . "How am I really going to change that big
> issue at the national level?"

The clergy who overcome this feeling have a strong interest in politics at the national level. In some instances they have had meaningful early encounters with the Washington offices. Many of the bonds between clergy and the Washington offices appear to be forged by the pastors themselves. Despite these ties, though, even the networked clergy are primarily involved with political work that does not require contact with the Washington offices.

CLERGY INVOLVEMENT IN THE WORK
OF THE WASHINGTON OFFICES

If networked clergy offer even tacit support for the Washington offices, they have the potential to serve as valuable conduits between the offices and the grassroots. Potential benefits for both sides would flow from such a relationship. Local churches would get to learn more about the work of their denominations, and Washington officials might come to feel less isolated from local churches.

The first question is whether the Washington officials receive or solicit input from clergy as they formulate their office's advocacy goals, agenda, and tactics. Although the Washington offices have elicited controversy over the years, the commentary they receive from clergy tends to be supportive. Hart's Episcopal office in particular had an effective way of heading off criticism: "We haven't heard a lot of complaints especially in recent years [because] I've tried to take into account the [church's] diversity. . . . when taking positions on issues and setting priorities. . . . Those issues that have passed 51 to 49 percent are probably not the ones we're going to be on the bleeding edge of at this point. We're trying to find those issues that [have] a little wider support in the church."

The UCC's Lintner said he tries to be realistic: "We listen very carefully to that response, some of which is crank. . . . The clergy generally let us know when they're not supportive, but there's [usually] a lot of support." As an illustration Lintner explained that in anticipation of the Senate's 1999 vote on the Comprehensive Test Ban Treaty, "We sent out . . . 4,000 action alerts. Then we started doing phone banking for those 4,000 people, and . . . did not get *one* [bit of] negative feedback."

My interviews confirm the accuracy of the Washington officials' impressions.[20] Since the Washington offices are not dealing with substantial resistance from clergy, perhaps they should invite pastors to contribute ideas for their work in Washington. The officials differed in their receptiveness to this idea. When asked if his office solicits opinions from clergy, the ELCA's Siler said succinctly, "No, we really don't." He and his colleagues have found such outreach to be too unwieldy and expensive. Hart of the Episcopal Church agrees, but for the slightly different reason that his denomination's General Convention—not he—sets his office's agenda. "That's our mandate and, frankly, our cover. . . . I'm not setting church policy. I'm merely providing a voice to it." Thus, he does not feel the need to solicit the opinions of clergy at the grassroots level. However, Washington officials have discretion to emphasize certain issues more than others. The Presbyterian Washington Office and the American Baptist Churches' Office of Government Relations do seek clergy input in making decisions about how to prioritize their lobbying efforts. And the UCC's Lintner wished his office could gather more clergy input.

The second question is whether the Washington officials feel it is important to incorporate the views of clergy as they set lobbying priorities and strategies. The Washington offices' action networks allow clergy and laity alike to request materials about the issues of their choice. However, none of the Washington officials had a clear sense of how many clergy actually belong to these networks, and several admitted the networks themselves are quite small. The fact that the offices maintain the networks at all, though, indicates that they feel it is important to maintain some level of contact with the grassroots.

But do the offices ever go further in their efforts to reach out to clergy, to solicit their views, or to mobilize them for political action? According to the American Baptist Churches' Ramsey-Lucas, "We ask people [who join our action networks] to share what interests they have and what issues concern [them]. . . . So in that sense, they do shape what we do and where we are on issues." Elenora Giddings Ivory of the Presbyterian Washington Office explained that because her agenda is set by the denomination's General Assembly, it "does not work directly with . . . the individual person if they come up with something new. . . . [But sometimes] a local clergy person . . . is instrumental [in] initiating an overture that goes to General Assembly and gets passed."

The Washington officials thought clergy were sometimes a hindrance to their offices' work. As the ELCA's Siler said, "Clergy can just as often be roadblocks or bottlenecks." The UCC Office sent a letter to its ten thousand clergy before the Persian Gulf War began, requesting their signatures for a newspaper advertisement in the *Washington Post* and the *New York Times* opposing any attack on Iraq. Lintner received two thousand responses from UCC pastors, each of whom contributed $20 along with an endorsement. While this might be seen as an extraordinary success, Lintner explained with some regret that UCC *laity* subsequently "beat me up . . . *furiously* because . . . the ad said 'UCC clergy.' The lay people wanted to be counted as well."

In short, the Washington offices are hesitant to say clergy play an integral role in their advocacy efforts. It is not surprising that clergy are not directly involved in the Washington offices' agenda-setting process, as denominational polity forbids the Washington offices from setting their own agendas unilaterally. However, the Washington offices can and do appeal to clergy during the lobbying process to enhance the denomination's grassroots voice on key issues. This strategy does not seem especially risky, because most pastors seem tacitly to support the offices and their work. Nevertheless, clergy do not appear to respond overwhelmingly to overtures made by the Washington offices. Consequently, Washington officials find themselves working in relative isolation from clergy, while clergy are doing their work at the local level without much contact with the Washington offices. Both parties are operating in separate political spheres: the Washington offices have a national and international focus, whereas the clergy have a local focus. A sort of equilibrium appears to exist between these two loci of mainline Protestant political outreach that is rooted in a lack of interaction.

COULD THE WASHINGTON OFFICES MOBILIZE CLERGY?

The picture that emerges to this point is one of a cordial but distant relationship between mainline clergy and their Washington offices. Even the networked clergy appear to be involved primarily in local-level political work. The Washington offices do try to mobilize clergy, yet they evince some skepticism about whether these efforts are likely to be effective. What would it take to strengthen the bonds between the offices and parish pastors?

Despite any mobilizational efforts by the Washington offices, ministers are unlikely to respond to a call from Washington unless they feel the offices facilitate their own political interest and involvement. Only 55 percent of the networked clergy said the Washington offices' work stimulates them politically. One especially enthusiastic pastor attributed his strong commitment to antipoverty work in a low-income urban area to his initial exposure to the United Methodist Office when he attended a conference as a teenager. A UCC pastor, however, made a more common statement: "I do more of my own thinking. If I'm going to address an issue in print or in the pulpit, [and] if they have material available, it will be one of the sources I look at, but usually not the primary one or certainly not the only one."

The randomly chosen clergy were much less enthusiastic about the Washington offices than their networked counterparts; only 33 percent of the random sample said the Washington offices stimulated their interest and involvement in politics.[21] One pastor said the office was useful "at least to the extent of trying to keep my conscience honest. . . . It doesn't always seem usable [or] relevant, but I keep trying to hang on and find the way that it will be." Nearly half (42 percent) said either that the offices made no difference in their lives or that they had too little knowledge to evaluate them. Again the predominance of local-level action emerges: "A lot of the work we do is much more local oriented, and [the Washington office is] much more national, global oriented."

The clear division that seems to exist between local and national political foci is the central reason for the absence of a stronger relationship between clergy and the Washington offices. The Washington officials attribute the emergence of this division between the local and national spheres to shifts in the public agenda. The issues that have come to dominate the agenda in recent years "are not as sharp as they once were," according to the Presbyterian Church's Ivory. "Now and then an issue will come along that will seem to catch the attention of local clergy," but she said this is a relatively rare occurrence.

Another reason why the Washington officials feel it has become difficult to mobilize clergy for political action on the national stage is that many current issues do not easily create consensus. Issues that do rally agreement, according to the ELCA's Siler, are frequently international in focus. He compared two issues—the international campaign against antipersonnel land mines and the domestic debate over health care reform—to make his point:

> You can talk about 120 million mines waiting to explode under the feet of a child wanting to play, a woman going to get water, a farmer going to till his land. That's easy [for people to understand in clear terms]. On the other hand, it's not nearly as easy to get people to march into their congressional office and say, "How come there are 5,000 children in your district alone who have no health insurance whatsoever when they have to go to the emergency room?" That's more confrontational.

But certainly the civil rights movement and the war in Vietnam were controversial domestic issues in their time, and mainline clergy rallied around them. The Episcopal Church's Hart observed that the protest issues of the 1960s and 1970s "had a clarity or a purity to them that [is] difficult to duplicate." Siler argued that the difference lies in a change in the political climate: "The climate in the sixties and seventies was much more confrontational." Still, clergy today who lobby city councils are certainly willing to be confrontational.

The political climate in the United States has undeniably changed since the 1960s; in large part this is due to the Reagan and Bush administrations' embrace of limited national government and resulting policy devolution. But the central reason why the Washington offices face significant challenges in mobilizing clergy is that pastors' focus on the local level is motivated by more than just their theological beliefs and their personal interests. Clergy today work diligently at the local level because such work benefits their churches—and, not insignificantly, the neighborhoods within which the churches are located. Ramsey-Lucas of the American Baptist Churches gets at the kernel of the matter by observing that "churches are in kind of a survival mode, with dwindling memberships, and clergy are focused on the immediate needs in their churches and communities."

It is eminently *rational* for clergy to make themselves as useful as possible to the people who immediately surround them. Local problems, especially poverty, create real human needs that require attention, and clergy are often among the few people in impoverished areas who have sufficient skills, resources, and willingness to address these needs.[22] Moreover, local political activity shapes churches' identities, which can help them attract and retain members.[23] National-level work, on the other hand, does not provide clergy with direct opportunities to address the immediate problems of the neighborhoods in which they live and work. National-level work is far more likely than local efforts to distract clergy from tending their own gardens, which is dangerous in this age of stiff, marketlike competition within organized religion. This is a particular concern for mainline Protestants, whose ranks have been hardest hit by the competition inherent in religious pluralism.

ARE THE WASHINGTON OFFICES WORTHWHILE?

The strong impetus for clergy to do local-level political work may suggest that the Washington offices, with their focus on national and international matters, have outlived their usefulness. Nevertheless, the overwhelming majority of the sixty-two pastors felt it was important to maintain the Washington offices—even though they seldom work in conjunction with them. And the randomly selected clergy were just as likely as the networked clergy to advocate preserving the offices. A common view was that "The church as a whole . . . needs to know it has a voice in that political arena even though each of us may not be individually involved." As one Episcopal priest put it, "It's money well spent. One of the things I like about it is it keeps me informed. . . . I've got my job here, so [I'm happy] our national budget can fund people who can do [work in Washington] in our name and on our behalf." A few clergy also expressed fear that the Washington offices would close: "I'd just hate to see it go. It seems like we in the mainstream [have] kind of given up all that territory, and so I'm glad we're hanging onto it."

Despite the fact that most of the pastors I interviewed appeared to be politically liberal, a few did express some concern about the offices' left-leaning politics: "They tend to be more liberal in terms of their concerns and their agenda. . . . They don't have to be more *radical* just to get more attention." Some pastors were also miffed because they felt the offices attempt to speak for the entire denomination. As one Lutheran minister explained, "We need to make our voice heard, [but] I think the best way to do it . . . [is] individually, congregationally." Pastors' feelings can and do change over time, though: "I didn't [think the office was a good idea] at first. I thought that was a little overkill. But given the way the country's politics works, [I decided] it doesn't hurt to have a lobby." These points of criticism are really quite minor considering that so many clergy seem to feel that their own work does not intersect with the offices' work. Evidently mainline clergy want the work of the Washington offices to be done, but they personally do not want to do it. Therein lies one of the more important bases of tacit support for the Washington offices among many mainline clergy.

Even more telling is the question of whether the mainline denominations ought to be staking out positions on political issues. This is, after all, one of the key functions of the Washington offices. If clergy think only local-level work is important, there should be no reason for them to support denomination-wide efforts to identify clear issue stances. Less than half (48 percent) of all the ministers interviewed agreed that the denominations *should* stake out positions on political issues. Many pastors argued that being clear on issues "is the job of the mainline church. . . . I don't know that the Presbyterian Church will ever be able to speak with a unified voice, but I do think . . . our gift to society is to grapple with the issues." They also expressed the sentiment that the mainline needs to be vocal to counteract the effect of the Christian Right. "We know that the right wing has hurt us. . . . The Falwells have . . . made Christian spokespersons a laughingstock and have damaged *our* ability to speak with integrity and authority because they are derided . . . from Jay Leno down to the pundit who draws the cartoons."

On the other hand, fully 26 percent of the sixty-two pastors felt that it was *inappropriate* for their denominations to take positions on political issues. This is particularly surprising, since mainline denominations are known for the time and effort they spend debating resolutions on various controversial issues. Clergy said they were particularly concerned about accommodating diversity within their denominations. Some pastors also worried that when their denominations made clear pronouncements on issues, people who might otherwise come to worship in mainline churches would begin to feel unwelcome:

The flavor of the denomination since the fifties on political stands has been very much in the liberal direction. . . . They may be the right stands on those particular issues, but unfortunately, I think we have become very much identified with a particular stance more than with the gospel which motivates those stands and people. . . . It's not an easy thing to pinpoint, but I . . . [wish] we were clearer that our motivation is our faith in God, our love for Christ, for each other, rather than being known as "Issues 'R' Us."

Even though I offered them ample opportunity to do so, the pastors did *not* put forth a call for their denominations to close the Washington offices. Inertia is one explanation for the pastors' support for the offices. Since the offices do not cause pastors any obvious problems, there may be no reason for pastors to feel any outrage. Still, it is reasonable to assume that if the offices have outlived their usefulness, at least a few of the clergy would have expressed this view.

The principal reason why mainline clergy believe the Washington offices should be preserved appears to be that they do fulfill a vital role for their denominations. They undertake political work that clergy cannot or will not do. To a great extent, the Washington offices and parish clergy operate in two separate spheres, but the fact is there *are two* spheres in which to operate. There is much work to be done at the local level, and clergy find plenty of opportunity and incentive to do it. But there is also a need for a political voice at the national level. Most local clergy do not have much opportunity to address international issues such as debt relief and nuclear testing. The Washington offices, however, are well equipped to speak and act on such matters as a result of their staffs' policy expertise and wherewithal in the political culture of Washington. This is not to say that clergy would put great energy into fighting for the preservation of the Washington offices, but much evidence suggests that they will not be leading a charge to abolish them in the near future. Meanwhile, the fact that parish clergy are not distraught about the Washington offices means that the offices themselves have a good measure of freedom to do their work without worrying about dissent from the grassroots.

FUTURE ROLES FOR THE WASHINGTON OFFICES

The mainline Washington offices seem to play an important role in the lives of their denominations. Their clergy support them, at least in a pro forma fashion. Thus, it is useful to consider how the offices might grow and adapt to change as they continue their work in the decades to come.

Perhaps alterations in the relationship between the Washington officials and parish clergy, for example, would assist the offices.

I asked each of the Washington officials whether having a different or in any way enhanced relationship with clergy would facilitate their work. All of them expressed a desire for deeper and more meaningful ties with clergy. The Episcopal Church's Hart observed: "We'd love to have all clergy . . . in our grassroots network. . . . Local clergy do have the capacity to raise awareness about the work of the office and encourage . . . participation." Additional funding would be the answer, according to the Presbyterian Church's Ivory: "[We need] to have more money to service them. . . . If we had more staff persons, then we could be more [involved] with some of their concerns and their needs." The American Baptist Churches' Ramsey-Lucas expressed an even more basic need for his office to raise awareness among clergy: "I think we certainly need to get the word out about the fact that we're here and the kind of resources we're able to offer." If the relationship between the Washington offices and parish clergy were antagonistic, these officials would not speak in such positive terms about the possibility of strengthening ties with pastors.

I also asked the networked clergy for suggestions about how the Washington offices might better assist them. Many requested that the offices provide more information. In particular, clergy would like to see more information on the Internet, more articles about the offices in denominational magazines, and more issue-specific bulletin inserts. In fact, despite the vast amount of mail that floods the average pastor's desk, some made it clear that they would not mind receiving a bit more.

Another theme that emerged among the clergy's suggestions was a desire to see further explanation of the offices' positions and stances on issues:

> I think mainly they seem to base their actions on previous resolutions
> of [the Episcopal Church's] General Convention. Many clergy in
> this part of the world tend to agree with me that a lot of the stuff the
> General Convention does is not well thought out and somewhat
> irrelevant. Maybe the Washington office could use other sources for
> their lobbying efforts. . . . There are other ways of approaching it than
> just [to] quote General Convention or some resolution that was
> passed x number of years ago.

The pastors also expressed a wish for more *theological* justification of the Washington offices' actions.

Many clergy said they would appreciate visits by Washington officials to their regions. One minister shared that the "most helpful [thing for me] has been the times when they come and participate in any kind of events regionally and we get a sense of who they are and can enter into dialogue with them and engage on different issues with them. . . . Part of the difficulty [is that] you're so separated, a world apart." Similarly, "When the people in the Washington office can be out in the Presbyteries talking about the Washington office, that makes the greatest impact. That has made the greatest impact in my life and I think the life of our Presbytery." While site visits might be ideal, the offices have neither sufficient funding nor staffing to accommodate this request. As the Presbyterian Church's Ivory explained, "My suitcase is [always] packed. . . . [And] each time I go, the group says, 'Well, we need you to come and see us *more*.' . . . I'm beginning to say, 'We can't be in all these places at one time.'" Such is the reality of the Washington officials' lives.

Nevertheless, clergy say they want the connections between themselves and the Washington offices to be tangible and relevant to their own work. Some say the Washington offices need to do "the listening project type work and then the educational work, so that they're listening to local church members and leaders and local church pastors . . . so you have a sense of who your constituency is." One suggestion was for Washington officials to listen to people in various regions and then share the information nationally with interested clergy: "[The offices could say] 'Here's what we're hearing from certain parts of the country. Is this something that is involving your area as well? If so, let us know.' Or 'Are there other arenas that you see that we might identify and check out with leaders in other parts of the country to help us form the opinion that we're bringing and, in effect, advocating or lobbying in Congress?'" Again, however, such an effort might prove nearly as costly and time-consuming as travel across the country.

Yet some clergy desire even more than a "listening tour"; they wish the Washington offices would provide leadership training. As one UCC pastor sees it, the offices need "to train clergy to effectively speak out and . . . mobilize at a local level folk to work on behalf of issues that are important to us. . . . [And] you need to begin to develop an understanding that it is essential for them to be involved in the process." Such leadership training would ensure that the Washington officials and clergy would "work more effectively together and therefore go out into the wider church with a clearer sense of mission and vision." Today mainline clergy are increasingly turning to private foundations such as the Industrial Areas Foundation for leadership training. Perhaps this indicates that more political leadership training may be needed in mainline seminaries.

Finally, a few clergy mentioned the possibility of establishing public policy offices at the state or regional level. The ELCA already has eighteen such offices scattered across the country. The Lutheran clergy who were networked with these state advocacy offices had only praise for them. One pastor said he depends on his state advocacy office whenever an issue that concerns him arises.

> My first thing to do . . . [is] call [my state office]. . . . Because of that I feel really well informed, because [the office director] is monitoring at that level. I don't really feel I need to know the specifics, there's just a network that enables me to know when I need to. . . . As soon as anybody in Washington knows [about an issue or situation of importance], it goes out to [my state office]. Then they get it in our hands so we can respond. . . . We don't have to go through mounds of information to try to get it.

Establishing offices at the state and regional levels would undoubtedly be time-consuming and expensive. In the ELCA, however, these offices seem to be worth the time and expense, because they link national-level work with the distinctive needs, cultures, and challenges of particular regions.

CONCLUSIONS

Mainline Protestant clergy and Washington officials increasingly are doing their political work in separate (local and national) spheres. Clergy who choose to be involved politically operate primarily at the local level, while the Washington offices' work is mostly national and international in scope. Does this divergence signal a problem for the mainline? Should changes be made to strengthen the connections between clergy and the Washington offices?

There was a time before mainline Protestantism even had that name when its churches and clergy enjoyed a good measure of social hegemony. Congregationalists, Episcopalians, and Presbyterians enjoyed a great measure of social influence, and used it to their advantage. They had few worries about filling either pews or coffers. But those days are now gone, thanks to the dramatic expansion of American religious pluralism. Increasingly Americans are attracted to evangelical Protestantism, with its doctrinal clarity and contemporary worship style, and to the many non-Christian faiths that are flowering in the United States today. Even though some may say mainline Protestantism is still the implicit "default" category for public religion in the United States, mainline Protestants have had a difficult time distinguishing themselves in today's crowded religious marketplace. At the same time that mainline Protestants have been fighting an uphill battle to maintain some small portion of their previous market share, they have diversified due to various regional mergers.

The clergy I interviewed reflected this diversity. One thing that unites these pastors, though, is their evident acceptance of Niebuhr's vision of Christ as cultural transformer. They said it is appropriate and important for clergy to be involved in political activity, particularly to ameliorate poverty. The message of social justice is alive and well among these pastors. Meanwhile, mainline Protestantism's diversity and flexibility allow clergy to choose their own political strategies to respond to the specific needs they encounter. Mainline clergy are equipped theologically and structurally to do work that is quite political, both independently and ecumenically. They can and do undertake activities from running meal programs in the church basement to joining or even creating local pressure organizations. And parish pastors with a political calling can fulfill their mission at the local level without consulting with the Washington offices.

Indeed, the day could soon come when the offices would no longer serve a valuable role. As ELCA's Siler proposes: "We would make sure [every new] congregation had social justice outreach as a part of their basic makeup, just the same way that they had to keep records of giving. [We should ensure] that this was right up on a par with the most important ministries they did. . . . That's what I wish for. Then our office could close up—literally close up." But even if every mainline Protestant pastor in the United States suddenly decided to become deeply involved in politics (which would by no means be an entirely positive development), the Washington offices should not "close up," because they would still serve a valuable function. Unlike clergy, the offices coordinate denominational political efforts. The officials have experience and expertise in working in the Byzantine political world that is Washington, DC. Unlike clergy, the offices focus keenly on issues of national and international importance. Just because the offices operate in a largely separate sphere from clergy does not mean they are not important. In fact, their separate mission makes them all the more vital. When clergy work at the local level and Washington officials work at the national and international levels, a division of labor results that allows the mainline to accomplish even more of the sociopolitical work that it values. Thus, the offices can simultaneously do important work in Washington and generate a substantial level of indifference among clergy.

Clear benefits accrue to clergy and the Washington offices because they work in separate spheres. Both are able to serve God, the church, and society in different but complementary ways. More pragmatically, their separate political spheres help them to preserve and protect their own interests.[24] The Washington offices, in order to survive in the challenging world in which they work, must have an indispensable and irreplaceable niche. This niche for them is national and international advocacy, which no other voice in the mainline could accomplish with as much authority or influence. Mainline clergy face an entirely different set of challenges. They need to keep people in the pews and money in the coffers, particularly in the face of strong competition from other religious traditions.

Pastors who feel a political calling can use local-level political advocacy not only to heed their calling but also to build unique identities for their churches. People are drawn to churches with clear missions and messages, and local-level advocacy helps churches define themselves. As one politically active Methodist pastor told me, "One of the problems I think the churches have is that they don't have a clearly enough defined mission statement. . . . [My church] has a very clear mission statement that we're committed to." This pastor and many others like him have found that the best way to make a difference in people's lives is through local-level advocacy.

Although the fact that they work in separate spheres may not be a problem in itself, enhanced communication could benefit both the Washington offices and the clergy. As Brian Steensland and Michael Moody (in chapters 8 and 9 of this volume) make clear, the relationship between the Washington office and local congregations varies by issue. Mainline clergy would benefit from clearer communication from the Washington offices, particularly on issues about which they agree. There is always the risk to the offices that communication could be costly both financially and in terms of criticism and controversy, but the pastors who are networked with the offices seem to support them and applaud their efforts. The Washington offices would also benefit from enhanced communication because it would allow them to connect more firmly with the grassroots they represent.

The characteristics mainline Protestants share—an open approach to Scripture and a non-authoritarian view of leadership—breed diversity rather than similarity. Mainline Protestantism's diversity means that its leaders, and especially its laity, embrace a wide variety of political attitudes and approaches. Its flexibility, which is guaranteed by the absence of uniform interpretations of Scripture and authoritarian approaches to leadership, means that mainline Protestants at all levels are free to act on their political dispositions in whatever ways are appropriate to the contexts in which they live, work, and worship.

NOTES

Thanks to each of the mainline Protestant clergy and officials who generously shared their time and insight. I also thank Bob Wuthnow, John Evans, Natalie Searl, Brad Wilcox, John Green, two anonymous reviewers, Wendy Cadge, Lynn Robinson, Brian Steensland, Marie Griffith, Ezra Kopelowitz, David Leege, Brian Kruger, Anna Looney, Sue Crawford, Paul Djupe, Mary Olson, Bob Olson, and the participants in the Religion and Culture Workshop at Princeton University for helpful advice and assistance.

1. On the types of political involvement clergy undertake, see Sue E. S. Crawford and Laura R. Olson, eds., *Christian Clergy in American Politics* (Baltimore: Johns Hopkins University Press, 2001); James L. Guth, John C. Green, Corwin E. Smidt, Lyman A. Kellstedt, and Margaret M. Poloma, *The Bully Pulpit: The Politics of Protestant Clergy* (Lawrence, KS: University Press of Kansas, 1997); Ted G. Jelen, *The Political World of the Clergy* (Westport, CT: Praeger, 1993); Laura R. Olson, *Filled with Spirit and Power: Protestant Clergy in Politics* (Albany, NY: State University of New York Press, 2000).

2. See James F. Findlay, *Church People in the Struggle: The National Council of Churches and the Black Freedom Movement, 1950–1970* (New York: Oxford University Press, 1993); Michael B. Friedland, *Lift Up Your Voice Like a Trumpet: White Clergy and the Civil Rights and Antiwar Movements, 1954–1973* (Chapel Hill: University of North Carolina Press, 1998); Allen D. Hertzke, *Representing God in Washington: The Role of Religious Lobbies in the American Polity* (Knoxville: University of Tennessee Press, 1988).

3. H. Richard Niebuhr, *Christ and Culture* (New York: Harper and Row, 1951).

4. On the "clergy-laity gap," which posits that mainline Protestant clergy are more liberal than most members of their congregations, see James L. Adams, *The Growing Church Lobby in Washington* (Grand Rapids, MI: Eerdmans, 1970); Jeffrey K. Hadden, *The Gathering Storm in the Churches* (Garden City, NY: Doubleday, 1969); Norman B. Koller and Joseph D. Retzer, "The Sounds of Silence Revisited," *Sociological Analysis* 41 (1980): 155–61. On liberalism among mainline clergy, see Guth et al., *Bully Pulpit;* and Robert Wuthnow, *The Restructuring of American Religion: Society and Faith since World War II* (Princeton, NJ: Princeton University Press, 1988). On the political lessons inculcated in seminary, see Jackson W. Carroll, Barbara G. Wheeler, Daniel O. Aleshire, and Penny Long Marler, *Being There: Culture and Formation in Two Theological Schools* (New York: Oxford University Press, 1997).

5. Ram A. Cnaan, *The Newer Deal: Social Work and Religion in Partnership* (New York: Columbia University Press, 1999); Crawford and Olson, *Christian Clergy in American Politics;* Olson, *Filled with Spirit and Power.*

6. Previous studies of these offices and their work include Adams, *Growing Church Lobby;* Luke Eugene Ebersole, *Church Lobbying in the Nation's Capitol* (New York: Macmillan, 1951); Hertzke, *Representing God in Washington;* Daniel J. B. Hofrenning, *In Washington but Not of It* (Philadelphia: Temple University Press, 1995); Matthew C. Moen, *Religion on Capitol Hill* (Tuscaloosa: University of Alabama Press, 1989).

7. Mission statements for the six mainline Protestant Washington offices are available on their websites: for the American Baptist Churches, <http://www.abc-usa.org/natmin/ogr/index.html>; for the Episcopal Church, <http://www.ecusa.anglican.org/peace-justice/Links.html>; for the Evangelical Lutheran Church in America, <http://loga.org/mission.html>; for the Presbyterian Church, <http://www.pcusa.org/pcusa/nmd/wo/info/what.htm>; for the United Methodist Church, <http://www.umc-gbcs.org/whoweare.htm>; and for the United Church of Christ, <http://www.ucc.org/staff.htm#OCIS>.

8. See <http://www.umc-gbcs.org/gbpro60.htm>; and <http://www.umc-gbcs.org/act24.htm>.

9. Jack Marcum, "Views on the PC(USA) Washington Office," <http://www.pcusa.org/rs/dcoffice.htm> (1999); John H. Adams, "Washington Office Little Noticed by Presbyterians or Politicians," *The Layman Online* (April 13, 1999), <http://www.layman.org/layman/news>.

10. See Adams, *Growing Church Lobby*; Hertzke, *Representing God in Washington*.

11. A recent survey of Presbyterians revealed that only 4 percent of all pastors felt "very well informed" about the Presbyterian Washington Office; 66 percent said they had had no personal contact with the office; and 46 percent were unable to assess the office's effectiveness; see "The Public Role of Presbyterians," *Presbyterian Panel*, August 1999, 3–4.

12. Whereas I interviewed the Washington officials in person, I spoke to the clergy over the telephone. The clergy serve in thirty-five different states plus the District of Columbia. Thirteen of the clergy (21 percent) are women; five (8 percent) identified themselves as African American, and two (3 percent) identified themselves as Hispanic American. All are ordained, and all but three were serving congregations. On average these clergy have been in the ministry for just over twenty years and have been serving their congregations for just over seven years. The interviews ranged in duration from fifteen minutes to over an hour.

13. I obtained the names of the "networked" clergy from Washington offices, state-level denominational officials, and denominational websites.

14. This difference between the two groups is statistically significant: *Chi-square* = 7.99; *p* = .02; *N* = 62.

15. On this point see Andrew Greeley, *The Catholic Experience: An Interpretation of the History of American Catholicism* (New York: Doubleday, 1967).

16. For a detailed discussion of why these issues are so important to mainline Protestant clergy, see Guth et al., *Bully Pulpit*, chapters 4–5.

17. In 1940 Saul Alinsky founded the Industrial Areas Foundation (IAF). His idea was to train people to reorganize and rehabilitate their own neighborhoods. Since its inception, faith-based organizations (such as churches) have been key players in IAF organizations. Other IAF-like organizing networks have also emerged, such as the Gamaliel Foundation, which is based in Chicago. See Saul D. Alinsky, *Reveille for Radicals* (New York: Random House, 1946); Jim Rooney, *Organizing the South Bronx* (Albany: State University of New York Press, 1995); and <http://www.gamaliel.org>.

18. My findings are consistent with those reported by Mark Chaves, "Religious Congregations and Welfare Reform: Who Will Take Advantage of 'Charitable Choice'?" *American Sociological Review* 64 (1999): 836–46; and Cnaan, *Newer Deal*, both of whom stress the role played by the federal government's Charitable Choice policy in organized religion's antipoverty work.

19. The difference between the two groups is statistically significant: *t* (55) = −5.40; *p* = .00; *N* = 62.

20. Only one of the sixty-two pastors, an Episcopal priest, expressed an openly negative attitude about the Washington offices. He was especially concerned about what he called the Episcopal Washington office's "considerably liberal viewpoint."

21. The difference between the two groups is statistically significant: *Chi-square* = 11.21; p = .01; N = 62.

22. See Olson, *Filled with Spirit and Power* for a wide-ranging discussion of this point.

23. James K. Wellman, *The Gold Coast Church and the Ghetto: Christ and Culture in Mainline Protestantism* (Urbana: University of Illinois Press, 1999), also makes this argument. More generally, see Roger Finke and Rodney Stark, *The Churching of America, 1776–1990: Winners and Losers in Our Religious Economy* (New Brunswick, NJ: Rutgers University Press, 1992).

24. For a different take on this concept, see Robert Wuthnow, *The Crisis in the Churches: Spiritual Malaise, Fiscal Woe* (New York: Oxford University Press, 1997), chap. 11.

The Generous Side
of Christian Faith
*The Successes and Challenges
of Mainline Women's Groups*
R. Marie Griffith

Laywomen's organizations have long played an important role in American Protestantism and in modern civic life more widely. During the nineteenth century, churchwomen within and across denominational boundaries worked together for slave emancipation, temperance, and female suffrage, to name only three of the most notable issues. Women's mission organizations helped transmit Christianity to peoples across the world and educated Protestants back home about distant cultures, all the while influencing American policy toward native and foreign populations alike. Later in the twentieth century, women's groups would continue to focus attention and resources on both national and global questions, interceding for victims of poverty and serving as strong advocates of such issues as international peace, women and children's rights, accessible health care, and racial justice.

In recent years, the work of mainline Protestant women's groups has received far less public attention than that of secular groups like the National Organization for Women or the Feminist Majority. The aims and activities of the faith-based groups—Church Women United, Episcopal Church Women, Presbyterian Women, United Methodist Women, and Women of the Evangelical Lutheran Church in America, among others—have not been well known outside their own constituencies. Even within the churches, especially at the congregational level, there has often been only a vague sense of what the women's groups do or did in the past. Are they support groups? Bible study fellowships? Mission and outreach organizations? Political advocacy associations? Or some combination of these? While this essay cannot hope to cover these organizations with the thoroughness they deserve, it attempts to illuminate their historical place within mainline Protestantism (and within the larger contours of American society) in the last third of the twentieth century, particularly the last decade. What kind of public role have such groups sought? How have their goals either succeeded or failed? How has this public role been affected by the more intimate, private role they have played in individual women's religious lives? Most important, perhaps, where do these groups stand today?

This essay derives its answers to these questions from textual as well as ethnographic research, blending information obtained from diverse printed sources and archival materials pertaining to women's groups with insights from interviews held with national and local leaders and participants between 1999 and 2000.[1] While no one familiar with these organizations would argue that they are either monolithic or identical to one another, there is enough significant overlap on their target issues, aims, strategies, and concerns to allow for an analysis that uses specific group cases to reach broader conclusions about mainline women's public activism. Three cases have proved especially salient for this project, each chosen because of its vibrant past, central position in American church life, and history of public activism: Church Women United, the major, ecumenical, mainline women's group of the twentieth century; United Methodist Women, directed by the Women's Division of the General Board of Global Ministries in the United Methodist Church; and Presbyterian Women, organized at all levels of the Presbyterian Church (USA) under the auspices of the Women's Ministry Unit of the General Assembly. A fourth group, Episcopal Church Women (ECW), has at times provided an interesting alternative example, since its recent trajectory, structure, and reason for existence are quite different from those of the other groups and have less to do with any construed "public role," although ECW shares many of the same tensions and challenges confronting the other organizations.

Mainline women in leadership perceive some of the challenges facing them and have ideas about how to increase their public role. Yet, for a variety of internal and external reasons, they are not always able to translate these ideas into successful practice in ways that would help spread their vision and maximize membership—both crucial tasks if these organizations are to thrive and have an impact on civic and political life. Adding to the perennial challenge of simply existing as activist women's organizations within church bodies that praise them as fund-raisers and nurturers, but may balk at a more public role, are the dramatic changes in women's roles over the past thirty years, especially the increased number of women in the paid labor force and, perhaps paradoxically, in ordained ministry. While such changes are often celebrated as marking progress for women, they have clearly had mixed effects on women's organizations, leaving potential constituents with decreased time and motivation to participate actively in mainline women's groups.

The story of faith-based women's associations is, then, most transparently a story of persistent obstacles to public activism, some created by denominational leaders concerned with upholding the public role of a unified church, others the consequence of time pressures for working women, and still others resulting from the expansion of women's religious leadership roles beyond unpaid volunteer work into the more prestigious sphere of the pastorate. Additional impediments arise out of tangled communication and disparate aims within the groups themselves, which may not agree on the best way to handle either external setbacks or internal adjustments. Indeed, the disjuncture between the aims of the national organizational offices and activities at the local level is perhaps the most critical trial now faced by these groups, the combined outcome of local independence, imperfect transfer of information, and shortage of funds. Yet even amid the dilution of resources such obstacles have sometimes entailed and the declining numbers of permanently active members, this is also a story of unexpected victories, skillful regroupings, and impressive resourcefulness in times of need.

HISTORY AND CURRENT CONFIGURATION

Mainline Protestant women's organizations have their own unique and complicated histories, dotted by mergers and reorganizations that partially correlate with the trajectories of their parent denominations while also being linked to women's movements in the wider society. In addition to the singular features of these histories, however, the groups share a common foundation in the American home and foreign mission movements of the late nineteenth century, when so many federations were formed to promote "woman's work for woman" in the United States and beyond. A brief sketch of these groups' histories, while not doing justice to their diverse activities over time, may at least serve as useful background to later discussion.[2]

Church Women United (CWU) looks back to countless hundreds of local interdenominational mission groups that ultimately came together in 1941 as the United Council of Church Women (UCCW). The UCCW raised funds for projects like ministries to migrant workers and Christian colleges in Asia and also worked for peace and social change during World War II. This tradition of activism continued after UCCW became incorporated as a department of the National Council of Churches (NCC) in 1950 (renamed United Church Women) and once again when the group separated from the NCC in 1966 to become Church Women United. Determined to implement equal rights for women in the churches, CWU also focused energy on passing the Equal Rights Amendment; eradicating the poverty afflicting millions of women and children across the world; and eliminating racism wherever it could be ferreted out, at home and abroad. After Vatican II, Roman Catholic women joined Protestants in CWU, muddying its designation as a mainline Protestant organization and bringing another vital tradition of social activism to the table. Today as always, notes former General Director Kathleen Hurty, CWU's social policy is "attuned to the generous side of Christian faith," consciously aimed at social justice work.[3]

Presbyterian Women (PW), United Methodist Women (UMW), and Episcopal Church Women (ECW) similarly look back to the nineteenth century, to the many women's mission societies, domestic relief associations, and ladies auxiliaries that were formed in the various Protestant denominations (including regional variants) extant at different times. Most of these predecessor societies focused on the Christianization of women and children, as the title of the Methodist periodical *Heathen Woman's Friend* (founded in 1869) suggests, and on helping both domestic and foreign populations by means of schools, hospitals, orphanages, and other relief-oriented institutions. Like that of Church Women United, the stated purpose of these denominational women's groups has evolved and shifted; the direct emphasis on "Christianization" has notably receded over time, but the primary focus on the lives of women and children has remained more or less stable. Since the 1960s, most of these groups have centered their efforts on the components of mission education, that is, informing their American constituents about the conditions under which women across the world live, especially in developing countries (or what some now call the "global south"); advocacy on behalf of women and children, in hopes of improving living conditions and prospects for long-term health and safety; spiritual nurture of their constituents, including the women with whom they work outside the United States; leadership development for women and girls, providing them with tools to make an impact on their churches as well as political and social institutions; and financial support for domestic and foreign ministries with women and children. How these aims are practically implemented, of course, has varied from group to group and across time.

The larger histories of the denominations have had mixed effects upon mainline women's groups. During the 1970s, for instance, the two major women's groups from the United Presbyterian Church in the USA and the Presbyterian Church U.S.—United Presbyterian Women (UPW) and Women of the Church, respectively—worked on creating a joint Bible study curriculum (issued in 1979) and, as the two churches grew closer to uniting, a framework for a unified women's organization. As time came closer to denominational unification, however, UPW opposed the Presbyterian Plan for Reunion, dismayed to think that their autonomous status could be eliminated in the reunited church (Women of the Church was not an autonomous entity, since its money was channeled through church treasuries). Though forced to compromise on such vital issues as representation to the General Assembly Council and staffing allocations, the merged group, Presbyterian Women, managed to retain control of impressive financial resources, including property holdings at the denominational headquarters in Louisville, Kentucky. Fiscally and politically savvy, yet long ambivalent about the costs of unification, PW became an official program of the General Assembly of the Presbyterian Church (USA)—part of the Women's Ministry Unit—rather than incorporating on its own.[4] And while leaders today speak mostly favorably about their arrangement under the General Assembly, the immediate years leading to that arrangement were painful ones.

Other women's groups have had similar missteps in their denominational dealings, some even more vivid. Episcopal Church Women, for example, looks back a bit ruefully at their misplaced trust in the Church's concern for women's issues, absent a coalition of congregational women's groups in place to keep them dutiful. The turning point occurred at the 1970 Triennial Meeting, when the Committee for Women allowed itself to be disbanded in favor of a denominationally run United Thank Offering Committee and a Standing Committee on Lay Ministry (later a Program Group on Lay Ministry). This was a heady, optimistic moment for such a move, as it followed the decision to amend the constitution so that women would be allowed to sit in the House of Deputies—which they immediately did, representing 4.3 percent of all deputies. With full gender equality apparently on the horizon, there seemed little reason not to abandon gender-specific work for the seemingly larger denominational tasks that crossed gender lines. Yet, as ECW's self-published history wryly notes, "It began to be obvious that the Lay Ministry Committee was unwilling to spend any time on its agenda on affairs of women."[5]

In a further irony, growing support during the 1970s and 1980s for women in ministry had the unforeseen effect of shifting attention and resources away from the needs and interests of laywomen qua women (a pattern replicated in virtually all denominational women's organizations), especially since many younger women who, in previous times, would have provided leadership for women's organizations instead chose the professional path. Though a National Board of ECW was eventually created and the national group reorganized in 1985, ECW still has no office at the Episcopal Church Center—its board members are dispersed throughout the country and work as volunteers—and, according to onetime president Jane Banning, has never fully recovered from that decision to disband.[6] As in the case of Presbyterian Women, the speech and writing of Episcopal Church Women leaders blend a potent sense of betrayal and regret with a realistic commitment to work within the bounds of the very denominations that have intermittently disappointed them.

Unlike Presbyterian Women and Episcopal Church Women, United Methodist Women—headed by the Women's Division—has retained tremendous power within its larger church body, flourishing semi-independently to a much greater degree than its sister organizations. Significantly, the Women's Division is incorporated as its own organization, making it fully autonomous, at least on paper.[7] Such independence hardly obviates tension with other church bodies, however; in fact, some UMW leaders note a certain envy on the part of other church and denominational representatives toward the national Women's Division budget along with local UMW budgets. (Pointed attempts to prevent funds raised by local UMW circles from being recycled into the churches rather than used for specific UMW projects have not always been successful, a problem to which leaders have given much attention.) In fact, UMW is authorized by its charter to accept and hold estates and funds bestowed in wills, which, like its endowment and appropriations money, denominational heads cannot touch.

United Methodist Women, like its predecessor organizations, has at times been criticized within the church for taking controversial stands. Peggy Billings, who headed the Women's Division Section of Christian Social Relations from 1968 to 1984, has recorded the ire aimed at resolutions calling for an end to the Vietnam War (1969); supporting striking textile workers (1978); speaking out against South African apartheid; and calling for recognition of China. In 1972, statements by the Women's Division on the divided independence movement in Rhodesia led critics to denounce the women's "irresponsibility," according to Billings, and to call for the entire Women's Division staff to resign (a recantation and apology was later issued). Ongoing tensions were also felt in 1973, when the Women's Division became one of the first groups to call for a House Judiciary Committee impeachment investigation of President Richard Nixon. "Whenever the Division met, some group in the church got a bad case of nerves!" writes Billings.[8] Despite these controversies, the Women's Division remains one of the most powerful and well-financed offices within the denomination, and the best-funded of the mainline women's organizations.

Perhaps the most notable (or, at least, most noticed) instance of denominational politics affecting Christian women's groups was the Re-Imagining Conference that took place in Minneapolis in November, 1993. Organized as part of the World Council of Churches' Decade in Solidarity with Women (1988–98), which in turn grew out of the 1985 celebration in Nairobi, Kenya, of the United Nations Decade for Women, the Re-Imagining Conference brought together about 2,200 participants from 32 denominations, 49 states in the United States, and 27 countries. The event became highly publicized when two journals representing conservative groups within the United Methodist Church and the Presbyterian Church (USA)—*Good News* and the *Presbyterian Layman*, respectively—published scathing reports of the gathering, accusing the women involved of participating in "pagan worship rituals," worshipping "the female goddess Sophia," promoting lesbianism, and rejecting the doctrine of the atonement. Fallout from the ensuing controversy polarized the mainline while heaping accusations of heresy upon the women who led groups like Church Women United, Presbyterian Women, and United Methodist Women, many of whom had supported or helped to organize the Minneapolis event. The forced resignation of Mary Ann Lundy, director of the Women's Ministry Unit in the Presbyterian Church (USA), was the clearest sign of the controversy's impact on women's ministries.[9] The current restrained (one might almost say wary) tone adopted by Presbyterian Women, quite striking when compared with that of United Methodist Women, Church Women United, and Episcopal Women, surely results not simply from the 1988 merger but also from the furor over women's theological work unveiled at Re-Imagining.

Even after the excitement mostly subsided, with subsequent Re-Imagining conferences smaller and devoid of church officials' blessing, questions about the meaning and legacy of this event remain. As all parties would agree, Re-Imagining rekindled a classic debate between mainline women's groups and denominational authorities: broadly speaking, Re-Imagining's supporters (including some but by no means all members of mainline women's groups) perceived the church as intractably suspicious of women's full rights and even women's speech, whereas the event's critics (including many women) objected to what they believed to be an effort to annul the basic theological structure of Christianity. The difficulty of sustaining a middle ground position amid this heated debate had immediate, injurious effects on mainline women's groups, and eight hundred United Methodist Women signed a statement that called critics to account for "criticizing the Women's Division and undermining the effectiveness of local units of United Methodist Women."[10] The long-term consequences of the controversy upon faith-based women's groups, at either the local or national level, while more complex and uneven, have been on the whole quite negative: despite the defiant reactions that have led some women into greater levels of activism, the event fortified the divide felt between feminist thinkers and activists, on the one side, and conservative traditionalists, on the other, while failing, by most accounts, to draw new constituents into the women's organizations. The mostly clear line that now exists between Re-Imagining and mainline women's groups is a product of the chasm created by the initial controversy, when theological differences suddenly took on new, even ominous, significance. Although women in mainline organizations may feel themselves to be finally escaping the shadow cast by Re-Imagining's critics, a major consequence of the controversy may be an ongoing tentativeness about the bounds of feminist theology—and of women's roles more broadly within the church.

Women's changing religious roles are nowhere more apparent than in the clergy. Whereas only 3 percent of clergy were female in 1970, the figure for 1990 was 10 percent and has climbed steadily ever since. Researchers have noted that over 30 percent of enrolled divinity school students are women, and in some denominations the figures are 50 percent or even higher.[11] Historically, of course, women's organizations played a very important advocacy role in gaining full clergy rights for women, a role that vastly amplified women's access to ordination and positions of religious leadership during the latter half of the twentieth century. Hence, one might expect mainline women's groups to have been strengthened by women's increasing prominence in the churches, and yet, as has already been suggested in the case of ECW, the reality is rather more mixed. While women interviewed for this project noted a good bit of support from female clergy for their activities, clergywomen were apparently too busy with other obligations to participate regularly in group meetings or activities. While they may be united in their interest in women's issues, such interest may be more symbolic than productive of actual cooperation on key issues. In other words, the relationship between women's groups and clergy-women is not unlike that between the groups and *male* clergy. Many women who may at one time have sought to fulfill their call to ministry through participation in a traditional women's organization now more of-ten enter seminaries and seek paid ministerial positions. It seems ironic that even as women have attained higher positions of authority and pres-tige within mainline churches, the status of laywomen's groups has ap-parently diminished, but such has unquestionably been the case.

In all, mainline women's groups have weathered their fair share of storms, both within and outside their own bounds. Long committed to the betterment of women and children's lives, they have sought in a variety of ways to sustain a public voice—a voice that would enable women at home and abroad to live in safety, freedom, and good health, their daily and long-term needs satisfied to the extent of human possibility. The dif-fering financial pictures of these groups, of course, allow them varying degrees of such influence and action: UMW's 2000 appropriations budget was nearly $20 million, received in undesignated giving from UMW mem-bers, with endowment funds in excess of $100 million, while PW's pro-grammatic budget was $600,000 per year, plus over $2 million in offerings going to special mission projects.[12] CWU's annual budget for the 1997–98 fiscal year, by contrast, was $1.9 million, up from $1.4 million in previous years.[13] While membership statistics are rather more difficult to attain (leaders from all three groups suggest that such numbers are misleading), a general estimate puts UMW at approximately 900,000, and active PW members at 12,000; the membership of CWU is impossible to calculate, since it does not keep statistics of active members, while counting women in all mainline organizations as part of their own membership. But while both money and membership make an obvious difference in terms of the numbers of mission projects supported, these factors may not make as big a difference in a group's ability to have a viable role in public policy and activism, since other factors—vision, energy, and concrete action, to name a few—are more crucial than sheer numbers alone. We turn now to take a closer look at how the shared aim of being a public voice in tune with the "generous side of Christian faith" has been translated into discrete goals and strategies.

GOALS AND IMPLEMENTATION AT THE NATIONAL LEVEL

What kind of public role do the national offices of mainline women's organizations aspire to fill? How well do they articulate and implement their goals for this public role? How clearly are these goals communicated among the different levels of each group? Finally, how do local participants throughout the United States come to embrace these goals and live up to the larger purpose of the associations to which they belong? The following two sections address these questions.

Most of these organizations have produced a fairly general statement of purpose, a typical example of which is this one from United Methodist Women: "The organized unit of United Methodist Women shall be a community of women whose purpose is to know God and to experience freedom as whole persons through Jesus Christ; to develop a creative, supportive fellowship; and to expand concepts of mission through participation in the global ministries of the church." National leaders of these organizations strive to balance personal nurture of their female constituency with mission and the political activism that may grow out of that sense of mission—but such a balance is not easy to achieve.

Presbyterian Women's national office offers a particularly strong program of spiritual nurture for its constituency, publishing yearly Bible studies in which most local circle meetings presumably take part. While some titles suggest a focus on justice issues, such as *Resistance and Restoration: The Message of the Prophet Jeremiah*, most tend to have a more individual focus, as befits the first three of the four principles guiding the organization: the value of the individual member; spiritual development and growth; and supporting the mission of the church (the fourth is community life). More than United Methodist Women or Church Women United, which have offices in Washington, DC, that work on advocacy and public policy, PW has tended to focus on the needs of the women inside its church walls and on raising funds for mission projects elsewhere. In 1988, when PW officially emerged out of its two predecessor organizations, one member of the working team organized to facilitate that merger wrote, "Presbyterian Women affirms, as does our new denomination, that the church's work is done primarily in the congregation. So the primary thrust of PW is to support women in each congregation as they do the work God calls them to do."[14] Though later in the same article this leader discussed "commitment to mission," the notion of justice, here and elsewhere in PW writings, remained only vaguely articulated. Emphasized instead were themes of spiritual nurturance, like "Sabbath: Seeking Order Out of Chaos," "Ministering to the Whole Person," "Healing Our Communities—Healing Ourselves," "Work and Family: Can Anyone 'Have It All?'" and "Boys to Men: Rediscovering Rites of Passage for Our Time."[15]

Balancing spiritual nurture and mission with justice imperatives has proven equally difficult in Church Women United, whose national office has chosen a rather different path from that of Presbyterian Women. The four Common Goals of Church Women United, adopted by the Common Council in 1989, stress both personal spiritual growth and social justice but emphasize the latter rather more pointedly than do the purpose statements of either PW or UMW. The three major group events that CWU sponsors throughout the year—World Day of Prayer, World Community Day, and May Friendship Day (recently renamed from May Fellowship Day)—center on worship programs with a strong justice orientation. In producing detailed curricula for local chapters to use at these events, CWU focuses its efforts, as it does in other areas, on education and advocacy work, rather than spiritual development or nurture.

These distinctive emphases have had quite obvious implications for each group's non-mission-oriented public role. Predictably, CWU's focus on justice has compelled it to retain a strong, activist voice, getting as much as it can out of its limited budget. The organization's Legislative Office in Washington, DC, is in charge, first, of monitoring, advocating, and educating on specific issues and pieces of legislation that relate to the quadrennial priorities chosen by the board, which for the 1996–2000 period were "Making the World Safer for Women and Children" and, admitting their own tenuous existence while working toward greater political effectiveness, "Strengthening and Enhancing CWU." Second, the Legislative Office participates in direct advocacy efforts aimed at Congress and the White House on the issues and the bills that most concern CWU constituents. Working in coalition with other (both religious and secular) organizations with common goals and priorities, CWU belongs to approximately fifteen working groups or task forces under umbrella groups such as the National Council of Women's Organizations and the Washington Interreligious Staff Community, focusing their efforts in the three areas of economic stability, peace and disarmament, and interpersonal violence. A bimonthly legislative newsletter, periodic action alerts posted on their website and sent out on e-mail, and periodic mailings to the fifty-state ecumenical action chairpeople are the primary ways that the office gets the word of its activities out to CWU constituents across the country. In all, CWU has impressive networks in place for filling its mandate as a faith-based social justice organization, focused on the global needs of women and children, even after the unexpected December 2000 dismissals of several high-level employees.

United Methodist Women, the most intentional among these three groups about integrating spirituality with mission and social justice, has created a range of published materials, from Bible studies like *Joshua and the Promised Land* and *Ecclesiastes: The Meaning of Your Life* to materials on public policy advocacy such as *Information on Legislation before Congress, State Legislatures and the United Methodist Women's Action Network*, and tracts on contacting and visiting congressional members. At the national level, at least, mission and social justice are far more highly prioritized than spirituality, though UMW's official magazine, *Response*, works to strike a balance between the three. There, articles on economic cooperative projects in India and Central America can mesh with accounts of UMW resolutions on hate crimes in the United States and visits to dioxin-producing municipal incinerators and, less often, with essays on worship or journaling. The magazine layout is colorful and personalized, with lots of photographs and sidebars listing resources for further reading and action.

Three UMW executive staff members are housed in Washington, DC, where they advocate changes in public policy. Pamela Sparr, recent executive secretary of the Office of Environmental Justice for the Women's Division, is proud of the various ways that UMW women get involved in policy work, from signing petitions to participating in hearings and submitting testimony for federal regulatory work, from participating in vigils and UN conferences to formulating shareholder resolutions and advocating corporate responsibility. In Sparr's account, this work occurs from the "very local level on up to the national, international level," such as the Kinko's "chlorine-free paper" campaign that involved women at all levels of UMW. Sparr is especially pleased with UMW's instrumental role in getting the Women, Infants, and Children (WIC) program to be public legislation, the Act for Better Childcare bill, and their ongoing role in the welfare reform debate. She also underlines a recent case where UMW did a "major public witness on health care issues," and while the legislation didn't pass as hoped, "many members of Congress, both Republicans and Democrats, publicly at a press conference lauded United Methodist Women for their dedication to lifting up the needs of people in the United States in terms of health care."

Presbyterian Women does not have a Washington office and does not, apart from the denomination, participate in direct advocacy or political activism. Yet the group is very clear in articulating its purpose, at least at the national level. In terms of a public voice, PW aims most of its efforts at leadership training, efforts directed toward a conglomeration of approximately one thousand PW volunteers called enablers. Enablers are meant to act as a resource for local church women, helping them plan programs, facilitating activities, and providing resources. In turn, enablers transmit information from the higher levels of PW and the denomination to local PW circles and to church pastors who want to know more about PW. In the words of Ann Ferguson, PW coordinator, each enabler is "an encourager and a teacher and really she helps put . . . all the pieces together for the congregation." Staking her hopes on the enabler network to carry out PW's purpose and increase its public role, Ferguson observes that PW does not have the same impact that it had some years ago. "If you look at the history of Presbyterian Women, and I expect other women's organizations in the churches, they were very active in the civil rights movement and then in women's rights and a lot of those issues. They don't seem to be that visible now, to me. But they are still in some ways, I think, doing that in the public realm." As an example, Ferguson mentions the account of one PW member in Alabama who convinced a congressional representative to support debt reduction as part of the Jubilee 2000 campaign. Even more, she notes the global mission work of "building hospitals and schools and encouraging women to get educations."[16] For her and others, mission work is "public" in ways that go beyond legislation and into people's everyday lives. More broadly, of course, PW plays an active public role by training women to be leaders and to think about pressing social issues, even when and where PW is not engaged directly in policy work.

Episcopal Church Women has traditionally been somewhat more reticent regarding the group's purpose and goals, noting that the organization is an umbrella for a diverse array of women's groups within the denomination. While this diversity may contribute to an overall sense of energy and creativity for Episcopal women, the lack of an overarching mandate also presents a problem that current and former leaders recognize and desire to remedy. Jane Banning, ECW president between 1997 and 2000, underscores the purpose of the group as "to carry out Christ's work of reconciliation in the world and to take our place as leaders in the church, in the life and governance and worship of the church." Yet at the same time, she remarks, "If somebody were to ask me, 'What is Episcopal Church Women? What do you do?' I can't tell you because it's so varied. It's different. We have so many ministries. Each group operates within their own parameters." Marjorie Burke, onetime chair of the Committee on the Status of Women in the Episcopal Church and former national president of ECW (1988–91), worries about this dilemma, wishing the group could come together around a common mission, as they did in the nineteenth century when the Episcopal Women's Auxiliary worked to create schools, health programs, and other public institutions. These days, she says, "I think we've kind of lost our focus and a purpose." A refurbished and much expanded website, launched in 2001, provides additional information to prospective constituents. Still, although ECW leaders are struggling to steer the course back to public issues, the organization continues to mean any number of different things to its uncounted participants.

In imagining what kind of public role their organizations fulfill, most mainline women's group leaders would probably echo the sentiment articulated by Kathleen Hurty, former general director of Church Women United, who depicts the public voice of CWU in this way: "It grows out of a faith perspective that is public, as well as a commitment to action that makes a public voice out of public faith." Constructing a public voice out of a faith-based commitment to action takes a prophetic vision for a just and peaceful world, a vision many leaders and participants in these groups certainly possess. It also requires, however, carefully conceived strategies of action, which are not often as clear or, if clear to people at the top levels of the organization and the Washington offices, are not always well translated into the participatory levels of these groups. We turn now to mainline women's associations at the local or congregational level, to examine participants' own sense of their public voice.

LOCAL ACTION

Many women locally involved in the mainline women's organizations echoed the perspective of Banning and Burke, remarking that their groups were so diverse that they could not be defined in terms of a clear function. Some women involved in local units of both United Methodist Women and Presbyterian Women are perfectly happy with this open situation; others complain that the lack of direction is afflictive and opens the way to spiritual narcissism. When asked in interviews to describe the purpose of their associations, virtually all focused on components like fellowship, spirituality, outreach, and mission, though these components—especially the last two—were defined in a variety of ways. Strikingly, only one local leader—from Church Women United—used the word *justice* in discussing the purpose of her organization, and even she had trouble imagining a faith-based women's group with any kind of public role, nationally or (especially) locally. Some local participants emphasized the efforts of their group on behalf of their local community—through rummage sales that provided inexpensive clothing to low-income families, for instance. Others focused more attention on the international mission projects that their organizational headquarters publicized in their magazines, such as supporting education or relief work in Africa. But most spoke first and foremost about their work vis-à-vis their local congregation, seeing their women's circle as more deeply connected to their fellow parishioners than to the mostly invisible organizational leaders in New York, Louisville, or Washington, DC.

Some of the group activities mentioned by local leaders and participants were rummage sales, mother-daughter banquets, luncheons for church staff and congregants, making ribbons for the church hymnals, and bake sales. Though the idea of having a public role appeared (surprisingly) to sound a new note, several suggested that their fund-raising activities had some potential in that regard. Rummage sale income from one local UMW group, one leader noted, was disbursed in 1999 to the African Christian Mission; the Appalachian service project; a Methodist student scholarship fund; a fund for flood victims; the local Church Women United summer camp fund; and local institutions, including a neighborhood center, soup kitchen, crisis center, and battered women's shelter. More money was distributed to the church caring committee, the pastor's discretionary fund, and the church's memorial fund—this despite the attempt by the Women's Division to prevent local UMW funds from being recycled into their congregations. Interestingly, one local co-coordinator of Presbyterian Women, in her third year of that office at the time of our interview, remarked that she had "absolutely no idea" how PW in her church determined which mission projects were funded or how funds were allocated. She suggested that while the local PW board controlled their own budget, paradoxically the local church leaders were the ones making the decisions as to where the money should go.

Without question, the difficulty most commonly raised by local leaders and participants was how to attract younger generations of women. Research data, such as a 1998 survey of *Horizons* (PW's official magazine) readers conducted by the Presbyterian Church, corroborate this as a problem: a full 52 percent of *Horizons* readers responding to the survey were age seventy or older.[17] Few participants interviewed for this project seemed to see much hope of drawing in many women under the age of fifty, nearly all citing contemporary work and family patterns as the reason for their groups' decline. PW and UMW circles tend to meet during the day, as do the programs sponsored by CWU; and even where attempts had been made to accommodate working women by creating evening meetings, these were not viewed as successful. One middle-aged woman, the new president of her local UMW and some years younger than the majority of participants, despaired at how little work had been done in recent years toward gaining new members: "When I got the information given to me from the past president, in the last five years there were maybe three new names on the roster. One was mine. You can't keep an organization strong if you don't pull in new members and get them to work for you! That's part of the problem." In this officer's view, the local UMW is "dying out," and even her best efforts to build it back up with fresh ideas and enthusiasm are not working.

What do younger women want? What would attract them to a mainline women's organization? Leaders and participants hold a variety of views on that question, though the amount of effort and research that has gone into solving it varies widely. Some, perhaps looking at the example of successful evangelical women's groups like the Women's Missionary Union of the Southern Baptist Convention or Women of Faith, suggest that younger women want a focus on spirituality, a way of reconnecting prayerfully with God in the midst of their increasingly hectic daily schedules. While a few leaders express frustration with this desire, as bespeaking a younger generation's self-absorption at the expense of neighbor love, others expect that by expanding the spiritual curriculum offered by local women's circles, they can direct participants into a broader sense of world mission and social justice. Small groups formed for Bible study and fellowship, it is hoped, have the capacity to reach outward into the community and the world.

The Presbyterians seem to have given this question of appealing to younger women the most careful attention, notably in the creation of the National Network of Presbyterian College Women (NNPCW) in 1991. Emerging out of the General Assembly–approved program "Witness to Women," the NNPCW works to develop resources that help college women think about and practice their faith and to train them for leadership positions within and outside the church. With twenty-three campuses directly affiliated with NNPCW, ninety more campuses indirectly affiliated, and numerous individual college women involved, the NNPCW serves as a network connecting young Presbyterian women across the country via a newsletter, a list server, and some local meetings. Other strategies for drawing in younger women have been employed by United Methodist Women, who in May 2000 claimed a nationwide total of teens and college/ university women of 6,795.[18] A survey sent out to members and prospective members in 1995 and a six-year membership campaign running from 1996 to 2002 have been used to expand UMW's base beyond the older women who are its major constituency, and the executive in charge of that campaign claims that it has been very successful so far, a claim that cannot yet be confirmed. While this process was not only aimed at drawing in younger women, the attempt to listen to members and potential members and the resulting action of streamlining local organizational structures signaled a desire to think of the constituency's needs and revise accordingly.[19] The recent addition of a new office—that of executive secretary for young women—further demonstrates UMW's concern for this area.

Church Women United leaders equally recognize the need to focus on younger women but have, not surprisingly, aimed their efforts toward advocacy work. Ann Delorey, the CWU legislative director in Washington, DC, between 1998 and 2000, spent a lot of time traveling in the field and meeting with local CWU groups around the country, most populated by women over sixty. She noted her discouragement, "as a young woman, to rarely see a young face in the audience. I think, 'What is the future of this movement?' There's so much about it I think that would appeal to young women . . . I mean, the issues that we're working on are so relevant." While she would have liked to extend her efforts to locate seminary and college women who might pursue internships in her office, problems of understaffing and scarce funds prevented her from doing very much. In 1999 Delorey was able to develop a hopeful pilot program for thirty-five young people between the ages of eighteen and twenty-seven. Participants in this event, the Young Adult Advocacy Program, came to Washington, DC, as part of the Interfaith Public Policy Briefing (an outgrowth of the now disbanded National Interfaith Impact) and met with members of Congress and the administration, received information on various issues, and participated in lobbying work. The hope was that the Young Adult Advocacy Program could be expanded in the future as a channel for bringing energetic young women back to organizations like CWU.

Local participants, though, of whatever age, often seem intentionally to avoid directing energy toward national issues of policy and legislation. Betty Anderson, a local PW leader, describes her group's function as a "support group," one that looks after its own people first and to individuals in need of mission work second. Indeed, the group appears far more focused on mission activities supported by the congregation than on anything suggested to them by the national office in Louisville. As to whether her group speaks to policy questions of any kind, Anderson says, "No. Well, I certainly don't. I don't think as a woman's group we particularly do." PW's role, in her view, was to serve as a nexus for Bible study and local mission outreach, the latter being directed to a number of worthy causes. Yet Anderson, concluding her third year of leadership, seems to feel somewhat badly at not supporting efforts of a more national or international significance. She recognizes that the national PW meetings (which she could not name) provide the impetus for good work, yet she has no interest in participating in them and so generates little energy in her local group for them. She knows this indifference is a matter of some concern for the higher levels: "I think [our church] has been accused of this [apathy] a lot as far as the women's association's concerned, because we tend not to be very participatory in the presbytery activities or the synod activities."

Anderson's words point to another significant issue, namely, the transmission of ideals, goals, and active implementation of strategies down the line from the national to the local level. Leaders at all points in the hierarchy are quite aware that the channels of communication often get clogged at the intermediate organizational levels—whether synod or presbytery, conference or district, state or region, province or diocese. National officers of these organizations all strive to maintain contact with officers at more concentrated levels, but it is not always easy. While national leadership positions are generally paid positions (with the exception of ECW), officers at every other level are volunteers, many of them working women who may have little time to devote to the group. Programs put in place to keep the national office in touch with its conference or state representatives seem fairly successful, but the closer one gets to the local level, the more difficult it is to maintain that momentum. For instance, United Methodist Women has a District Visitations program, meaning that district officers should visit all local UMW units in any given year. When asked if they had heard from their district representatives, however, most local women had not and needed to look in their files to recall the names of their representatives. One mentioned that "someone at Presbytery" had called her, but she had no clear sense of who this person was.

In the case of Church Women United, one local president interviewed for this project was also a state officer, giving her local chapter a direct link to the state CWU office and the benefit of having a unit president whom they could expect to be particularly well informed about national advocacy work. Yet when local members were asked about programs and activities occurring at the national level, none seemed to have any specific information; they seemed more at ease talking about the current worship program or local CWU activities like the summer camp fund for low-income children than national initiatives. Whether constituents are actually not receiving any information from this local president or simply not processing the information received is difficult to say; but the result—lack of concrete knowledge about national policy initiatives—is the same in either case. This does not necessarily mean that local women are opposed to national forms of political activism—indeed many, especially CWU women, seemed quite proud of the broad-based public work their organizations performed—but they do seem to feel that this type of activity is not in their purview.

As this discussion suggests, intermediate leaders probably have the hardest job of all, charged with disseminating national mandates to the local groups and with communicating local concerns to the higher levels—all of this in unpaid, volunteer positions taken on by women who have other jobs and obligations to fulfill. No matter how good the women's intentions, this intermediate work is virtually impossible to do well, the result being that national leaders seem to be (and are) out of touch with their constituencies, while local participants feel much more connected to their congregations than to a group of unknowns headquartered elsewhere. Grassroots rhetoric to the contrary, these are top-down organizations, with all indicators pointing to the coordinating levels of the organizations as the most reliable places where public activism takes place. Indeed, if the local groups examined here are at all representative of other local groups across the country, then these organizations are profoundly divided between the national and local levels—not an atypical state of affairs in similar associations but one that leaders of faith-based women's groups do not like to admit. How to get local women to think beyond their congregations and imagine themselves as part of a national organization that can be a unified, effective voice for public action is the challenge, and it remains to be met.

The challenge for national leaders, on the other hand, may be to think more realistically and positively about the "non-public" kinds of activities that occur at the local level. Local service activities (including rummage sales whose proceeds go to congregations) and self-help activities (including prayer and support groups) can be interpreted as excessively inner-directed and insufficiently attentive to larger questions of justice. On the other hand, however, such activities are the stuff of what Robert Wuthnow calls "loose connections," the growing tendency of Americans to join together in short-term, task-specific projects and therapy groups rather than long-term, multipurpose affiliations. As Wuthnow's research demonstrates, even very busy people continue to find time and energy for temporary coalitions and short-term volunteer work around particular issues that concern them; moreover, such coalitions depend, for the most part, on the continued presence of the older membership groups like the mainline women's organizations studied here. Both sporadic, single-purpose endeavors and meetings devoted to the spiritual sustenance of modern overworked citizens, however different these activities may look from those organized by more traditional civic or religious groups, are vital forms of public work in modern American society and ones possibly less subject to burnout and discouragement than older forms of association. Above all, as suggested earlier, training women to be leaders, even of small, "private" groups or one-time projects, has ongoing and profoundly important public consequences.[20]

RESOURCES AND RECOMMENDATIONS

Kathleen Hurty once spoke of Church Women United as "one of the best untold stories," an organization whose work for social justice has global impact on women and children and whose impact could be strengthened if only people inside and outside of the churches knew more about it. Lack of media coverage has been a problem for virtually all mainline Protestant institutions and subgroups, as other essays in this volume demonstrate. For women's groups, however, the consequences of public ignorance seem especially severe, particularly in a social climate where disdain is more readily directed toward feminism (even among those reaping its benefits) than is praise. Perhaps to compensate, the materials produced by mainline women's organizations (including websites) follow heroic plotlines about the positive role they have long played in church and society while taking little stock of their internal vulnerabilities. In interviews, national leaders outline with pride their groups' effective outreach and advocacy on behalf of women and children, even as they admit concern about the future of their efforts as fewer women join and remain active. To be sure, Church Women United, Presbyterian Women, and United Methodist Women have inspiring stories to tell about their successes, each possessing its own unique strengths and gifted visionaries, and all have managed to speak and act publicly on issues important to both church and society.

Correspondingly, each organization does some things less effectively than it could, and leaders at all levels do well to be informed of the failures as well as the successes evident in these histories. Single-purpose groups, such as those dedicated to bettering the lives of women and children, are important if such efforts are to reap fruit; and yet it remains true that some work better than others. Various points of weakness in mainline women's groups, such as structural positions within larger church bodies, cannot be easily remedied. And certain factors, such as the wide dispersal of organizational headquarters—Church Women United and United Methodist Women in New York, Presbyterian Women in Louisville, Episcopal Church Women scattered throughout the country, and so forth—may work to disadvantage all groups alike, complicating efforts of leaders to learn from counterparts in their sister organizations and to work together on issues of shared concern. The problem of trying to draw in younger women is likewise common to all, addressed by a wide range of programs, and typical too are the fatigue and burnout potentially created by the daunting proliferation of group-supported issues. But each group has significant resources that, sufficiently utilized, have the potential to carry them well into the future. If there are features of Church Women United, United Methodist Women, and Presbyterian Women that remain untold or untapped, details that could increase the efficacious public role to which these groups aspire, then the groups must be ready both to communicate and to utilize them more directly than they have in the recent past.

A major obstacle to mainline women's public activism is evident in the Washington offices, where staffing is so sparse as to increasingly force mainline women's public advocacy into virtual invisibility. Ann Delorey of Church Women United emphasized that her office could not even hire an administrative assistant to handle such details as ordering office supplies or dealing with technicians when computers, copiers, or fax machines break down. She and her fellow legislative director typed all their own materials, including correspondence, and published their newsletter from the DC office, striving to stay in touch with constituents across the country as well as with key legislators, lobbyists, and a host of advocates from other women's organizations and denominational boards. Volunteer help ranged from scant to nonexistent, the hours spent training newcomers often wasted as well-meaning helpers got too busy, or too infirm, or simply drifted away. According to Delorey, she often had to miss briefings and official meetings in order to keep the office running, and she had no time to cultivate relationships with media representatives who could publicize the kind of work her office performed. To make matters worse for CWU's legislative efforts, Delorey herself resigned her post during the summer of 2000 to return to seminary and start a new family. Her move only begins to illustrate the frequent displacement of talent and dedication from the women's organizations to the clergy, and there are other kinds of displacements as well: in December of the same year, seven national CWU staff members, including Kathleen Hurty, were terminated by CWU's National President, Jerrye Gray Champion, and the Board of Directors, a move that generated a great deal of anger and confusion among constituents that, at this writing, has yet to be thoroughly resolved. As these different cases suggest, both the lack of staffing resources and the apparent crises of leadership within the organization itself have inhibited Church Women United's public presence on women's justice issues in direct and visible ways.

There is also a pressing need to address questions directed toward women's organizations, implicitly or explicitly, by denominational parties that sympathize with their goals yet are dubious about the efficacy of promoting separate, all-female groups to pursue them. Why, given the struggle facing denominational bodies to fulfill a substantial public role in contemporary society, do women's associations not simply work to channel women's energy and money into policy initiatives being developed at higher denominational levels? Should women's groups focus their efforts on fund-raising for programs run by denominational offices, rather than spending money on their own office, administrative, and programming costs? Mainline women involved in these organizations offer a decisive "no" to such queries, pointing out that their work is to consider first the needs of women and children, needs that other denominational offices address only indirectly when they work to end poverty or racism. If the system works properly, the organizations should have myriad ways, from printed matter to e-mail, to get the word of their advocacy out to women in congregations across the nation. While women could feel burdened by calls to support multiple programs, many may well be *more* inclined to support programs that emphasize a positive impact on women and children's health than those that do not—an emphasis that, especially for more conservative women or others less inclined to advocacy, can be read as a mission program instead of a piece of feminist activism. The long history of women's mission organizations, in that sense, provides an ongoing example and justification for female activism, even among more conservative Protestant women who shun the label of feminist.

Yet women's groups at all levels need ways to frame their activities so as to attract attention and support. Protestant women are not always comfortable with what might be seen as boasting, and some surely prefer to hide their light under a bushel. But if such groups are to attract attention and resources and appeal to women who might become (more) active members, publicity about their activities in the secular as well as church media is critically important. National leaders have some media experience, even if they don't always have the time and staff to follow through on what they know; and they would do well to impart some of these skills to local chapters and circles, showing women at all organizational levels how, in this media-saturated age, to get a hearing for their projects. A public presence that is virtually invisible does not seem like much of a presence at all.

For Church Women United, the problem of maintaining a public presence is most acute, particularly in an era when ecumenical work is at the margins of denominational consciousness. Women involved in denominational organizations like United Methodist Women or Presbyterian Women seem little interested in or cognizant of CWU's activities, while CWU women themselves, though deeply loyal to the group, do not always appear confident about articulating what is unique about its work. What local CWU women do say is that UMW and PW units are now so inward-focused as to no longer have any real activist focus to them: CWU, in other words, is perceived as the *only* faith-based group that really works for the betterment of women and children's lives, rather than making ribbons for church hymnals or organizing potluck suppers. In terms of what CWU does that a non-faith-based group like the National Organization for Women or the League of Women Voters does not do, one local CWU president asserts the need to deal with "the religion question . . . in politics" in a way that these groups do not, constructing an alternative to the Religious Right's use of the political process and working to rid the world of religious warfare. At the same time, as Ann Delorey of CWU's Legislative Office put it, CWU is largely "unique within the religious community" for emphasizing the impact of public policies on women and children. Working to clarify these unique contributions is a vital imperative for CWU as well as the denominationally distinct women's organizations.

Beyond the immediate impediments, the challenge for the future is to tap effectively into resources at all levels of mainline women's organizations, getting the best from the national and local levels alike. Rather than see the shifting balance away from national successes to local successes as a sign of decline, for instance, these groups can be proud of the positive impact of their efforts on local communities. And they can celebrate the "loose connections" that often bind people together on short-term, task-specific projects that have lasting value, from rummage sales and battered women's shelters to the encouragement achieved through small group involvement. It does little good to wax lyrical in lament for the large numbers of women who committed enormous amounts of time and energy to these groups in the past; the demographic realities of today's working women make a return to those days impossible. Still, as Wuthnow and his team of researchers have shown, there is much to value in current arrangements of time and energy. Even when struggling to attract and retain new members, these groups fill a vital role for the many sympathizers who are too busy to attend regular meetings yet read about their activities and occasionally contribute money and labor to specific initiatives. Leaders ought to think about the changing roles of their groups in a more positive light and work creatively to tap into those sideline resources more effectively.

To combat fatigue and complacency, it remains crucial to convey to all participants and leaders the concrete impact their individual actions can have upon women and children's lives throughout the nation and the world, both in terms of direct "mercy" or relief work and through changes in law and public policy. Task-specific projects, moreover, can affect the latter, even on the national level, as surely as they can bring immediate help to local women and children in need. The moral of recent CWU initiatives of this kind, for Delorey, is that if more people at the national as well as the local level could have the experience of visiting their elected representatives, more would recognize the importance of such seemingly small efforts as writing letters to legislators. However small or mundane such work might seem to groups that regularly lobby Congress to pass legislation, conveying the message that each individual and local unit has the potential to make an impact and fulfill a public role is critical for faith-based women's groups that want to extend the generous side of Christian faith. Says Delorey, "It's like participating in your own democracy."

Further integrating spirituality with social justice would be another way of appealing to younger women who ostensibly want more of a spiritual focus in these groups, while not losing the mandate for public justice work stressed by national leaders. Cindy Bartol, former Province Three representative to the national board of Episcopal Church Women (and onetime chair of ECW's Social Justice Committee), gives a potent definition of spiritual nourishment as "skill building and justice issue building and community building." If women's groups could move further in the direction of articulating such a vision of the spiritual life that begins with private Bible study or journaling and then uses such tools to expand outward into larger questions and issues, they could go farther in their intent to appeal to women from all walks of life and with varying levels of time and energy to spend in a women's group. Bartol's own suggestion—give the women a concrete action to do and don't oblige them to attend monthly meetings—might work less in the cause of spirituality but could also facilitate local groups' awareness of themselves as having a tangible public role, both in their local communities and in the world at large.

How much has changed over time? During the early 1980s, in preparation for the creation of Presbyterian Women out of its predecessor organizations, pastors and congregants were surveyed about the women's groups' strengths and weaknesses. The results, initially reported in 1985, are interesting to read today. Respondents praised the two women's organizations for their attention to direct, concrete service; their structure from the local to the national level; the degree of nurturance available there; their impact on local communities; their funding resources; their relative autonomy in setting agendas; and the esteem in which the organizations were held by their respective churches. Weaknesses of the organizations highlighted by the survey included the schizophrenia of being both "old and dull" and "on the cutting edge"; lack of communication between local and regional staff; pastors' ignorance of the organizations' purpose and functioning; poor leadership training and resources; and the lack of time for building personal relationships.[21] Interview data for this project record echoes from those earlier respondents, making clear the ongoing trials facing women's groups within church bodies that do not always see their public value beyond local fund-raising.

Perhaps the most daunting challenge now is the shift that has taken place over the past thirty years in public understanding of the role of religion in the political process. Countless observers from these groups have watched that shift take place, as media-savvy conservative groups have pushed mainline Protestant organizations out of the public spotlight. Mainline Protestants' confidence in their capacity to fulfill a broad public role for social justice is not as high as it could be at the moment, as the evidence here and elsewhere shows. Yet at the same time, women inspired by the range of feminist models that have opened up in this period have arguably become *more* confident of the need to bring a gender-conscious perspective to public issues beyond ministerial ordination, from the environment to the economy. Ultimately, the legacy of mainline women's groups like Church Women United, Presbyterian Women, and United Methodist Women may not simply be their own activism, or whatever new numbers they can attract to their ranks, but the tangible commitment to justice for women and children they can inspire in the church bodies that surround them.

NOTES

1. Interviews were conducted with the heads of each mainline women's organization and various high-ranking staff officials located in the national or Washington, DC, offices. Local women were selected through phone calls to fifteen congregations in the northeastern United States: approximately half of these did not have enough currently active women in their organizations to warrant further pursuit. Interviews were mostly restricted to the remaining congregations, where local groups remained active and connected to their official headquarters. With permission, I have quoted women using real names; in other cases, I have used pseudonyms.

2. Each of these organizations keeps careful records of its history, and all have printed numerous accounts of their founding and trajectory over time. Information about current projects and contact information is readily available on group websites; for Church Women United, http://www.churchwomen.org; for United Methodist Women, http://gbgm-umc.org/umw; for Presbyterian Women, http://www.horeb.pcusa.org/gathering; and for Episcopal Church Women, http://www.ecusa.anglican.org/ecw. Another useful reference source is Sarah Slavin, ed., *U.S. Women's Interest Groups: Institutional Profiles* (Westport, CT: Greenwood Press, 1995).

3. This and subsequent quotations are taken from interviews. (My interview with Hurty took place more than a year before she was terminated from her position in December 2000.) More historical information on CWU appears in Gladys Gilkey Calkins, *Follow Those Women* (New York: Church Women United, Office of Publication and Distribution, 1961); and Margaret Shannon, *Just Because: The Story of the National Movement of Church Women United in the U.S.A., 1941 through 1975* (Corte Madera, CA: Omega Books, 1977). See also Virginia Lieson Brereton, "United and Slighted: Women as Subordinated Insiders," in William R. Hutchison, ed., *Between the Times: The Travail of the Protestant Establishment in America, 1900–1960* (Cambridge: Cambridge University Press, 1989), 143–67.

4. Discussions of the proposed merger and its potential impact upon these Presbyterian women's organizations in the United Presbyterian Church (USA), and the Presbyterian Church, U.S., took place in a special issue of *Concern* magazine in February, 1977. The issue, entitled "Two Goodly Heritages: Presbyterian Women, How Does Our Past Inform Our Future?" told the histories of the two groups, compared their similarities and differences, and tried to lay the groundwork for unification. See also Annette Chapman-Adisho, *Years of Strong Effort: The Development of Women's Organizations in the Presbyterian Churches, 1967–1993* (Louisville, KY: Women's Ministries Program Area, National Ministries Division, Presbyterian Church [USA], n.d.); and Barbara McDonald, *Bound Together in Love: The Creation of Presbyterian Women, 1978–1988* (Louisville, KY: Presbyterian Women, 1991).

5. Anne Bass Fulk, Marylyn Adams, Marcy Walsh, Marjorie Burke, and Ginger Paul, *A Short History of the Triennial Meetings of the Women of the Episcopal Church* (n.d., n.p.), 36.

6. Episcopal Church Women is a separate entity from Women in Mission and Ministry in the Episcopal Church.

7. Describing the practical difference this different structure makes, Ann Ferguson, PW coordinator, notes that PW depends on the General Assembly Council for staff, while UMW pays for its own staff. In her words, "The organization [PW]

determines its own program budget, determines its own programs, elects its own leadership all the way through, from the congregation on to the church-wide level. But we don't work outside of the denomination at all."

8. Peggy Billings, *Speaking Out in the Public Space: An Account of the Section of Christian Social Relations, Women's Division, the United Methodist Church, 1968–1984* (New York: Women's Division of the United Methodist Church, 1995), 13.

9. On Lundy's resignation, see "The Plight of the Presbyterians," *Christian Century* June 1–8, 1994, 565–66.

10. For a brief account of this statement, see "Women's Conference and a 'Theological Crisis,'" *Christian Century*, March 23–30, 1994, 306–7.

11. Mark Chaves, *Ordaining Women: Culture and Conflict in Religious Organizations* (Cambridge, MA, and London: Harvard University Press, 1997), 1.

12. The total amount received from mission pledges in a single year, according to Ann Ferguson, was $35 million. Anything above PW's annual program budget (approved in three-year cycles) remains in the unified fund for the denomination, given to the Presbyterian Church to do with as its leaders see fit.

13. According to CWU's published information, the breakdown of funding for that fiscal year was as follows: World Day of Prayer offerings (24%), individual gifts (9%), World Community Day offerings (7%), state unit support (7%), denominational support (3%), sales of CWU materials and resources (13%), foundation grants (23%), and other (14%).

14. Sylvia Washer, "A Dream Called Presbyterian Women," *Horizons*, July/August 1988, 2.

15. Titles are taken from the cover stories of *Horizons* magazine, all from issues published in 1999.

16. The Women's Ministry Program Area also staffs an Office of Women's Advocacy, which, though separate from Presbyterian Women proper, participates in justice and peace activities.

17. With 52 percent of respondents age seventy or older, 28 percent were 60–69; 10 percent were in their fifties; 7 percent were in their forties; 2 percent were in their thirties; and none were under thirty. As the survey concludes, "*Horizons* subscribers are an educated, yet elderly group. . . .Because of the age of its readers, *Horizons'* circulation will continue to decline as these women reach the age at which they can no longer read it or death takes them. To prevent the eventual demise of the magazine, radical changes are needed." From "*Horizons* Reader Survey," May 1998, 5, 9; available from Research Services of the Presbyterian Church, Louisville, KY.

18. Long claiming a U.S. membership of a million women, UMW leaders now acknowledge that their numbers are probably no longer that high; as with the other groups, however, leaders are reticent about actual figures. Published data from the United Methodist Church shows that UMW had 1.4 million members in 1974, 1.2 million in 1980, and 905,000 in 1998. If these figures are correct, UMW membership is declining at a faster rate than overall denominational membership. In 1980, there were 9,548,284 members of the United Methodist Church and 1,241,622 members of UMW, meaning that 13 percent of Methodists were members of UMW. In 1990, 12 percent were members, and by 1998, just 10.7 percent of Methodists were members of UMW. Figures are from the general minutes of the United Methodist Church, published by the General Council on Finance and Administration.

19. Local units henceforth were allowed to opt for a minimum-function structure (with two elected offices), a basic structure (with six), or the expanded struc-

ture (with eleven). Some titles of elected offices were also revised: for instance, the former "mission coordinator for Christian personhood" became the "mission coordinator for spiritual growth."

20. Robert Wuthnow, *Loose Connections: Joining Together in America's Fragmented Communities* (Cambridge, MA and London: Harvard University Press, 1998).

21. Chapman-Adisho, *Years of Strong Effort*, 55–56; McDonald, *Bound Together in Love*, 28.

4 Religious Variations in Public Presence

*Evidence from the
National Congregations Study*

Mark Chaves, Helen M. Giesel,
and William Tsitsos

Religion and religious organizations are enjoying (or, perhaps, enduring) renewed attention from scholars and public officials. This renewed attention probably does not represent increased appreciation of religion qua religion—spirituality, theology, ritual, worship, or other core religious operations or concerns. Rather, it is largely driven by interest in what religion, and religious organizations, might contribute to the world outside the walls of churches, synagogues, mosques, and temples. How does religion enhance individuals' civic skills and participation? How do religious organizations contribute to a vital civil society or enrich public discourse? How do they partake in movements for social change? Many now see religion and religious organizations as springs of voluntarism, community resources, and civic skills that can be deployed in a wide variety of secular arenas. This volume, with its focus on the public presence of mainline Protestantism, can be placed in the context of this wider concern with religion's civic significance.[1]

Discussions of civic participation often note that not all voluntary associations contribute positively to civil society, not all community resources are deployed to advance the public good, and not all voluntarism is outward-looking. In one influential formulation, the political scientist Robert Putnam distinguishes between "bonding" and "bridging" forms of civic participation. "Bonding" civic participation tends to keep individuals within the groups or associations to which they are primarily attached. "Bridging" civic participation, by contrast, tends to build connections between groups or associations. This chapter focuses on religious differences in various kinds of bridging civic activities engaged in by American congregations. Such bridging activity is one important way that religion and religious organizations might have a public presence.[2]

Religious groups vary in the extent to which they value, pursue, or encourage public activities. Previous research suggests that, among Christians in the United States, such variation is systematically tied to long-standing differences among liberal or mainline Protestants, conservative or evangelical Protestants, and Catholics. Mainline Protestants, when they are active churchgoers, are more likely to join nonreligious voluntary associations, work actively in those organizations, and volunteer in support of secular activities and organizations. They are more likely to be on the boards of secular hospitals. Mainline congregations, at least historically, appear to have been much more likely than congregations in other traditions to give rise to secular associations of various sorts. In other words, liberal or mainline Protestantism appears to encourage more bridging forms of civic engagement than either conservative/evangelical Protestantism or Roman Catholicism.[3]

Previous research on this question has mainly examined individuals' activities. In this chapter, we examine *congregations'* activities. Are the same patterns we see in individuals' activities visible among congregations' collective activities? Though a correlation between individuals' civic participation and the civic activities of their congregations may seem obvious, it is not. The fact that Presbyterians, on average, volunteer more than Pentecostals for secular organizations does not in and of itself imply that Presbyterian congregations engage in more social service activities *as congregations*. However, our examination of thirty-eight concrete congregational activities bearing on the question of public presence—understood here as bridging kinds of activities—shows that mainline Protestant congregations do indeed engage in most of these activities at higher rates than do other Protestants and, to a lesser extent, Catholics. Political activity is the most important exception to this pattern.

What type of connection might there be between a congregation's bridging activities and the bridging activities of the individual people in that congregation? On the one hand, congregations might be gatherings of like-minded people who together use the congregation as a vehicle for activities that they might anyway engage in but which are more effectively or efficiently pursued through an organization. On the other hand, congregations might provide individuals with the information, rationale, and opportunities that lead them to pursue civic and public activities that they might not otherwise pursue. These two types of connection between congregations' and individuals' public activity are not, of course, mutually exclusive, and we suspect that they work together in a positive feedback loop. We are not able, in this chapter, to discern the relative importance of these mechanisms in producing the patterns we describe below. Still, by establishing that congregations within different religious traditions are "public" in distinctive ways, and that mainline Protestants are, in general, more likely than others to sponsor activities that build bridges extending outside their congregations, we add one piece to the emerging picture about religious variations in public presence and civic participation.

DATA AND METHODS

The National Congregations Study

This chapter draws on data from the National Congregations Study (NCS), a survey of a nationally representative sample of religious congregations in the United States. This survey had its genesis in the 1998 General Social Survey, a representative sample of non-institutionalized, English-speaking adults in the United States that included a set of items asking respondents who say they attend religious services to report the name and location of their religious congregation. Data about each of these congregations were collected via a one-hour interview with a key informant, such as a minister, priest, rabbi, or other staff person or leader. Data were collected for 1,236 congregations, a response rate of 80 percent.[4]

The NCS data can address two different kinds of questions: (1) What percentage of *congregations* have particular characteristics? (2) What percentage of *people* attend congregations with particular characteristics? Although answers to both kinds of question are often substantively interesting, this chapter focuses on congregational characteristics in terms of the percentage of people attached to them rather than in terms of congregations as organizational units without respect to size. When it comes to congregations' public presence, it is more useful to focus on how many people are in congregations engaging in certain kinds of activities than it is to know how many congregations engage in those activities. For the purposes of this chapter, for example, it is more relevant to report that 75 percent of religious service attenders are in congregations that have social service projects than to report that only 57 percent of congregations have such projects.

Measuring Religious Tradition and Congregations' Public Presence

There is no single correct way to define "mainline Protestantism." In this chapter we follow the convention of the volume as a whole and include six denominations in the "mainline": United Methodist Church, Presbyterian Church (USA), Episcopal Church, Evangelical Lutheran Church in America, American Baptist Churches, and the United Church of Christ. When we say "other Protestants," we mean Christian congregations that are neither Roman Catholic nor associated with one of these six denominations—an appellation that includes conservative and evangelical Protestants, but also other Protestant groups as well. We limit our analysis to Christian congregations because, although the NCS contains data on non-Christian congregations, there are too few such congregations within any one tradition to have a high degree of confidence in the reliability of statistics based on these subsamples.[5]

The NCS gathered data on a wide range of congregational activities and characteristics. For this chapter we scoured the NCS data to identify items that we could reasonably interpret as indicators of bridging activities. Casting a wide net, we found thirty-eight relevant items, which we organized into six groups:

1. The *social service* group includes items indicating whether or not congregations participate in any social service programs, and whether or not they have programs in any of five substantive areas: food, housing, clothing, health, and homelessness. It also includes an item indicating whether or not the congregation has had a representative of any social service organization as a visiting speaker within the past twelve months, and another item indicating whether or not the congregation had a group, or meeting, or event in the past twelve months focused on organizing or encouraging people to do volunteer work.

2. A group of *education* items examines whether or not the congregation has an elementary or high school; whether or not it contributes money to any college, university, or seminary; and whether or not it had an academic or professor as a visiting speaker in the past twelve months. Items indicating whether or not the congregation has any ongoing education programs (not including religious education), any youth mentoring programs, or any congregational small groups focused on educational themes (again not including religious education) are also included.

3. A *religion* category includes activities that might connect a congregation with other congregations or expose its members to other religious traditions: whether or not clergy from another congregation were visiting speakers within the past year; whether or not, within the past year, the congregation had a group or class that met to discuss or learn about a religion other than their own; whether or not, within the past year, the congregation had any joint worship services with other congregations; and,

if it did, whether or not it had one with a congregation from another religious tradition and whether or not it had one with a congregation of a different racial or ethnic makeup.

4. A *culture* category includes activities through which the congregation might connect, or at least expose its people, to secular art worlds. Items identifying these activities include the following: Has there been a group, meeting, class, or event within the past year focused on discussing a book other than the Bible, or one to organize a trip to see a live musical or theatrical performance outside the congregation? Has the congregation, within the past year, hired any singers or musicians to perform at a worship service? Do visitors ever come to view the architecture or artwork of the worship space? Have any outside groups used the congregation's building for rehearsals or performances of musical or theatrical work? Have any used the building for art exhibits?

5. A *community* category includes these items: whether or not, within the past year, any group, program, or event with no connection to the congregation used or rented space in the congregation's building; whether or not the congregation has had any groups, meetings, classes, or events to talk about race relations, to talk about environmental issues, or to assess community needs. This set of items also includes one with a different valence than the others: whether or not the congregation has special rules or norms regarding what sorts of outside groups its members can join. Whereas most of the other items used in this chapter indicate the presence of bridge-building kinds of activity, this item indicates the presence of barriers between the congregation and the world outside it.

6. Finally, a *politics* category contains items indicating various ways a congregation might engage in or encourage political activity: Within the past year has there been a group, meeting, class, or event to discuss politics, to organize or participate in efforts to lobby elected officials, to organize or participate in a demonstration or march concerning some public issue or policy, or to get people registered to vote? Has the congregation ever distributed voter guides? Are people told during worship of opportunities for political activity? Has an elected government official or someone running for office been a visiting speaker at the congregation within the past year?

We attribute no particular theoretical significance to this way of grouping activities, nor do we claim that these thirty-eight items or six categories exhaust the meaning of congregations' public presence. We claim only that these items represent a fairly broad range of activities bearing on congregations' public presence, and that we have found it helpful to organize the specific items into these six categories.[6]

Although we have emphasized bridging activities as a form of congregations' public presence, the items listed above are not equally apt as indicators of congregations' connectedness to the world around them. Having a school, for example, although clearly indicating a kind of public presence for a congregation, does not so clearly indicate a congregation's effort to connect itself or its people to other parts of the community. A religious school might indicate just the opposite: an attempt to keep a congregation's children isolated—or, from the congregation's point of view, protected—from the wider community. Without knowing more about how a congregation's school actually operates, it is difficult to know, from the mere fact of its existence, whether to interpret it as a bridge-building or barrier-erecting kind of activity.

Although this and other legitimate interpretive questions might be raised about some of these thirty-eight items, we see value in examining a broad range of activities that might bear on the question of congregations' public presence. We also should note that we selected these items without respect to what the data show about religious differences on them. As we will see, differences among mainline Protestants, other Protestants, and Roman Catholics are strikingly consistent across these items, and we want to emphasize that this consistency is not a consequence of any selective choosing of items on our part.

Our analysis strategy is straightforward. We compare the percentages of mainline Protestant, other Protestant, and Roman Catholic congregations that engage in each of these thirty-eight activities. In line with this volume's theme, we focus our analysis and discussion on the comparison of mainline versus other congregations. We present in detail only these basic percentages, but we also report some results from analyses that examine differences across religious traditions while controlling for a variety of congregational and neighborhood characteristics. Results from these analyses do not change the basic patterns evident in the percentages we present below. Readers may focus solely on the simple percentages without fear of being substantively misled.

RESULTS

Table 4.1 displays our basic results. This table gives the percentages of people in mainline, other Protestant, and Catholic congregations who are in congregations with the specified activity. The table also reports whether

Table 4.1. Differences in Congregations' Public Presence, by Religious Tradition

Activity	Members Attending Congregations Engaged in Specified Activity (%)			Statistical Significance of Mainline Effects[a]	
	Six Mainline Protestant Denominations[b] (n = 283)	Other Protestants (n = 604)	Roman Catholics (n = 299)	Significance Level for Difference between Mainline Congregations and All Other Congregations Combined	Significance Level for Mainline Difference, Controlling for Other Variables[c]
Social Services					
Any social service, community development, or neighborhood project	88	65	82	**	**
Hosted representative of a social service organization as visiting speaker	61	25	46	**	**
Held group/meeting/class/event to organize or encourage people to do volunteer work	62	45	79	n.s.	n.s.
Sponsored or participated in any:					
Food programs	62	39	59	**	**
Housing programs	53	23	33	**	**
Clothing programs	21	15	19	n.s.	n.s.
Homelessness programs	19	13	17	+	n.s.
Health programs	13	5	14	n.s.	n.s.

Education					
Have an elementary school or a high school	3	14	55	**	**
Gave money to any college, university, or seminary	57	45	39	**	**
Hosted academic/professor as visiting speaker	43	34	38	+	n.s.
Held small group whose purpose for meeting was education-related (not including religious education)	4	2	11	n.s.	n.s.
Sponsored or participated in educational program, not including religious education	16	8	8	**	**
Sponsored or participated in mentoring program	6	2	2	**	**
Religion					
Held group/meeting/class/event to discuss or learn about another religion	40	26	25	**	**
Hosted clergy from another congregation as visiting speaker	72	77	61	n.s.	n.s.
Participated in joint worship with another congregation	75	66	60	**	**
Participated in joint worship with a congregation of another religious tradition[d]	41	21	49	**	*
Participated in joint worship with a congregation of a different racial or ethnic makeup	31	33	27	n.s.	n.s.

Table 4.1. (continued)

| Activity | Members Attending Congregations Engaged in Specified Activity (%) | | | Statistical Significance of Mainline Effects[a] | |
	Six Mainline Protestant Denominations[b] (n = 283)	Other Protestants (n = 604)	Roman Catholics (n = 299)	Significance Level for Difference between Mainline Congregations and All Other Congregations Combined	Significance Level for Mainline Difference, Controlling for Other Variables[c]
Culture					
Hired singers or other musicians to perform at a worship service	59	43	56	**	**
Had visitors view the building's architecture or artwork	63	42	68	**	n.s.
Held group/meeting/class/event to discuss a book other than the Bible	66	35	33	**	**
Organized group/meeting/class/event to attend a live musical or theatrical performance outside the congregation	63	55	40	**	**
Permitted outside groups to use the building for rehearsals or performances of musical or theatrical works	45	19	33	**	**
Permitted outside groups to use the building for exhibits of paintings, photography, or sculpture	19	6	12	**	**

Community					
Permitted outside groups to use or rent space in the building	85	55	**	73	**
Held group/meeting/class/event to:					
Plan or conduct an assessment of community needs	52	43	n.s.	53	n.s.
Discuss pollution or other environmental issues	24	7	**	16	**
Discuss race relations in our society	31	18	**	21	*
Have special rules or norms regarding what sorts of outside groups congregants can join	3	25	**	23	**
Politics					
Held group/meeting/class/event to:					
Discuss politics	19	8	**	13	**
Organize or participate in efforts to lobby elected officials	10	6	n.s.	23	n.s.
Organize or participate in a demonstration/march concerning some public issue or policy	12	14	**	42	*
Get people registered to vote	7	13	**	16	n.s.
Informed people at worship services about opportunities for political activity	38	30	n.s.	45	n.s.
Distributed voter guides	19	31	**	26	n.s.

Table 4.1. (continued)

Activity	Members Attending Congregations Engaged in Specified Activity (%)			Statistical Significance of Mainline Effects[a]	
	Six Mainline Protestant Denominations[b] (n = 283)	Other Protestants (n = 604)	Roman Catholics (n = 299)	Significance Level for Difference between Mainline Congregations and All Other Congregations Combined	Significance Level for Mainline Difference, Controlling for Other Variables[c]
Hosted elected government official as visiting speaker	16	12	8	*	n.s.
Hosted someone running for office as visiting speaker	8	6	3	n.s.	*

NOTE: Congregations were asked if most of these activities and programs had occurred within the past year.

[a]n.s. = p ≥ .10; + = .10 > p ≥ .05; * = .05 > p ≥ .01; ** p < .01.

[b]This category includes six denominations: United Methodist Church, Presbyterian Church (USA), Episcopal Church, Evangelical Lutheran Church in America, American Baptist Churches, and the United Church of Christ.

[c]Based on logistic regressions with the following control variables: logged size; logged amount of annual income; theologically conservative, liberal, or right in the middle; percentage of regular participants living in households with annual income under $25,000; percentage of regular participants living in households with annual income higher than $100,000; percentage of regular adult participants having at least a four-year college degree; racial composition; geographical region; rural/nonrural location; located or not in a census tract where more than 30 percent of the people fall under the official poverty line; percentage of regular adult participants younger than thirty-five; percentage of regular adult participants older than sixty; and founding date.

[d]These numbers slightly overstate the level of ecumenism among congregations. Congregational informants sometimes reported a joint worship service that occurred with a congregation that was not Protestant, Catholic, or Jewish, even though the joint service at issue was in fact with a Protestant congregation. We were not able to adjust for these mistaken reports of inter-religious worship before this volume went to press.

the percentage of mainline congregations engaged in each activity is statistically different from the percentage of all other congregations engaged
in that activity. Unless the percentage difference is not statistically significant (indicated by "n.s." in the table), one may be reasonably confident
that people in mainline congregations are indeed more (or less) likely to
be in congregations engaged in an activity than are people in non-mainline
Protestant congregations. The table also gives significance levels for the
mainline difference in more complex analyses which control a variety of
congregational and neighborhood characteristics. We will say more about
these analyses below. Our main focus, however, is on the simple percentages displayed in table 4.1.

In regard to social service activities, a clear picture emerges. Mainline
congregations are significantly more likely to be engaged in five of the
eight social service items. On the activities where this overall difference is
not present—organizing or encouraging volunteer work, participating in
clothing programs or in health-related programs—mainline congregations
are noticeably more likely to do these things than are other Protestant
congregations, but the overall mainline difference is washed out because
Catholic congregations are at least as likely as mainline Protestants to
engage in these activities. When it comes to organizing or encouraging
volunteer work, Catholic congregations are substantially more likely to do
this than mainline Protestants.

Some of these differences are sizeable. Sixty-one percent of people attending mainline congregations, for example, are in a congregation that
had a representative of a social service organization as a visiting speaker
within the past year, compared to 46 percent of people attending Catholic
congregations and only 25 percent of people attending non-mainline Protestant congregations. In general, the differences between mainline and
non-mainline Protestants are larger than the differences between mainline
Protestants and Catholics. For some kinds of activities—hearing someone
from a social service agency speak, participating in some kind of housing
activity (often a Habitat for Humanity project), sponsoring or participating
in some kind of health-related program—mainline congregations are more
than twice as likely as other Protestant congregations to expose their members to these ventures.

A similar pattern is evident in the education items. Mainline congregations are significantly more likely than other congregations to engage
in four of the six activities: giving money to an institution of higher education, having had an academic or professor as a visiting speaker, and
sponsoring or participating in education-related and youth mentoring pro-

grams. Mainline congregations do not stand out from other congregations when it comes to having small groups who meet around educational purposes (not including religious education).

Given the long history of Catholic schooling in the United States, the priority given to school-building by Missouri Synod (but not ELCA) Lutherans, and the more recent emergence of private schooling among evangelicals and fundamentalists, it is not surprising that mainline congregations are least likely to sponsor elementary or high schools. More than half of all Catholics are in congregations that sponsor schools, compared to 14 percent of non-mainline Protestants and only 3 percent of those in mainline congregations. From one perspective this could be seen as a dimension of public presence on which mainline Protestant congregations fall behind other groups. From another perspective, as discussed earlier, to the extent that school sponsorship indicates wagon-circling rather than bridge-building, this result is consistent with the larger pattern in which the public presence of mainline congregations is more likely than that of other congregations to result in connections to other parts of the community. Mainline congregations are less likely to build enclaves for their people.

Reflecting on the meaning of religious schools prompts another observation. Institutions or practices that begin as efforts to separate a religious community from the surrounding world may develop into institutions or practices that enhance the connectedness of the religious community to others. The fact that some urban Catholic elementary schools, which began as an effort to shield Catholic children from public schools dominated by Protestants, now educate large numbers of non-Catholic children from the surrounding neighborhoods is, perhaps, a case in point. Religious institution-building, it always is worth mentioning, can generate long-term consequences that are unintended and unforeseen by their founders.

The set of items indicating bridging to other religious communities presents a slightly more mixed picture, but one that is broadly consistent with our developing theme. Although mainline congregations are not distinctive when it comes to having clergy from another congregation as a visiting speaker, the religious connections that they pursue are more likely to cross important religious boundaries than are the religious connections pursued by other kinds of congregations. Mainline congregations are significantly more likely than others to have a group, or meeting, or class to discuss or learn about another religion. They also are more likely than other congregations to expose people to joint worship with another congregation, and they are about twice as likely as non-mainline Protestant congregations to expose their people to joint worship with a congregation from another religious tradition (meaning a Catholic or non-Christian congregation). Interestingly, mainline Protestant, other Protestant, and Catholic congregations are equally likely to have joint worship that crosses ethnic or racial boundaries: about 30 percent of the people within each group are in congregations that have had such a joint service in the past year.

The culture and community items tell an unambiguous story. Mainline congregations are substantially more likely than other congregations to connect to secular art worlds in various ways, from hiring musicians to perform in worship, to organizing groups to attend live performances, to allowing outside groups to use the congregation's building for rehearsals, performances, or exhibits. They are also more likely—by substantial margins—to have outside groups using or renting space in their buildings, and they are more likely to have groups, meetings, classes, or events to discuss environmental issues or race relations. On only one of the culture and community items are mainline congregations statistically indistinguishable from other congregations: they are no more or less likely to have a group or meeting focused on assessing the surrounding community's needs. Strikingly, only 3 percent of participants in mainline Protestant congregations are in congregations reporting special rules or norms regarding what sorts of outside groups people can join, compared to 25 percent in other Protestant congregations and 23 percent in Catholic congregations. On this rather direct measure of whether or not congregations actively discourage other kinds of civic engagement, mainline Protestants are clearly far less likely than others to receive such discouragement from their churches. All in all, these results, like those in the other categories, support the conclusion that mainline congregations are substantially more likely than others to create and encourage connections between churches and their surrounding communities.

Only when it comes to political activities does the picture look dramatically different. Here, mainline congregations are significantly more active only on two of eight types of political activity: having a group, meeting, class, or event to discuss politics, and having an elected government official as a visiting speaker. This second difference disappears when other things are controlled, and on all the other political activities there is either no difference, or the difference is the opposite of what we have been seeing. Mainline congregations, for example, are significantly *less* likely than other congregations to organize or participate in a demonstration or march, get people registered to vote, or distribute voter guides. Interestingly, unlike most other kinds of bridging activities examined in this analysis, Catholic congregations seem to lead the way on several sorts of political activity.[7]

Overall, these results point to a simple but important conclusion: Mainline congregations engage in more public activity of every sort we have examined, *except political activity*. Political activity is likely to represent taking sides in a partisan conflict, even when, as with encouraging voter registration or distributing voter guides, the activity is ostensibly educational and nonpartisan. Given this, the fact that mainline congregations do more of every activity except explicit political activity suggests that not only are mainline congregations in many ways among the most public of all congregations, but they also tend to be public in ways that encourage bridging and nonpartisan connections between congregations and other community segments.

Throughout this section we have emphasized the ways in which mainline congregations stand out from Christian congregations of other sorts. It is worth noting, however, that on some kinds of activities the key fault line seems to be between Protestants and Catholics, while on other activities Catholics and mainline Protestant congregations appear to be fairly similar when compared to non-mainline Protestants. Catholics, for example, are substantially more likely than either mainline or other Protestants to be in a congregation that organizes or participates in lobbying efforts, demonstrations, and marches. When it comes to social services, by contrast, Catholic congregations are closer to mainline Protestant congregations, with other Protestant congregations notable for their lower levels of participation. The general, though not universal, pattern is that mainline Protestant congregations are most likely to expose people to bridging activities, other Protestants are least likely, and Catholics are in between. Although it would be tedious to inventory every possible comparison and all of the exceptions to the general pattern, some of these exceptions bear closer examination for what they might tell us about the distinctive cultures of public presence carried by religious traditions.

CONCLUSION

We have shown that mainline congregations' public presence is of a different sort than the public presence of Catholic and other Protestant congregations. Mainline congregations are more likely to engage in and encourage activities that build connections between congregations and the world around them. They are more likely to engage in social services, encourage educational activity (except sponsor their own elementary or high schools), interact with other congregations across traditional religious boundaries, connect or expose their people to art worlds, and open their buildings to community groups. They are not, in general, more likely to engage in politics. Mainline congregations may not have more of a public presence than other congregations, but they clearly have a public presence of a distinctive sort. Were we to interpret our results expansively, we might say that mainline congregations appear more likely than congregations in other traditions to act as stewards of civil society rather than as one component of civil society.

The basic contours of religious variation in public presence that we discern among congregations are, as we indicated in the introduction to this chapter, consistent with much scholarship on long-standing religious differences in the United States. Interpreters of American religion have offered a variety of explanations for these differences. Robert Wuthnow has suggested that one source of the difference, at least among Protestants, is that denominations with European roots as territorial churches re-created in the United States their systems of associations and federations, thereby reproducing their deep involvement in civic affairs. The historian Peter Dobkin Hall attributes the difference, in part, to regional differences in institutional culture and to a broader contrast between pro- and anti-institution-building ideologies carried by different religious traditions. Sociologists John Wilson and Thomas Janoski have hypothesized that higher levels of otherworldly religious beliefs among non-mainline Protestants might be responsible for lower levels of concern with, and participation in, community outside the congregation.[8] Generally lower levels of civic activity in Catholic congregations, compared to mainline congregations, might be an institutional residue of historic attempts to build an encompassing set of Catholic institutions and associations whose purpose was to maintain enclaves rather than bridge to other communities.

An explanation somewhat less sanguine about high levels of mainline civic activity might emphasize the fact that, for much of American history, white mainline congregations were more or less coterminous with a civil society that quite effectively excluded others from full participatory citizenship. If "your" people in fact control public schools, there is no reason to use your congregations to build schools. If the surrounding civil society is mainly composed of associations, federations, and organizations that "your" people lead, there is no reason to discourage congregants from participating in them. Perhaps higher levels of mainline civic activity are a by-product of mainline Protestant domination of civil society, and lower levels of civic activity by other congregations are a long-term consequence of social exclusion from that Protestant Establishment. Congregations perhaps become vehicles for civic activity for groups already wholly embedded, by other means, in the secular institutions of civil society; they perhaps become enclaves and vehicles for achieving social closure for groups that do not have such easy access to the opportunities for action offered by secular civil society. From this perspective, mainline civic distinctiveness is less a product of any internal features of mainline religion and more a product of the position traditionally held by mainline congregations within communities' civic hierarchies.

We are not able to fully assess the validity of any of these explanations, but we think none of them are likely to be adequate by themselves. A strong correlation among denominations between civic participation and historical roots as a state or territorial church is unlikely. Neither Methodists nor American Baptists have these roots, for example, yet their congregations are among the most civically engaged. Nor do regional or theological differences, as we describe below, fully explain the different patterns of civic activity observed across religious traditions. Catholic efforts to build enclaves may explain earlier Catholic versus Protestant differences in civic activity, but why would Catholic levels of such activity remain lower than mainline levels some three or four decades after full Catholic assimilation into middle-class America? As for the Protestant Establishment thesis, it works better, prima facie, for some kinds of activities than for others. It is plausible that "establishment" congregations would be less likely to build schools and more likely to do things like let outside groups use the building, have representatives of community groups as visiting speakers, and support educational programs. But why would links to a broader civic establishment make a congregation more likely to participate in or sponsor social service programs, build or rehabilitate housing for poor people, sponsor soup kitchens, hold meetings about race relations or the environment, or hold joint worship services that cross major religious boundaries? Why would exclusion from a civic establishment make a congregation less likely to do these things?

Results from our more complex analyses are relevant here. If the mainline distinctiveness evident in the percentage differences of table 4.1 disappeared, or became much smaller, when relevant variables were controlled, this would suggest that the historic and long-noted differences between religious traditions in civic participation might be attenuating as the Protestant Establishment erodes and as congregations in all religious traditions face similar pressures arising from suburbanization, high divorce rates, increased numbers of families where the adults work two and three jobs, and so on.

The fascinating reality, however, is that the basic patterns of religious variation evident in table 4.1 are *not* much explained by other congregational characteristics. The rightmost column shows the significance level of the difference between mainline and other congregations in a logistic regression equation including controls for a congregation's size, annual income, theological leanings, social class composition, racial composition, age composition, geographical region, rural/nonrural location, location in a poor neighborhood, and founding date. On only four items where mainline Protestants are significantly more publicly engaged than others is that difference explained away by these controls.[9] Thus, the verdict reached from inspecting the simple percentages is sustained by more sophisticated analysis: mainline congregations are more likely than other congregations to have a public presence encompassing activities that create or maintain connections between churches and communities. The mainline propensity to encourage these kinds of public activities apparently is not reducible to differences in congregational size, urban/rural location, region, racial composition, social class composition, or other factors we were able to control.

Among the variables we examined in the more complex analyses is a congregation's theological bent: whether informants described their congregation's theology as more on the conservative side, more on the liberal side, or right in the middle. The results associated with this variable suggest that, above and beyond connection to one or another denomination, a culture of theological liberalism or conservatism is associated with congregations' civic activities. In general, self-described liberal congregations do more civic and bridge-building activities than other congregations, whatever their denominational affiliation.[10] Not only are congregations associated with mainline Protestant denominations more likely to build bridges beyond themselves but, *within* each religious tradition, theologically liberal congregations are more likely to build these bridges than theologically middle-of-the-road congregations, and middle-of-the-road congregations are more likely to build these bridges than conservative congregations. Not incidentally, the point we made above concerning congregational characteristics in general applies here as well: although a congregation's theological culture often has its own independent correlation with civic participation, theological variations among congregations do *not* account for the denominational differences in public presence. Those differences remain substantial even when self-described theology is controlled. These results—the joint presence, in the face of controls, of both denominational and theological effects on a wide range of civic activities—suggest to us that religious variations in public presence are not reducible to any single feature of demography, organization, ideology, or historical background. We are not sure how to account for these differences, but we are struck by how deep and stable they appear to be.

We conclude with one further observation. The relationship between a congregation's founding date and civic activities is provocatively suggestive about a possible trend in congregations' public presence in American society. More recently founded congregations are *less* likely to engage in many of the bridging activities examined here.[11] It is difficult to know whether this implies a trend toward less civically engaged American congregations, or whether it means only that newer congregations, at any point in time, are less publicly engaged than older congregations. Perhaps a congregation's early years require more inward than outward focus as people work to create a stable organization, and perhaps today's newer congregations will become more publicly engaged as they become more established in their communities. If this is what is happening, we need not worry that, in the future, America's congregations will, as a whole, be less publicly engaged than today's congregations. If, however, the other interpretation is the correct one—if more recently founded congregations are less civically engaged at their core and will remain so even as they age and become more established—then we will see a future in which congregations, collectively, engage in and encourage less civic activity than is currently the case. If we are in the midst of such a trend, then more attention should be paid to what a declining Protestant mainline might portend for both American religion's public presence and, more broadly, for civic engagement in our society.

NOTES

1. See, for example, Robert Putnam, *Bowling Alone: The Collapse and Revival of American Community* (New York: Simon and Schuster, 2000); Sidney Verba, Kay Lehman Schlozman, and Henry E. Brady, *Voice and Equality: Civic Voluntarism in American Politics* (Cambridge, MA: Harvard University Press, 1995); Virginia A. Hodgkinson and Murray S. Weitzman, *From Belief to Commitment: The Community Service Activities and Finances of Religious Congregations in the United States* (Washington, DC: Independent Sector, 1993); Mayer N. Zald and John D. McCarthy, "Religious Groups as Crucibles of Social Movements," in *Sacred Companies: Organizational Aspects of Religion and Religious Aspects of Organizations*, ed. N. J. Demerath III, Peter Dobkin Hall, Terry Schmitt, and Rhys H. Williams (New York: Oxford University Press, 1998), 24–49; and Theda Skocpol and Morris Fiorina, eds., *Civic Engagement in American Democracy* (Washington, DC: Brookings Institution Press and New York: Russell Sage, 1999).

2. For discussions of the extent to which voluntary associations might detract from as well as contribute to civil society, see, for example, Putnam, *Bowling Alone,* chap. 22; Alejandro Portes, "Social Capital: Its Origins and Applications in Modern Sociology," *Annual Review of Sociology* 24 (1998): 1–24; Michael W. Foley and Bob Edwards, "Escape from Politics? Social Theory and the Social Capital Debate," *American Behavioral Scientist* 40, no. 5 (1997): 550–61; and Morris P. Fiorina, "Extreme Voices: A Dark Side of Civic Engagement," in Skocpol and Fiorina, *Civic Engagement in American Democracy,* 395–425.

3. For recent research on religious differences in civic participation, see, for example, Robert Wuthnow, "Mobilizing Civic Engagement," in Skocpol and Fiorina, *Civic Engagement in American Democracy,* 331–63; Peter Dobkin Hall, "Vital Signs: Organizational Population Trends and Civic Engagement in New Haven, Connecticut, 1850–1998," in Skocpol and Fiorina, *Civic Engagement in American Democracy,* 211–48; Peter Dobkin Hall, "Religion and the Organizational Revolution in the United States," in Demerath et al., *Sacred Companies,* 99–115; David Schwartz, "Secularization, Religion, and Isomorphism: A Study of Large Nonprofit Hospital Trustees," in Demerath et al., *Sacred Companies,* 323–39; Dean R. Hoge, Charles Zech, Patrick McNamara, and Michael J. Donahue, "The Value of Volunteers as Resources for Congregations," *Journal for the Scientific Study of Religion* 37, no. 3 (1998): 470–80; John Wilson and Thomas Janoski, "The Contribution of Religion to Volunteer Work," *Sociology of Religion* 56, no. 2 (1995): 137–52; cf. Christian Smith, *American Evangelicalism: Embattled and Thriving* (Chicago: University of Chicago Press, 1998), 40–42; Mark Regnerus, Christian Smith, and David Sikkink, "Who Gives to the Poor?" *Journal for the Scientific Study of Religion* 37, no. 3 (1998): 481–93.

4. For more detail about National Congregations Study data and methods, see Mark Chaves, Mary Ellen Konieczny, Kraig Beyerlein, and Emily Barman, "The National Congregations Study: Background, Methods, and Selected Results," *Journal for the Scientific Study of Religion* 38, no. 4 (1999): 458–76.

5. There are fifty congregations in the NCS that are either non-Christian or of indeterminate religious affiliation. This set of fifty congregations includes Jewish synagogues, Moslem mosques, and Buddhist temples, as well as other types of congregations. Reporting statistics for such a heterogeneous category seems unwise, and looking at each of these groups separately would, of course, reduce the case base even further.

6. Additional details about the exact question wordings and coding procedures underlying these variables are available from the authors upon request.

7. Our finding that, among congregations, religious variations in political activity look different than religious variations in other kinds of civic and public activity are very similar to Wuthnow's findings from analyses of individuals; see Wuthnow, "Mobilizing Civic Engagement."

8. See Wuthnow, "Mobilizing Civic Engagement"; Hall, "Religion and the Organizational Revolution"; Wilson and Janoski, "Contribution of Religion to Volunteer Work."

9. Moreover, the mainline difference usually is not much reduced by the presence of controls. In only four regression equations is a coefficient indicating that mainline congregations are more likely to engage in a public activity reduced by as much as 25 percent when all controls are added. Additional details about our multivariate results are available from the authors upon request.

10. In sixteen of the thirty-eight regression equations, theological culture had a significant effect (at least at the .10 level). In all but one of these, the effect is in the same direction: self-described theologically liberal congregations are more pub-

licly engaged than self-described conservative or middle-of-the-road congregations. The exception is having a school, which liberal congregations are less likely
to do. As we discuss in the main body of the text, running a school may or may
not bridge a congregation to the community.

11. The coefficient associated with a congregation's founding date is negative
in thirty of the thirty-eight regression equations. In nine of these it is significant
at least at the .10 level. The founding date coefficient is never significantly positive.

5 Connecting Mainline Protestant Churches with Public Life

Nancy T. Ammerman

The terms *mainline* and *civic* have long been seen as nearly synonymous. As earlier chapters in this volume have shown, churches in the historic Protestant "mainstream" have drawn on both their theological heritage and their position at the center of American culture to make unique contributions to the well-being of our society.[1] That legacy—and possible threats to it—prompt our attention at this moment in history. Are mainline churches still playing significant public roles, and if so, how?

It is becoming clear from a number of studies that many individual congregations, across the theological spectrum, engage in a wide range of activities in an effort to benefit their communities. From the informal handout given to a needy person at the door to massive programs of education, community development, and social service, congregations house significant portions of the overall public service activity undertaken in the United States.[2] However, even more numerous than these congregationally sponsored programs are the networks of other organizations to which congregations are connected by way of money, volunteers, space, and more intangible means of support. Congregations do much of their work in the public arena not by organizing their own programs, but by contributing their energy and resources to the efforts of others.

This essay offers an initial mapping of that network of organizations, describing especially what mainline Protestant congregations are doing in partnership with others. Encompassing more than simply "parachurch" organizations and religious nonprofits, this web of connection extends from informal local coalitions out into public sectors not usually considered religious. The work of mainline Protestantism draws congregations into a wide set of public relationships and draws an equally wide group of partner organizations into the mission of churches in the world. When we ask about the "public role" of mainline Protestantism, these seemingly mundane, everyday connections cannot be ignored.

THE DATA

This essay draws on data gathered as part of the Organizing Religious Work project, funded by the Lilly Endowment and headquartered at the Hartford Institute for Religion Research at Hartford Seminary. During 1997 and 1998, our team of researchers interviewed representatives, usually the pastor, of 549 congregations, 191 of which are within eleven mainline denominations (including the six that are the focus of the Public Role of Mainline Protestantism project). Our research sites included five urban areas—Seattle, Albuquerque, Nashville, Chicago, and Hartford—and two rural areas—clusters of counties in central Alabama and in central Missouri.[3] Taken together, these seven sites approximate the religious and demographic distribution of the United States as a whole, and we have weighted our cases to approximate the size and denominational distribution found in the National Congregations Study.[4] A full description of our sample is included in the appendix.

Because we interviewed representatives of congregations from across the religious spectrum, we will seek to bring the distinctiveness of the mainline tradition into sharp relief by comparisons to the conservative Protestant, historically African American, and Catholic congregations in our study. Our interviews asked about each congregation's history, activities, and sense of mission, probing especially for information about the organizations—including denominations—on which they depend for support, for resources, and for partnership in the work they do beyond their own four walls. In addition to this open-ended interview, lasting usually about an hour, the respondent completed a brief questionnaire giving basic demographic and statistical information on the congregation; and researchers collected a variety of written materials, from Sunday bulletins to budgets and annual reports. Beyond the congregation-level data, in a total of thirty-two churches we distributed individual surveys to Sunday attenders, providing us with responses from 4,012 persons, 874 of whom belong to mainline Protestant congregations.

THE WORK OF CONGREGATIONS: WHAT MATTERS MOST

We begin this excursion by placing the public work of congregations in the context of their overall mission. Most churches do not exist primarily as social service agencies or policy advocates (in spite of the apparent wishes of some politicians, theologians, and church bureaucrats). They exist primarily as places of worship and fellowship, where building up the spiritual and moral lives of their own members is at the heart of what they do. Across Christian traditions, the leaders we talked with agreed that the spiritual well-being of their members was the single thing their congregations most strongly valued. They pursue that goal both in corporate worship and in actively supporting individual spiritual growth. These spiritual activities are the two highest priorities for mainline Protestant congregations, and they are rated even higher among other Christian traditions. Also very near the top is the goal of providing for the social and communal needs of a congregation's members. Whether providing a "family-like atmosphere" or "fellowship activities," all four families of U.S. Christians are equal in the high value they give to taking care of the spiritual and social needs of their own members.[5]

Even these foci, however, should not be seen as utterly lacking in public significance. To the extent that congregations are providing strong, face-to-face communities, fortified by spiritual strength, they are generating social capital and often civic skills that can potentially be transferred into other arenas.[6] Social capital flows from all the relationships that build up trust and facilitate the functioning of our society, including the relationships nurtured in congregations. Civic skills are the experiences and practices that facilitate political participation, and they are enhanced in all the opportunities for advocating, planning, and leading offered by congregational life.[7] Many congregations in fact understand their primary public role to be the formation of good persons who will individually take seriously their roles as citizens.

The public and civic character of the work inside congregations is seen directly in two other priorities that especially distinguish mainline Protestant congregations. More than in other traditions, mainline leaders say their congregations value doing things democratically. People want to be involved in decision making, to have their voices heard. They also want their religious traditions to inform their everyday lives, to have opportunities to make connections between what their churches teach and the values that guide their decisions outside the church. Thinking hard about how to live, valuing individual decision making, and providing places to talk about what matters most—these are things the leaders of mainline Protestant churches claim they do. This pattern of church support for individual social responsibility is what Roozen, McKinney, and Carroll called a "civic" mission orientation, and it is a strong emphasis in the mainline Protestant churches we surveyed.[8]

But what about more direct action outside the church family? Mainline Protestant congregations are much less committed to these goals, according to the leaders we interviewed. The congregations most likely to say they support the promotion of social change, service to the poor and needy, and working with others to improve the community are not either of the predominantly white Protestant traditions, but African American groups, with Catholics not far behind. The same pattern is seen among the individuals we surveyed. Individual African American church members are much more supportive of community activism than are any other tradition's members. While mainline pastors want their members to lead responsible lives, they report that their congregations are less committed to corporate congregational activity in the pursuit of social change and community betterment than to the spiritual and moral well-being of their members.

THE PREVALENCE OF PUBLIC PARTNERSHIPS

Given these assessments of mission priorities, we need to ask just what these congregations are actually doing. Here we turn specifically to the question of congregational partnerships with other community organizations. While the congregation itself *is* a "public," a new kind of relationship is formed when the congregation seeks out others with whom to work toward a common goal.

We draw here both on what congregations told us about their connections—all 5,849 of them—and on interviews with just over two hundred of the organizations they named.[9] Our subsample consists of 3,905 connections that are oriented toward or include service to nonmembers and are directed through an organizational mechanism that is neither internal to the congregation itself nor tied to its denominational structure. We look closely at what these connections facilitate in the community and what this partnership between religious groups and public activity looks like.

As table 5.1 shows, extra-congregational partnerships are by no means rare. In each of the Christian congregations we surveyed, there are, on average, nearly six inter-organizational connections through which outreach work is done. Within that total level of activity, however, there are significant differences. All kinds of Christian congregations are involved in extra-denominational partnerships, but mainline Protestants are far more involved than anyone else. Whatever pastors may have told us about

Table 5.1. Congregational Involvement with Outside Organizations, by Religious Tradition

	Mainline Protestant	Conservative Protestant	African American Protestant	Catholic	Weighted Total[a]
Average number of connections with outside organizations, per church	8.7	5.1	4.7	6.5	5.9
Churches with at least one community connection	93%	90%	84%	91%	87%
Churches that provide volunteers to at least one outside organization	86%	73%	65%	77%	74%
Average number of outside organizations to which churches send volunteers	3.71	2.54	2.21	2.91	2.80
Churches that provide space to at least one outside organization	72%	51%	66%	76%	57%
Average number of outside organizations to which churches provide space	3.06	1.30	1.35	2.33	1.76
Churches that donate material goods to at least one outside organization	49%	23%	28%	28%	30%
Average number of outside organizations to which churches donate material goods	.85	.35	.30	.60	.48
Churches that donate money to at least one outside organization	67%	41%	27%	27%	45%
Average number of outside organizations to which churches donate money	4.32	1.95	1.59	2.73	2.53
Average total contributions to nondenominational outreach organizations	$3,404	$4,199	$727	$4,878	$3,538

[a]Included in total but not in the other columns are fourteen "other Christian" cases, ten Jewish synagogues, and eleven other non-Christian groups.

their perceptions of congregations' priorities, the reality is that mainline churches are nearly twice as active in forming partnerships as are churches in other sectors of Christianity.

Across traditions, nearly everyone is connected to at least one outside organization. Only among the most sectarian groups (Mormons and Jehovah's Witnesses, for instance, who are not included in these analyses) and the groups newest to American soil (Hindus and Muslims, for instance, who are also not included here) is it common to find congregations that have no connections outside their own religious world. Partnerships between congregations and other community organizations have simply been institutionalized as an expected pattern in most of American religion.

The substance of these relationships is multifaceted and varies enormously in the degree of its centrality to the congregation's sense of mission. Rarely does a partnership involve a whole congregation on an ongoing and intense basis. But rarely is it something about which they know or care little. Less than 10 percent of all connections involve only money, for instance, and less than 15 percent involve only providing space. We examined these connections, and in about half the cases we were able to discern some countable measures of what is being invested. Where our informant did not know the answers to our questions about volunteers, contributions, and other aspects of the connection, we have erred on the conservative side and counted as if no such contributions exist. The numbers in table 5.1, therefore, clearly underestimate the amount of contributions being made by congregations to their outreach partners.[10]

Still, even with incomplete information, the numbers are substantial. Seventy-two percent of mainline congregations allow at least one outside organization to use space in their buildings (either donated outright or made available at minimal cost), and the average number is three such organizations for every congregation. Each mainline congregation contributes, on average, volunteers to nearly four organizations, and 86 percent of mainline congregations report that they send volunteers to help in at least one group. The median number of volunteers per group supported is five, with a few reporting literally dozens of routine volunteers. That, of course, does not begin to count the number of groups in which individual members work, not as official representatives of their congregations, but at least in part because their congregation encourages such activity. It also does not count the projects taken on by intrachurch groups (such as Sunday School classes or women's groups) about which our informant did not know. On average, four organizations receive monetary contributions from each mainline congregation, for an average of over $800 per organization per year. And most churches supplement their monetary contributions to at least one organization with other material goods—food, clothing, furniture, Christmas gifts, and the like—collected by the members.

Across all aspects of participation, the level of activity in mainline congregations is roughly double that in conservative, African American, and Catholic churches. They send volunteers to, provide space for, and give money and goods to roughly twice as many organizations. Providing space and sending volunteers, however, are patterns that are nearly as prevalent (if not as numerous) in the other traditions. Proportionately as many churches are involved, but they do not invest in as many different groups. In fact, the total funds contributed in Catholic and conservative Protestant churches is substantially more than in mainline ones, meaning that they give, on average, about twice as much to each of the groups they support. In part, then, the high level of mainline connection represents spreading a smaller number of dollars among many more groups. Churches in the other traditions do not, however, send more volunteers to the groups they support. Across all the traditions, the average number of volunteers per group is the same. Given that mainline churches support many more groups, their total number of volunteers is therefore considerably larger than the total coming from other traditions. Measured in personpower, as well as in the number of different connections, the mainline is a significant partner in the work of community organizations.

Having noted that mainline groups are more broadly involved with public organizations, we must pause to ask whether demographic or other social variables can account for such differences. Do mainline churches simply have more resources and therefore have the luxury to use those resources in forming community alliances? Table 5.2 shows the results of an analysis that tests the effects of various factors on the number of connections a congregation has. Other things being equal, are mainline churches really different?

Table 5.2 shows that resources are indeed a significant part of the story. The more money a congregation has in its budget, the more connections it is likely to form; and the more high-income parishioners it has—over and above the size of the budget—the more connections it can sustain. Money, not sheer size, is what makes a difference. Regional context has no effect, but churches in rural areas are less involved in outside partnerships than are urban ones.[11] The educational and racial composition of the congregation makes no difference, other things being equal.[12] And our informants' rating of the church's emphasis on community cooperation has, ironically, no relationship to actual community activity; nor does the

Table 5.2. Effects on Congregational Involvement in Community
Partnerships

	Effect on Total Number of Connections (Betas)
Resources	
Budget size	+.13
Average number of attenders	n.s.
Context	
Northeast	n.s.
Rural	−.18
Demographics	
Proportion with more than college education	n.s.
Proportion with high income	+.14
Predominantly African American	n.s.
Religious tradition	
Mainline	+.34
Mission emphases	
Community cooperation	n.s.
Social change	n.s.

NOTE: n.s. = p > .10; N = 385 congregations; R^2 =.22.

emphasis on organizing for social change. Some of these demographic, missional, contextual, and resource factors have an effect, then, but being a part of the mainline tradition has the greatest single effect on the number of connections a congregation has.[13] The differences we have seen are partly a matter of money and context—bigger churches with bigger budgets do more—but more than that, there are real differences based in a particular religious tradition. Forming alliances with groups beyond one's own doors is an organizational strategy that exists in virtually all Christian (and Jewish) congregations, but it is a pattern set by the congregations in the mainline tradition.

PUBLIC ACTIVITIES FOR COMMUNITY GOOD

With a basic picture of the number and quality of the public partnerships congregations have formed, we can turn our attention to the question of just what all those organizations are doing. What are congregations supporting when they cooperate with outside organizations, and how are mainline churches distinctive in their choices of partners? We have grouped the activities congregations are supporting into the broad categories shown in table 5.3. With a few exceptions, these categories follow the groupings outlined in the 1994 Giving and Volunteering Survey.[14] Human Services includes organizations providing food, clothing, shelter, and other direct aid, while Community Benefit includes the neighborhood and civic groups that do work aimed at the general betterment of their communities. Policy Advocacy groups are those whose primary goal is changing public policies, and Civic Services are official activities, such as hosting a polling place, undertaken in behalf of towns and cities. Health, Education, Culture, and Youth Organizations are groups that provide opportunities for individual enhancement, learning, and recreation. Self-Help and Growth groups have many of the same educational goals, but are structured as mutual support environments, rather than classroom or performance events.[15] From our long list of connections between congregations and outside organizations, we created about sixty categories of activity being supported and then grouped them under these six broad rubrics.

Mainline members told us that serving the needy was very important to them, and indeed the average mainline congregation has between three and four connections to community organizations that provide immediate relief to people in need. Mainline members who reported in the Religion and Politics Survey that their congregations sponsored soup kitchens and homeless shelters, probably had these connections in mind.[16] Through such connections, runaway teens are housed; battered women and children find a safe place; people who are homeless find temporary shelter; and thousands and thousands of hot meals are served to people who are hungry. While many of these organizations also do advocacy and work on long-term solutions, their primary task is simply to relieve immediate suffering. Each community has dozens of such agencies. Here are a few of the organizations that mainline congregations support:

- In Middletown, Connecticut, near Hartford, St. Vincent de Paul Place provides hot meals, clothing, and "supportive housing," a program aimed at helping homeless people get the services they need in order to stay off the street.

- In Nashville, Room in the Inn includes both shelter facilities and a "Guest House" unit for people who are too intoxicated to be admitted to the shelter. When they sober up, counseling and medical assistance are available.

- In Chicago, a representative of Hesed House told us, "We feed, clothe and shelter very poor homeless people. And hopefully, try to give them reason to hope again."

Table 5-3. Types of Public Activities Supported by Local Congregations through Partner Organizations

Type of Activity	Mainline Protestant		Conservative Protestant		African American Protestant		Catholic	
	Average Number of Connections per Church	Churches with at Least One Connection (%)	Average Number of Connections per Church	Churches with at Least One Connection (%)	Average Number of Connections per Church	Churches with at Least One Connection (%)	Average Number of Connections per Church	Churches with at Least One Connection (%)
Human services	3.29	89	1.35	60	1.28	55	1.82	65
Community benefit	.76	51	.43	27	.63	42	.85	56
Policy advocacy	.32	20	.11	8	.26	9	.53	29
Civic service	.06	6	.04	4	.12	12	.28	24
Health, education, culture, and youth organizations	2.63	80	1.14	58	1.08	48	1.99	71
Self-help and growth	.81	53	.39	25	.18	18	.47	38

- In Albuquerque, the director of Storehouse rattled off these numbers for yearly contributions to poor people in the community: "Somewhere between 38,000 and 42,000 bags of clothing. We're projecting over 100,000 meals. We will help 250 families with furniture."

- In Seattle, Northwest Harvest provides food and meals, but its major task is serving as the primary distribution system for other shelters and feeding programs around the state, buying truckloads of beans and cargo containers full of rice, in addition to receiving food donations from dozens of churches and businesses. The director explained that the total "amounts to close to 15 million pounds of food a year. We distribute only through nonprofit 501(c)(3) organizations. . . . They in turn give it to people who present themselves in need."

In rural areas the organizations are smaller and sometimes less formalized, but the infrastructure is there, as well. The single concern most likely to draw congregations into public activity is the effort to tend to the most vulnerable of society's members. People in congregations of all sorts want to salve some of society's wounds, and most of them recognize that they cannot respond to all the need around them with only their own resources. They need to work with others, pooling money, personpower, and expertise that can go beyond a quick handout at the door.

Ongoing efforts to build up the strength of a community are captured in our Community Benefit category. While only about a quarter of conservative Protestant churches participate in such civic-minded activities, around half of the mainline, African American, and Catholic parishes have at least some tie to a group working for community betterment (see table 5.3).[17] Most such organizations are all-purpose associations—block watch groups, neighborhood associations, civic clubs, and the like. They take on tasks as mundane as trash pickup and as complicated as policing issues. In addition, their very existence as public gatherings of concerned citizens makes them important players in the creation of "social capital."[18] Whether the church simply participates as a regular member, provides space for the meetings, or signs on to assist with a specific project, these community groups do at least some of their public work with the help of congregations.

Some of these community benefit activities attempt to implement longer-term changes that are needed to make the community a better place to live. Providing permanent affordable housing, for instance, has become a widespread concern, and the premier organization that has mobilized the energies of churches and others in behalf of this cause is Habitat for Humanity.[19] Forty-one percent of all the mainline Protestant churches in which we interviewed had some connection to Habitat. Catholic parishes were not far behind (33 percent). Conservative and African American churches are involved, but at much lower levels (11 and 8 percent, respectively).

No other form of community economic development activity has anything like the presence of Habitat among churches. The next most prevalent organization (with nearly 10 percent of mainline churches involved) is Heifer International, an Arkansas-based ministry that provides livestock as a means of economic self-sufficiency in communities around the world. While most of the churches that named Heifer International are within the mainline, a few African American and conservative churches participate as well. World Vision is the only other development organization with a significant base of support among the congregations we surveyed, and unlike Heifer, it was stronger among conservative churches than within the mainline.

Roughly a quarter of the mainline churches we surveyed had links to some national or international organizations that do human service, community benefit, educational, and other good work in the larger world. Among these partners, for instance, was Food for the Poor, which "seeks to link the church of the First World with the church of the Third World in a manner that aids both the materially and spiritually poor."[20] Childreach is a similar organization "striving to achieve lasting improvements in the lives of poor children worldwide, primarily through child sponsorship."[21] Several churches also supported activities of the National Council of Churches' Church World Service, especially disaster relief, refugee resettlement, and SERRV International crafts sales.

Like World Vision and Heifer International, these organizations work primarily overseas; local economic development partnerships are considerably more rare. Only eleven mainline congregations (6 percent) named locally oriented economic development groups (other than Habitat) as organizations to which they contribute. African American churches were more than three times as likely (22 percent) to name a local economic development group as a partner. While the idea of "community development corporations" is getting a good deal of attention these days, it is the rare church that has taken on this sort of economic partnership.[22]

In addition to these on-the-ground efforts to build up community social and economic life, a few congregations also make connections with organizations that allow them to give voice to public policy concerns. From the environment to health care and from civil rights to animal rights, mainline

Protestant congregations sometimes pursue the cause of justice in this world through advocacy organizations that include Amnesty International, the Audubon Society, the Sierra Club, Earth Ministry, the Center for Prevention of Sexual and Domestic Violence, the Children's Defense Fund, the Fellowship of Reconciliation, Gay Pride parades, Simple Justice (an advocacy group for gays and lesbians), Interfaith Alliance, Physicians for Social Responsibility, Protestants for the Common Good, the Union of Concerned Scientists, and United Power for Action and Justice.

In addition to this list of perhaps predictable alliances, a few mainline churches were supporting the March for Jesus and other Right to Life activities, causes more commonly supported, not surprisingly, by conservative Protestant and Catholic churches. Classic civil rights organizations such as the NAACP and Southern Christian Leadership Conference (SCLC) are only supported, among the churches where we interviewed, by African American congregations. Those same African American churches were the only ones to report alliances with specifically political or voter-education organizations. Their members, in turn, were also the most likely to report participation in political activities in the community.[23]

Another common encounter between mainline churches and the political arena comes on election day. A small contingent of the churches where we interviewed serve their communities as polling places (an activity we placed in our Civic Service category). In this seemingly simple exercise, congregations transform themselves into public spaces in which the basic work of U.S. democracy is done. On some additional occasions, churches also serve as gathering places for a whole community in times of celebration or crisis. One local ministerial association recounted, for instance, "We had a major snowstorm that wiped out all electricity, and the village called us" to arrange for churches to serve as shelter space.

These, then, are the kinds of activities and connections we normally mean when we think about the church's "public" role. As we have seen, by working with community partners, most congregations are significantly involved in the delivery of social services to people in need. Nearly all mainline churches, and over half of all the others, join forces with service agencies of all sorts to feed, clothe, and house those who are falling through the cracks of government programs and economic hard times. Less common are alliances that seek more long-term solutions, and mainline churches are less distinctive in those activities. It is a staple of mainline church life to be linked to shelters, food pantries, and emergency assistance agencies where mainline members spend volunteer energy, and their churches provide critical financial, material, and network support.[24]

PUBLIC ACTIVITIES FOR INDIVIDUAL
AND COMMUNAL ENRICHMENT

Human service and community benefit efforts are not the only activities that bring mainline and other congregations into contact with the public outside their doors. In at least as many cases, the public in question seeks personal growth and enrichment, rather than the fulfillment of basic needs. Everywhere you look in mainline churches, there are scout troops and nursery schools, senior centers and sports leagues, music programs and self-help groups—all existing independently of any single congregation but often housed and supported by churches, along with others in the community.

The average mainline congregation has two or three connections to groups that provide for the educational, spiritual, and cultural enrichment of people within and beyond their membership (see table 5.3). As with human service activities, this is a distinctive mainline practice. Mainline churches have roughly twice as many education and culture-related connections as do any other Christian groups. Just as churches have institutionalized participation in networks of care for the needy, they have also institutionalized the practice of providing for the educational, health, and cultural enhancement of people in their communities by supporting the wide range of organizations and alliances that provide those services. From after-school tutoring to performances of Bach cantatas and blood pressure screening, they combine forces with other community organizations to make the world a better place.[25]

A closely related set of activities are those that fall into the Self-Help and Growth category. Here persons with a given concern gather to help themselves and each other to deal with the problem. By far the best known and most widespread, of course, are the Alcoholics Anonymous (AA) and other twelve-step groups for narcotics addicts, overeaters, and even "sex and love addicts." Congregations across the religious spectrum provide support for these groups, but mainline churches are especially likely to be involved. Over half of the mainline churches in which we interviewed have at least one AA or twelve-step group meeting in their buildings. Conservatives and Catholics are somewhat less likely to support self-help groups, and African American churches almost never do (see table 5.3). In most cases, the congregation has little connection with the group beyond the provision of space for meeting, but that in itself is significant. As a regional AA staff member told us, "We're really grateful that so many churches have opened up their doors, and they tend to keep fairly low rent. We do meet in places other than churches . . . but boy we can really tell the difference in rent cost, because those places are so much more expensive." An infrastructure of congregations is an assumed part of what makes such groups possible.

As numerous as AA groups are in the basements and parlors of American churches, there are an equal number of other support and spirituality groups, as well. Beyond the church's own Sunday School classes and men's bowling groups, about one in three congregations also hosts or provides resources to a support and growth group that includes people from beyond its own membership. These include the usual religiously focused groups like Bible study and prayer groups. In about 5 percent of mainline congregations, for instance, the list includes a local chapter of Promise Keepers. But even more common are support groups for people encountering both mundane and extraordinary challenges in living. There are parenting groups for Mothers of Preschoolers (MOPS) and weight-control groups, including Take Off Pounds Sensibly (TOPS) and Weight Watchers. There are groups dealing with birth defects and disability, as well as groups for people who have encountered less common difficulties—Tourette's syndrome, Lyme disease, and incest, to name a few of those we found. There are groups for transvestites and for Christian motorcycle enthusiasts, for people recovering from divorce and people who are victims of violence.

As Wuthnow has argued, our highly fragmented and mobile society has found small groups to be an effective means for sustaining social and emotional bonds and promoting mutual aid.[26] When one or two church people see a need, they often make their interest known through and beyond their own congregation. They draw on the church's networks of knowledge and communication and often end up housing the resulting group in the church building. Again, the resources of congregations facilitate the creation of social capital that sustains the common good by helping citizens to help each other.

Both in efforts to support individuals and in efforts to change structures and systems, mainline Protestants are very likely, then, to link with organizations beyond the congregation as a way of fulfilling their sense of mission in the world. The largest proportion of their energy goes into providing relief for people in need, but nearly as much is directed at the education and self-improvement of others who may be less immediately needy. Relatively little is directed to economic development or policy advocacy, and almost none to overtly political groups. The public role of mainline congregations is much more a matter of cooperative action on behalf of needy persons than a matter of political lobbying or economic boycotts. It is, nevertheless, a significant role. By combining efforts with other organizations, aid and services are provided far beyond what any one congregation could do and with a far more diverse set of partners than would be possible if such work were confined to denominational channels alone.

WHO ARE THE PUBLIC PARTNERS
OF MAINLINE CONGREGATIONS?

We might suppose that the primary links between congregations and outside organizations would be to religious nonprofit organizations—the so-called parachurch. Organizations such as Heifer International and World Vision and countless local groups from Agape House to Tabitha House embody religiously inspired charitable impulses throughout the country and the world and are indeed frequent vehicles through which congregations work. But nearly as often, congregational partners are secular nonprofits such as the Audubon Society or the Red Cross. And still other organizations are nearly impossible to classify. They embody a mix of religious and secular motives, origins, ideas, funding, and identities.[27] A closer look at the organizations with which mainline (and other) congregations work reveals the ambiguity of our usual distinctions between secular and religious. Especially among the mainline churches, doing good in the world may begin within the community of faith but quickly involves partnerships that transcend confessional boundaries.

Just what sorts of organizations are these? Our first discovery is that many of the "organizations" through which congregations do their work are not formal organizations at all (see table 5.4). They are often simply partnerships between two or more churches, partnerships that have no staff of their own and often no distinct name. Many food pantries and clothes closets are run this way. A group of churches agrees informally that one will collect, store, and distribute furniture, while another will take care of the food, and a third will collect clothing. They may notify various social service agencies of the arrangement so that needy persons can be referred to the right place. This network of caring may never show up on anyone's annual report, but it is a critical link in the safety net in many communities. In Chicago, such inter-congregational sharing of responsibility was eventually made more formal in the Public Action to Deliver Shelter (PADS) system. By 1998, more than sixty-five congregations were serving as overnight shelters on a highly organized and well-supported

Table 5.4. Types of Organizations with Which Churches Cooperate in Public Activities, by Religious Tradition

Type of Organization	Mainline Protestant		Conservative Protestant		African American Protestant		Catholic	
	Average Number of Connections per Church	Churches with at Least One Connection (%)	Average Number of Connections per Church	Churches with at Least One Connection (%)	Average Number of Connections per Church	Churches with at Least One Connection (%)	Average Number of Connections per Church	Churches with at Least One Connection (%)
Informal coalition	1.76	71	1.63	63	1.34	56	1.05	59
Religious nonprofit	2.85	80	1.69	68	1.30	46	1.88	63
Secular nonprofit	3.02	82	.92	47	1.07	49	2.23	80
Governmental unit	.49	34	.40	26	.54	39	.72	44

rotating schedule. But the idea started with the same sort of informal relationships that we found among churches in every one of our sites.

Equally informal are the people who share a common interest or concern and form a self-help or support group. Rather than being part of a formal national network (like AA, for instance), many are simply church and community folk who decide to get together. We found Alzheimer's groups, disability support groups, and groups that gather to practice Aikido, Irish step dancing, or Zen meditation, for instance. Many (although not all) of the sports leagues we encountered were similarly informal. They have an ongoing existence and a recognizable identity, but little if any financial or legal infrastructure defines the group.[28] They are as religious or as secular, as private or public, as the individuals in them choose to make them at any given time.

By far the most important of these informal groups are the clergy associations that are present in nearly every community. Some are dormant and do little more than gather for an occasional social lunch. Most, however, have a strong component of prayer and fellowship, offering clergy an opportunity to share their burdens with others who understand. As one Missouri pastor put it, "There's a lot of times that you struggle along in ministry, and in a lot of ways you are very individualized. It seems like you're fighting against the world, and there's no connection to any outside sources until you get together. And then you see that you're all in the same work, doing the same thing within your own local locations."

Often the praying is specifically directed at needs and concerns in the community, and the concerns expressed in prayer spill over into concrete actions the group may undertake. In rural Missouri, for instance, the ministers got together to form a food pantry when they discovered that more people seemed to be in need: "When the government stopped that assistance program [distributing commodities] like that, then it kind of fell to the local communities to start working with either food banks or food pantries and try to bring it together."

Not only does this county ministerial association maintain a food bank, they also have arrangements with various local businesses to provide gasoline, medicine, groceries, and the like. Similarly, the president of a suburban Chicago Ministerial Association told us,

> Instead of having Mr. and Mrs. X coming to your door and saying, "We need money," and then going to the next church and getting money, and the next church, we came up with a voucher system where we have a checking account and each church donates in various

ways. . . . We have an agreement with a local hotel, the local gas station, the local grocery store and restaurant. And then if Mr. X comes to your door, . . . we provide for them a night stay at a hotel, meals, gas and some groceries.

This was a familiar refrain. Churches are obvious stopping points for people in need, but it is hard for a pastor (or a church secretary) to make a judgment about what is best when someone knocks on the door. By banding together, and by enlisting the help of local merchants, churches establish some semblance of rationality in a situation they find otherwise frustratingly ambiguous. They want to help, but do not always know the best way. If all the churches cooperate, each has a sense that appropriate help is being delivered.

Ministerial alliances also sometimes serve as an all-purpose civic arm for the churches. The same suburban Chicago leader noted that their members take turns offering prayer at the town council meetings and writing a column for the town newspaper. When there are crises, the town is likely to call on them to mobilize the resources of the churches as needed. And when other celebrations or events need the blessing of a minister, the ministerial alliance is the clearinghouse that sends someone. Ministerial associations seem to be a common vehicle for linking the religious and charitable impulses of the churches with the needs and resources of a larger public. They raise their own money from the churches, set their own agendas, and respond to needs as they choose—usually without any formal staff. Through such informal alliances, business, government, social service agencies, and churches can be brought together for the good of the community.

Sometimes the work of these ministerial associations leads to more ongoing and formal organization. Today the Church Council of Greater Seattle, for instance, supports over a dozen programs that address everything from homelessness to care for the elderly and from urban youth to concern for the people of Iraq. It still brings official church bodies together for mutual support and to address public issues, but its role in the community has shifted over its eighty-year history from a focus primarily on churches themselves to a focus on the community and its needs. In the process, the structure has gotten considerably larger and more formal.

Formal, religious, nonprofit organizations are, in fact, the dominant sector through which congregations do their work in the community. Once they incorporate as separate entities, however, religious nonprofits are faced with the question of just how religious they will be. The answers varied enormously among those where we interviewed. As is evident from the names of some of the organizations—Room in the Inn, St. Vincent de Paul—religious motives are often very close to the surface, even if they are now formally organized as nonsectarian entities. The stories we heard about their origins made these religious impulses especially clear. Northwest Harvest was described to us this way:

> It was strictly a religious-based, ecumenical movement, pretty much designed with people power—no going after government funds or anything else. The churches to the rescue. . . . We were doing this according to St. Matthew 25:40, "Inasmuch as you do it unto the least of these you do it unto me." What that to us meant was that each person that came, if you requested food they received food, not an investigation. Not an invasion of their privacy, but rather to make them welcome and show kindness that would also feed their spirit as well as the food for their body.

This was not the only time we heard Matthew 25:40 cited. Jesus' admonition to care for the hungry, the thirsty, the stranger, the naked, the sick, and the imprisoned was a theological mandate for many of those we talked to.

In addition to the ideological and spiritual motivation provided by the churches, the value of church network connections is also apparent in the founding stories of these service organizations. Loaves and Fishes is one of the primary feeding ministries in Hartford. When it started in the mid-1980s, church connections built both the desire and the infrastructure. "There were a couple of women from several different churches. From Asylum Hill Congregation, from Trinity Episcopal, from Immanuel, who had a great interest in doing something about a soup kitchen on Asylum Hill. And when they realized—they all knew each other as friends—that they were representative of different churches, they decided to try to make this an ecumenical effort." The civic concerns and connections already present in mainline churches make them an especially fertile seedbed for the sprouting of new religious nonprofits.[29]

Sometimes the religious connections and motivations eventually fade as an organization takes on professional staff and seeks nonreligious funding sources.[30] That was the case at Seattle's Teen Hope Shelter. Begun by a network of mostly church-based folk, it almost immediately became a secular, professionally run organization with little connection to churches, church people, or religious ideas. A similar story was told by an agency in Albuquerque.

For the first twenty or twenty-five years, this was a shelter for kids, and it was funded and staffed largely by volunteers and by church people and [was] that kind of a coordinated effort. Over the years that started to change, and we got more and more kids who got more and more kind of difficult. They were not just little babies anymore. They were older with behavioral and mental health problems, and we had to start moving increasingly into a professional sphere, and that became more expensive. And the churches could not manage all of that, and volunteer help was not adequate when you need therapists and psychiatrists and that sort of thing. So we started getting other dollars and state monies and city monies and United Way monies and all sorts of other dollars to supplement the volunteer help and the church dollars.

More common, however, are religious nonprofits that retain some sense of their religious identity and mission, which means hiring staff that share that mission. St. Vincent de Paul Place, in Connecticut, for instance, was founded by women religious and is still staffed by them. Loaves and Fishes' director said simply, "I am a Christian, and I felt very strongly on acting on my Christian beliefs in a way that was helping other people." What is important for the staff carries over into the experience of the volunteers as well. At the Storehouse in Albuquerque, we heard, "One of the volunteers said it best. She said, 'You know, I never hear God's presence like I do when I'm around here in this circle.' And I said, 'Why?' And then she said, 'Because I think it's because somehow when I'm here I just, I can't, I just give everything I have . . . ' And she didn't finish it. That's all she said. She said, 'I give everything I have.'"

That sense of embodying God's presence in service to the poor is very strong among many of those we interviewed, even when they do not openly talk to their clients about their faith. At Hesed House in Chicago, for instance, we were told, "If you don't believe that God is present in your offering of bread, in your words, in your hospitality, then God isn't going to be there because you say some prayers."[31] In some organizations, talk about faith permeates the services rendered. In others, faith is in the background, but no less present.

While faith may be a central ingredient in the identity, mission, and ongoing motivation of most religious nonprofits, few of them exist solely on money from religious sources or volunteer energy that comes only through religious channels. The following description of support for St. Vincent de Paul Place in Connecticut is typical of what we heard.

The bishops' annual appeal funds us a certain amount for the salaries of the staff every year. And then the rest of the financial resources

come from a few grants, a little out of donations. We have a lot
of individual donations. . . . The business community and the civic
organizations are very good support for us along with the churches.
We can't—the churches are our staple. They do the meal program
on Sunday. They have food drives for us. . . . Lots of money—we have
churches that send us $100 and $500 and $750 every quarter, every
month.

For a time, they received state funds, but that program got caught in state
and city politics and was shut down. Since then, they have been cautious
about governmental money, a caution that was echoed in what we heard
at Northwest Harvest. The paperwork and verifications that are necessary
when state money is involved are enough to keep some religious nonprofits
from seeking it. They want to be able to look a needy person in the eye
and make their own assessments about whether and how to help. Many
other religious nonprofits, however, do receive various forms of public
money to assist in their work—a practice that was common long before
the current discussion about Charitable Choice.[32]

Still, religious nonprofits receive a solid base of material support
through religious channels, especially, as we have seen, mainline Protestant churches. When we asked individual attendees in the congregations
we surveyed about their community involvement beyond the church, the
extent to which churches contribute more than budgeted donations was
evident. Seventy percent of the individuals in mainline congregations say
they participate in community service organizations at least a few times a
year; 46 percent say that they gave more than one hundred dollars in 1997
to religious groups beyond the congregation; and 59 percent gave at least
that much to secular charities. Both these individual contributions and the
corporate involvement of congregations form a foundation that most religious nonprofits recognize as essential to their work. At Hesed House,
they said, "We define ourselves as an ecumenical center for ministry, supported—our major support is the churches. That's not even a strong
enough way—we *are* the work of the churches."

Note the word *ecumenical*. While many churches may support ministries that are exclusively the work of their own denominations, almost all
of the religious nonprofits about which we are concerned here span religious groupings. Even an identifiably denominational group, such as Catholic Charities or Lutheran Social Services, is likely to have tangible support
from persons and congregations outside that denomination. The work of
religious nonprofits is not only public in the object of its service; it is also

public in the coalitions of religious, civic, governmental, and business groups that support the work.

Secular nonprofits, of course, are even more clearly public in their activities and diverse in their base of support. While they may have some congregational donors and volunteers that come through religious channels, their work is defined primarily in secular terms. About one-third of all the human service, community benefit, and culture/education/health connections of mainline congregations involve explicitly secular organizations.

In spite of their secular identity and mission, even some of these organizations have church connections that are quite pervasive. PFLAG (Parents and Friends of Lesbians and Gays) in Seattle describes its mission as the support of gay, lesbian, and transgendered persons and their families. They operate as a support group and sometime lobbying organization. But they also have a volunteer who works as a liaison with churches, offering educational programming and garnering support. They meet in a church building, and congregations advertise PFLAG meetings. Similarly, in Albuquerque, we heard about (and witnessed) the pervasiveness of church volunteers at a food and jobs agency. It is staffed by secular professionals. The funding is from government, business, and civic groups. And the programming is guided by basic social work standards. But the people who cook and serve the meals every day are overwhelmingly groups based in churches who are quite clear that what they are doing is a ministry.

While some mainline human service work is done through secular groups, religious nonprofits are more the norm. The opposite is the case with education and self-help work. Here goals are more often accomplished through secular groups. In addition to groups like Boy Scouts and AA, schools, colleges, nursing homes, hospitals, and the like often provide educational and service activities for which congregations serve as partners. At the county hospital in Rolla, Missouri, for instance, a corps of local pastors and retired ministers serves the chaplaincy needs of the hospital, and they often recruit their members for other volunteer jobs at the hospital. The Hartford Conservatory regularly uses church space for rehearsals, performances, and lessons. Similarly, the Loyal Heights Preschool uses otherwise unoccupied space in a Seattle congregation. These institutions serve a thoroughly nonsectarian public but draw resources of various sorts from congregations. Congregations, in turn, are able to help provide for the educational, cultural, and health needs of the community by assisting these institutions in their work. It is worth noting that main-line Protestant congregations are much more likely to make connections to secular nonprofits than are conservative, African American, or even Catholic churches (see table 5.4). Similarly, the members of mainline congregations give more generously to secular charities than do the members of other groups.

The other activity in which secular nonprofits are the dominant players is policy advocacy. As we saw above, mainline congregations provide support to groups as diverse as Amnesty International, the Sierra Club, and Physicians for Social Responsibility. Such secular groups are considerably more common than religiously based ones (such as Interfaith Alliance or Bread for the World) in the advocacy partnerships cited by mainline churches. And congregational support for denominational advocacy is even less common. While there are, of course, both regional and national denominational groups that take on political and educational efforts on behalf of social policy change, only two of our 191 mainline congregations mentioned such efforts as a denominational benefit they especially valued. Indeed, social policy positions were much more likely to be mentioned as a problem standing between the congregation and support for national denominational work. At least from the vantage point of congregations, what little support exists for advocacy work is channeled largely through secular more than religious groups, and through parachurch groups almost to the exclusion of denominational ones.

That does not mean that congregations are not involved with the government, however. Rather, their involvement with governmental institutions is in more immediate efforts to improve the well-being of persons and communities. Most common are connections between churches and schools, and most often those connections involve churches in tutoring and other support programs. In addition, congregations are often partners in public projects that are run by parks departments, police departments, and chambers of commerce. In Chicago, for instance, a number of congregations participate in the CAPS (Chicago Alternative Policing Strategy) program. One church in Hartford provides resources for special activities at the public library. And in both of our rural locations, churches have especially close working relationships with the county welfare office. Social workers know which churches to call when there are emergency needs. In Alabama, a Christmas gift-giving operation has been set up and run by volunteers, virtually as an adjunct to the Department of Social Services, which provides the names and screens the families. Where governmental programs and services fall short, social workers, police, teachers, and even librarians have often called on mainline (and other) congregations to fill the gap. Such cooperation with governmental entities is by no means rare. Over a third of mainline congregations provide space, volunteers, and other support to the efforts of city governments and agencies.

SUMMARY

Looking at this network of organizations affords a critical perspective on the question of the relationship between mainline churches and public life. The "parachurch" and nonprofit sectors have increasingly become the organizational vehicles through which individual compassion is channeled and social services are delivered.[33] What this study has uncovered is the extent to which this network of organizations does not exist on its own as a replacement for traditional institutions. Rather, it is connected in complex ways to existing religious organizations and their members. Our data do not suggest, for instance, that connections to these extradenominational outreach organizations have any negative effect on a congregation's giving to their own denomination or to their sense of identification with it. The more denominationally loyal are no less active than the more independent-minded. The impulse to do work through a variety of organizational channels is so embedded in American culture—and in the mainline tradition especially—that complementarity more than competition seems to describe the situation. Congregations have simply adopted social service organizations into their organizational network. This pattern is true across the Christian traditions, but especially so, as we have discovered here, in the Protestant mainline.

Overwhelmingly, inter-organizational public involvement by mainline Protestant congregations is aimed at assisting the needy and providing services that enhance the well-being of local communities. *Local,* however, means much more than immediate neighborhoods. These congregations are not, for the most part, "parishes" tending to those within walking distance of the church. Rather, they are participants in metropolitan and countywide organizations that link them in cross-town relationships as much as in neighborhood ties.

Some work for the public good is done by individual congregations, and much of it is done because congregations encourage their individual members to be good citizens. But a significant portion of the mainline's public engagement takes the form of cooperative activity. By creating informal coalitions, providing seedbeds for and resources to religious and secular nonprofits, and by serving as partners to governmental organizations, mainline congregations enter into the vast network of care through which social services are delivered and public engagement takes place. In the encounter with diverse groups of recipients and diverse groups of coproviders, mainline congregations and their members are drawn into the practical, everyday dilemmas of public life: who should be served, what services are needed, how can we pay for them, and how can we work together?

Almost all congregations participate in this work to one degree or another, but mainline ones are distinctive both in the amount and in the types of their participation. They are simply more connected than other Christian churches, and they are more likely to make connections with organizations that are not explicitly religious in their identity and mission. The practice of working across religious and secular boundaries is part of the mainline heritage, as is the habit of tending to the material needs of those beyond their own membership. They are more involved than other churches in immediate relief efforts and in providing educational, cultural, and self-help programs for their communities. Together with African American and Catholic churches, they exceed conservative churches in forming alliances for community benefit and policy advocacy.

If we were looking for extensive political activism or community organizing, we did not find it here. The mainline congregations in which we interviewed are rarely involved either in links to religious and secular lobbying and advocacy groups or in vocal support for their own denominations' activities. Still, the work in which they are engaged is significant, not only for the public good it does, but also for the social capital that is generated in the process. While the local soup kitchen may not usually count when instances of "civic engagement" are being assessed, the volunteers who meet there and the participants who eat there are a "public" in which notions of the common good are being negotiated. The fact that volunteers represent local congregations spreads the effects beyond the individuals who are directly involved. When congregations establish links to others in the community, they not only provide necessary resources to those community groups, but also expand and redefine the very nature of their own membership and citizenship. The boundaries crossed by these inter-organizational linkages allow religious values and religious caring to pass freely between mainline churches and public life. As the director of Albuquerque's Storehouse said to us, "We are, in a real sense, also a ministry to the churches." Nurturing the values embodied in Matthew 25:40 is a task jointly pursued by mainline Protestants and their many public partners.

APPENDIX: DESCRIPTION OF THE SAMPLE

The sample from which this paper draws was constructed for the project called Organizing Religious Work and oversampled congregations in eight "focus" denominations, of which four were mainline Protestant (noted below). After that oversample was drawn, congregations from all other traditions in seven representative locations were randomly selected. In our two rural areas, researchers used a number of sources to compile, we believe, nearly complete lists of congregations, from which we sampled. In the urban areas, the congregations were selected from lists compiled using both denominational directories and the American Yellow Pages on CD-ROM. Churches, synagogues, and "religious organizations" are listed there if they have a phone. They do not pay a fee to be included. Still, a list of groups with phones disproportionately misses the smallest and least "organized" groups. Weighting our cases to approximate the size and denominational distribution of the National Congregations Study alleviates that bias.[34]

Note that this analysis includes only the Christian congregations. Excluded are the 2 percent of our sample that was Jewish, the 2 percent representing other non-Christian congregations, and the 3 percent in certain sectarian groups such as the Church of Jesus Christ of Latter-Day Saints and Jehovah's Witnesses, whose internal and external dynamics are significantly different from those of other Christian denominations.

Note also that "mainline" includes a broader group than just the six that are the focus of the Public Role of Mainline Protestantism project. Included are the following:

Denomination	No. of Churches (unweighted numbers)
*United Methodist	54
Presbyterian Church, USA	21
*Episcopal Church	35
Evangelical Lutheran Church	15
*United Church of Christ	38
American Baptist Churches	4
*Reformed Church in America	14
Disciples of Christ	1
Unitarian	4
Friends	1
Mennonite (General Conference)	4
Total	191

*Represents an oversampling for our focus denominations.

The four categories of Christian traditions used in this essay closely follow those recommended in Brian Steensland et al., "The Measure of American Religion: Toward Improving the State-of-the-Art" (*Social Forces* 79, no. 1: 291–318). Included in the Conservative category are the Southern Baptists, Lutheran Church Missouri Synod, Assemblies of God, Churches of Christ, non-denominational and independent churches, as well as churches from about two dozen other evangelical and pentecostal groups. Included in the African American category are churches from the seven historic black denominations, such as the National Baptists, the

African Methodist Episcopal, and the Church of God in Christ. Included in the Catholic category are both Roman Catholic parishes and various Orthodox bodies.

NOTES

1. Peter Dobkin Hall lays out the theological and historical connections in *Religion and the Origin of Voluntary Associations in the United States*, Working Paper #213 (New Haven, CT: Program on Non-Profit Organizations, Yale University, 1994).

2. See Chaves, Giesel, and Tsitsos, chapter 4 in this volume, as well as Virginia A. Hodgkinson and Murray S. Weitzman, *From Belief to Commitment: The Community Service Activities and Finances of Religious Congregations in the United States*, 1993 ed. (Washington, DC: Independent Sector, 1993), 22–51. Ram Cnaan reports that the historic congregations they surveyed provided services through an average of four programs, including those independently run; see Ram A. Cnaan, "Social and Community Involvement," final report to Partners for Sacred Places (Philadelphia: University of Pennsylvania School of Social Work: Program for the Study of Organized Religion and Social Work, 1997).

3. Because of the demands of the larger study, we also added a small sample of Reformed Church in America congregations in rural upstate New York. See the appendix to this chapter for a full description of the sample.

4. Mark Chaves, Mary Ellen Konieczny, Kraig Beyerlein, and Emily Barman, "The National Congregational Study: Background, Methods, and Selected Results," *Journal for the Scientific Study of Religion* 38, no. 4 (1999): 458–76.

5. Penny Becker reports parallel findings about cultural models for congregational life in her *Congregations in Conflict: Cultural Models of Local Religious Life* (Cambridge: Cambridge University Press, 1999).

6. This argument is elaborated in Nancy Tatom Ammerman, *Congregation and Community* (New Brunswick, NJ: Rutgers University Press, 1997), chap. 9.

7. Sidney Verba, Kay Lehman Schlozman, and Henry E. Brady, *Voice and Equality: Civic Voluntarism in American Politics* (Cambridge, MA: Harvard University Press, 1995).

8. David A. Roozen, William McKinney, and Jackson W. Carroll, *Varieties of Religious Presence* (New York: Pilgrim Press, 1984).

9. The interviews were conducted in a randomly drawn sample from the list of organizations to which congregations were connected. Because our original sample of congregations was also randomly selected, this list should represent the range of activities and types of organizations in which congregations in these seven regions are invested. It is not a comprehensive survey of social service organizations or nonprofits. Nonprofits that have no connection with congregations would not show up on this list. In turn, not all of the organizations on the list are engaged in public community activities, and not all are nonprofits.

10. Our undercount is probably less serious in the mainline congregations than in others. Mainline congregations were much more likely to give us copies of annual reports and other written documents from which we could often glean precise information. Our impression is that the generation of such reports, and the willingness to share them with researchers, is more common among mainline Protestants than among other groups.

11. Peter Dobkin Hall argues that the Northeast is distinctive in its Calvinist heritage and that this heritage has resulted in distinctive patterns of organizing in the nonprofit sector. See his "Religion and the Organizational Revolution in the

United States," in *Sacred Companies: Organizational Aspects of Religion and Religious Aspects of Organizations,* ed. N. Jay Demerath III, Peter Dobkin Hall, Terry Schmitt, and Rhys Williams (New York: Oxford University Press, 1998), 99–115. The Northeast certainly is more dominated by mainline groups than are other regions, but once we take that fact into account, there is no remaining effect of the regional culture itself.

12. African American pastors reported that their churches place fairly strong emphasis on promoting social change and working together in the community, but this emphasis does not translate into higher levels of connection in those churches. These results suggest that the primary explanation for that fact is resources—both the number of well-off people in the congregation and the overall size of the church's budget.

13. Similarly, in an analysis not shown, when we compare conservative Protestant churches to all others, and hold the same external factors constant, the negative effect ($b = -.23$) of being within that tradition remains.

14. Our categories closely mirror those developed by Virginia A. Hodgkinson, Heather A. Gorski, Stephen M. Noga, and E. B. Knauft in *Giving and Volunteering in the United States,* vol. 2, *Trends in Giving and Volunteering by Type of Charity* (Washington, DC: Independent Sector, 1995), as cited in Robert Wuthnow, "Mobilizing Civic Engagement: The Changing Impact of Religious Involvement," in *Civic Engagement in American Democracy,* ed. Theda Skocpol and Morris P. Fiorina (Washington, DC: Brookings Institution Press, 1999), 331–63. Our Human Services category almost exactly conforms to theirs. We have separated out Policy Advocacy and Civic Service from their larger category of Public Benefit (which we call Community Benefit). And we have combined their four Health, Education, Culture, and Youth Organizations categories into one. We have, however, placed Recovery and Self-Help groups into a separate category.

15. A given organization may engage in several kinds of activities, so our categorization depends on the particular activity the congregation supports, not necessarily on a global characterization of the organization itself. For instance, a congregation may cooperate with the local Red Cross in conducting a blood drive (something we classified as a health enhancement activity), or it may channel disaster-relief contributions through the national Red Cross office (something we classified as a human service activity).

16. See Robert Wuthnow, "Beyond Quiet Influence? Possibilities for the Protestant Mainline," chapter 15 in this volume.

17. Our results are generally parallel to those offered in Wuthnow, "Mobilizing Civic Engagement." He notes that people in mainline churches are more likely than those in evangelical ones to be members of and volunteer for nonreligious civic organizations.

18. See Robert D. Putnam, "Bowling Alone: America's Declining Social Capital," *Journal of Democracy* 6, no. 1 (January 1995): 65–78.

19. Jerome Baggett has documented the work of Habitat for Humanity in *Habitat for Humanity: Building Private Homes, Building Public Religion* (Philadelphia, PA: Temple University Press, 2000).

20. Information can be found at http://www.foodforthepoor.com.

21. See http://www.childreach.org/globaled/index.html.

22. Links between churches and economic development are explored by Richard Wood in "Faith in Action: Religious Resources for Political Success in Three Congregations," *Sociology of Religion* 55, no. 4 (winter 1994): 397–417. See also Stephen Hart, *Cultural Dilemmas of Progressive Politics: Styles of Engagement among Grassroots Activists* (Chicago: University of Chicago Press, 2001).

23. There is an extensive literature on the involvement of African American churches in political and civil rights activity. One of the more interesting recent contributions is Mary Pattillo-McCoy, "Church Culture as a Strategy of Action in the Black Community," *American Sociological Review* 63 (December 1998): 767–84. Her findings about the role of church culture in political organizing are paralleled by the findings of Richard Wood in "Religious Culture and Political Action," *Sociological Theory* 17, no. 3 (November 1999): 307–32.

24. See Robert Wuthnow, *The Crisis in the Churches: Spiritual Malaise, Fiscal Woe* (New York: Oxford University Press, 1997), chap. 10, and his *Acts of Compassion: Caring for Others and Helping Ourselves* (Princeton, NJ: Princeton University Press, 1991).

25. This is consistent with the patterns of religiosity described in Nancy T. Ammerman, "Golden Rule Christianity: Lived Religion in the American Mainstream," in *Lived Religion in America*, ed. David Hall (Princeton, NJ: Princeton University Press, 1997), 196–216.

26. Robert Wuthnow, *Sharing the Journey* (New York: Free Press, 1994).

27. Thomas Jeavons has written helpfully on the complications of identifying the religious dimensions of an organization in "Identifying Characteristics of 'Religious' Organizations: An Exploratory Proposal," in *Sacred Companies*, ed. Demerath et al., 79–96.

28. See Wuthnow, *Sharing the Journey*, chap. 5, for a discussion of organizational structure in small groups.

29. Carl Milofsky and Albert Hunter, "Where Nonprofits Come From: A Theory of Organizational Emergence," paper presented to the Southern Sociological Society, April 1995.

30. Zald's study of the YMCA is the classic examination of this process; see Mayer N. Zald, *Organizational Change: The Political Economy of the YMCA* (Chicago: University of Chicago Press, 1970). For a discussion of the implications of institutional differentiation for the religious organizations themselves, see Patricia Wittberg, "Declining Institutional Sponsorship and Religious Orders," *Sociology of Religion* 61, no. 3 (fall, 2000): 315–24.

31. For a similar story, see Courtney J. Bender, "Kitchen Work: The Everyday Practice of Religion, Cooking, and Caring for People with AIDS," Ph.D. diss., Princeton University, 1997.

32. Lester M. Salamon, "Partners in Public Service: The Scope and Theory of Government–Nonprofit Relations," in *The Nonprofit Sector: A Research Handbook*, ed. Walter W. Powell (New Haven, CT: Yale University Press, 1987), 99–117.

33. Robert Wuthnow, *Loose Connections: Joining Together in America's Fragmented Communities* (Cambridge, MA: Harvard University Press, 1998).

34. Mark Chaves et al., "National Congregational Study."

6 The Changing Political Fortunes of Mainline Protestants

Jeff Manza and Clem Brooks

In the first two decades after World War II, the political worlds of mainline Protestants were remarkably stable. Mainline voters regularly provided a large and stable bloc of votes for Republican candidates in national elections. In particular, they provided key support for the Eisenhower/Nixon/Rockefeller "liberal" wing of the Republican Party, with its characteristic combination of support for civil rights and fiscal conservatism. This political and ideological alignment could be traced back to the nineteenth century, enduring through the political upheavals of the Progressive and New Deal eras.

This pattern began to change in the middle 1960s. Increasingly partisan conflicts over civil rights legislation and the Republican Party's nomination of Barry Goldwater in 1964 presented new dilemmas for mainline voters. The growing liberalism of mainline clergy beginning in the 1960s—particularly with regard to civil rights legislation and opposition to the Vietnam War—generated new tensions within mainline denominations. Although the decline of the social movements of the 1960s and the return to dominance (at the national level) of moderate Republican leaders such as Nixon and Ford provided a temporary halt to such conflicts, they have reemerged since the late 1970s to shape the experience of the mainline Protestant community. These tensions have included conflicts generated by the Christian Right, as well as the emergence of a dominant conservative wing within the Republican Party since the presidency of Ronald Reagan, in the face of a continuing liberal shift within many mainline denominations.[1]

These events provide the background against which to understand one key finding of this chapter: traditionally robust support for the Republican

Party among mainline voters has declined. In recent elections, mainline voters have voted in much the same way as the rest of the electorate, marking a significant shift to the political center since the 1950s. At the same time, the impact of mainline Protestants in the American electoral arena has diminished significantly because of their steady decline in membership and size (relative to other religious groups). We have estimated elsewhere that whereas mainline voters constituted nearly half of the entire electorate (46 percent) in 1960, they had fallen to under 28 percent by 1996.[2] As a result of *both* declining size and electoral support for the Republican Party, mainline Protestants are a significantly reduced bloc of voters within the Republican coalition. However, their increasing receptivity to the Democrats has not produced a large impact on the Democratic electoral coalition or on the activities of party leaders, because it has occurred at the same time as membership declines.

In this chapter, we argue that these trends have—in the last few decades—led to a significant erosion of the influence of mainline Protestants in American politics. We start with a brief discussion of the relationship between religious group memberships and political behavior to provide the necessary background for the discussion and analysis developed in the rest of the chapter. Next, we present a series of analyses that examine three related questions. First, to what extent have the political alignments of mainline voters shifted, in comparison both to conservative Protestants and to the rest of the electorate, since the 1960s?[3] Second, what ideological differences in attitudes explain these trends? Third, how have changes in the relative size of the mainline electorate and their political alignment affected the Republican and Democratic Party coalitions respectively? By presenting comparisons with conservative Protestant and all other voters, we situate changes affecting either or both Protestant groups within a broader comparative framework, thereby distinguishing trends that have affected mainline (and conservative Protestant) voters from trends that have affected *all* voters. The analyses presented in this chapter utilize data from two regularly administered national surveys of adults in the United States, the National Election Studies (NES) and the General Social Surveys (GSS).[4]

THE RELIGIOUS CLEAVAGE IN AMERICAN POLITICS

The role of religion in American politics has long been understood to be important. Tocqueville's famous analysis of democracy in America emphasized the strength of voluntary associations rooted in religious organizations and highlighted their contribution to the vitality of American democracy.[5] Whatever its virtues for holding civil society together, religion has frequently been deployed as a weapon in partisan political conflicts as well.[6] The "new political history" that developed in the 1960s and 1970s vigorously established quantitative historical evidence of the importance of religious-based cleavages for voting behavior and the formation of party coalitions throughout the nineteenth century. "Ethnoreligious" cleavages, as they came to be known in the literature, reflected both ethnic differences in the churching of immigrant groups as well as broader denominational differences. They provided a source of political division well understood by contemporary actors and analysts.

Controversies over the disestablishment of official state churches provided the earliest source of religious political division, beginning virtually at the founding of the Republic. Supporters of state churches, especially the Congregationalists, were generally aligned with the Federalist Party, while members of lower-status churches challenging the hegemony of the traditional churches were more likely to line up with the Jeffersonian Democratic-Republicans. The antebellum period (1828–60) appears to have been loosely characterized by the alignment of voters from "liturgical" or "ritualist" religious traditions with the Democratic Party of Andrew Jackson, and voters from pietist or conservative Protestant denominations with first the Whig Party and later the Republican Party. In the period after the Civil War, party competition in the North and Midwest was even more decisively structured by ethnic and religious divisions. Until 1896, the Republican Party received very strong support from Episcopalians, Congregationalists, New School Presbyterians, Methodists, and black Protestants; the Democrats, meanwhile, drew support most heavily from Catholics, and less broadly from Lutherans and Unitarian-Universalists.[7] In the "system of 1896," Republican domination of the North and Midwest involved strong support from nearly all Protestant denominations in those regions, while with rare exceptions the Democrats were limited to the votes of Catholics and the relatively small, unionized working class outside the South.[8] The post-Reconstruction South was, of course, a very different matter: there the Democratic monopoly through World War II made religious differences of little electoral consequence.

With the coming of the New Deal, many analysts assumed that the sharp ethnoreligious cleavages in the North would decline in strength as class factors appeared to grow in importance. But it seems instead that the increase in class divisions during the New Deal largely developed alongside, rather than in place of, traditional religious cleavages. Roosevelt generally performed better among all social groups than Democratic candidate Al Smith did in 1928, leaving largely unchanged the *relative* differences in the levels of support received from most key religious groups.[9] The core of the Democratic coalition continued to be defined by working-class Catholic and Jewish voters in the North and Midwest and white voters of all religious backgrounds in the South. The greatly weakened Republican coalitions of the 1930s and 1940s, by contrast, continued to receive disproportionate support from northern mainline Protestants.

The early post–World War II period was one of unusual stability in the religious world, but by the late 1960s and early 1970s important changes were taking place in nearly every major religious denomination.[10] Mainline Protestant denominations had been losing religious market share for many decades, and beginning in the late 1960s this decline accelerated. Long associated with the political and economic status quo, mainline denominations were deeply influenced, as well as thrown into turmoil, by the great moral crusades of the period: the civil rights movement and the demand for racial justice, protests against the war in Vietnam, and the women's movement. A growing split between liberal Protestant clergy who supported civil rights and other sixties movements and a more conservative laity appeared to generate intra-denominational (and/or intrachurch) tensions.[11] Conservative Protestant churches also reacted sharply—but very differently—to the social and cultural movements of the period. Resisting most of the trends of the period, many leaders of conservative Protestant churches became involved in organizing or promoting new Christian Right movements and discourses which sought to defend "traditional values" against the onslaught of "secular humanism."[12]

In the wake of these and other political upheavals linked to religious mobilizations in the late 1970s and early 1980s—including more broadly the fundamentalist Islamic revolution in Iran, the active role of the Catholic Church in the Solidarity movement in Poland in 1980–81, and the public prominence of "liberation theology" movements in Latin America— a substantial amount of new empirical work on contemporary religious influence in recent American political life has appeared. A central question within this literature concerns the political effects of membership in religious denominations, and whether these have changed in any significant way.

THE CHANGING POLITICAL BEHAVIOR
OF MAINLINE PROTESTANTS

Given our focus on mainline Protestants, we begin our analysis in this chapter by examining political trends among mainline voters in comparison to conservative Protestants, and then contrast both groups with all other (nonblack) respondents in our datasets. The appendix includes a table summarizing variables in all the analyses presented here. We focus on presidential elections in analyzing trends in voting behavior. We also consider trends in group attitudes across a range of different issues, including attitudes toward race, gender equality, abortion, gay and lesbian rights, and attitudes toward government intervention to reduce poverty and assist African Americans. We employ a version of the now conventional scheme for distinguishing the two mutually exclusive and exhaustive groups of Protestant voters, using the information provided in the national surveys we analyze. Our scheme thus classifies members of denominations such as Episcopalians, Methodists, Presbyterians, and Lutherans (except Missouri Synod Lutherans) as members of mainline denominations, and such groups as Baptists, the Assemblies of God, Pentecostals, and Missouri Synod Lutherans as members of conservative Protestant churches.[13]

The analyses in this chapter are limited to nonblack respondents in the surveys we examine. The reason for this restriction is straightforward. Our main interest lies in the impact of religion on voting behavior. Since African Americans of all religious identities are overwhelmingly Democratic, there is little that can be gained by directly including them in this analysis. To be sure, the religious and political distinctiveness of African Americans raises important issues, but we cannot engage them here.[14]

We begin by considering the changing alignment of Protestant voters with the Democratic and Republican parties. Despite their other differences during the 1960s, conservative and mainline Protestants shared a similarly strong level of support for Republican presidential candidates, a phenomenon we have analyzed elsewhere.[15] Figure 6.1 reveals subsequent changes, showing the predicted *log-odds* of supporting the Democratic candidate. Because the scores for the three groups sum to zero,[16] negative scores indicate a *relative* tendency to vote Republican, and positive scores indicate a relative tendency to vote Democratic (in each case, relative to the other two groups). In other words, at the midpoint of zero, a group exhibits the same voting behavior as the rest of the electorate.

The results shown in figure 6.1 document a dramatic shift in the political alignment of mainline Protestants. In comparison to the electorate as a

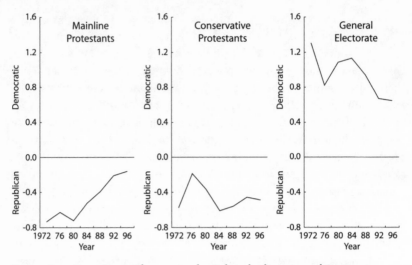

Figure 6.1.   Long-Term Changes in the Political Alignment of Protestant Groups, 1972–1996. SOURCE: Data are from the National Election Studies.

whole, mainline voters have moved steadily from a very strong Republican alignment toward the political center. Conservative Protestants, by contrast, have remained in a strong Republican alignment, punctuated only by their exceptionally high levels of support for born-again Democratic candidate Jimmy Carter in 1976 (and to a lesser extent in 1980). Aside from these two elections, conservatives' voting behavior has been relatively stable and strongly Republican.

With the movement of mainline Protestants toward the political center, an important and interesting cleavage has emerged *within* the ranks of Protestant voters. In the 1960s, and even in the early 1970s, mainline and conservative Protestants exhibited similar levels of support for Republican candidates. To be sure, conservative Protestant voters were more likely to be drawn to the conservative wing of the party in this period, represented especially by Goldwater and Nixon's 1968 "Southern Strategy," while mainline voters may have remained in Republican alignment more out of partisan loyalty than enthusiasm for the emerging conservative movement. However, by the 1990s, a clear electoral separation of the two Protestant groups had emerged.

Most commentators—journalists, political strategists, and academic voting analysts—have attributed this split to the increasing conservatism of conservative Protestants. Our results, by contrast, suggest that such analyses have misread the trends: conservative Protestants appear to become more conservative after 1976 only if one treats that year as the benchmark against which to judge the later trend. Results for 1972 (and similar results for the 1960s) demonstrate that conservative Protestants have been in a Republican alignment for a long period of time, indicating that it is the steady drift of mainline voters toward the political center that has created the observed cleavage among Protestant voters.

What impact have these changes had on the Democratic and Republican electoral coalitions? Analyzing group contributions to electoral coalitions is complicated by the possibility that group-specific political alignments are mediated by the relative size of the groups involved.[17] Table 6.1 considers this issue, comparing the relative size of the mainline Protestant group in comparison to conservative Protestants and to the remainder of the (nonblack) electorate. The sample estimates from the NES data show that the group of mainline voters has decreased in size from 40 percent to 30 percent of the entire electorate, while non-Protestants have increased from 36 percent to 46 percent during the years from 1972 through 1996. Even steeper declines in the relative size of mainline Protestants in the electorate as a whole can be observed if we extend the time series back further. For instance, using the NES data we have estimated elsewhere that mainline Protestants were about 46 percent of the entire electorate in 1960.[18]

Combining the information from our analyses of changes in both group size and alignments, table 6.2 shows the contributions of mainline, conservative Protestant, and non-Protestant voters to the major party coalitions. The top half of the table summarizes the results for the Democratic coalition, which show that changes in the relative size and political alignments of mainline Protestants, conservative Protestants, and non-Protestants have had only a minor impact on the Democratic coalition: mainline voters constitute approximately 27 percent of the Democratic coalition during the twenty-four-year period covered by the analyses, whereas conservative Protestants represent roughly one out of five Democratic presidential voters. Although mainline voters have become much more Democratic in recent elections, their declining proportion of the electorate as a whole has reduced the potential impact of that shift on the Democratic coalition.

The most startling story in table 6.2 can be seen in the steadily declining contribution of mainline voters to the Republican coalition. We estimate that mainline voters provided 45 percent of Republican votes in 1972, falling to 40 percent in 1984, and declining further to just 33 percent in 1996. In the space of just twenty-four years, this represents a substantial

Table 6.1. Protestants as a Percentage of the U.S. Nonblack Electorate, 1972–1996

	1972	1976	1980	1984	1988	1992	1996	Net Change (%)
Mainline Protestants	40	38	36	36	36	30	30	−10
Conservative Protestants	25	23	22	22	25	23	24	−1
All others	36	38	42	42	40	47	46	+10

SOURCE: Data are from the National Election Studies.

Table 6.2. Partisan Representation of Mainline and Conservative Protestants (%), 1972–1996

	1972	1976	1980	1984	1988	1992	1996	Net Change
Democratic coalition								
Mainline Protestants	28	31	29	30	30	26	27	−1
Conservative Protestants	20	21	19	17	19	18	18	−2
All other nonblack voters	52	48	52	53	51	56	55	+3
Republican coalition								
Mainline Protestants	45	45	41	40	39	35	33	−12
Conservative Protestants	27	24	23	24	29	29	30	+3
All other nonblack voters	28	31	36	36	32	36	37	+9

SOURCE: Data are from the National Election Studies.

net decline of 12 percent. These changes are even larger when we use an earlier election as the baseline for our comparisons. In 1960 and 1964, mainline voters represented 59 percent and 52 percent of the Republican coalition; net change in the representation of mainline voters within the Republican coalition thus declined 26 percent between 1960 and 1996. During the same period, conservative Protestants experienced a slight increase

(3 percent) and non-Protestants, a larger increase (9 percent) in their contribution to the Republican coalition.[19]

Ideological Differences and Their Political Effects

What factors can help us better understand the sources of political change among mainline Protestants and their divergence from conservative Protestants during this period? Our data enable us to examine attitudes toward a number of hotly contested issues over the entire time period to see their significance for explaining changing trends among mainline and conservative Protestant voters. We begin with some of the issues that have been the focus of sharp policy and partisan conflicts since the 1960s. The first two relate to attitudes toward African American civil rights and to women's rights (see the appendix for exact question wording). Using data from the General Social Surveys, figure 6.2 shows trends and differences in the respective attitudes of mainline and conservative Protestants, as well as non-Protestants, since the 1970s.

Prior to the 1990s, mainline and conservative Protestant attitudes toward civil rights and women's rights show some notable differences, with mainline respondents being more liberal than conservative Protestants, and non-Protestants being the most liberal of the three groups. However, during the past ten years, the GSS data show an increasing degree of convergence, especially with regard to attitudes toward the civil rights of African Americans. While the attitudes of all three groups have moved steadily toward greater support for civil rights, conservative Protestant attitudes have closed a significant portion of the ideological gap with mainline Protestant and the non-Protestants, resulting in greater similarity in their respective attitudes. Given the similarity of these trends and the evidence for ideological convergence, attitudes toward African American civil rights and women's rights are thus limited candidates for explaining political differences among Protestants in recent years.[20]

Figure 6.3 presents the corresponding differences and patterns of changes over time in attitudes toward gay/lesbian civil rights and toward abortion. As before, non-Protestant respondents are generally the most liberal of the three groups, but with average levels of support for gay/lesbian civil rights and for legal abortion that are very similar to those of mainline Protestants. Conservative Protestants' attitudes are showing modest signs of convergence with the other two groups on gay/lesbian rights, although all three groups' attitudes have clearly moved in a liberal direction since the 1970s on those issues.

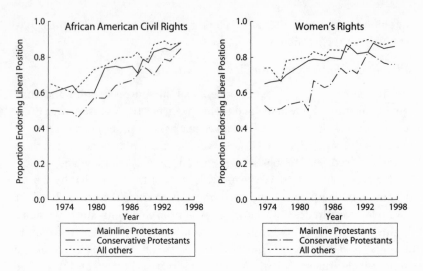

Figure 6.2.   Changing Attitudes toward African American Civil Rights (1972–1998) and Women's Rights (1973–1998). SOURCE: Data are from the General Social Surveys.

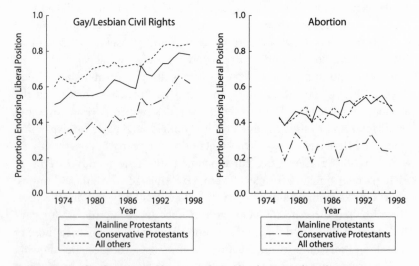

Figure 6.3.   Changing Attitudes toward Gay/Lesbian Civil Rights (1973–1998) and Abortion (1977–1998). SOURCE: Data are from the General Social Surveys.

Differences in abortion attitudes provide the most noteworthy evidence of divergence among Protestants on social issues. Whereas conservative Protestants' attitudes toward abortion show fluctuation over time but no liberalizing trend, both mainline and non-Protestants' attitudes show increases in support for abortion rights. Ideological differences among the two groups of Protestant respondents increased from the 1970s through the 1990s, with mainline attitudes converging with those of non-Protestants.

What about attitudes toward social provision and race-targeted social policies? We examined two issues involving different interpretations of the proper role of the federal government in reducing poverty or providing assistance to African Americans (see the appendix for exact question wording). Although these issues are an important source of difference between the Democratic and Republican parties (and voters' perceptions of the parties), the three religious groups are quite similar in their attitudes. As shown in figure 6.4, non-Protestants are consistently the most liberal of the three groups, but their differences with both groups of Protestants are minor, and the differences between mainline and conservative Protestant attitudes are even smaller. Religious differences in attitudes toward social provision and racial policy undoubtedly exist, but the latter are to be found either *within* denominations or at a more disaggregated level of analysis than the broad categories of "mainline" and "conservative" Protestants permit.[21]

We are now in a position to better understand the ideological sources of differences in the political alignments of mainline versus conservative Protestants. More specifically, our analyses of between-group ideological differences suggest the importance of attitudes toward issues of gay/lesbian civil rights and abortion. Figure 6.5 presents the results of a simple test of this hypothesis. For these analyses, we use a statistical model to predict whether a respondent voted for a Republican or Democratic presidential candidate by examining the mainline or conservative Protestant denominational membership, but adjusting the figures to take into account the changes described above in attitudes toward abortion and gay rights. (This model thus resembles the earlier model employed in the analyses summarized in figures 6.2 and 6.3, except that we use the GSS data and its items measuring these attitudes.) If our hypothesis is supported, then we expect to observe *smaller* differences between the political alignments of mainline and conservative Protestants (and also less divergence among mainline voters from the Republican Party) once we control for differences

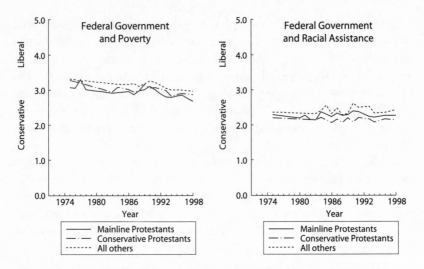

Figure 6.4. Changing Attitudes toward Federal Government and Public Policy, 1975–1998. SOURCE: Data are from the General Social Surveys.

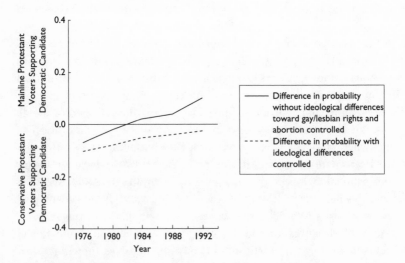

Figure 6.5. The Impact of Ideological Differences on Mainline versus Conservative Protestant Political Alignments, 1976–1992. SOURCE: Data are from the General Social Surveys.

in attitudes toward abortion and gay/lesbian civil rights. Conversely, if we observe no such changes, then these results provide evidence against this hypothesis.

The results in figure 6.5 are consistent with the hypothesis. The solid line shows the predicted difference in the probability of supporting the Democratic over the Republican candidate when we *ignore* ideological differences between the attitudes of mainline versus conservative Protestants toward gay/lesbian civil rights and abortion. The estimates connected by the dashed line, however, directly take into account ideological differences in mainline versus conservative Protestant attitudes, showing considerably *smaller* differences in political alignment once those attitudinal differences are controlled. These results confirm findings we have reported in earlier work, showing that voting differences between these two groups have increased steadily.

CONCLUDING REFLECTIONS

The results presented in this chapter have broad implications for understanding the changing character of denominationally based religious conflict and the changing religious composition of the Democratic versus Republican party coalitions. The headline-grabbing story over the past two decades has been that a new conservative political mobilization among conservative Protestants has caused them to shift sharply into Republican political alignment. The sudden emergence of the Christian Right (CR) in the late 1970s as a factor in U.S. politics and the visible role of some early CR groups such as the Moral Majority in the 1980 elections seemed to herald a new type of political conflict in which conservative religious values were becoming increasingly important in the political system. Fears about the CR have periodically been expressed in dystopian novels such as Margaret Atwood's *The Handmaid's Tale,* and major media representations of the CR have frequently been alarmist as well; a *Time* cover story in 1994 featured a report on Ralph Reed and the Christian Coalition's strategy for "taking over" American politics, which it proclaimed to be "working."[22]

The analyses we have developed here (and elsewhere) cast doubt about the existence of such a shift, at least at the denominational level. Instead, the story most worthy of consideration is not about conservative Protestants, but rather about mainline Protestants and their political realignment. We believe the results presented here should firmly establish that mainline voters are no longer a Republican bloc, voting much the same way as the electorate as a whole in recent presidential elections.[23] This represents a substantial shift from the historic pattern that characterized their political behavior during the nineteenth century and first half of the twentieth century, and this shift provides the sharpest and most unambiguous evidence of change in the alignment of religious groups and political parties.

The shift of mainline voters to the political center follows, but does not match, the shift among mainline clergy and church hierarchies, which have become increasingly liberal in recent years. Over the past thirty-five years, the mainline churches have increasingly endorsed liberal positions not only on questions of economic justice but also on such rights-related issues as race, gender, gay/lesbian rights, and abortion. The laity, however, has experienced liberal trends only with respect to these last issues.

The existence of liberal opinion trends is not restricted to the religious groups investigated in this study. In keeping with the large body of evidence from opinion research, we find that the attitudes of social groups tend to be affected similarly by large trends, resulting in groups experiencing similar patterns of change over time.[24] Indeed, the majority of the issues we have investigated reveal such a pattern, with several also indicating clear evidence of convergence between the attitudes of mainline and conservative Protestants, as well as non-Protestants. However, the issues of abortion and gay/lesbian civil rights are also notable in suggesting enduring ideological differences between mainline versus conservative Protestants. These differences showed little sign of shrinking during the 1990s.

The Political Impact of Mainline Voters

Group-based alignments represent an important source of continuity to parties when they provide a loyal source of voters in elections. Accordingly, shifts in group alignments can significantly alter the electoral calculations of politicians, who must subsequently decide how to attract new party supporters or how to reformulate appeals so as to win back defectors.

Our focus on mainline versus conservative Protestant voters in presidential elections provides a telling example of this pattern. Since the 1960s, the representation of these groups within the Democratic coalition shows extensive stability, with no more than a net 3 percent change in the respective position of mainline Protestant, conservative Protestant, and non-Protestant (and nonblack) voters from 1972 through 1996. These minor changes suggest that little change has occurred in the religious bases of support for Democratic candidates. This stability appears to coexist along-side the changing identity of the contemporary Democratic Party and its growing focus on endorsing (and partially implementing) rights for as-criptively defined groups such as African Americans, women, and gays and lesbians. In dramatic contrast, the representation of religious groups within the Republican coalition reveals a substantial change. Whereas mainline Protestants once represented a near-majority of Republican voters, their presence within the Republican coalition has declined by over 10 percent from 1972 through 1996, and by over 25 percent since 1960.

As the relative size and Republican loyalty of mainline voters has de-clined, there is increasingly less incentive for ideological and political en-trepreneurs within the Republican leadership to modify conservative pol-icy positions that would require support for conservative Protestant ideas or initiatives. Without the moderating ideological influence of mainline voters, more conservative religious voters and activists have been able to exert greater influence and experience less opposition within the Repub-lican Party. Had the religious composition of both political parties remained unchanged since mid-century, it seems unlikely that the Christian Right would have found the same opportunities for electoral influence in the Republican Party of the 1980s and 1990s.

What does the future hold for the political fortunes of mainline Prot-estant denominations? In general, as long as current alignments persist, we would expect that the drift of mainline Protestants away from the Republican Party will either stabilize or continue to grow. However, Re-publicans will not necessarily continue to endorse the socially conservative positions that contributed to the shift of mainline Protestants away from that party. These positions have reduced support for Republican candidates as a whole, as we have documented elsewhere.[25] The Republican Party's partial (and at times substantial) embrace of the Christian Right platform is driving other socially liberal segments of the electorate into centrist or Democratic alignments. Moderation on such issues could potentially shift mainline Protestants back into their historic alignment with the Republi-can Party, but only if the enduring images that these and other voters have of party differences come to be altered as well.

Such considerations suggest an important picture of the increasingly asymmetrical political influence of conservative and mainline Protestants on the two major U.S. political parties. Although conservative Protestants have not become more Republican in their political alignment, their actual influence on the GOP has nevertheless increased since the 1970s. By con-trast, the influence of mainline voters on the Democratic Party shows little sign of growth. Ironically, as mainline voters have shifted to the political center while their numbers diminished, they have lost their political distinctiveness in the American political system. The Democratic coalition contains virtually no more mainline Protestant voters now than in the 1960s or 1970s, and as a result, there has been no palpable increase in the incentives for Democratic politicians to endorse principles or implement policies that would have disproportionate appeal to mainline voters. Smaller groups, notably Jews, African Americans, and union workers, are often able to parlay higher levels of loyalty into political influence within the Democratic Party. With divided political loyalties that no longer lead to a consistent alignment with one party, members of mainline churches (and denominational leaders who speak for them) are unlikely to appear to face significant obstacles to achieving similar political influence in the foreseeable future.

APPENDIX: VARIABLES IN THE ANALYSIS

Note: The information on religious group membership (first item) and major party vote choice (last item) was included in analyses of both General Social Surveys (GSS) and National Election Studies (NES) data.

VARIABLES (FROM GSS)

Religious Group Membership

Mainline Protestant	Congregational/United Church of Christ
	Episcopalian/Anglican
	Methodist (except Nazarene/Free Methodist)
	Unitarian/Universalist
	Presbyterian
	Lutheran (except Missouri Synod Lutheran)
	Evangelical and Reformed Protestants
	Reform, Dutch Reformed, or Christian Reformed
	Protestants, not elsewhere classified
	"Christian," not elsewhere classified
Conservative Protestant	Baptists (including Southern Baptists and Primitive/Free Will Baptists)
	Pentecostal/Assemblies of God
	Holiness/Church of God

Plymouth Brethren
Seventh-Day Adventist
Missouri Synod Lutheran
Fundamentalist, not elsewhere
  classified
Church of the Nazarene

All other respondents

African American Civil Rights
  Agree
  Disagree

"White people have a right to keep (Negroes/Blacks/African Americans) out of their neighborhoods if they want to, and (Negroes/Blacks/African Americans) should respect that right."

Women's Rights
  Yes
  No

"Women should take care of running their homes and leave running the country up to men."

Gay/Lesbian Civil Rights
  Yes
  No

"And what about a man who admits that he is a homosexual? Should such a person be allowed to teach in a college or university, or not?"

Abortion
  Yes
  No

"Please tell me whether or not you think it should be possible for a pregnant woman to obtain a legal abortion if the woman wants it for any reason?"

Federal Government and Poverty
  1 = People should take care of themselves
  2
  3 = Agreed with both
  4
  5 = Government should improve living standards

"Some people think that the government in Washington should do everything possible to improve the standard of living of all poor Americans. . . . Other people think it is not the government's responsibility, and that each person should take care of himself. . . . Where would you place yourself on this scale, or have you not made up your mind on this?"

Federal Government and Racial Assistance
  1 = Should not be giving special treatment
  2
  3 = Agreed with both
  4

"Some people think that (Blacks/Negroes/African Americans) have been discriminated against for so long that the government has a special obligation to help improve

5 = Government should improve living conditions	their living standard. Others believe that the government should not be giving special treatment to (Blacks/Negroes/African Americans). Where would you place yourself on this scale, or have you not made up your mind on this?"
Major party vote choice	Republican candidate choice
	Democratic candidate choice

NOTES

Both authors contributed equally to this chapter. We thank Mark Chaves, John Evans, and John Green for helpful suggestions on an earlier draft of the chapter.

1. For a recent overview and documentation of the leftward shift of the major mainline denominations, see Thad Williamson, "True Prophecy? A Critical Examination of the Sociopolitical Stance of the Mainline Protestant Churches," *Union Seminary Quarterly Review* 51 (1997): 79–116.

2. See Jeff Manza and Clem Brooks, *Social Cleavages and Political Change: Voter Alignments and U.S. Party Coalitions* (New York: Oxford University Press, 1999), chaps. 7, 8. Our estimates are based on National Election Study survey data, but other surveys corroborate the declining proportion of mainline voters in the electorate.

3. There is a debate over what to call Protestants who are not mainline. While scholars traditionally use the term *evangelical,* we use the more general term *conservative Protestants,* following Robert D. Woodberry and Christian S. Smith, "Fundamentalism et al.: Conservative Protestants in America," *Annual Review of Sociology* 24 (1998): 25–56.

4. NES: Center for Political Studies, *American National Election Studies, 1948–1994* (Ann Arbor, MI: Institute for Social Research, and Inter-University Consortium for Political and Social Research, 1995), machine-readable data files and codebooks; and Center for Political Studies, *American National Election Study 1996: Pre- and Post-Election Surveys* (Ann Arbor, MI: Inter-University Consortium for Political and Social Research <www.umich.edu/nes>), machine-readable data files and codebooks. GSS: James Davis and Tom W. Smith, *General Social Surveys, 1972–1996.* [machine-readable data file and codebook] (Storrs, CT: Roper Center for Public Opinion Research, 1997), machine-readable data file and codebook.

5. Tocqueville argued that "I have already said enough to put Anglo-American civilization in its true light. It is the product (and one should continually bear in mind this point of departure) of two perfectly distinct elements which elsewhere have often been at war with one another but which in America it was somehow possible to incorporate into each other, forming a marvelous combination. I mean the spirit of religion and the spirit of freedom"; see Tocqueville, *Democracy in America,* vol. 1 (Garden City, NY: Anchor, 1969), 46–47.

6. The journalist William Safire has put the point nicely, commenting on the 1992 national party conventions in terms that are widely applicable in the history of U.S. politics: "The name of the Lord is being used as a symbol for the other

side's immorality, much as the American flag was used in previous campaigns as a symbol for the other side's lack of patriotism"; see William Safire, "God Bless Us," *New York Times*, August 27, 1992, A23, quoted in Stephen Carter, *The Culture of Disbelief* (New York: Basic Books, 1993), 47.

7. For a concise summary of the main findings from the literature on partisan alignments of religious voters in the nineteenth century, see Richard Swierenga, "Ethnoreligious Political Behavior in the Mid-Nineteenth Century: Voting, Values, Cultures," in *Religion and American Politics*, ed. Mark A. Noll (New York: Oxford University Press, 1990), 146–71.

8. For a broad overview of the alignments of this period, see Walter Dean Burnham, "The System of 1896," in *The Evolution of American Electoral Systems*, ed. Paul Kleppner (Westport, CT: Greenwood Press, 1981), 147–202.

9. The major exception was Jewish voters, who realigned sharply during the 1920s and 1930s toward the Democratic Party. See for example Gerald Gamm, *The Making of the New Deal Democrats* (Chicago: University of Chicago Press, 1986), 45–74.

10. For a good general summary of the changes within the major religious traditions during the 1960s and beyond, see Wade C. Roof and William McKinney, *American Mainline Religion* (New Brunswick, NJ: Rutgers University Press, 1987), 11–39; and, more generally, Robert Wuthnow, *The Restructuring of American Religion* (Princeton, NJ: Princeton University Press, 1988).

11. For analyses of the growth of liberalism within the Protestant mainline and the tensions it generated, see, for example, Harold Quinley, *The Prophetic Clergy: Social Activism among Protestant Ministers* (New York: Wiley, 1974); Jeffrey Hadden, *The Gathering Storm in the Churches* (Garden City, NY: Anchor, 1969); and Richard Neuhaus, *The Naked Public Square* (Grand Rapids, MI: Eerdmans, 1984), esp. chap. 3.

12. For useful overviews of the Christian Right mobilization, see Steve Bruce, *The Rise and Fall of the New Christian Right* (New York: Oxford University Press, 1988); Jerome Himmelstein, *To the Right: The Transformation of American Conservatism*, 97–128; and William Martin, *With God on Our Side* (New York: Broadway Books, 1996).

13. Because of a failure in the early years of the National Election Study to distinguish among Baptists, to maintain consistency we have placed all Baptist respondents in our "conservative Protestant" category. This will tend to produce slightly more conservative estimates of the differences between the groups. See the appendix for details about our scheme for coding Protestant denominations.

14. An alternate strategy is to analyze statistical models and measures that directly take into account the specific linkages between religious group memberships and political alignments among African Americans; however, this strategy would result in considerably more complex analyses, and we adopt the simpler strategy in this study.

15. See Manza and Brooks, *Social Cleavages*, chap 4, esp. figure 4.2 and accompanying text.

16. In technical terms, we are employing a zero-sum normalization for identification purposes, in which at every election the scores of all groups will sum to zero.

17. A third relevant factor affecting party coalitions is the rate of voter turnout for a given social group. Differences in the turnout rates of U.S. religious groups have generally been stable since the 1960s, and to simplify the current analyses, we do not analyze the impact of this factor on party coalitions. See Manza and

Brooks, *Social Cleavages*, figure 4.3, for these trends. For a general overview of the issues in analyzing group contributions to party coalitions, see our "Group Size, Turnout, and Alignments in the Making of U.S. Party Coalitions, 1960–1992," *European Sociological Review* 15 (1999): 369–90.

18. See Manza and Brooks, *Social Cleavages*, chap. 7.

19. For analyses of the trends going back to 1960, see our *Social Cleavages*, table 7.5 and accompanying text.

20. These analyses of mean differences in attitudes should be treated with some caution. They do not tell us how *salient* these views are, or whether respondents are willing to translate these attitudes into support for particular kinds of public policies. Mainline respondents could differ from conservative Protestants in either regard. For recent debates about the so-called "principle-implementation" gap with regard to racial attitudes, see David Sears, Jim Sidnaius, and Larry Bobo, eds., *Racialized Politics* (Chicago: University of Chicago Press, 2000); and Jeff Manza, "Race and the Underdevelopment of the American Welfare State," *Theory and Society* 31 (2000): 482–505. For analysis of the growing political salience of attitudes toward civil rights principles among all U.S. voters, see Clem Brooks, "Civil Rights Liberalism and the Suppression of a Republican Political Realignment in the U.S., 1972–1996," *American Sociological Review* 65 (2000): 482–505.

21. See Wuthnow, *Restructuring of American Religion*, for this argument.

22. Novels invoking the CR threat are cited in Clyde Wilcox, "Premillennialists at the Millennium: Some Reflections on the Christian Right in the Twenty-First Century," *Sociology of Religion* 55 (1994): 243. For an overview and critique of some common general media stereotypes of conservative Protestant voters, see J. David Woodard, "Evangelicals and the Media," in *Contemporary Evangelical Political Involvement*, ed. Corwin Smidt (Lanham, MD: University Presses of America, 1989), 119–31.

23. It is informative in this context to consider changes in the magnitude of the coefficient measuring change over time in mainline Protestants' political alignment (.18) when their ideological differences from conservative Protestants are taken into account (.08). The reduction in coefficient size indicates that attitudinal differences between the two groups account for approximately 55 percent of mainline Protestants' divergent political alignment from the 1972–1992 presidential elections.

24. Benjamin Page and Robert Shapiro, *The Rational Public: Fifty Years of Trends in Americans' Policy Preference* (Chicago: University of Chicago Press, 1992); Tom W. Smith, "Liberal and Conservative Trends in the United States since World War II," *Public Opinion Quarterly* 54 (1990): 479–507.

25. See Brooks, "Civil Rights Liberalism."

Part II

INVOLVEMENT IN
PUBLIC ISSUES

7 Furthering the Freedom Struggle

Racial Justice Activism in the
Mainline Churches since the Civil Rights Era

Bradford Verter

For He hath made of one blood all the nations of the
world to dwell on the face of the earth together.

Acts 17:26

About ten years ago Old Northbury Congregational, a church with an exclusively white membership located in a wealthy Connecticut suburb, entered into a partnership with Mt. Pisgah, a black Baptist church serving a poor community in Hartford. John Biggs, chair of Old Northbury's social action committee, was in on it from the beginning. The partnership was initiated by his pastor, an affable, soft-spoken, concerned man in his early fifties, whom Biggs described as "a real Garrison Keillor type of guy." The pastor was an earnest advocate of social justice. He gave sermons on peace, on the environment, and on race. Throughout the 1990s he kept close tabs on *Scheff v. O'Neill*—the suit that would eventually alter the state tax code to equalize educational funding across school districts—as it wended its way through the Connecticut court system. He saw the partnership with Mt. Pisgah as a way to get his congregation involved in racial justice and reconciliation. The congregation of Old Northbury gave a portion of its tithes, amounting to between $10,000 and $15,000 a year, to the Hartford church. Old Northbury also set up a food pantry, running groceries over to Mt. Pisgah for the inner-city church to distribute. As chair of the social action committee, Biggs organized joint activities with Mt. Pisgah, picnics and field days involving the children of both congregations. Several times a year the pastors of the two churches would swap pulpits, and delegations of one church would visit the other.

But the partnership did not work out. Different worship styles had something to do with it. "We're a traditional, staid, Protestant, New England Yankee church," Biggs noted. "They hated coming to our church. It was boring. . . . Going to their church was a gas. A lot of singing, dancing, jumping up and down. . . . They kept inviting people to be saved. It was fun but it was weird." More problematic, however, was the social gulf that separated the two churches and made their relationship unequal:

> The black church lost interest. They weren't so into reciprocity. They were dealing with a lot of difficult issues—drugs, alcohol, poverty, and stuff. They weren't very well organized. Organizing with a white suburban church probably was not high on their list of priorities. . . . They were feeling like we were the suburban rich people coming in to do good with them. . . . They resented the discrepancy, the hierarchical relationship. . . . It's hard not to get into the role of the benevolent giver and the needy recipient. . . . It's hard to transcend that divide.

In the end, the two churches drifted apart, and the social action committee of Old Northbury turned its attention to other projects. "We tried," said Biggs's wife, Amy. "But they just weren't interested."[1]

Many white, liberal Protestants today who try to bridge the racial gap share the frustration and sense of failure voiced by John and Amy Biggs. They know that thirty-five years after the civil rights movement, the country is still deeply split along racial lines. Divided responses to the stories of Rodney King, O. J. Simpson, Louis Farrakhan, Amadou Diallo, and a thousand other news bulletins bear ample testimony to the persistence of racial polarization in America. The members of the mainline know that racism is a sin, a cancer in the body of Christ—this they've heard in church often enough. They want to do something, to join a white "we" and a black "they" into an interracial "us." They try reading books, attending workshops, entering into partnerships with black churches, recruiting minorities. But nothing they do seems to work. After decades of aggressive outreach programs, minorities still compose between only 2.2 and 7.8 percent of the membership of the major Protestant denominations. Mainline congregations remain as divided as they were in 1956, when Rev. Martin Luther King Jr. proclaimed eleven o'clock on Sunday morning "the most segregated hour of Christian America." And when they look at the statistics, they see that the differences between blacks and whites with regard to such key social indicators as health, education, employment, residency, arrest, and imprisonment are wider now than they were in the 1960s. They do not understand what went wrong.[2]

For their part, African Americans have grown increasingly frustrated with the persistence of the racist structures that perpetuate inequities. As several recent studies and numerous memoirs have attested, middle-class blacks may feel this disaffection most acutely, compelled by the precariousness of their privileged position to suppress their rage and despair at the corrosive indignities of everyday racism. Few African Americans place the white churches at the vanguard of the struggle for justice; and even within these institutions, blacks consistently voice their disappointment at the mainline's insufficiency as a base for status, dignity, or recognition. In the 1960s, King was increasingly outspoken about his disappointment with the denominations. "As the Negro struggles against grave injustice, most white churchmen offer pious irrelevancies and sanctimonious trivialities," he told an interviewer. Today his dream of building the beloved community on an interracial bedrock of faith seems more distant than ever.[3]

The recent history of mainline activism for racial justice is a story of good intentions but discouraging results. Liberal Protestants articulate a progressive vision of integration and equality, but their efforts at breaking down the system of American apartheid are largely symbolic. The mainline churches, as numerous studies have demonstrated, are the most segregated institutions in the United States, and thus serve to maintain the structures of white privilege. In order to effect genuine change, members of the churches would have to relinquish power to the populations from whose exploitation they benefit, and this they are unwilling to do. Paternalism and social distance are two of the deepest faults of the liberal program. By ignoring black concerns and failing to establish bonds of reciprocity, whites have defined an agenda for racial justice that not only fails to redress inequities but even helps to perpetuate them. By striving separately to tear down racial barriers, well-meaning activists have unwittingly erected new ones.[4]

PATERNALISM AND THE SEGREGATION OF ACTIVISM

Paternalism is the means by which dominant groups within a society maintain their position without recourse to physical violence. "The agenda for dominant groups," according to sociologist Mary R. Jackman, "is to create an ideological cocoon whereby they can define their discriminatory actions as benevolent." Paternalism (defined as acts "in which one person, A, interferes with another person, S, in order to promote S's own good") serves this purpose, perpetuating relations of inequality by obfuscating strategies of social control through expressions of affection and concern. Whether expressed as "compassionate conservatism," "tough love," or (as John Biggs noted) occasional gifts of charity, paternalistic intervention presumes the superior moral competence of the dominant group, and affirms an implicit status hierarchy: the donor supposedly knows what is best for all concerned. Truly disinterested compassion, Jackman suggests, is impossible in relations between unequal groups. Although donors may feel genuine sympathy, and recipients real gratitude, the dynamics of paternalism inevitably sustain the social asymmetries benevolence is ostensibly designed to redress. Frustration and resentment are the natural results, as witnessed by the members of both Old Northbury Congregational and Mt. Pisgah.[5]

Does this mean whites who replicate biased patterns of behavior and pursue inequitable policy goals under the guise of fighting racism are hypocrites? Not necessarily. Jackman argues that individuals may hold beliefs that are in opposition to their interests; but they will act according to their interests, not according to their beliefs. Their positive feelings render their discriminatory actions invisible even to themselves. This helps to explain recent findings that although whites are decreasingly likely to express prejudicial attitudes overtly, they are also increasingly likely to oppose concrete measures to overcome racial disparities. They affirm the principles but reject the program.[6]

Opinion among Presbyterians on affirmative action offers a good example of the dichotomy between abstract and applied ethics. Since 1973 the General Assembly of the Presbyterian Church (USA) has issued a number of statements in favor of affirmative action, buttressing its repeated appeals with political, economic, and theological arguments. But these official declarations appear to neither reflect nor direct the behavior of the people in the pews. According to a 1999 survey, over 75 percent of members and elders in the PCUSA oppose the preferential hiring and promotion of African Americans. Presbyterians are unexceptional in their general opposition to affirmative action; this is the majority opinion among whites in the United States. Nevertheless, the gap between the talk and the walk is striking and demands explanation.[7]

The case against affirmative action is founded on one of the core values of Protestant theology: the principle of individualism. "Reverse discrimination" and other shibboleths draw their power from this consensual ideal. The principle of individualism supports social asymmetries by discouraging policies that would benefit subordinate groups. As a number of scholars have argued, individualistic values serve to redefine the concept of equality—a widely shared norm—as equal rights and opportunities instead of equal outcomes, and to depict as illegitimate such redistributive programs as affirmative action. Jackman goes so far as to call individualism "the hallmark cry of dominant groups under challenge." Not surprisingly, blacks are more likely than whites to articulate policy goals based on collective ideals.[8]

The ideology of individualism also means that the prophetic witness of the Presbyterian Church in assembly has something less than the force of law—certainly there are no institutional penalties for heterodox opinion. In keeping with the traditional Protestant emphasis on personal autonomy, the resolutions and statements of social principles that mainline denominations pass at their regular church-wide meetings, however forcefully expressed, are defined as guides for church policy, not as mandates for personal decision making. When it comes to ethical matters, modern Protestant theology tends to emphasize the process of sincere introspection, guided by faith; the verdict itself is secondary.

Individualistic principles have also led white activists to pursue a separate agenda from that of their black counterparts. Social hierarchies, Jackman argues, are dependent upon both spatial segregation and role separation. In the case of racial justice, activist ideologies and practices are also differentiated by race. Unlike blacks, whites tend to express their visions of racial justice in abstract rather than practical terms, and to define racism as an individual sin rather than a systemic problem. These differences are reflected on the national level in the divergent political platforms of black and white churches. More significantly, perhaps, they are also reflected on the local level in the social agendas of mainline congregations. As John Biggs noted, while members of Old Northbury were examining their own racial assumptions and trying to forge ties of friendship with members of the black church on occasional Sundays, the members of Mt. Pisgah, normally isolated residentially, economically, and socially, were grappling with substantive issues—"drugs, alcohol, poverty, and stuff." They were too busy to "celebrate diversity" or work toward "racial healing," objectives defined by white reformers. Black and white activists may look toward the same ultimate goal, but they face in opposite directions.[9]

MAINLINE ACTIVISM AFTER THE BLACK MANIFESTO

The weak moral authority of the church and the paternalistic approach of the mainline denominations with regard to racial justice are products of the collapse of the civil rights movement, whose shadow looms over contemporary efforts at racial reconciliation. In American memory, the freedom struggle represents liberal Protestant activism (and black political influence) at its peak. At no time before—or since—had the mainline supposedly enjoyed such a unity of commitment, such a solidarity of purpose, such an effectiveness of presence. Linking arms with their African American counterparts, denominational clergy, ecumenical administrators, and laypeople strove together to rectify the gross injustices of segregation. That golden image of collective effervescence has been tarnished somewhat by recent scholarship highlighting the tensions and disagreements that existed among movement activists, but it still stands as the high-water mark against which subsequent denominational mobilization has been measured. What has set the black and white churches, which once fought together for racial justice, so far apart today that conversation partners now talk past each other? To understand the process of division, one must examine the debates that followed the civil rights era. The 1970s saw a struggle over racial policy, the most lasting result of which was the virtual withdrawal of white activists from the field of racial justice for over a decade.[10]

At the heart of the issue was the question of power—the power to set agendas, to allocate resources, to make decisions, to represent oneself. The mainline denominations deserve great credit for their heroic labors during the freedom struggle of the 1950s and 1960s. But they did not initiate the battle for civil rights; that honor goes to members of the black churches. Whites fought, but it was African Americans who led the charge. White involvement in the civil rights movement was a top-down phenomenon, "an elitist effort initiated largely by ministers and church bureaucrats," according to historian James F. Findlay. When racial tensions developed within the movement over who should lead, mainline leaders were unwilling to surrender their privileged positions, leaving themselves vulnerable to black critiques of the limitations of white liberalism. The awkward response of denominational officials to black demands for self-determination dictated the troubled path of racial justice activism over the next several decades. As African Americans demanded recognition, respect, and autonomy, whites abandoned direct engagement and reverted to ineffective symbolic overtures and patriarchal intervention. As one long-term activist recalled, "White liberals were no more committed to major changes in power and control than were conservatives."[11]

By the mid-1960s, a number of the mainline denominations had boards in place to articulate policies on racial justice, race relations, and ministries for racial and ethnic minorities. Among them were the Episcopal Society for Cultural and Racial Unity (ESCRU), the United Presbyterian Church's Commission on Church and Race (COCAR), the United Church of Christ's Commission for Racial Justice (CRJ), and the Methodists' Commission on Religion and Race (CORR). These boards, most of which were chaired by

African Americans, were notable for being biracial, but their activities involved only a small number of clergy. In 1966, an informal ecumenical group, the National Committee of Negro Churchmen, crafted a statement that defended "black power" and demanded a larger role for black clergy: "Without [the] capacity to participate with power—i.e., to have some organized political and economic strength to really influence people with whom one interacts—integration is not meaningful." By 1969, African American clergy and laity in each mainline denomination had organized separate black caucuses.[12]

The black power statement and the organization of African American clergy did not prepare white officials for the shock of the Black Manifesto. Promulgated in 1969 by veteran Student Nonviolent Coordinating Committee (SNCC) activist James Forman, the document outlined a radical vision of African American self-determination, vociferously rejecting "the racist white Christian Church with its hypocritical declarations and doctrines of brotherhood," and demanding reparations of $500 million (later expanded to $3 billion) from white churches and synagogues. Forman ensured that his critique would not pass unnoticed by walking down the aisle of Riverside Church—flagship of liberal Protestantism, located directly across the street from the headquarters of the National Council of Churches (NCC)—and presenting his demands to the minister and parishioners assembled for Sunday services. Startled by this attack from outside their precincts, mainline church leaders were thunderstruck when Forman's vituperative critique was echoed by more carefully articulated but equally passionate voices from within. The ecumenical committee of black clergymen that had issued the black power statement of 1966 now ratified Forman's claim that "white churches and synagogues undeniably have been the moral cement of the structure of racism in this nation and the vast majority of them continue to play that role today." Since 1963, Reverend Gayraud S. Wilmore had headed COCAR, the racial justice arm of the United Presbyterian Church, and had worked closely with the NCC and other ecumenical councils to further the struggle for civil rights. In his theologically grounded response, Wilmore confirmed the assertions of the Black Manifesto; noted that $500 million was "actually [a] modest sum"; derided "bland, liberal theology"; and compared Forman to a prophet. "It may well be for all his vehemence and rudeness, James Forman is being used by God to declare to the churches, 'This night your soul is required of you; and the things you have prepared, whose will they be?' (Luke 12:20)."[13]

The Black Manifesto and the strong support it elicited from African

American leaders within the mainline evoked a crisis of confidence among denominational officials. Many whites had been vocal supporters of the struggle for civil rights, but these demands for reparations and self-determination struck at the heart of paternalistic leadership. Blacks were asking not for handouts, not for expressions of support, but for institutional authority. "The fact is that black and white church officials have unequal voices when they speak," noted one clergyman. "As long as everyone was talking simply about money, we were missing the real point," said another. "The overriding issue is now redistribution of power." African American spokespeople conceived of the redistribution of power not only in temporal but also in spiritual terms. Albert B. Cleage, James H. Cone, Vincent Harding, and other prophetic critics argued that the white vision of Christian theology was Eurocentric, misguided, and fundamentally oppressive. In its stead they offered a politically and spiritually liberating reading of the New Testament based on the suffering, social activism, and deliverance of Jesus. "Whether whites want to hear it or not," Cone proclaimed, *"Christ is black, baby."* To some whites, this theological development represented the last straw; if blacks and whites had separate discourses even about God, then what hope would there ever be for moral reconciliation?[14]

Within the denominations, black demands were met with resistance and retrenchment. Conservative factions within the United Presbyterian Church and other mainline denominations sought to decentralize national governance by cutting staff and deposing liberal activists from leadership positions. Most of the racial justice offices established during the 1960s—COCAR, CORR, the CRJ—continued, but in a marginal capacity as isles of color in a sea of white bureaucracy. Some closed shop altogether. ESCRU disbanded in 1970 after eleven vigorous years. Under the funding structure of the NCC, members were allowed to specify which programmatic activities their contributions should support, and during much of the 1970s, the ecumenical organization's social action unit ran at a deficit. During the 1970s, the NCC, along with a number of mainline denominations, including the United Church of Christ (UCC), the United Presbyterian Church in the United States of America (UPCUSA), and the Episcopal Church, USA (ECUSA), significantly reduced funding to progressive causes. Another round of cuts in 1978 compelled the NCC to lay off five of the sixteen remaining staff in its social action unit, including its associate for racial justice issues.[15]

Bitter disputes over racial policy wracked the churches. In 1971, for example, the United Presbyterian Church was divided over the decision of

COCAR to grant $10,000 out of the church's Emergency Fund for Legal Aid for the defense of Angela Davis, a radical activist arrested on charges of murder, kidnapping, and conspiracy. Davis was a member of the Black Panthers and avowed herself a Communist and an atheist. But according to UPC official Edler Hawkins, this was beside the point. Defending the council's decision before the General Assembly in 1971, he insisted that the higher cause of racial justice was more important than the particulars of the defendant's political views. But his argument failed to persuade a vocal segment of the church; thousands of letters protesting the action poured in. The Presbyterian Lay Committee, founded in 1964 by a group of Presbyterian businessmen (including J. Howard Pew) who disapproved of the church's "meddling in secular affairs," led an attack on the mission programs of the national denomination. To keep the peace and rebuke the church though their witness, twenty black Presbyterians repaid the grant with their own money. But this action did not mollify critics, and the church remained badly shaken by the controversy.[16]

After the Angela Davis debacle, the UPC continued to issue statements supporting the major issues of the day—busing (1972, 1976), affirmative action (1973), and the Wilmington Ten (1976, 1977). But these were rare and isolated overtures during a period characterized by silence. The contrast with the previous decade was so stark that, as early as 1975, internal critics were proclaiming that the mainstream denominations, having relinquished their role as social witness, were now culturally insignificant. By 1978, President Carter, not noted as a progressive in racial matters, expressed his concern to the NCC about the "growing quiescence in the churches" on the subject of racial justice.[17]

The mainline's retreat from racial justice in the 1970s was reflected also in its shift to new programmatic concerns. The civil rights movement inspired new struggles for liberation by women, Chicanos, Native Americans, and gays and lesbians. These and other progressive initiatives—the environment, education, world peace—provided a liberal rationale for denominational officials to turn their attention from black demands. Throughout the decade, the churches broadened (and, some claimed, diluted) their social witness, creating new bureaus, reorganizing staff, and reallocating budgets. The unfinished cause of racial justice was (some said, gratefully) abandoned.

Take the American Baptist Churches (ABC), for example. In 1968 the ABC's General Council acknowledged the demands of a newly organized black caucus for fuller participation in leadership. But the following year, the denomination's Board of National Ministries turned its attention to other ethnic groups, forming a Division of Missions to focus on Native American and Hispanic issues. (Later, the board would appoint a director for Asian Ministries and a director of Hispanic Ministries, but not a director for Black Ministries.) In 1970, American Baptist Indians and Hispanics formed separate caucuses. In 1971, the denomination formed task forces on ecology and justice. Asian American Baptists formed a caucus in 1972. Responding to the challenge presented by the evangelical revival, Baptists inaugurated in 1973 a three-year revitalization program emphasizing an "Evangelistic Life-Style." In 1975, women within the church initiated a new program, Feminism and the Church Today (FACT). In the second half of the decade, the Board of National Ministries focused on charitable works, establishing new ministries for housing, and domestic disaster response. It was not until June 1980 that the ABC's General Board Executive Committee (GBEC) acknowledged that it had retreated from addressing issues of racial justice, and it took over a year and a half for the denomination to convene a Racial/Ethnic Justice Research Team to examine its policies. The ABC's decision to recommit itself to racial justice was not met with universal acclaim. When the denomination finally adopted a policy statement on racism and justice in June 1983, it was over the opposition of 11 percent of the delegates to the General Board.[18]

Though the mainline churches were quiet with regard to racial justice issues during the 1970s, they were not entirely somnolent. Denominational officials continued to pursue a liberal agenda in a paternalistic mode, restricting their witness for racial justice to the arenas they were most comfortable with, and to which they had privileged access: the narrow corridors of established power. A first step was taken by the NCC, which responded to the Black Manifesto's demands for reparations by instituting in 1970 a program of socially responsible investing. Over the next few years, the other mainline denominations followed the NCC's lead, establishing similar bureaus to monitor corporate responsibility in the United States and abroad. In the mid-1980s, these boards would become more activist as churches used their financial power to combat apartheid in South Africa. To promote racial justice at home, the mainline relied primarily upon Project Equality, an interfaith agency devoted to promoting affirmative action by helping businesses to diversify their workforce and compiling lists of vendors who complied with Equal Employment Opportunity standards. The churches also maintained the offices in Washington, DC, that they had established during the 1960s, lobbying Congress and filing *amicus curiae* briefs in support of Angela Davis and other, less controversial, cases. Their lobbying efforts were also enhanced through their support of ecumenical organizations such as Interfaith IMPACT, which pooled the resources of the mainline along with Catholic and Jewish organizations to promote an array of social justice issues, including affirmative action.[19]

As African Americans' demands for representation increased, the mainline churches made some attempts to redress institutional racism within their own denominational structures. Throughout the 1970s, Congregationalists, Methodists, and Presbyterians sought to diversify their leadership and staff at both national and regional levels. In the 1980s, Baptists, Episcopalians, and Lutherans adopted similar measures. Each denomination modified its constitution repeatedly in efforts to ensure proportional representation on its committees and governing bodies. However, these goals were met in ways that were ill designed to redistribute power.

Within the national headquarters of a given denomination, people of color tended to be clustered in units devoted to minority concerns, minimizing their influence over greater church policy. And there tended to be great disparities between organizational diversity at the national and regional levels. "When you go to General Assembly you get the impression that this is a fairly integrated church," noted the Presbyterian Church's racial justice director in 1985. "But as you go down from the General Assembly level to the next levels of the church, the church gets whiter and whiter." The difference between an integrated central bureaucracy and a segregated laity raised concerns over tokenism and the depth of commitment to genuine change. A joke among African American Episcopalians had it that "it's easier for a black priest to get elected bishop than to become rector of an all-white congregation." The American Baptist Churches provide an interesting counterexample because, among the mainline denominations, it has always had the highest proportion of nonwhite congregants. Today, approximately 44 percent of American Baptists are people of color. But this does not mean that the ABC is more integrated than other denominations. Black Baptists and white Baptists worship in separate congregations, and the executive staff in the national and most regional offices are disproportionately white. Occasional staff audits taken during the 1980s and 1990s reveal that achieving organizational diversity within the mainline churches is still an ongoing process.[20]

Not only have the denominations so far failed to reallocate decision-making authority in meaningful ways, but in some quarters the churches' record with regard to institutional racism actually has worsened. For example, since the late 1980s, black leadership in the Episcopal Church has declined. Edmond Lee Browning of Hawaii had a reputation as a liberal and a vocal opponent of apartheid in South Africa when he was elected to the office of presiding bishop of the ECUSA in 1985 (defeating the first black candidate for the post, Bishop John Walker of Washington, DC). Under his leadership, the church appointed African American clergy to key positions in the 1980s, most notably Barbara Clementine Harris, who was consecrated Suffragan Bishop of Massachusetts in 1989. Browning established a church commission on racism in 1988. But a few years later, he overrode protests to allow the 1991 General Conference of the church to take place in Arizona, a state that at the time refused to recognize Martin Luther King Day. In 1992, Edward Rodman, coordinator of the Episcopal Urban Caucus, called attention to the fact that senior black clergy were being redeployed from their positions in key pulpits, including Trinity Parish, New York City, and the University of the South in Sewanee, Tennessee (which had been segregated until the 1960s). When Browning was elected presiding bishop, twenty-four African Americans served in his appointed staff; in 1995, a decade later, only six remained. Browning's supporters justified this by pointing to cuts in the denomination's central budget, but many observers interpreted the pattern of staff reduction in more ominous terms.[21]

THE MAINLINE'S SYMBOLIC RETURN

After a decade of "benign neglect," the liberal churches began to rededicate themselves to the ideals of racial justice. The process was slow and piecemeal, however, and failed to address the problems of institutional racism. Racial activism during the 1980s and 1990s seldom departed from the paternalistic model: only rarely did mainline churches attempt to bridge the social gap that divided them from the populations whom they sought to help. This period was characterized by a singular lack of focus and an absence of cooperation as the different denominations pursued separate agendas dictated by the winds of political change and whatever happened to be in the current headlines. With rare exceptions, the churches responded rather than led. This resulted in a diffusion of resources, as churches divided funds among a range of continuously fluctuating priorities. The churches outlined a broad vision, but they pursued evanescent issues; they pointed to the roots of prejudice, but spent their energy on pruning the branches. "Qualis patria, talis ecclesia," mourned Episcopalian Harold T. Lewis: "As goes the nation, so goes the church." As a result, the actions of the mainline frequently appeared reactive rather than prophetic, symbolic rather than substantive. The churches "talk God but don't move with God," complained civil rights leader Benjamin F. Chavis Jr. after he left the United Church of Christ to take the helm of the NAACP. They "talk justice, but don't seek justice."[22]

It took a wave of racial violence in the late 1970s to jar white denominational leaders into recognizing the persistence of racism. In 1979, members of the Ku Klux Klan shot participants in a march led by the Southern Christian Leadership Conference (SCLC) in Decatur, Alabama. Later that year, the Klan killed five protesters in Greensboro, North Carolina. These were uncomplicated atrocities that the churches could deplore without fear of criticism from either its black or its white constituencies. Between 1979 and 1981, the mainline denominations and the National Council of Churches issued statements on these and other specific incidents. Soon they issued more expansive, theologically grounded policy statements on racism and the need for racial justice. The United Methodist Women adopted a charter for racial justice in 1978, which formed the template for a similar charter ratified by the General Conference in 1980. In 1978 the southern Presbyterians confessed the denomination's "unfaithfulness" in legitimizing an unjust social order. In 1981, the northern church examined its witness in racial justice and similarly found itself wanting. Then, in 1983, the newly unified denomination resolved to pursue a comprehensive agenda for racial justice. Other mainline churches followed suit, as did the NCC, which issued statements in 1984 and 1985 and offered the definition, now widely cited in faith communities, of racism as "racial prejudice plus power."[23]

Since the 1980s, the churches have launched a multifront assault on racism. They have formulated theologically based position papers ranging from policy statements on such broad issues as welfare, immigration, hate speech, and police brutality to ad hoc pronouncements on current events such as California's Proposition 187, a 1994 bill that denied social services to undocumented immigrants, and the depredations of hurricane Georges, a 1998 storm that caused widespread destruction in the Caribbean and the southern United States. Their public policy offices have continued to lobby Washington and keep affirmative action concerns alive. The mainline churches also have sought to promote awareness by developing and circulating a wide range of educational materials, from the United Church of Christ's weekly *Civil Rights Journal,* to the Evangelical Lutherans' youth video, *The Family of God,* and the United Methodists' recent series of antiracism booklets. In addition to participating in national interfaith efforts like the NCC, the Interreligious Foundation for Community Organization, and the Southern Christian Leadership Conference, the mainline churches have contributed denominational resources to local efforts such as Interfaith Action for Racial Justice in Baltimore, Maryland. Each denomination has also sponsored numerous grant programs, disbursing funds for community improvement, youth ministries, church growth, college scholarships, and other vital projects. Clearly, the problem is not that the mainline churches have been inactive.

Why then has progress been so minimal? One problem is that the churches' efforts have been too diffuse. In theory, a widespread and varied effort should be a source of strength, a way of extending the churches' witness into every aspect of life. But in practice, because the resources of the mainline are finite, a scattered effort produces uneven results. Choosing the issues is important because money is tight, and getting tighter. In recent years, financial declines have severely affected the budgets of the National Council of Churches, the United Methodist General Commission on Church and Race, and every other racial justice agency within the mainline. In 1985, Jovelino Ramos, the director of the Presbyterian Council on Church and Race, voiced what was then and remains today a common complaint—that there is a gap between what the church preaches and what it is willing to spend on: "The church has been very reluctant in running an economic risk for the sake of racial justice." But as church membership has declined, congregations have had to retain a larger portion of the funds that they might otherwise send to the national headquarters. As a result, denominational agencies have not been able to fund fully the programs they would like to support.[24]

An example of a racial justice initiative that has suffered in recent years is Project Equality, an interfaith advocacy group that for more than twenty-five years served as the mainline's most important agent for the promotion of affirmative action. Founded in 1965 by the National Catholic Conference for Interracial Justice, Project Equality received a major grant from the Ford Foundation that ran through the mid-1970s. At a time when many religious organizations were scaling back their social justice initiatives, Project Equality continued the fight. In 1976, Maurice Culver, a Methodist minister, took over as executive director and solicited commitments from the mainline churches, which became and have remained the organization's major source of funding.

Project Equality promotes affirmative action by certifying vendors who agree to maintain minimum equal employment opportunity (EEO) standards regarding hiring and promotion. These vendors range in size from national corporations such as Ameritech, Toys 'R' Us, and Sears to local businesses such as Engineered Pump Services of Mukwonago, Wisconsin. The PCUSA, the Chicago Episcopal Diocese, and Shepherdstown Presbyterian Church of Shepherdstown, West Virginia, are among the two thousand national, regional, and local institutions that have made a commitment to affirmative action by requiring all of their vendors to validate their EEO practices with Project Equality.

Project Equality also sponsors diversity training programs and aggressively pursues companies that engage in discriminatory practices. It was one of the major organizations in the mid-1990s to pressure Texaco to redress its racial shortcomings. Staffing limits have prohibited Project Equality from checking up to ensure that businesses maintain their agreements, which has led to some flaws in their efforts. The Adam's Mark hotel chain, investigated by the Department of Justice in 1999 for a long history of discriminatory practices, had been listed in Project Equality's buying guide since 1987. But these oversights have not reduced faith in the organization's basic efficacy. When Adam's Mark settled its suit in March 2000, the Justice Department assigned Project Equality the task of monitoring the hotel chain's compliance.[25]

However, in recent years Project Equality has fallen on hard times. In 1972 the organization boasted twenty-two offices around the country. Today there are only three: headquarters in Kansas City, and branches in Milwaukee and Chicago. The major reason for this decline is lack of funding, a situation not unique to Project Equality. Due to changing budget priorities, the PCUSA, UCC, and UMC curtailed their funding in 1995 to Interfaith IMPACT for Justice and Peace, an interdenominational agency founded in 1970 to promote affirmative action and other social justice policies. In response, the board of Interfaith IMPACT terminated all paid staff, including its executive director; the organization soon folded.[26]

These budgetary cutbacks were only partly due to a decline in the overall wealth of the denominations. For as the mainline was scaling back its support for groups like Interfaith IMPACT and Project Equality, it was investing funds in a shifting array of new top priorities. An example of the churches' programmatic inconsistency is the African American Male Project instituted by the PCUSA in 1990. Following several studies that defined "the African American male" (imagined to be uniformly poor, young, and inner-city dwelling) as a population "at extreme risk," the church resolved to spend one million dollars over five years to develop outreach programs, provided it could raise the money. "The church said in new dollars, meaning not from existing resources," Racial Justice Director Otis Turner noted. "We knew then that one million dollars was not forthcoming." This fanciful figure represented approximately eight times the amount actually allocated over the same period to support affirmative action programs such as Project Equality. In 1995, the Assembly reaffirmed its programmatic emphasis on African American males, but still did not allocate funds. The program for the 2000 General Assembly had only dim echoes of this once-central mandate. Given current statistics and recent news stories, the situation seems no less dire now than it did ten years earlier, but the church's energies have been redirected. "Our attention span for issues, that's short," admitted the director of the United Methodists' racial justice division.[27]

There have been times, however, when the mainline churches have awakened from their reactive roles and taken on prophetic ones. As one staff officer of the National Council of Churches noted, mainline churches have the potential to focus attention on subjects that might otherwise escape public notice. In the mid-1990s, the NCC took the lead in defining a mysterious rash of black church burnings as a racial justice issue. In 1996, the organization placed ads in the *New York Times*, the *Los Angeles Times*, the *Washington Post*, and *USA Today* alerting readers to an epidemic of incendiarism. Over the course of the year, the NCC raised over $7.5 million in cash as well as donations of goods and services for its Church Rebuilding Project, helped to reconstruct ninety African American church structures, and galvanized other agencies to take up similar projects. The organization lost some credibility after an independent task force presented its conclusions in 1997 that racism was a primary motive in only a small percentage of 429 reported incidents. But this did not detract from the larger value of the NCC's work, which was to revitalize a public dialogue on racism.[28]

Perhaps the most important accomplishment of the mainline denominations in this regard, at least in the past thirty years, is identifying environmental racism as a problem and fostering a movement to combat it. Before the United Church of Christ became involved in environmental justice, other agencies and activists had noted a correlation between race, income, and the zoning of hazardous waste. But the UCC crystallized the issue by commissioning and publicizing a study on environmental racism in 1987. And the Church made resistance to environmental discrimination feasible by sponsoring leadership summits, training workshops, development grants, and protests, helping to transform what had started as a local complaint into a nationwide issue. The National Council of Churches inaugurated its Eco-Justice Working Group soon after the publication of the UCC report, and the other mainline denominations swiftly followed suit.[29]

Benjamin F. Chavis Jr., the former director of UCC's Commission on Racial Justice, widely credited with coining the phrase "environmental racism," was one of a small group of African American leaders within the mainline churches who strove to keep their denominations focused on issues of racial justice throughout the period of retrenchment and budget cuts. Chavis had been serving as a field officer of the commission in 1971 when he was convicted along with nine other activists for burning a white-owned grocery store during a riot in Wilmington, North Carolina. Earning a doctorate in divinity while in prison, Chavis was released in 1979, ordained in 1980, and succeeded Charles E. Cobb as executive director of the commission in 1983. Under Chavis's leadership, the Commission on Racial Justice became more visible and vocal in the public sphere. Chavis championed such causes as asylum for South African refugees and voter registration for blacks in Alabama. In 1991, he helped to draft the UCC's pastoral letter on racism, only the third pastoral letter the denomination had issued in thirty years.[30]

Chavis had his analogues in each of the mainstream churches: Edler Hawkins, Harold T. Lewis, Jovelino Ramos, James Foster Reese, Barbara Ricks Thompson, Otis Turner, Woodie White, to name but a few. Within each denomination, black leaders have served as prophetic witnesses to the persistence of racism, goading their white brethren to extend the work of reform. For example, in 1990, protesting the Episcopal Church's plans to hold its triennial assembly in a state that refused to honor Martin Luther King Day, black bishops issued a statement lamenting that "we have confessed Jesus Christ as Lord and Savior, but our confession has not always been sufficient to accord us full acceptance among others who make a similar confession." Their action prompted a survey in 1991, which confirmed an enormous gap within the church between black and white perceptions of racism. After contemplating these findings for several years, the House of Bishops promulgated a pastoral letter in 1994 on "the sin of racism." But this gesture did not satisfy the Rev. Canon Edward Rodman. In a long meditation on the O. J. Simpson verdict and the Million Man March, Rodman urged the church to move beyond symbolic gestures to build bridges of understanding through a national dialogue on racism. In response, the church prepared materials for a national dialogue on anti-racism in time for Martin Luther King Day in 1997.[31]

The churches' reliance on an African American cadre within their ranks to serve as their voice of conscience is, however, a sign of the maldistribution of power that still characterizes these institutions. Transcending the paternalistic model means allowing people of color to participate on equal terms in all levels of denominational leadership. Concentrating African Americans in one office not only conceives of racial issues in the narrowest terms possible, but also exemplifies what environmental justice activist

Robert D. Bullard calls "the WHOM (We Have One Minority) scenario"—upholding a disenfranchised and underfunded representative as a token concession to minority-group interests. The same critical disengagement also accounts for the consistent failure of the mainline churches to forge ties with the wider black community. The relationship between John and Amy Biggs's Old Northbury Church and Mt. Pisgah reflects in microcosm the relationship between liberal churches and black churches more generally. The same criticisms that African American leaders leveled against white liberals in the 1960s and 1970s are continuously repeated today: developing programs for people of color without engaging them in the decision-making processes denies them agency and thus only exacerbates the problem. In 1998, the United Methodist Church, having initiated discussions with three African American Methodist denominations about the possibility of unification, prepared a guidebook without consulting any of the black leaders—"yet another example of systemic racism," one African American pastor sighed.[32]

The failure of the mainline churches to enter into genuine partnerships with African American groups to foster racial justice has led to programmatic agendas that to critics seem irrelevant, and to resolutions that seem largely symbolic. The best example of this approach is the wave of dramatic recantations launched in 1994 under the banner of "racial reconciliation." After the Promise Keepers and the Southern Baptist Convention apologized for supporting racism, many mainline churches responded by making similar confessions. The Evangelical Lutheran Church in America issued a declaration rejecting the anti-Semitic writings of the faith's founder, Martin Luther, and the United Methodist Church issued a formal apology for the 1864 Sand Creek massacre of Cheyenne and Arapaho Indians, accepting responsibility for the fact that the group of soldiers responsible for the incident was led by a Methodist lay preacher, Col. John Chivington of the First Colorado Cavalry. The self-flagellatory mood has affected even the Catholic Church, which has taken the opportunity to express its regrets for oppressing women, martyring Protestants, and failing to oppose the Holocaust. Regional bodies have also joined the cavalcade of repentance. In June 1999, the West Ohio Conference of the United Methodist Church extended its apologies for slavery and other racial wrongs.[33]

But African Americans are tired of apologies and promises of reconciliation. "The pieties of the 1960s are not going to help produce change—not even with a garnish of jargon from the eighties," wrote one Episcopalian layman after reading the 1994 pastoral letter on racism. "We need to look around for chapter two—not to keep re-reading chapter one." Indeed, even in the 1960s, chapter one had lost its novelty. In a short story Langston Hughes first published in the mid-1950s, Jesse B. Semple, Hughes's plain-spoken black Everyman, vents his frustration:

> Some white church convention . . . have resolved ["that all men are borned equal and everybody is entitled to life and liberty while pursuing happiness"] all over and the Golden Rule, too, also that Negroes should be treated right. It looks to me white folks better stop resolving and get to *doing*. They have resolved enough. *Resolving ain't solving*. . . . They have been *resolving* for two hundred years. I do not see how come they need to *resolve* any more. I say, they need to *solve*.

In 1969, Gayraud Wilmore expressed in more elegant terms a similar conviction: "No institution in American society has made more confessions of guilt for its involvement in the sin of slavery and in segregation and discrimination against Black people than has the Christian Church. No institution in America has issued more high-sounding pronouncements of the principles of a commitment to social justice." Blacks had had enough of words, Wilmore concluded; now it was time for action. As early as 1968, the PCUS Assembly had defined reconciliation as "cheap grace." Twenty-five years later, the mainline churches have returned to reconciliation as their vision of racial justice. Predictably, black audiences have been unimpressed. A number of African American pastors recognized the West Ohio Conference's apology as a meaningless gesture: "We ought not to reflect on the past, but look to the future," one said. Alexis Thomas, senior pastor of the Pilgrim Rest Baptist Church, a predominantly African American congregation in Phoenix, Arizona, said that his members were "just looking to be fed, to be helped." Solving the race problem was "way down" on their list of priorities: "In my opinion, there are other issues that are much more pressing, the numbers of our young men going to prison, the economic situation in our community. Having affordable housing, dealing with police issues, those are the issues we deal with. We don't wake up in the morning thinking about racial reconciliation." Black political leaders have agreed. Deriding what he termed "touchy-feely" approaches to racial reconciliation, Reverend Jesse Jackson called for concrete political action. "If we're going to reconcile, let it be on some agenda of structural substance," he said.[34]

The new banner of multiculturalism is similar to racial reconciliation in terms of being out of touch with the systemic sources of racial injustice that concern black Americans. The rhetoric of multiculturalism unwittingly reifies racialized thinking by presenting ethnic groups as naturally distinct, and race as an essential characteristic of individual identity rather than, say, a social construction or a political condition. By representing denominational membership as a rainbow, a quilt, or some other comforting image, multiculturalist discourse redirects attention away from questions regarding the organization and distribution of power. Multiculturalism also inevitably invokes the affective distance that, according to sociologist R. Stephen Warner, characterizes theological liberals. Whereas mainline publications emphasize cultural diversity, evangelical publications emphasize spiritual unity. Compare any mainline publication "celebrating the differences among us" with the statement of John K. Groves, a black Pentecostal pastor in San Diego: "We don't see the color of the skin. We're not looking for the texture of the hair. We care less about the slant of the eyes. Our ambition at Omni Community Christian Church is to teach the gospel so plainly until every man and woman can only see Jesus." By continuously reaffirming the status of ethnic and racial others as a category discrete from whites, the language of reconciliation divides as it seeks to unite.[35]

Liberal distance is reflected also in the churches' paternalistic model of corporate charity. Looking outward to perform acts of charity assumes a fundamental gap between the giver and the recipient. Sociologist Robert Wuthnow notes that emotional detachment is a necessary defense mechanism for individuals who volunteer for altruistic causes. A similar process transpires at the institutional level. In 1998, for example, the United Methodist Church granted almost $1 million to sixty-two projects and programs under its Minority Group Self-Determination Fund. On the one hand this benevolence represents an admirable level of commitment to the ideals of racial justice, and to the demands of African Americans for programmatic autonomy. On the other hand, charity is dispensed from a point of superiority, not of equality. And charity without service removes whites from direct participation in the process. As Warner notes, "Benevolence creates a barrier." Only by meeting each other in a position of equality and striving together at ground level will whites and blacks begin to bridge the gap.[36]

WALKING LOCALLY

House speaker Tip O'Neill's famous remark that all politics is local applies also to racial politics. Racial reconciliation will come not through pronouncements made by administrators at a denominational assembly, but through continuous and sustained face-to-face interactions between individuals. Racial justice will come not by issuing checks from a dwindling treasury, but by working together in the trenches. In the late 1980s, and increasingly in the 1990s, the mainline has placed increasing emphasis on fostering interracial harmony at the congregational level. These efforts have not been uniformly successful, but they do point the way.

Numerous studies by Gordon Allport, Thomas F. Pettigrew, and other social psychologists testify that interracial contact—on equal terms—is the best way to overcome prejudice. Overcoming segregation is the crucial step. In 1968, a landmark report by the Kerner Commission observed that the United States was comprised of "two societies, one black, one white— separate and unequal." In their widely acclaimed study of the social system that they term "American apartheid," sociologists Douglas Massey and Nancy Denton argue persuasively that the continued separation of black and white society fuels the cycle of racial inequality and prejudice:

> For America, the failure to end segregation will perpetuate a bitter dilemma that has long divided the nation. If segregation is permitted to continue, poverty will inevitably deepen and become more persistent within a large share of the black community, crime and drugs will become more firmly rooted, and social institutions will fragment further under the weight of deteriorating conditions. As racial inequality sharpens, white fears will grow, racial prejudices will be reinforced, and hostility towards blacks will increase, making the problems of racial justice and equal opportunity even more insoluble.

As the most segregated institutions in America, mainline congregations are de facto agents of racial apartheid. Their affective, geographical, social, economic, and political distance from populations of color fosters the paternalistic modes of control that serve to maintain the structures of white privilege.[37]

But how to break down the barriers of religious segregation? One tactic the mainline denominations have explored is the aggressive evangelization of African Americans and other underrepresented groups. In 1987, the Evangelical Lutheran Church of America set a ten-year goal of expanding its membership of ethnic or linguistic minorities to at least 10 percent. The Presbyterians and United Methodists have set similar goals. Forsaking statistical realities, the United Church of Christ redefined itself as a "Multiracial and Multicultural Church" in 1993. Two years later, the UCC published the *New Century Hymnal*, collecting songs from a wide array of cultures to reflect the denomination's new commitment to diversity.

African American church leaders have not greeted this effort with enthusiasm. They have tended to regard mainline missions to minorities at best as a desperate ploy to reverse the dramatic declines in their member-ship, and at worst as a sinister attempt to alienate people of color from the cultural heritage and separate institutions that have long served as their pillars of political strength. "Whites own the schools, the newspapers, the businesses, the government. But we own our churches," said one Pente-costal minister in Aurora, Colorado. "I am committed to worship that is Afrocentric and music that is Afrocentric," noted another clergyman, "I don't want to be absorbed by the dominant society." Reverend Gayraud Wilmore pointed out that the churches' vision of integration is not recip-rocal: "Whites have rarely been willing to integrate Black institutions and neighborhoods, except when the latter acceded to White control."[38]

Because people of color are disenfranchised within the mainline churches, relatively few have been attracted through these evangelical drives. After ten years of effort, the ELCA was unable to raise its minority membership above 2.2 percent. On the face of it, the United Church of Christ has been more successful at increasing congregational diversity. Caucasians still compose the vast majority of members in the UCC—92.2 percent in 1997—but the number of ethnic minority members increased by 11.7 percent from 1987 to 1997. However, this demographic shift owed as much to white attrition as to minority growth. During the same ten-year period, white membership in the UCC declined by 15.3 percent.[39]

In addition to attempting to diversify their ranks, the churches have sought to promote racial healing by raising consciousness through edu-cational programs, diversity workshops, and anti-racism training pro-grams. The Evangelical Lutherans and the Presbyterians hired consultants to lead workshops for their entire executive staffs, and every denomination has prepared extensive materials to promote discussion of racism and racial justice among its congregations. The churches promote interracial dialogue as a particularly promising practice. (This was also the conclusion of Pres-ident Clinton's 1998 One America initiative on race.)

Although this approach has obvious appeal, it has many limitations. First, these workshops and training sessions are of extremely limited du-ration. They may open doors of perception, but it is hard to gauge how widely or how long the portals stay ajar. "Often we get together superfi-cially, but don't really talk to each other and break down walls," lamented the leader of the Clergy Committee for Racial Justice in Columbus, Ohio. Parishioners know what approved racial attitudes are, so some find further sermons tedious. "My pastor sometimes lectures us on racism," admitted a member of a Chicago-area United Methodist congregation. "[It] makes you feel guilty for a while. . . . But then that's what you expect to hear in church." Others react negatively at what they perceive as a "politically correct" program that places all the blame on whites. "Salvation through condemnation," is how a Presbyterian clergyman from Royal Oak, Michigan put it.[40]

Another problem is that, because racial politics are local, a number of churchwide initiatives fail to be implemented at the congregational level. For example, Dan Price, an Episcopalian pastor serving an all-white congregation in rural Massachusetts, was mandated to read the pastoral letter on racism in 1994. But five years later he could not remember ever having looked at it. "It didn't have much of an impact that I can see," he said. John Biggs did not pay attention to many of the directives that came to him when he was serving as chair of his congregation's social action committee. "I made announcements sometimes, entered them in the minutes if I had to. Our minister was really into that stuff."[41]

Finally, it is worth noting that, though whites may find confronting their racist assumptions through cross-cultural dialogue to be spiritually cathartic, many African Americans find it exasperating. Teaching whites about racism is a relatively low priority for black activists. Basing a program of reconciliation on more talk instead of more action implicitly subordinates black goals to white ones. Forging partnerships between white and black churches, as John Biggs's congregation did, is an extended exercise in interracial dialogue, but one that also perpetuates an unequal relationship.

A third strategy is the practice of appointing a black pastor to tend a white flock. The racial tensions this inevitably raises can be too heavy a cross for some to bear. In 1989, Joan Salmon Campbell was the first black woman to serve as moderator of the General Assembly of the PCUSA.[42] The following year she was called to pastor Old Pine Presbyterian Church, a prestigious white, affluent congregation in Philadelphia, but she resigned after only twenty-one months, complaining of racism, sexism, and classism. She moved to another pulpit in Cleveland, but found that similarly dissatisfying. In 1997 she renounced her ordination, and left the denomination altogether. When members of Berkshire Congregational called Robert Barr to the pulpit in 1991, they were impressed with the African American minister's laid back, folksy manner and his Yale Divinity degree. But breaking with UCC tradition, the white pastor whom Barr had replaced began attending services and making unfavorable remarks. Seven years later, after numerous reconciliatory meetings, Barr left the ministry to take up an administrative post within the denomination. Even at Riverside Church, perhaps the most prominent pulpit within the mainline, a cross-racial appointment can lead to friction. The church appointed its first black pastor, James A. Forbes, in 1989, a time when the minority membership of the congregation was growing. Several years later the congregation exploded in controversy. Critics within the church disliked the length and style of the service (Forbes was raised in a Pentecostal church). "To me the preaching is fundamental, thin fare indeed for someone seeking understanding and enlightenment," wrote one prominent member; "I do not need to return to the Sunday School of my youth; I need a thoughtful adult perspective." Forbes survived his critics, and today heads a vibrant, multicultural congregation. But the path was not easy.[43]

Forbes's eventual success is a sign of hope, and indeed some congregations have managed to foster genuine diversity. One signal success story is the Oakhurst Presbyterian Church in Decatur, Georgia, where the congregation is 54 percent black and 45 percent white, and includes rich and poor, young and old, gay and straight. The church was not always so diverse. Founded in 1921, Oakhurst Presbyterian was all white in the 1960s, when its membership peaked at 900. But its membership shrank quickly in the 1970s as African Americans moved into the neighborhood and whites fled to the suburbs. When Rev. Gibson "Nibs" Stroupe and his wife, associate pastor Caroline Leach, took over the pulpit in 1983, there were only 80 people in the pews. Stroupe and Leach, both white, altered the church to reflect the community. They installed images of black angels and a black Jesus to match the white ones, and they included music from African American traditions in their services. They expanded the social ministry of the church to include a wide array of community services, including literacy programs, social service programs, and a prison outreach program. In ten years they doubled the membership. Today, the congregation stands at almost 250, and shows every sign of continued growth.[44]

Riverside Church and Oakhurst Presbyterian are not unique. Other successful interracial congregations thrive: the McCabe Roberts Avenue United Methodist Church in Beaumont, Texas; Lakeview Presbyterian in St. Petersburg, Florida; Cedar Grove United Methodist Church and Northwoods United Methodist Church, both in Atlanta; and a growing number of others. But while these churches offer hope for the possibility of genuine racial healing in the United States, they do not offer a panacea. Interracial congregations are difficult to start, and even more difficult to maintain. A recent study by sociologists Michael O. Emerson and Christian Smith indicates the reasons why churches tend to be racially homogeneous. Religious pluralism in the United States, they argue, has led to balkanization at the congregational level. In a crowded spiritual marketplace, churches cater to specific demographic niches. Faced with a choice, people generally will opt for the church whose ideological, socioeconomic, ethnic, and racial profile matches their own. By constructing and sustaining symbolic boundaries, membership in a homogeneous group reinforces an individual's distinct cultural identity, and this in turn fosters social solidarity and institutional stability. Demographically uniform churches are stronger because they mirror the members' sense of themselves and meet their perceived needs. Heterogeneous congregations, on the other hand, do not maintain a distinct identity, and thus foster relatively weak social ties. Because it seems less natural, membership in a mixed church requires greater effort; diverse congregations are thus vulnerable to centrifugal forces and typically suffer from attrition. Racially uniform churches, therefore, are likely to remain the norm.[45]

Interracial churches, then, are not the answer to the problem of race in America. But they do offer models for a solution. One of the most important factors contributing to the success of Oakhurst Presbyterian was the willingness of the white pastors to share administrative authority. Stroupe was quick to delegate leadership roles to African American members of the church. "Power had to be taken away from some white folks who were holding all the power," he recalled. "They were willing to let black folks in, but not willing to let them lead."[46]

Stroupe's relinquishment of control may have been a difficult sacrifice for someone accustomed to taking a leadership role, but it was a necessary one. Mainline officials have long recognized that black autonomy will always be limited in institutions created for and maintained by whites. "Irrespective of motives," noted the United Presbyterian Church in 1981, "often the final impact of our institutional styles of organization and management serve to exclude racial/ethnic groups from full and just participation." As Episcopalian Bishop Harold T. Lewis observed, diversifying denominational staff is not enough; token appointments alone do not suffice to make an organization truly multicultural. Stroupe's sacrifice addressed the long-standing complaints generated by white paternalistic leadership. His model for surrendering administrative power to people of color might be followed both at the national and the congregational level.[47]

For example, rather than relying on their own instincts to establish priorities and formulate programs to further racial justice, the most segregated institutions in America might follow the agenda set by the African American churches. Denominational leaders and local activists might ask: What program should we help fund? What issue should we be focused on?

What boycott should we publicize? Where should we march? Rather than inviting members of a poor black church to a dialogue on racism or presenting them with an annual check, members of mainline congregations might volunteer for the social programs and participate in the political campaigns the black churches already have established. The crucial shift here is one from a model of benevolence to one of equality; from doing things *for* blacks to doing things *with* blacks.

Related to this is a second lesson from Oakhurst Presbyterian—the importance of developing interracial networks through intense and continued contact across ethnic lines. Stroupe and Leach took care to extend relationships among their congregation beyond the worship service. They instituted a churchwide breakfast on Sunday mornings, and a supper club, where black and white members would visit each other's homes. Their social ministries served a dual purpose in this respect. They developed strategies to enable black and white congregants to work together and across ethnic lines outside of church, fostering an interracial network devoted to addressing issues of racial justice in a spirit not of charity but of equality.[48]

Social psychologists are unanimous in concurring that interracial relationships reap positive changes in white attitudes only when the blacks whom they meet are of equal or higher status. The extent of contact is another vital factor. However intimate, one cross-race friendship is not enough. Involvement in an interracial network, on the other hand, ends the isolation that generates prejudicial stereotypes. This suggests the importance for all congregations, but especially those characterized by a high degree of racial homogeneity, of walking locally. Participating meaningfully in the voluntary efforts of African American congregations may allow white Christians to forge not one but many affective bonds with their black brothers and sisters and thus take a crucial step toward dismantling the insidious structure of American apartheid.[49]

A final lesson from Oakhurst Presbyterian is that racial justice takes commitment—of time, of money, of concentrated effort. It took Stroupe and Leach more than fifteen years to increase the membership of their church to 250—a sizable growth, to be sure, but still considerably smaller than it was in the 1960s when the congregation was all white. As one mainline racial justice leader notes, "Reconciliation is a process, not an event." It is a process in the sense that it depends upon the continuing interaction of individuals striving together for racial justice. It is also a temporal process. Rome, as they say, was not built in a day; dismantling Babylon will take a long time indeed.[50]

NOTES

Among the several people who commented on an earlier draft of this essay, let me single out for particular thanks Leslie Callahan, Jennifer Delton, Vincent Di-Girolamo, John H. Evans, Elenora Giddings Ivory, Michael Moody, Edward Rodman, Alex W. Willingham, my two anonymous reviewers, and especially Otis Turner, whose extensive and detailed comments greatly strengthened the themes of my analysis. Responsibility for errors of fact or interpretation remains mine alone.

1. Interview with Amy and John Biggs. Most of the people I spoke with for this essay are identified by their real names, with their permission. Others, including Amy and John Biggs, Old Northbury, and Mt. Pisgah, I have elected to identify by pseudonyms.

2. Martin Luther King, "Paul's Letter to American Christians," in *The Papers of Martin Luther King, Jr.: Birth of a New Age: December 1955–December 1956*, ed. Clayborne Carson et al. (Berkeley: University of California Press, 1997), 3: 417; Gerald D. Jaynes and Robin M. Williams Jr., eds., *A Common Destiny: Blacks and American Society* (Washington, DC: National Academy Press, 1989); Melvin L. Oliver and Thomas M. Shapiro, *Black Wealth/White Wealth: A New Perspective on Racial Inequality* (New York: Routledge, 1995); *A Changing America: Indicators of Social and Economic Well-Being by Race and Hispanic Origin* (Washington, DC: Council of Economic Advisers for the President's Initiative on Race, 1998); Neil J. Smelser, William Julius Wilson, and Faith Mitchell, eds., *America Becoming: Racial Trends and Their Consequences* (Washington, DC: National Academy Press, 2001).

3. Jennifer L. Hochschild, *Facing Up to the American Dream: Race, Class, and the Soul of the Nation* (Princeton, NJ: Princeton University Press, 1995); Joe R. Feagin and Melvin P. Sikes, *Living with Racism: The Black Middle-Class Experience* (Boston: Beacon Press, 1994); Ellis Cose, *The Rage of a Privileged Class* (New York: HarperCollins, 1993); Sam Fulwood III, *Waking from the Dream: My Life in the Black Middle Class* (New York: Anchor, 1996); Martin Luther King Jr., "Playboy Interview," in *A Testament of Hope: The Essential Writings of Martin Luther King, Jr.*, ed. James Melvin Washington (New York: Harper & Row, 1986), 345.

4. I here focus exclusively on relations between blacks and whites. A number of scholars and activists (including officers within the mainline denominations) have argued for a conception of racial justice that looks beyond a biracial model to examine conflict between and among multiple racial and ethnic groups. My decision to pursue a narrower course was determined by the centrality of black/white relations to both the historical and the current efforts of the churches. Previous research into the dynamics of racism concentrating on the African American experience has provided valid models for understanding the experiences of other people of color. Thus neither the validity of the insights gained from the present study nor the possibility of their broader application should be compromised by my focus on black/white relations as a starting point for analysis.

5. Mary R. Jackman, *The Velvet Glove: Paternalism and Conflict in Gender, Class, and Race Relations* (Berkeley: University of California Press, 1994), 14, 12. The definition Jackman quotes here is from Donald VanDeVeer, *Paternalistic Intervention: The Moral Bounds of Benevolence* (Princeton, NJ: Princeton University Press, 1986), 12.

6. Howard Schuman, Charlotte Steeh, and Lawrence Bobo, *Racial Attitudes in*

America: Trends and Interpretations (Cambridge, MA: Harvard University Press, 1985), 99–195. Further insight into this discrepancy is offered by Bourdieu's notion of the *habitus,* the deep-rooted nexus of attitudes and dispositions that delimits individual behavior. The product of complex processes of socialization and profoundly resistant to change, the *habitus* precedes conscious thought, structuring people's action by defining what choices are "reasonable" or "commonsensical." It may be argued that the logics of racism are fundamental to the *habitus* shared by American whites, guiding their behavior even against their wishes. See Pierre Bourdieu, *The Logic of Practice,* tr. Richard Nice (Stanford, CA: Stanford University Press, 1980), 52–65; Paul Connolly, "Racism and Postmodernism: Towards a Theory of Practice," in *Sociology after Postmodernism,* ed. David Owen (London: Sage, 1997), 65–80.

7. Presbyterian Panel, August 1999. What is notable, in addition to the radical disjuncture between institutional policy and popular consensus, is the gap between clerical and lay opinion. According to the same survey, only 16 percent of members and 17 percent of elders in the PCUSA support affirmative action; however, a startling 49 percent of pastors and 63 percent of specialized clergy (administrators, educators, etc.) say they support preferential hiring and promotion of African Americans. This gap between the professionals and the pews is reflected in other assessments of racial attitudes. Clergy are significantly more likely than laity to believe that racial issues are central to church concerns, to claim that racial issues within the church are still largely unresolved, to assert that focusing on racial matters is not detrimental to church unity, and to believe that the quality of leadership in the church would be improved by hiring more black elders, pastors, clergy, and professional staff.

8. Jackman, *Velvet Glove,* 222–26, cit. at 225; Donald R. Kinder and David O. Sears, "Prejudice and Politics: Symbolic Racism versus Threats to the Good Life," *Journal of Personality and Social Psychology* 40 (1981): 414–31; William A. Gamson and Andre Modigliani, "The Changing Culture of Affirmative Action," *Research in Political Sociology* 3 (1987): 137–77.

9. Jackman, *Velvet Glove,* 127–38; Schuman, Steeh, and Bobo, *Racial Attitudes in America;* James R. Kluegel, "Trends in Whites' Explanations of the White Gap in Socioeconomic Status, 1977–1989," *American Sociological Review* 55 (1990): 512–25; Michael O. Emerson and Christian Smith, *Divided by Faith: Evangelical Religion and the Problem of Race in America* (New York: Oxford University Press, 2000).

10. Recent works examining internal conflicts within the civil rights movement include Taylor Branch, *Parting the Waters: America in the King Years, 1954–1963* (New York: Simon & Schuster, 1988), and *Pillar of Fire: America in the King Years, 1963–65* (New York: Simon & Schuster, 1998); James F. Findlay, *Church People in the Struggle: The National Council of Churches and the Black Freedom Movement, 1950–1970* (New York: Oxford University Press, 1993); and Michael B. Friedland, *Lift Up Your Voice Like a Trumpet: White Clergy and the Civil Rights and Antiwar Movements, 1954–1973* (Chapel Hill: University of North Carolina Press, 1998).

11. Findlay, *Church People in the Struggle,* 223; Otis Turner, personal communication.

12. National Committee of Negro Churchmen, "Black Power," in *Black Theology: A Documentary History, 1966–1979,* ed. Gayraud S. Wilmore and James Cone (New York: Orbis Books, 1979), 25–26.

13. Findlay, *Church People in the Struggle,* 184, 199–236; James Forman, "The Black Manifesto," in *Black Theology,* ed. Wilmore and Cone, 80–89, cit. at 88, 84;

National Committee of Black Churchmen, "Response to the Black Manifesto," in *Black Theology*, ed. Wilmore and Cone, 90–92, cit. at 90–91; Gayraud S. Wilmore, "A Black Churchman's Response to the Black Manifesto," in *Black Theology*, ed. Wilmore and Cone, 93–99, cit. at 96, 98, 99.

14. Edward B. Fiske, "Forman's Demand for 'Reparations' Spurs Power Struggle among Protestants," *New York Times*, 27 July 1969, 1, 54; James H. Cone, *Black Theology and Black Power* (New York: Seabury, 1969), 68 (emphasis in original); Wilmore and Cone, eds., *Black Theology*, 135–43.

15. Findlay, *Church People in the Struggle*, 213; Harold T. Lewis, *Yet with a Steady Beat: The African American Struggle for Recognition in the Episcopal Church* (Valley Forge, PA: Trinity Press International, 1996), 150–54; Cornish Rogers, "Copping Out on Social Action," *Christian Century* 90 (1973): 524–525; Gary L. Chamberlain, "Has 'Benign Neglect' Invaded the Churches?" *Christian Century* 91 (1974): 448–51; Constance D'au Vin, "Black and White Clerics Differ on Integration of Churches," *Washington Post*, 10 March 1978, A28; Marjorie Hyer, "Council of Churches Staff, Programs Cut," *Washington Post*, 15 September 1978, C14.

16. Dean R. Hoge, *Division in the Protestant House: The Basic Reasons Behind Intra-Church Conflicts* (Philadelphia, PA: Westminster Press, 1976), 36–40, 106–15; Gayraud S. Wilmore, "Identity and Integration: Black Presbyterians and Their Allies," in *The Presbyterian Predicament: Six Perspectives*, ed. Milton J. Coalter, John M. Mulder, and Louis Weeks (Louisville, KY: Westminster/John Knox Press, 1990), 127–30.

17. UPCUSA, *General Assembly Minutes*, 1971, 515; PCUS, *General Assembly Minutes*, 1972, 176; UPCUSA, *General Assembly Minutes*, 1973, 504–8; UPCUSA, *General Assembly Minutes*, 1976, 157, 158; UPCUSA, *General Assembly Minutes*, 1977, 123; John Fry, *The Trivialization of the United Presbyterian Church* (New York: Harper & Row, 1975); D'au Vin, "Black and White Clerics." For a critique of Carter's racial policy, see Manning Marable, *Race, Reform, and Rebellion: The Second Reconstruction of Black America, 1945–1990*, 2nd ed. (Jackson: University Press of Mississippi, 1991), 168–74.

My discussion of Presbyterian Church policy here and in subsequent paragraphs owes much to the summaries compiled in James D. Beumler, "Social Teachings of the Presbyterian Church," *Church and Society* 75 (November/December 1984): 27–35, and Dieter T. Hessel, "Race and Racial Justice," *Church and Society* 81 (November/December 1990), 28–36, as well as the social witness policy compilation prepared by the Advisory Committee on Social Witness Policy and PresbyTel, online at http://horeb.pcusa.org/folio/om_isapi.dll.

18. Until 1972, the Board of National Ministries was called the American Baptist Home Mission Society (ABHMS). Of the 172 delegates to the General Board in 1983, 153 voted for the policy statement on racial justice, 15 against, and 4 abstained; see Richard Schlosser, "Chronological History of the Board of National Ministries, 1817–1994," *American Baptist Quarterly* 14 (June 1995): 139–57; Paul W. Light, "Race and Ethnicity in the ABC: Summarizing a Research Process and Report," *American Baptist Quarterly* 5 (March 1986): 36–48.

19. Finlay, *Church People in the Struggle*, 217–20; Maurice Culver, interview.

20. Jed Emerson, "Discerning the Racism of the Eighties: An Interview with the Reverend Jovelino Ramos," *Church and Society* 75 (May/June 1985): 28–35, cit. at 29; Barbara Ogilby, "Can Blacks Find a Home in the Episcopal Church?" *Episcopal Life/The Pennsylvania Episcopalian*, March 1998, D–E; Pin Yao, personal communication. See also the 1983 data in Light, "Race and Ethnicity within the ABC," 40–42.

21. Emmet Pierce, "Episcopalians Moving in Liberal Direction," *San Diego Union-Tribune*, 15 September 1985, A3; Lewis, *Yet with a Steady Beat*, 165, 167–69.

22. Lewis, *Yet with a Steady Beat*, 164, 147; "Chavis: Civil Rights Requires Repentance," *Christian Century* 110 (1993): 1042.

23. UPCUSA, *General Assembly Minutes*, 1979, 62; PCUS, *General Assembly Minutes*, 1979, 127; PCUS, *General Assembly Minutes*, 1978, 187; UPCUSA, *General Assembly Minutes*, 1981, 201; PCUSA, *General Assembly Minutes*, 1983, 458–60. Texts of the NCC's resolutions are available in *American Baptist Quarterly* 5 (March 1986): 52–68; the definition of racism is on p. 55.

24. "Paying the Price of Racial Justice," *Christian Century* 110 (1993): 423; Sammy Toineeta, interview; Emerson, "Discerning the Racism of the Eighties," 31–32.

25. Joe Popper, "In Fight for Equality, Quiet Warrior Persists," *Kansas City Star*, 7 December 1996, A1; Maurice Culver, interview; Kirk P. Perucca, interview; Shari Devonish, interview; http://www.projectequality.org.

26. *James M. Bell v. Presbyterian Church (U.S.A.) et al.*, United States Court of Appeals for the Fourth Circuit, no. 96–1297 (1997).

27. PCUSA, *General Assembly Minutes*, 1990, 784; PCUSA, *General Assembly Minutes*, 1995; Otis Turner, personal communication; Chester R. Jones, interview.

28. Sammy Toineeta, interview; Religious News Service, "Church Rebuilding Project Shifts Focus," *Los Angeles Times*, 14 June 1997, B4.

29. See Moody, chapter 9 in this volume; also Eileen Maura McGurty, "From NIMBY to Civil Rights: The Origins of the Environmental Justice Movement," *Environmental History* 2 (1997): 301–23; United Church of Christ, Commission on Racial Justice, *Toxic Waste and Race in the United States: A National Report on the Racial and Socioeconomic Characteristics of Communities Surrounding Hazardous Waste Sites* (New York: United Church of Christ, 1987); Charles Lee, ed., *Proceedings: The First People of Color Environmental Leadership Summit* (New York: United Church of Christ, 1992).

30. Lena Williams, "Church Official Presses Rights Battles of the 80's," *New York Times*, 18 August 1986, A15.

31. Harold T. Lewis, ed., *But We See Jesus: Pastoral Letter from Black Episcopalian Bishops* (n.p.: Executive Council, 1990); Clayton P. Alderfer, *Race and Ethnic Relations in the Episcopal Church: A Report on the Racism Audit from the 1991 General Convention* (n.p.: NTL Institute, 1992), 14; Edward Rodman, *A Lost Opportunity? An Open Letter to the Leadership of the Episcopal Church*, http:// www.AfroAnglican.org/UBE/resource/; Louie Crew, "Black Priests in the Episcopal Church," http://andromeda.rutgers.edu/lcrew/blkpr.html.

32. Robert D. Bullard, "Race, Equity, and Smart Growth," *Transportation Equity* 3, no. 1 (fall/winter, 2000), online at www.ejrc.cau.edu; "Report on Racism Lacks Minority Voices," *Christian Century* 109 (1992): 959; Linda Green, "Some Remain Skeptical about United Methodist Repentance Plans," United Methodist News Service, 24 November 1998.

33. Felix Hoover and Dennis M. Mahoney, "A Step Towards Reconciliation: Black Churches Call Methodist Apology a Good Starting Point," *Columbus Dispatch*, 11 June 1999, D1.

34. Langston Hughes, *The Best of Simple* (New York: Hill & Wang, 1961), 80–81 (italics in original); Wilmore, "Black Churchman's Response to the Black Manifesto," 97–98; PCUS, *General Assembly Minutes*, 1968, 99; Hoover and Mahoney, "Step Towards Reconciliation"; Maureen Jenkins, "Making a Promise

to End Racism: Christian Men's Group Presses for Diversity," *Arizona Republic*, 23 October 1999; "Church Rebuilding Project Shifts Focus," *Los Angeles Times*, 14 June 1997, B4.

35. Michael Omi and Howard Winant, *Racial Formation in the United States: From the 1960s to the 1990s*, 2nd ed. (New York: Routledge, 1994); Michael A. Omi, "The Changing Meaning of Race," in *America Becoming*, ed. Smelser, Wilson, and Mitchell, 243–63; R. Stephen Warner, *New Wine in Old Wineskins: Evangelicals and Liberals in a Small-Town Church* (Berkeley: University of California Press, 1988); John K. Groves, "Segregation Lives—In Our Churches," *San Diego Union-Tribune*, 29 March 1987, C3.

36. Robert Wuthnow, *Acts of Compassion* (Berkeley: University of California Press, 1992), 204–12; Joretta Purdue, "Minority Group Self-Determination Fund Grants Aid Many," United Methodist News Service, 30 September 1998; Warner, *New Wine in Old Wineskins*, 293.

37. Gordon Allport, *The Nature of Prejudice* (Reading, MA: Addison-Wesley, 1954); Thomas F. Pettigrew, "Intergroup Contact Theory," *Annual Review of Psychology* 49 (1998): 65–85; Thomas F. Pettigrew and Linda R. Tropp, "Does Intergroup Contact Reduce Prejudice? Recent Meta-Analytic Findings," in *Reducing Prejudice and Discrimination*, ed. Stuart Oskamp (Mahwah, NJ: Erlbaum, 2000), 93–114; Otto Kerner, *Report of the National Advisory Commission on Civil Disorders* (New York: Bantam Books, 1968), 1; Douglas S. Massey and Nancy A. Denton, *American Apartheid: Segregation and the Making of the Underclass* (Cambridge, MA: Harvard University Press, 1993), 235–36.

38. Virginia Culver, "On the Seventh Day, Segregation Won't Rest," *Denver Post*, 10 November 1996, A33; "Mainliners and Minorities," *Christian Century*, 110 (1993): 200; Gayraud Wilmore, "Neighborly Fences and Hostile Walls," http://www.pcusa.org/wo/theology/wilmore.htm.

39. *The State of the UCC*, Research Office, United Church Board for Homeland Ministries, August 1998.

40. Religious News Service, "Evangelical Lutherans Adopt Anti-Racism Measures," *Los Angeles Times*, 4 September 1993, B4; "Clergy Committee Seeking Ways to Improve City's Race Relations," *Columbus Dispatch*, 6 May 1999, 8C; Janice Cara (pseudonym), interview; Julian Shipp, "Peacekeeping Conferees Confront Racism Through Crossroads Ministry Workshop," Presbyterian News Service, 24 July 1997.

41. Dan Price is a pseudonym.

42. Though SalmonCampbell was the first black woman to serve as moderator of the PCUSA, she was not the first to lead a Presbyterian convention. The UPC-USA, which merged with the PCUS in 1983 to form the present church, elected Thelma Adair as moderator of its 188th General Assembly in 1976.

43. Berkshire Congregational and Robert Barr are pseudonyms. Yvonne Samuel, "Renowned, Controversial Clergywoman to Leave Post," *St. Petersburg Times*, 19 September 1992, 6E; Ari L. Goldman, "Riverside's Pastor at Center of Turmoil," *New York Times*, 18 May 1992, B1; Peter Applebome, "Integration Steps into the Pulpit," *New York Times*, 2 January 1995, 1–8.

44. Holly Crenshaw, "Divine Diversity," *Atlanta Journal and Constitution* 17, February 1994, A1; Nibs Stroupe and Inez Fleming, *While We Run this Race: Confronting the Power of Racism in a Southern Church* (Maryknoll, NY: Orbis, 1995); Caroline Leach, interview.

45. Mark Potok, "Two Segregated Churches Merge in Race 'Milestone,'" *USA Today*, 20 February 1996, 3A; Nicole Piscopo, "Church Prides Itself on Long Tradition of Interracial Harmony," *St. Petersburg Times*, 29 June 1996, 6B; Charles R.

Foster and Theodore Brelsford, *We Are the Church Together: Cultural Diversity in Congregational Life* (Harrisburg, PA: Trinity Press, 1996), 66–86; Emerson and Smith, *Divided by Faith*, 135–51.

46. Foster and Brelsford, *We Are the Church Together*, 71.

47. UPCUSA, *General Assembly Minutes*, 1981, 201; Lewis, *Yet with a Steady Beat*.

48. Foster and Brelsford, *We Are the Church Together*, 71.

49. Pettigrew, "Intergroup Contact Theory"; Pettigrew and Tropp, "Does Intergroup Contact Reduce Prejudice?"; Mary R. Jackman and Marie Crane, "'Some of My Best Friends Are Black': Interracial Friendships and Whites' Racial Attitudes," *Public Opinion Quarterly* 50 (1986): 459–86; Emerson and Smith, *Divided by Faith*, 106–9.

50. Otis Turner, "The Pitfalls of Reconciliation," *Church and Society* 87 (July/ August 1997): 120–26, cit. at 124.

8 The Hydra and the Swords

Social Welfare and Mainline Advocacy, 1964–2000

Brian Steensland

Religious institutions took center stage in the rhetoric of America's fight against poverty in the 1990s. Over the course of the decade, both political liberals and conservatives increasingly came to view churches and other faith-based organizations as uniquely effective providers of social services for the poor. In their first major policy speeches of the 2000 presidential campaign, Democratic and Republican candidates Al Gore and George W. Bush each praised the virtues of shifting more welfare delivery responsibilities to religious organizations.[1] While a host of factors produced this bipartisan consensus, the "charitable choice" provision of the 1996 welfare reform bill served as the immediate catalyst that started this scramble toward faith-based service for the poor. This provision broadened to an unprecedented extent the explicit possibilities for government welfare money to flow directly to religious organizations for the delivery of public assistance services.[2] Among its significant implications, charitable choice focused attention on the relationship between religious institutions and welfare, and thus created a point of entry for mainline Protestants to raise questions about the American welfare system.

Mainline Protestant organizations have a long-standing concern for poverty-related issues and were well-positioned to enter into national discussions about welfare. They have historically been among the largest nonprofit providers for the poor (who composed 14 percent of the population—about 36 million people—in 1995).[3] Mainline leaders have also frequently been aligned with those most critical of unrestrained capitalism because of the social inequalities it produces. For either of these reasons, one might have expected a substantial mainline presence in the welfare reform debates in 1996 and the following years. Yet their voice, by most accounts, was weak. Few press accounts or subsequent works by scholars mentioned mainline organizations as significant players in the debates.[4] Still, their role was considerably larger than these accounts would lead one to believe. The relatively unseen nature of the mainline community's involvement was due to the particular approaches to advocacy they adopted over time in response to changes in the political environment, the public understanding of poverty, and the fortunes of the mainline itself.

Based on interviews with leaders from mainline organizations and a review of denominational and ecumenical publications, this chapter examines the mainline's recent advocacy on welfare-related issues and traces its development from the 1960s.[5] This research shows that the welfare system and the politics surrounding it touch on many aspects of American life—work, family structure, race relations, urban decline, gender roles, and free market capitalism. Much like fighting the Hydra, the multiheaded monster of Greek mythology that grew two new heads every time Heracles cut one off, combating poverty requires diverse and sustained efforts against a seemingly irrepressible foe. Mainline organizations have consistently taken a holistic perspective on the problem of poverty by recognizing its complex causes and multifaceted implications. Advocacy for the poor within the mainline community reflected this holism by calling for a variety of ways to help the needy. Such diverse advocacy goals also exemplified the internal diversity of mainline Protestantism, which houses a wide-ranging arsenal for fighting poverty. At any given time, groups within the mainline community pressed toward numerous remedies for poverty and hunger in America, yet a dominant approach usually established the primary course for welfare activism.

In broad terms, mainline Protestant advocacy changed in three ways from the late sixties to the late nineties: Advocates and denominational officials (1) scaled back calls for sweeping reform programs in favor of more moderate and incremental goals, (2) worked increasingly within broad-based (often secular) coalitions, and (3) relied more and more on the technical language of policy evaluation rather than theologically informed moral justifications for support of their policy goals. Taken together, these trends diminished the mainline's distinctive public *voice* in welfare debates, even while their public *involvement* in welfare activism remained robust. In light of future challenges, however, the mainline community's voice may be what is most necessary.

THE BEST AND THE GOOD

The Christian church's heritage of concern for the poor has deep biblical roots, but it took modern shape for the mainline during the Social Gospel movement at the turn of the twentieth century. Active engagement in social improvement was the norm, but providing charitable services for the needy was more prevalent than formal lobbying on their behalf. Most mainline organizations did not directly advocate on poverty issues until the growth of federal social welfare programs in the early 1960s, when poverty was "rediscovered."

During the 1940s and 1950s, discussions of poverty were nearly absent from the national agenda, despite the fact that by the end of the fifties 22 percent of the American population lived in poverty.[6] Mainline organizations were among the few groups to express concern for the disadvantaged sectors of society that the nation's postwar prosperity had left behind. In 1958, the National Council of Churches (NCC), the mainline's most politically prominent organization, issued a statement expressing concern for domestic public assistance programs. Among other things, it called for eligibility requirements to be less degrading to recipients, higher and more nationally uniform benefits levels, and increased involvement of church members at the local level of government decision making. The NCC also issued statements during these years addressing related concerns about unemployment, adequate housing, labor-management relations, and health services, all of which reflected the mainline community's recognition of the multidimensional nature of poverty.[7]

Intellectual currents among scholars and government officials in the late fifties and early sixties gradually pushed the issue of poverty back into mainstream consciousness. This renewed attention eventually led to President Johnson's War on Poverty programs, most of which were included in the Economic Opportunity Act of 1964 and Social Security Act of 1965. These bills were the first large-scale assault on American poverty since the Depression, and they initiated jobs programs, educational training, and Medicaid. Together with other preexisting programs, such as Aid to Families with Dependent Children (AFDC), food stamps, and public housing, they composed (until 1996) the core group of public assistance programs in America.[8]

The new legislative focus on fighting poverty gave mainline organizations opportunities to enter into a national dialog that had not previously existed, and they responded by taking positions on a host of social welfare issues. Combining theological justifications with analyses of economic and social trends in the nation, denominations and ecumenical groups called for the elimination of poverty through programs that increased opportunities for the poor, provided services and benefits that softened the effects of the free market economy, restored dignity to the disadvantaged, and recognized the interdependence of the nation's citizens.[9] These positions were politically liberal, calling for an expansive role of the federal government, but they were not radical. Like Johnson's programs, they emphasized opportunity ("a hand up and not a handout"), appealed to core American values like individualism and the work ethic, and operated according to the general principles established by Franklin Roosevelt's New Deal policies in the 1930s.

Several factors led mainline organizations to refashion their goals and strategies over the course of the next decade. One was increasing national criticism of Johnson's antipoverty programs in the years following the passage of the Economic Opportunity Act of 1964. The dramatic growth in the number of people on public assistance, increasing news coverage of fraudulent abuses among recipients, and complaints about gross inefficiency within the welfare bureaucracy all cast doubt on the efficacy of the welfare system. These concerns were exacerbated by the sporadic but often violent urban disturbances that swept across the country from 1964 to 1968.

Currents within the mainline were at play as well. Ideologically, mainline intellectuals increasingly adopted ideas from Marxism and liberation theology that made them more critical of America's economic regime and more attuned to the plight of the powerless. This trend was apparent in the shifting emphasis in coverage of poverty-related issues in *Christianity and Crisis*, a leading liberal Protestant periodical of its day. Proposals for alleviating poverty in the early 1960s worked within the established postwar framework of corporate liberalism, emphasizing remedies such as tax cuts and expanded social and legal services. Over the course of the next decade, the magazine's coverage grew to emphasize empowering the poor through community organizing, such as the Mobilization for Youth project in New York City and calls for a poor people's movement similar to the workingmen's movement in the 1930s. A prominent rallying cry was that "the economy should serve society, and not the other way around."

In the political arena, the growing alliance between mainline leaders and the civil rights movement amplified the intellectual currents within mainline thinking. It inclined the clergy more than ever to see social inequality from a racial viewpoint, and the role played by the white clergy in the movement set up grand expectations for continuing social change in the name of justice and equality. The outgrowth of these trends led mainline leaders to join civil rights activists, leftist academics, and public-interest lawyers to lobby for the next stage in this apparent revolution: a legally prescribed set of economic rights secured through guaranteed income policies. An early debate over these policies in *Christianity and Crisis* in 1966 presaged this new goal, and it became a focus for mainline leaders.[10]

These efforts found an unlikely champion in newly elected President Nixon. In 1969, he proposed a guaranteed income plan that broke sharply with the New Deal philosophy of temporary, service-based welfare programs that Johnson's programs had largely followed. Nixon's Family Assistance Plan (FAP) promised a minimum income—in effect, a right to welfare—to all families with children. Mainline organizations, along with Catholic and Jewish groups, lent their strong support to this principle. Beginning in 1968, the NCC and individual denominations issued statements arguing for a guaranteed minimum income as a fundamental right of citizenship and one of the best ways to ensure the dignity of the poor.[11]

Once Nixon publicly announced the FAP and the frequently heated debates over the proposal unfolded in Washington, the NCC's political stance shifted to the left of all but the most radical groups involved. While still favoring the principles of guaranteed income, it gradually withdrew its support for the FAP, at first through sympathetic criticism but ultimately by flatly opposing the legislation because its welfare benefits were deemed far too low. Mainline advocates called for a benefit level almost three times as high as the administration's proposal. Daniel P. Moynihan, the main proponent of the FAP in the Nixon administration, attributed the mainline's unrealistic financial demands and surprising objections to the FAP to the increasingly close alliance between liberal Protestant leaders and the National Welfare Rights Organization, a social movement largely comprised of black welfare recipients.[12] Though the House approved the FAP on two different occasions, the legislation languished and ultimately died in the Senate, a result that Moynihan blamed partly on the Protestant mainline's opposition.[13] A longtime advocate, recalling the mainline's inflated demands and political naïveté at the time, lamented: "We did all the wrong things for all the right reasons."

In 1977, President Carter placed a comprehensive welfare reform plan at the center of the nation's domestic agenda once again. Carter's plan, like Nixon's before it, proposed to guarantee a minimum income for those who could not work, but it also contained a more extensive public jobs component. Before developing the details of the new plan, the Carter administration solicited recommendations from a wide variety of civic interests, including representatives from the mainline community. The mainline community welcomed a second opportunity to improve on the shortcomings of existing antipoverty programs. Mindful of the lessons learned from Nixon's failed FAP, mainline Protestant advocates proceeded in a more measured fashion in the legislative arena. NCC director James Hamilton expressed three immediate concerns that characterized sentiments among the mainline toward the existing welfare system: its damaging impact on human dignity; its perverse incentives, which broke up or discouraged marriages; and the prevalence of work disincentives. Hamilton added that adequate income should be a right for America's citizens, not the haphazard end-product of charity, and that the churches supported the long-term goal of both full employment and guaranteed income policies.[14] Through this strategic pairing of incremental change set against the backdrop of comprehensive reforms, Hamilton found a balanced position that had been largely absent in the advocacy of the Nixon era.

Subsequent welfare legislation looked similar in many ways to the policy Hamilton had in mind, including guaranteed income and guaranteed jobs components. The proposal did not fare very well during the 1978 Congressional session, however, and the Carter administration was forced to offer a more incremental, scaled-down bill. This more moderate legislation created a dilemma for liberal mainliners similar to the one that characterized the FAP debates: whether to oppose the weak legislation because they felt it did not go far enough in practice, or to support the minor improvements as a hopeful first step toward more substantial reform in the future. Gradually the mainline developed a rough consensus. The new bill, without further amendments, provided enough tangible improvements in providing national standards and the coverage of two-parent families that it warranted their lukewarm support. While even this moderate legislation ultimately stalled amidst opposition in congressional committees, the mainline had learned to "not let the best be the enemy of the good."[15]

BUILDING BARRICADES IN THE "WAR ON WELFARE"

By 1981, the legislative terrain in Washington had changed considerably, and mainline advocates were forced into an entirely defensive posture on social welfare issues. This marked the transition from Johnson's War on Poverty to a period that historian Michael Katz terms the "war on welfare."[16] During the early eighties, the Reagan administration scaled back public assistance programs through its manipulation of the federal budgetary process and by shifting welfare administration to the states, thus circumventing the usual legislative channels in which mainline organizations played a role. As a result, advocates devoted most of their energies on broad welfare issues to trying to protect existing programs and benefit levels however they could.

A burgeoning conservative movement among intellectuals gave the political aims of the Reagan administration a sound ideological footing from which to advance its agenda. George Gilder's influential book, *Wealth and Poverty*, came to be known as "the Bible of the Reagan administration," and it circulated widely among government officials and business leaders.[17] Among other things, the book was an early manifesto for supply-side economics and a paean to the entrepreneurial spirit of risk-taking. A review in *Christianity and Crisis* appropriately described it as articulating the "theology of capitalism."[18] In essence, Gilder depicted a society in which human worth is measured by individual earnings, value is established by price, and faith is located in the workings of the free market. Accordingly, he opposed almost all government efforts to interfere in how the market distributes wealth. He targeted public assistance programs in particular, arguing that the poor "need the spur of poverty" to overcome their refusal to work hard. Along the way, he derided the notion that racial discrimination might damage the work opportunities of minorities and argued that women have little desire to work because of their biological differences from men. Such explanations provided the reader with the flip-side of praise for wealth and accumulation—a justification for poverty, the theodicy of capitalism.

Gilder's book was one of the most prominent examples of the mounting critique of government-sponsored assistance for the needy that forced the mainline Protestant community to the barricades to defend an unsatisfactory—or, at best, barely satisfactory—status quo. Though demoralizing at the time, this bunker mentality proved productive in some long-term ways. Groups such as the Coalition on Human Need—an influential organization and partner with the Protestant mainline—formed in the early 1980s as a direct response to attacks on antipoverty programs. And for mainline leaders, Reagan's initiatives forced the recognition that it was essential to develop alternatives to the theodicy of capitalism that legitimated the assault on the poor.

The United Church of Christ (UCC) was prominent among mainline denominations in developing through its national assembly a framework by which to evaluate economic systems. In 1983, UCC leaders commissioned a group of pastors, scholars, and business people to produce a "public theology of economics." After a six-year development process, the General Synod of the UCC adopted the "Pronouncement on Christian Faith: Economic Life and Justice" in 1989. (During the same period, the Presbyterian church [PCUSA] published an in-depth study paper and report on economic justice, and the National Conference of Catholic Bishops published a pastoral letter on the economy.)[19] While the "Pronouncement" ranged widely over a multitude of domestic and international issues— including resource depletion, the global debt crisis, and military waste— it was remarkable for its attention to poverty in America. As part of its recommendation for fighting poverty, it called for an "economic bill of rights" which included a guaranteed national minimum income, a national health care program, and rights to employment and affordable housing.[20]

Academics and policy analysts worked simultaneously with these broad-based efforts of the Protestant mainline to heighten national awareness that economic marginalization did not affect everyone equally. While overall poverty rates fell from 1960 through the 1970s, it was increasingly apparent that women, blacks, children, and urban residents were overrepresented among the poor. Research showed an increasing divergence between men's and women's poverty rates, particularly among the young and elderly. Households headed by single women had grown to compose half of the total poor population, and these women were more likely to be black. The percentage of children living in poverty grew from 15 percent in 1970 to 23 percent by the early 1980s. And while poverty had decreased in suburban and rural areas since 1960, it had increased in urban areas. For the mainline, as for other advocates for the poor, the implications of these trends meant that legislative activism would focus more attention on improving the economic status of particular groups through targeted programs and less on broad economic and labor-market reforms.

By the second Reagan administration, conservatives realized that they could not dismantle the welfare state as they had hoped. Despite the substantial cuts in AFDC and food stamps, there was public and congressional resistance to cutbacks to other public assistance and social insurance programs. The administration and its legislative allies instead focused on reshaping the welfare system to suit their ends. New ideas for welfare reform developed out of a sense that programs such as AFDC had been too permissive and that the government had been giving assistance to the poor without asking anything in return. In principle, this represented a shift toward paternalism and social monitoring (particularly toward women) and a greater emphasis on ending "dependency." In practice, it meant increasing work requirements for mothers and stronger child-support enforcement for fathers. In exchange, job training and child care were to be expanded and benefits extended to two-parent families. These ideas represented a new bipartisan consensus among many politicians and policymakers, and welfare reform was high on the legislative agenda in the mid-eighties. During the policy formulation process in congressional committees, however, many of the more liberal aspects of the legislation were removed, and bipartisan support waned. The end product was the Family Support Act of 1988, the first significant piece of welfare legislation to become law in two decades.

During preliminary congressional hearings on the bill, the mainline Protestant community's views were represented by advocates from the UCC, the Lutheran Office of Governmental Affairs, and an ecumenical coalition, Interfaith Action for Economic Justice. Their testimony reflected some of the changes that had occurred in mainline advocacy over the previous two decades. Reference to large-scale social transformation was nearly absent, as were theologically based visions of a just social order.[21] More prevalent was the technocratic language of program evaluations, incentive programs, and national poverty statistics. The mainline advocates each raised common themes that were not as salient in testimony from other liberal-leaning groups: an emphasis on welfare reform that focused on reducing poverty rather than reducing welfare rolls; attention to programs that enhanced human dignity; and a reminder that welfare reform is always driven by value judgments, even if these values are cloaked in different rhetoric. In the end, however, only one of the three advocates raised the more long-range policy goals of the mainline churches. The ultimate passage of the Family Support Act, many elements of which the mainline did not endorse, set the terms of debate in the following decade.

FIGHTING HUNGER, HELPING CHILDREN

One of the defining themes of Bill Clinton's 1992 presidential campaign was his promise to "end welfare as we know it." Clinton recognized the widespread dissatisfaction with the existing welfare system, and his agenda for reform advanced the basic set of ideas developed during the Reagan and Bush administrations. Clinton's proposal struck a compromise between conservative and liberal perspectives—conservative because it required welfare recipients to be working within two years after receiving benefits, and liberal because it increased funding for childcare, job training, transportation, and other services that could ease the transition from welfare to work. Despite finding elements of his welfare agenda disagreeable, mainline church leaders viewed Clinton as a welcome ally in the White House because of his concerns about poverty as governor of Arkansas. Clinton aimed to create a "national dialogue" about welfare, a dialogue in which mainline organizations could actively participate. And indeed, after being virtually shut out of conversations on welfare issues with the Reagan and Bush administrations, mainline advocates and their allies maintained an exchange of ideas with the Clinton White House in subsequent years. Despite these conversations, however, national mainline leaders were disappointed with many aspects of welfare reform once the policy details took shape in 1996, and they spent the last years of the decade trying to improve the implementation of the bill at the federal and state levels.

The renewed welfare debates in the 1990s took place in a national environment significantly different from the Carter years. Though Clinton was a Democrat and his party controlled Congress during his first two years in office, the country's mood was more economically conservative, as reflected in the centrist agenda of the "New Democrats" in power. There was little public desire for either extensive economic reform or expansion of social programs, as Clinton discovered early on in his failed attempt to create a universal health care program. In 1994, Republicans took control of Congress for the first time in forty years in what was perceived as a popular mandate against big government, and they developed a new political vision they called the "Contract with America." Welfare reform was one of ten items in this new agenda. The Contract with America argued that Johnson's Great Society programs had "bred illegitimacy, crime, illiteracy, and more poverty," and that the aims of reform should be to "reduce illegitimacy, require work, and save taxpayer money."[22] These three goals framed the specifics of the reform plan. There were almost no references to lowering poverty rates or reducing hunger. It was Gilder's theology of capitalism in a slightly different guise.

The advocacy situation in Washington had also changed. The ecumenical movement was considerably weaker than it had been in the seventies. The influence of the National Council of Churches was declining, and significant ecumenical advocacy groups such as the Washington Interreligious Staff Community and Interfaith IMPACT were either weakening or defunct. Advocates found it increasingly necessary to work within broad coalitions of religious and secular groups. In such diverse coalitions, theological rationales were often scaled down to least-common-denominator ethical arguments, and technical, "pie-chart" evaluations of poverty came to the forefront because expertise from think tanks such as the Center on Budget and Policy Priorities was readily available.

More generally, the combined effects of the national mood and the emerging research on poverty from the eighties meant that rather than focusing on changes within the economy and labor market, such as full-employment policy or minimum-income proposals, advocates gave more attention to targeted, remedial goals, such as fighting hunger and decreasing child poverty. Responsibility for welfare advocacy in the mainline churches shifted to denominational divisions dealing with hunger or women's issues rather than economic justice offices. For instance, the Hunger Action Program of the UCC began on a small scale in 1975 as an outgrowth of the World Food Conference in Rome in 1974. Over time it became entirely financed by special offerings, and, as other welfare-related initiatives within the UCC diminished, the Hunger Action Program emerged as a primary way the denomination addressed welfare issues. The PCUSA and NCC conducted much of their welfare-related work through similar hunger programs and task forces.

Focusing on children was another way mainline denominational organizations lobbied on welfare issues in the 1990s. Advocates noted the irony that federal welfare programs were originally devoted primarily to children's well-being (in the form of Aid to Dependent Children in 1935) and yet contemporary welfare debates rarely identified children's nutrition and health as a high priority. The mainline focus on children attempted to redress this oversight and also concentrate energies on an issue about which there was universal concern. (Some advocates suggested that focusing on children's issues was also a "stealth" strategy for addressing more controversial institutional reform issues.) Within the United Methodist Church (UMC), many welfare-related issues were addressed from the Women's Division because of the obvious relationship between women's and children's issues, and welfare advocacy took on a strong family and gender perspective. Children's issues also served as a strong basis for coalition work. The UMC's Women's Division and the Children's Defense Fund (CDF) cooperated extensively, sharing data and materials. For instance, the Women's Division coordinated the denominations' participation in the CDF's annual Children's Sabbath, a program that encouraged congregations to involve themselves in children's issues through prayer, education, volunteering, contributions, and advocacy. Within the ecumenical community, the Food Policy Working Group, an active coalition on Capitol Hill that focused on policies such as school lunch and children's nutrition programs, grew out of the Justice for Women and Families ecumenical taskforce in the early 1990s.

The focus on hunger and poor children played to the strengths of the mainline. In the 1960s and 1970s, many mainline organizations supported welfare reform proposals that called for government intervention in labor markets and the economy. According to mainline advocates, these ideas were often not well-received among policymakers because the church's authority on economic issues was arguable. The church's concern for the hungry and powerless, on the other hand, was beyond reproach. When asked about the advantages of lobbying on welfare issues on behalf of mainline organizations, advocates did not primarily point to their ability to use religious rhetoric or the fact that a quarter of the American population affiliates with the mainline Protestant tradition. Instead they emphasized the credibility that stemmed from the church's tradition of concern for the poor and its extensive experience at the grassroots of caring for the needy through service programs.

Because of the mainline community's involvement in providing services to the poor, legislators saw advocates as a valuable source of information on trends and problems at the local level. Political scientists have long recognized that providing information is one way groups can influence policy development aside from money and votes, and the churches played a unique role in passing on information from the grassroots. For instance, mainline representatives and allies provided some of the earliest assessments of how the 1996 reform bill affected the poor. Second Harvest, the nation's largest network of food banks and a major mainline partner, reported that 21 million people used their food programs in 1997, a 17 percent increase from previous years, and that 40 percent of these clients were from working families. Reports such as these provided important policy feedback considerably more quickly than the first major report from the USDA over a year later that found the same trend.

The mainline's focus on hunger and children did not make them unique on Capitol Hill, however, since its short-term lobbying agenda on welfare issues was similar to that of advocacy organizations such as the Children's Defense Fund and the Food Research Action Center. The main difference that mainline Protestant advocates themselves identified was their holistic perspective on social problems and their solutions. This emphasis on holism served as a kind of touchstone for the advocates and they used the term in several ways. First, holism meant paying attention to the multiple dimensions of an individual's existence—from basic needs of food, shelter, and clothing to more existential needs such as dignity and a sense of purpose. Second, welfare advocates were motivated by a concern for the entire constellation of factors related to poverty and economic injustice, ranging from improvements in society's safety net (food stamps, health care, and childcare) to lobbying for a "living wage," implementing a full-employment policy, and strengthening the bargaining power of unions. Third, and even more broadly, these "justice" issues were seen as related to constellations of other issues revolving around peace and the environment. Advocates distinguished these holistic concerns from the narrow, often single-issue, concerns of typical lobbyists.

The holistic perspective taken by mainline advocates had strengths and weaknesses. Concerns for the whole person appeared distinctly positive and made the mainline's approach relatively unique in Washington. Rather than seeing individuals narrowly as taxpayers, shareholders, or employees, advocates tried to evaluate public assistance programs in light of their effects on the complete person and their contribution toward a more just society. Advocates felt this strengthened their credibility because legislators did not view them as "just another special-interest group." On the downside, advocates voiced concerns that one of the mainline's weaknesses was the tendency to view "the whole world as the problem." Too much concern with the proliferation of social problems, and how they reinforce one another in seemingly intractable ways, sometimes threatened to lead to a diffusion of limited resources for organizations and feelings of inefficacy for advocates and laypersons. Within denominations, holism sometimes resulted in welfare issues being addressed through a number of different divisions: economic justice, race and civil rights, women and children, labor and business, or hunger and nutrition. A Presbyterian leader enumerated seven different denominational programs or offices within the PCUSA that dealt with welfare-related issues. While this flexibility may have been beneficial in some cases, it also meant that welfare advocacy lacked a sustained focus. An advocate for another denomination suggested that their hunger program had been weakened considerably for exactly this reason once it was integrated into a larger peace and justice network. And in most denominations, welfare responsibilities floated across divisions and offices more than issues such as civil rights, the environment, and international peace. Therefore advocates who dealt with welfare tended to have less long-term knowledge of the issue than their counterparts in these other divisions.

Strategically, mainline church advocates employed a wide range of tactics to bring their holistic perspective to bear on legislation. In order to illustrate the process, one Washington advocate had created a chart diagramming eighteen possible avenues of action for his office on any particular legislative issue. The approach ultimately chosen depended on the level of public interest, available resources, and the nature of the issue. On welfare, advocates seldom lobbied solely on behalf of their denominations. Direct lobbying of this type was more likely to involve issues in which a denomination's immediate interests were at stake, such as on matters pertaining to religious freedom or church-state relations. In the fight against poverty, working in coalitions was the norm.

A number of advocates pointed to Washington's Food Policy Working Group as an exemplary coalition for capitalizing on coalition strengths while avoiding potential weaknesses. The group was primarily an interfaith coalition that included Catholics, Jews, and a wide array of Protestant groups. It additionally included representatives from Bread for the World, an interfaith organization that fights hunger worldwide, and the Food Research Action Center, a Washington-based antihunger advocacy organization. These two organizations added a well-defined focus on hunger issues and the institutional resources to "staff out" the coalition by providing high-quality research and information. The group met nearly weekly in the Senate cafeteria to strategize and then make congressional visits concerning whatever hunger-related legislation was up for congressional action during that week. Their visits usually included between seven to ten coalition members, and they developed close relations to members of Congress active on nutrition-related committees. The group combined the moral voice, policy expertise, consistent focus, and action orientation that characterized effective coalition work.

The mainline worked through a variety of coalitions such as this during the period leading up to the 1996 welfare reform bill. Republicans in Congress, following the proposal outlined in the Contract with America, sought to substantially transform the welfare system, including ending the entitlement status of most public assistance programs and devolving the administrative power over welfare programs to the states through block grants. The proposed block grant program, Temporary Assistance for Needy Families (TANF), would replace AFDC and consolidate a number of other programs into a single payment made to state governments to fund their own public assistance programs. States would generally have the flexibility to experiment with programs; however, families would have a five-year lifetime limit on receiving benefits. The mainline community opposed many of these provisions and fought the legislation by participating in numerous coalitions, including the Coalition for Human Need, which brought together many other interests, such as the Children's Defense Fund, the Center on Budget and Policy Priorities, Catholic Charities, social work organizations, labor unions, and public-interest law firms. One of the aspects of the welfare bill that caught the coalition most off guard was the proposal to include nutrition programs like food stamps in the TANF block grant. Advocates were concerned that food stamp benefits would be susceptible to the same time limits as other programs.

Clinton vetoed two versions of the Republican legislation but signed a third version in August of 1996, despite firm opposition from the mainline churches. However, these broad-based coalitions successfully fought the inclusion of food stamps in the TANF grants, therefore retaining their status as a federal entitlement. Mainline advocates identified this as one of their most significant welfare successes of the 1990s and considered their moral voice on hunger as an important contribution to this effort. Passage of the welfare bill in 1996 marked a paradigm shift in welfare provision that refocused much more attention on the states than ever before. The mainline denominations had been slow historically to develop state-level advocacy offices, but nevertheless worked toward expanding their presence in state capitols in the wake of reform.

The "charitable choice" provision was another element of the 1996 welfare bill that held important implications for the mainline churches. It broadened the range of ways that state governments could explicitly contract with faith-based organizations for the provision of social services. None of the mainline denominations took a formal position on charitable choice, but personal opinions toward it among national officials ranged from ambivalence to cynicism. They agreed that the potential pool of financial resources had been greatly expanded through the provision, but that the price the churches might have to pay for this additional funding might be too great.

The most salient concern stemmed from constitutional issues regarding the appropriate relationship between the churches and the government. Many leaders worried about threats to religious freedom, and most felt that court cases stemming from the charitable choice provision would ultimately be decided in the Supreme Court. Despite universal agreement on these church-state concerns, mainline attitudes toward the provision were considerably deeper and more complex. Many leaders felt the mainline churches' approval of charitable choice would send the wrong message to the nation, since most church leaders supported the principles of government responsibility for caring for the poor. Therefore there was concern that receiving government money would be equivalent to participating in the government's abdication of its responsibilities. Moreover, almost everyone familiar with church social service programs recognized that churches, contrary to the opinions of many conservatives, did not have the institutional capacity to care for the nation's poor.[23]

Mainline service agencies also worried that increasing the provision of basic necessities for the needy, like food and shelter, would lead to an unproductive shift in church focus. They felt the churches could best provide services that required developing time-intensive, one-on-one relationships with clients, such as drug rehabilitation and mentoring programs. Churches are especially suited to deal with these sorts of problems because solutions involve addressing the spiritual needs of clients. On the other hand, activities like stocking food pantries and overseeing homeless shelters do not require either the relational or spiritual dimension of service provision, but rather large staff, adequate space, and substantial financial resources. Leaders felt that government agencies were better suited for dealing with these basic aspects of public assistance. Philosophically, leaders expressed concerns that receiving government money would dampen the critical public voice of the church, since it is often directed at the government. In effect, funds made available through charitable choice might co-opt the mainline churches. Finally, there was a related fear that if churches participated in charitable choice they would have to change their relationship with the poor as they moved from providing charitable services to being an arm of the state. One mainline official described this as a shift from the church acting as an agent of grace to acting as an agent of judgment, because faith-based workers would be required to terminate recipients' benefits if they didn't comply with the broad variety of new regulations.

While mainline church leaders opposed the passage of the 1996 reform bill, lay parishioners generally supported it. Despite efforts by church leaders to debunk myths about welfare recipients and highlight weaknesses in the legislation, most Americans, including mainliners, were sympathetic to the core aspects of the bill. As one advocate lamented, "It's much easier for the mainline to write policy statements than change the minds of people in the pews." Denominational officers agreed that the linchpin of success on economic justice issues was the laity. They felt that lay members needed to be educated on the appropriate relationship between churches and the government. Calls for political activism by pastors or advocacy coordinators cannot be effective if church members feel that injecting religious or theologically derived arguments into matters of public policy is inappropriate or unconstitutional. Leaders also recognized, with more direct relevance to welfare issues, that educational materials needed to draw a more explicit link between biblical principles and concrete issues of hunger and poverty.

Mainline organizations took many approaches to educating the laity.

The ELCA included a detailed discussion of poverty in a major study of economic life published in 1996. Typical of the mainline respect for diversity of opinion within its ranks, the discussion outlined five prevailing explanations for why people are poor—ranging from "poverty is the result of choices individuals have made" to "poverty is the failure of the economic system." It then proceeded to unravel some of the basic values and assumptions implicit in each perspective and asked readers to form their own conclusions about how antipoverty policies should be constructed.[24] Some national leaders in the American Baptist Church chose an approach that was more centered on members' own economic lives. Using study guides that integrated biblical teachings with discussions of personal finance, they hoped that through thoughtful consideration, participants would see the broad social influences in their own lives—such as corporate downsizing and globalization—and translate this understanding to the social situations of the less fortunate.

This work in the national offices to forge direct links between Christian faith and modern economic life was an effective counterbalance to the widespread view among the Washington advocacy community that lay members would become involved in welfare advocacy if they were simply supplied with the pertinent information. This advocacy assumption was most apparent from the structure of the "action alerts" that denominations and ecumenical organizations distributed. These one- to two-page flyers outlined the broad background and implications of legislation pending before Congress, and ended with a call for action. While these alerts often succinctly described the issues, they rarely contained substantial biblical or theological justification for concern about the issue generally or for the church's stance in particular. Thus they overlooked the fact that most people attend church not to become activists but for spiritual growth and Christian fellowship. This advocacy assumption seems at least partially accountable for what has been called the "75 percent gap" observed in some denominations: the fact that around 85 percent of church members participate in direct service ministries while only 10 percent participate in advocacy. Service is viewed as a Christian manifestation of stewardship and care for others, while advocacy apparently is not.

Washington offices were more successful at debunking many of the prevalent myths about the nation's welfare population. One common point within denominational and ecumenical publications was that it is difficult to generalize about the welfare population: most of the stereotypes of welfare recipients—for instance, that they are black, lazy, promiscuous, and on welfare for generations—were shown to be statistically inaccurate and very misleading. Yet these prevalent beliefs significantly affect the way Americans think about welfare policy.[25] On this issue, the mainline played an important role in attempting to counterbalance many of the inaccurate images and depictions of welfare recipients in the media and political rhetoric.

At a broader level of public education, the mainline Protestant advocacy community came to recognize the power of the media during the 1996 welfare debates. In the following years, there were discussions of formulating an orchestrated media strategy as a means to inject a stronger moral voice into debates over issues that welfare brings to the forefront of American consciousness, such as community, family, compassion, and responsibility. For instance, the NCC convened a consultation on welfare reform in 1998, and its title, "Shaping the Values That Shape Us," suggested the approach of many of the speakers. They discussed the ways in which views of welfare depend on the links that are drawn between welfare recipients, social programs, and American values. The 1996 welfare bill, they argued, was framed by the media and politicians as a way to reduce dependency on welfare checks, and thus to reduce welfare rolls. It focused on ending welfare, not ending poverty. Subsequent evaluations of the consequences of the legislation measured success by reductions in state welfare caseloads rather than reductions in the number of poor people. By focusing on dependency, this perspective privileged American values like individualism and the work ethic. Speakers at the consultation instead proposed a strategy in which welfare policy goals could be redefined as being concerned mainly with reductions in poverty, and in which progressive reforms were reframed to appeal to equally strong American values such as fairness, mutual responsibility, and human rights.[26]

RAISING THE QUESTIONS

The welfare situation in America changed over the decades of the late twentieth century, and mainline advocacy changed along with it. Johnson's programs represented a high point of public concern about poverty, followed by fifteen years of growing skepticism toward welfare programs and their increasing attachment to issues such as dependency, illegitimacy, the feminization of poverty, and the urban underclass. The Reagan administration initiated a retrenchment in welfare policymaking that culminated in program cuts, administrative devolution, and the suspension of benefit entitlements in 1996.

At times, mainline organizations took up the vanguard of welfare activism—expressing concerns about public assistance programs in the 1950s when the rest of America seemed oblivious to poverty; arguing the merits of guaranteed income programs years before Nixon put them on the national agenda; and formulating an alternative perspective on the economy during the supply-side Reagan years. But more often, mainline churches seemed to be at the mercy of broad oppositional forces.

On the whole, advocacy goals shifted from institutional reform in the late sixties and seventies toward residual assistance in the subsequent years, from trying to transform the structure of the economic system toward assisting the most vulnerable who fall through its cracks. To the extent that institutional reform remained a long-term aim, it was cloaked in "stealth" advocacy on hunger and children's issues. Over the same period, the mainline's unique moral voice became weaker as more technical, "pie-chart" advocacy came to be prominent. Yet these trends should not be overstated. Some groups within mainline organizations continued to lobby for structural reforms, such as full-employment policies, and goals such as these remained officially on the books. Likewise, policy justifications continued to draw on theological language at least occasionally. Nonetheless, most of the mainline church community's writing on poverty was virtually indistinguishable from that found in secular publications such as the *New Republic* or the *Nation*.

The mainline's success on welfare issues is difficult to gauge, particularly when definitions of success are not entirely clear. Should success be defined as winning legislative victory, setting the terms of political debate, being invited to the bargaining table, educating lay parishioners, or decreasing the number of people living below the poverty line? What should be expected of the church's role in politics? Compounding this difficulty is the fact that most mainline advocacy regarding welfare policy was undertaken in conjunction with other groups, making any assessment of its individual contribution all but impossible. Rather than debating the merits of mainline involvement according to any of these criteria, it may be more fruitful to probe a unique strength of mainline Protestant organizations: their role in raising theologically informed moral questions about hunger, poverty, work, and the American economy.

Why Raise These Questions?

Instead of speaking out about sources of social injustice as they perceive them, mainline organizations could more quietly continue their efforts toward residual assistance for poor children and the hungry. Advocacy could continue to work comfortably within the established system, and social services could be provided for those whom society leaves behind. Undoubtedly, the quality of many lives would (and will) be improved by these efforts. Yet this scenario overlooks a deeper relevance of the mainline churches. If nothing else, churches are repositories of values. The history of mainline welfare advocacy can be viewed as a struggle to inject a particular set of moral and holistic values into debates hostile to these values. As the NCC welfare consultation emphasized, the dominant approach to welfare reform asks how to decrease welfare rolls, increase the work ethic, save taxpayer dollars, and unfetter the free market. These questions are rooted in the theology of capitalism, and they appear natural and obvious to most Americans. (Social commentators, in fact, have argued that the ideology of the free market occupies the position formerly held by God in earlier centuries.[27]) Mainline organizations have worked hard to articulate an alternative set of standards by which to judge economic and social systems. If these moral and theological concepts are not mobilized to their fullest through raising questions, the mainline community will have packed a very large suitcase for a very short trip.

This moral and theological voice also provides a model for public discussion that extends beyond self-interest. A recent study of civic engagement suggests that Americans have a difficult time discussing politics and engaging in advocacy explicitly for the public good. Even when activists are motivated by public-spirited concerns, they generally revert to narrow, self-interested justifications for their claims once they engage in public talk about the issues. For instance, the study followed activists motivated to protest toxic waste for global environmental reasons, yet noted that they justified their actions in public forums by citing their concerns as "parents" and "property holders" (rather than as public-minded citizens). In other words, Americans can readily use and understand arguments based on individualism and self-interest, while arguments based on "other-oriented" concerns for the larger society seem odd and suspicious.[28] The mainline's holistic vision in discussing the merits of various welfare policies provides a rare template for engaging the political process in such public-spirited ways. If, as the study suggests, "we make the road by walking it," the mainline is a member of the advanced guard.

Who Should Raise the Questions?

A division of labor within mainline organizations can make the process of raising the questions more effective. Many church leaders recognize that advocacy offices tend to be reactive, responding to whatever issues bubble up from the legislative cauldron. National offices, on the other hand, are typically more prospective because they function at a considerable remove from the pressing day-to-day concerns of the advocacy community. Denominational leaders plan for the future rather than react to the political moment. Mainline organizations can self-consciously structure themselves to take advantage of these preexisting differences in function: advocates can position themselves as pragmatists working on realistic legislative gains, while national offices can focus on large-scale issues in a more visionary way, such as articulating moral justifications for full employment, a family allowance, or national childcare programs. In effect, this division of labor positions the mainline community both within and outside the system it is trying to change.

The strategic pairing of these two voices can serve a number of important functions for mainline organizations. Advocates in particular could couple immediately feasible goals with more ultimately desirable ones, employing a double-barreled language in which advocacy goals are located within the larger context of the churches' biblical mandate. This approach minimizes the possibility that short-range victories might become the sole aim of advocates. Strategic pairing also allows all of the sometimes competing pragmatic and prophetic voices within the church body to be heard. Rather than attempting to reconcile a host of diverse perspectives, each would be granted productive outlets. And pairing diverse voices within the mainline is likely to be more politically effective in the long run. The civil rights movement serves as a useful model. Despite long odds against it, the movement was successful largely because it coupled moderate approaches to reform—such as the "inside" legal strategies of the NAACP—with more radical "outside" approaches, including sit-ins, mass demonstrations, and other unconventional strategies.

Who's Listening?

Mainline church organizations necessarily must address multiple audiences on issues of poverty, including legislators, lay parishioners, and the general public. Each of these audiences plays an important role in welfare advocacy and requires a different communication strategy. Legislators seem to respond to advocates when they speak with strong (but not aggressive) moral language, provide information from their grassroots involvement in service provision, and can mobilize influence in the legislator's district. For these reasons, the Protestant mainline should consider how to make the best *rhetorical* use of the public platform that charitable choice provides, regardless of their views toward actual participation in the programs. The challenge with lay parishioners requires forging explicit connections between theology and public policy without necessarily pre-scribing consensus on policy positions. Diversity is inherent in the main-line, but if given the proper outlets, it can advance productive work toward any number of useful welfare goals. Making inroads into public conscious-ness, on the other hand, requires a well-formulated public relations strat-egy involving the media. Because participation in secular coalitions can dampen the mainline's moral voice, ecumenical coalitions are likely to be crucial in these efforts. As with legislators, it will be important to establish credibility among the media by drawing attention to the mainline com-munity's experience in service provision.

In some ways the welfare situation in the late 1990s was similar to that of the late 1950s. During both periods, America was in the midst of an economic boom, middle-class citizens enjoyed economic prosperity, pov-erty was perceived to be receding, and the mainline Protestant agenda for helping the needy was left-of-center while still working largely within the prescribed confines of the system. Yet in the 1950s, if one looked just beneath the surface, signs of social turmoil were readily apparent, and within mainline organizations, strategies for more visionary pursuits were in formative stages. Social unrest in the following years provided an op-portunity for mainline leaders to raise their voices and be heard. In the opening years of the twenty-first century, processes as varied as growing church-state partnerships and global inequality may provide a new plat-form for the mainline's voices. Leaders and parishioners must be ready to articulate them.

NOTES

I would like to thank Bob Wuthnow, John Evans, Paul Lichterman, Lester Kurtz, and Mark Chaves for helpful comments and suggestions on earlier drafts of this chapter. I am also grateful to the National Council of Churches for allowing me access to the records in their New York City and Washington, DC, offices, and to the Center for the Study of Religion at Princeton University for generous financial support of this research. Most of all, I would like to thank the many mainline officials who took time to speak with me and pass on relevant research materials. These people and institutions bear no responsibility for the views expressed in this chapter.

1. Kevin Sack, "Gore Backs Money for Church Social Service Programs," *New York Times*, May 25, 1999, A23; Adam Clymer, "Filter Aid to Poor Through Churches, Bush Urges," *New York Times*, July 22, 1999, A1.

2. Specifically, the statute reads that religious organizations should be permit-ted to receive government funding "on the same basis as any other non-governmental provider without impairing the religious character of such organi-zations" (Personal Responsibility and Work Opportunity Reconciliation Act of 1996, sec. 104). Since religious organizations have long received governmental

funding for various service activities (e.g., through the Church World Service for the resettlement of refugees), the extent to which the charitable choice provision actually expanded funding opportunities for churches is a matter of debate. Nevertheless, the explicitness of the statute in regard to religious organizations is a marked change in policy approach.

3. Jim Castelli and John D. McCarthy, "Religion-Sponsored Social Service Providers: The Not-So-Independent Sector," working paper, Aspen Institute, 1997; Sar A. Levitan, Garth L. Mangum, and Stephen L. Mangum, *Programs in Aid of the Poor,* 7th ed. (Baltimore, MD: Johns Hopkins University Press, 1998), 11.

4. A computer-based media search of news articles written about welfare reform in the months preceding the signing of the welfare bill suggests that Catholic and evangelical Protestant organizations received the majority of press attention among religious groups. Call to Renewal and Bread for the World, two antipoverty organizations that include mainline members, received some attention, as did Lutheran Social Services.

5. I conducted sixteen in-depth interviews with denominational officials in national headquarters and advocacy offices, and at Bread for the World and the Food Research Action Center. At the national offices, I interviewed officials who dealt most closely with welfare issues; the Washington advocates I interviewed typically worked on a wide range of policy issues, not just those relating to welfare.

6. Levitan et al., *Programs in Aid,* 10.

7. National Council of Churches, "The Church's Concern for Public Assistance," June 4, 1958; see also, "The Churches' Concern for Housing," November 18, 1953; "The Moral Crisis in the Labor Union Movement and in Labor-Management Practices," December 5, 1957; "Christian Concern about Unemployment," June 4, 1958; and "The Churches' Concern for Health Services," February 25, 1960.

8. Sometimes all these programs together are referred to as welfare programs. More frequently, the term *welfare* refers more narrowly to means-tested income-maintenance programs such as AFDC. Unless otherwise indicated, I use the more inclusive meaning in order to reflect the mainline's holistic orientation toward advocacy.

9. For instance, National Council of Churches, "The Church and the Anti-Poverty Program," December 3, 1966; United Church of Christ, "Support of Domestic Anti-poverty Programs, July 5, 1966.

10. Ben B. Seligman, "Guaranteed Incomes and Negative Taxes: Pro"; and Robert Lekachman, "The Guaranteed Annual Income: Con," *Christianity and Crisis,* January 24, 1966.

11. For instance, National Council of Churches, "On Guaranteed Income," February 22, 1968; United Church of Christ, "The Family Assistance Plan," March 1970; United Presbyterian Church (USA), "United Presbyterians and Income Maintenance," May 27, 1970.

12. Daniel P. Moynihan, *The Politics of a Guaranteed Income: The Nixon Administration and the Family Assistance Plan* (New York: Random House, 1973).

13. Ibid., 302.

14. Joseph Califano to James Hamilton, letter dated February 8, 1977; and James Hamilton to Joseph Califano, letter dated February 22, 1977, National Council of Churches, Washington files.

15. Hyman Bookbinder, quoted in Moynihan, *Guaranteed Income,* 300.

16. Michael B. Katz, *The Undeserving Poor: From the War on Poverty to the War on Welfare* (New York: Pantheon Books, 1989).

17. George Gilder, *Wealth and Poverty* (New York: Basic Books, 1981). On the influence of Gilder's book, see Katz, *Undeserving Poor*, 143–47.

18. Winston Davis, "The Gospel According to Gilder," *Christianity and Crisis*, February 1, 1982.

19. Presbyterian Church (USA), "Christian Faith and Economic Justice" (ms., 1984), and "Toward a Just, Caring, and Dynamic Policy Economy" (Office of the General Assembly, 1985); National Conferences of Catholic Bishops, *Economic Justice for All: Pastoral Letter on Catholic Social Teaching and the U.S. Economy* (Washington, DC: United States Catholic Conference, 1986).

20. United Church of Christ, "Pronouncement on Christian Faith: Economic Life and Justice" (General Synod, July 1989). For a discussion of the formulation of the document, see Rebecca Blank, *Do Justice: Linking Christian Faith and Modern Economic Life* (Cleveland, OH: United Church Press, 1992).

21. The lack of reference to these issues was particularly notable in the oral testimony when compared to the written statements submitted to the Committee on Ways and Means, House of Representatives, "Welfare Reform," Serial 100–14 (Washington, DC: U.S. Government Printing Office, 1987), 493–530.

22. Republican National Committee, *Contract with America* (New York: Times Books, 1994), 65–77.

23. For an example of this conservative argument, see Marvin Olasky, *The Tragedy of American Compassion* (Washington, DC: Regnery, 1992).

24. Evangelical Lutheran Church in America, "Give Us This Day Our Daily Bread: Sufficient, Sustainable Livelihood for All" (Division of Church and Society, 1996).

25. Martin Gilens, *Why Americans Hate Welfare: Race, Media, and the Politics of Antipoverty Policy* (Chicago: University of Chicago Press, 1999).

26. National Council of Churches, "Shaping the Values That Shape Us: A National Consultation on Welfare Reform," transcript of presentations (New York: National Council of Churches, 1998).

27. One recent example is Harvey Cox, "The Market as God," *Atlantic Monthly*, March 1999, 18–23.

28. Nina Eliasoph, *Avoiding Politics: How Americans Produce Apathy in Everyday Life* (New York: Cambridge University Press, 1998).

9 Caring for Creation

*Environmental Advocacy by
Mainline Protestant Organizations*

Michael Moody

CAN PROTESTANTS BE ENVIRONMENTALISTS?

Prominently displayed inside the Episcopal Church's famous St. John the Divine Cathedral in New York City is a huge quartz crystal. A plaque says the crystal is "200 Million Years Old" and is placed there "To Honor the Beauty of God's Creation and Our Sacred Stewardship of Planet Earth."

Such a display celebrating a Christian role in preserving the environment departs from the once-popular opinion about Christianity's attitude toward "planet earth." In a famous 1967 essay in *Science*, UCLA historian Lynn White Jr. claimed that Judeo-Christian teachings were in fact a primary *cause* of the contemporary "ecologic crisis."[1] Specifically, White pointed to the belief, taken from a reading of Genesis 1:26, that man should have "dominion" over all creation, in the sense that creation existed for man's use and control. This "Christian arrogance toward nature," White argued, justified the modern technology-driven depletion of the earth's resources.[2]

White's thesis sparked much debate but was widely influential. Many activists in the then-emerging environmental movement adopted White's view and labeled Judeo-Christian religion an enemy of nature.[3] However, while some Christians surely adopted the "dominion" stance, many others embraced a goal of "caring for creation"—translating "dominion" as "holding" or "keeping" the earth—even before White made his argument. Some theologians and ethicists worked to promote an alternative "ecological" theology, while many Christian institutions, especially the national organizations of the mainline Protestant denominations, developed a range of pro-environment advocacy programs.

In fact, these mainline Protestant environmentalists sustained some form of public and political activity throughout the ups and downs of environmental issues over the next three decades. They advocated in Washington, DC, for stringent environmental regulations like the Endangered Species Act. They mobilized a religious presence at major international summits on the environment from Stockholm in 1972 to Kyoto in 1997. They sent educational and liturgical materials to thousands of their member congregations encouraging local "eco-justice" action. And they were early proponents of the need to fight "environmental racism," helping to launch the new "environmental justice" submovement.

While these Protestant environmental advocates often sound much like secular environmentalists, they have also sought to offer an explicitly religious voice on environmental problems. In fact, they feel they have a distinctive calling to protect the environment *because* they believe that environment is "God's creation." As the American Baptist Churches' central policy statement on ecology puts it, "God created the Earth, affirmed that it was good, and established an everlasting covenant with humanity to take responsibility for the whole of creation." The mainline groups have also repeatedly asserted that ecological concerns are inextricably tied to their traditional concerns of social justice and human well-being, and they made such "justice" connections before most secular environmentalists.

In general, despite what one would predict from White's thesis, mainline groups have been a consistently active force in pro-environment advocacy. Their impact on environmental policy, the environmental movement, issue awareness, and grassroots mobilizing has been "quiet" and limited, yet occasionally notable. The purpose of this chapter is not to celebrate this faith-based environmental advocacy but to chronicle it, assess its impact, and draw attention to this neglected area of public influence by mainline Protestantism.

The research described here focuses on the environmental advocacy activities of the six major mainline Protestant denominations which are the focus of this volume, as well as those of the National Council of Churches of Christ in the USA (NCC) and a key interfaith group, the National Religious Partnership for the Environment (NRPE). I examine their work over the past thirty years, roughly the duration of the modern environmental movement. The data comes from in-depth interviews, a wide variety of documents and materials produced by the groups, and historical research.[4] The analysis focuses on: (1) the organizational, political, and other public activities and tactics of the mainline groups; (2) the arguments they make, the environmental issues they focus on, and what they feel provides their legitimacy; and (3) how and why the mainline has been successful or had an "impact" (however they define that impact).[5]

HISTORY OF ADVOCACY AND SUMMARY OF PROGRAMS

The Initial Call for "Eco-Justice"

Lynn White's 1967 essay highlighted the connection of religion with ecological concern at a time when the ethics and politics of ecology were just emerging as key public issues. Many philosophers of ecology who came to prominence in the late 1960s and early 1970s—for example, René Dubos, E. F. Schumacher, Wendell Berry—made links to religious ethics and helped establish the "eco-theology" that informs many Protestant environmentalists today.[6] But even before this, religious organizations were addressing what later would be called "environmental" issues. For example, the NCC's Committee on the Church and Economic Life sponsored a report on natural resources by the famous economist Kenneth Boulding in 1966.[7]

By the time of the first Earth Day in 1970, many congregations and individual members were involved with the budding environmental movement and were beginning to connect it to their religious lives. Activity also expanded considerably in the national mainline organizations. In 1972, some officials from U.S. mainline groups attended the seminal International Conference on the Human Environment in Stockholm. At home, influential publications like *The Limits to Growth* in 1972 inspired more Protestant leaders to focus attention on environmentalism.[8]

The most significant development in these years, however, was the creation and elaboration of the notion of "eco-justice" by early mainline environmental activists. This is significant because it shows how, from the very beginning, environmental concerns were connected with the traditional social justice (gender, race, economic justice) mission of the mainline churches. It also predates—by more than a decade—the widespread recognition within the secular environmental movement of the importance of highlighting justice connections. The term was initially offered as part of a strategic planning effort for the Board of National Ministries of the American Baptist Churches, which brought together a group of young, socially committed scholars and consultants, some of whom were inspired by their participation in the Stockholm summit. Discussions during this process kept returning to the important links between the ecological and justice goals of the National Ministries program—solving global environmental problems was necessary, but the standard solutions tended to affect the poor disproportionately. So the planning team developed a notion of "eco-justice" to guide their approach to these interrelated concerns. A program combining these goals was not without its critics, though. Some feared "eco-justice" would detract from the church's primary commitment to other forms of justice. But the promoters of eco-justice insisted the two missions were inseparable.[9]

This term stuck among mainliners and was soon adopted by many other churches attempting to make similar connections. Local eco-justice task forces emerged in religious communities around the country in the early 1970s. Eco-justice came to be defined broadly to include a call for solidarity with all creatures, sustainable lifestyles and development, a norm of "sufficiency" in consumption, participatory decision-making processes, and so on. While acknowledging the church's primary mission of social justice, the proponents of eco-justice sought to avoid making it into an "anthropocentric" argument for environmental protection. As Rev. Doug Hunt of the United Church of Christ Network for Environmental and Economic Responsibility explained in our interview, the goal was instead to expand the traditional justice mission "to all of God's creatures, the ones that breathe, and ones that don't. . . . They too, by dint of being created by God and declared good at the same time we were, deserve justice." Or as the Presbyterian Church's major study paper on eco-justice puts it, "The great new insight of our time is that nature has become co-victim with the poor, that the vulnerable earth and the vulnerable people are oppressed together. It has become necessary to understand justice as eco-justice."[10]

Contemporary mainline environmentalists recognize this early conceptual development of eco-justice as seminal, though it is largely unknown outside this community.[11] The term and the broad emphasis never caught on much beyond the religious community, despite some efforts to promote eco-justice to leaders of environmental organizations like the Wilderness Society. When similar connections between environmental problems and race and poverty issues were eventually brought to the fore of the secular environmental movement in the mid-1980s, the terms "environmental racism" and "environmental justice" were used, and the issues covered were more limited.

Early Program Development

The early eco-justice program development in U.S. denominations in the 1970s and early 1980s was influenced considerably by related programmatic developments in the World Council of Churches (WCC). The WCC adopted a program focus called "Just, Participatory, and Sustainable Society" in 1975 and became a prominent international advocate for connecting global ecological protection with social justice concerns—for example, justice for indigenous people, for poor countries, and for women. In 1983, the WCC World Assembly in Vancouver remodeled the program under the title "Justice, Peace, and the Integrity of Creation," highlighting more centrally the need for a theological basis for preserving "God's creation."

In the United States, the National Council of Churches was also becoming more vocal and active in environmental advocacy. A proponent of "safe energy" since the Eisenhower Administration, the NCC in the mid-1970s came out strongly against nuclear energy, especially after the Three Mile Island meltdown in 1979. They also focused considerable effort on educating members about alternative solutions to the "energy crisis." Then, another major environmental scandal, Love Canal, focused Protestant organizations on the health consequences of environmental hazards. Mainline environmental advocacy also addressed many international issues (e.g., deforestation, sustainable development) during these years, partly on the advice of returning missionaries. And in 1981, mainline denominations joined other environmental groups in fighting the appointment of James Watt as Reagan's Secretary of Interior, trying specifically to counter Watt's insistence that his Christian belief in the imminent Second Coming made environmental protection useless.

One area of particular focus for the NCC and its members in this period was the connection of environmental issues with hunger relief and poverty. Arguing that persistent hunger was not simply the result of insufficient agriculture and problems of drought, but also of a nonsustainable *lifestyle* by the most affluent people, a coalition of mainline Protestant staff coordinated their work in the 1970s and early 1980s as the "Responsible Lifestyle Task Force." This task force was reorganized in 1983 as the "Eco-Justice Working Group" of the NCC, which remains today the primary interdenominational Protestant group working on environmental issues.

Individual denominations were also developing their own programs on environmental issues during these years. They passed resolutions affirming a general commitment to environmental stewardship, and on specific environmental issues (e.g., energy, disposal of hazardous wastes). They occasionally engaged in direct legislative advocacy through their Washington offices. They convened eco-justice conferences for pastors and laity, and provided information and resources to member congregations. Along with the Baptists' National Ministries program on eco-justice, the Presbyterians were very active on a national level, establishing a Presbyterian Eco-Justice Task Force and hiring national environmental program staff.

The United Methodist Church had been addressing environmental and energy issues in some form since the early 1930s, and in 1972 the Methodists took the major step of adding the category called "The Natural World" to their "Social Principles," the core statements of belief for the denomination. The UMC also organized a Department of Environmental Justice and Survival in the DC office in 1980.[12] The Episcopal Church had a Task Force on Energy and Environment during the 1970s and 1980s, and Dean James Park Morton of the Cathedral of St. John the Divine promoted a number of "sacred ecology" programs there, inviting ecological thinkers like René Dubos and James Lovelock to give guest sermons.[13]

The Challenge of the Environmental Justice Movement

In the mid-1980s, however, the "discovery" of "environmental racism" and the development of a movement for "environmental justice" led to contentious changes in the secular environmental movement, and a mainline denomination was centrally involved in this discovery. This is perhaps the clearest example of Protestants having a direct and major impact on secular environmentalism or environmental policy. But as we will see, it did not result in Protestants becoming primary leaders in the secular environmental movement, or in their broad notion of eco-justice becoming widespread.

As the now well-known story goes, in 1982 the largely African American and low-income residents of Warren County, North Carolina, discovered that the state had targeted their community as a dumping site for a huge load of waste containing toxic PCBs, waste that officials had been unable to dump elsewhere. Community residents in Warren County began organizing themselves into a grassroots force opposing this environmental health hazard. They utilized their existing community institutions, such as their churches, and eventually enlisted the help of the United Church of Christ's (UCC) national Commission for Racial Justice, then directed by an activist with North Carolina ties, the Rev. Benjamin Chavis Jr. There were major protests later in 1982 with more than four hundred arrests, including that of Rev. Chavis. This major confrontation focused national attention on the problem of toxic waste sites' being placed predominantly in poor and minority communities—what came to be called, using a term coined by Chavis and the UCC commission staff, "environmental racism."[14] The UCC commission set up a Special Project on Toxic Injustice and launched a multiyear study that produced a now famous report in 1987, *Toxic Wastes and Race in the United States.*[15]

Following Warren County and the widely cited UCC report, grassroots activists fighting community toxic risks throughout the country—including Lois Gibbs, the mother who had organized in Love Canal—began to organize nationally under the general rubric of "environmental justice." The UCC commission was active in facilitating the early development of this movement by sponsoring the First National People of Color Environmental Leadership Summit in Washington, DC, in 1991. This summit is considered a seminal event and the "Principles of Environmental Justice" forged there have become the basic orienting guidelines for the movement. The first of these principles begins with the religiously flavored statement, "Environmental justice affirms the sacredness of Mother Earth." After this summit, the environmental justice movement began to establish itself as a nationwide movement, though they eschewed becoming national in the sense of having a centralized movement structure. They sought to coexist with, but also openly challenge, the mainstream environmental movement, which has always been overwhelmingly white and upper-middle-class.

Besides the UCC, other mainline groups were involved in the early stages of this new movement. Several passed resolutions on toxics and race in these years, and tried to encourage legislation on environmental racism. And the NCC's Eco-Justice Working Group, inspired by environmental justice organizing, underwent a major reorganization in 1988 to try to make itself more diverse—that is, to involve more people of color and more local community leaders. They also began close program collaborations with new groups such as the Southwest Organizing Project, a nationally known environmental justice group in New Mexico.

However, although the mainline environmentalists saw the new environmental justice movement as in line with their existing focus on eco-justice, the leaders of the new movement did not adopt the mainline's term or its generalized orientation, preferring instead to focus their efforts explicitly on "injustice" in terms of the distribution of toxic risks. The new movement is also clearly much more focused on grassroots organizing and local injustices than on global eco-justice issues or on developing a general conceptual grounding (e.g., the philosophy of justice for all creatures).

Over the years, though, the mainline denominations have for the most part eagerly welcomed and participated in the emergence of this promising new submovement. Mainline environmentalists have even come to use both terms, retaining "eco-justice" as a general term and using "environmental justice" as a more specific term. However, with the exception of the UCC Commission for Racial Justice, mainline groups are not considered primary leaders of the environmental justice movement.[16]

Program Expansion Amid Global Environmentalism

The emergence of environmental justice as a prominent submovement in the United States in the late 1980s and early 1990s coincided with a significant escalation of environmentalism into a truly global movement focused on global problems.[17] At the same time, all mainline denominations greatly expanded their environmental advocacy programs.

This period of expansion for both secular and faith-based environmentalism came as the stagnation of U.S. environmental policy under Reagan and Watt left the nation unprepared to respond to growing global environmental problems like depletion of the Amazonian rainforest. In 1988, *Time* magazine declared the "Man of the Year" to be the earth itself. In 1989, the world watched oil-drenched birds dying on television after the Exxon Valdez spill, and Pope John Paul II warned of an "ecological crisis." And in 1990, the movement made a media splash for the twentieth anniversary of Earth Day. At the same time, the United Nations Environment Programme began planning a major Earth Summit in Rio de Janeiro.

On the international stage, the World Council of Churches hosted a Conference on Creation Theology and Environmental Ethics in Annency, France, in 1988, and then convened a major ecumenical gathering, the World Convocation on Justice, Peace, and the Integrity of Creation in 1990 in Seoul. Building on the community formed at these events, the WCC organized a large delegation to go to Rio in 1992 for the historic United Nations Conference on Environment and Development—the Earth Summit. Several mainline groups in the United States sent large delegations to Rio, and these people participated in the NGO (Non-Governmental Organizations) Summit that stole some of the thunder from the main UN gathering. The WCC also called together a Working Group of Religious Communities at Rio that involved 176 people from 54 countries.[18]

Rio became a key rallying point for American mainline environmentalists who geared up their national programs just before 1992, and/or came back inspired to establish programs and work on a wider range of issues like global biodiversity. All U.S. mainline denominations expanded their environmental programs in the late 1980s and early 1990s. Several denominations passed major policy statements in these years, setting official policy on the theological basis for "caring for creation." They also passed numerous resolutions on a wide range of environmental issues (e.g., acid rain, biodiversity, water quality, air pollution, overpopulation, ozone depletion, etc.). Each denomination also committed additional resources for staffing, membership outreach and organizing, and national and global policy advocacy. These developments are reviewed briefly by denomination below.

- *American Baptist Churches:* The General Board approved a core statement, the "Policy Statement on Ecology: An Ecological Situational Analysis," in 1989. This focused the existing National Ministries eco-justice program (now combined with the racial justice program) on three goals—awareness and education, forming networks among ecologically committed members, and advocacy.

- *The Episcopal Church:* The General Convention in 1991 approved a statement of principles on environmental stewardship, created a new program that is now part of the Jubilee Ministries for Justice, Peace, and Integrity of Creation, and convened a national Environmental Stewardship Team involving networks of active members and clergy.

- *Evangelical Lutheran Church of America:* In 1992, a program area of environmental stewardship was added to the existing Hunger Education Program, and the Churchwide Assembly passed a Social Statement, "Caring for Creation: Vision, Hope and Justice," in 1993. The ELCA's combination of hunger and environmental programs has led them to a distinctive emphasis on issues such as community gardens.

- *The Presbyterian Church (USA):* The Presbyterian Eco-Justice Task Force and national environmental staff that was so active in the 1980s put together an influential resource paper called *Keeping and Healing the Creation* in 1989, which led the General Assembly to pass the official policy statement, "Restoring Creation for Ecology and Justice," in 1990. In 1994, a group of pro-environment Presbyterians formed a national volunteer fellowship called Presbyterians for Restoring Creation which now has about four hundred members.

- *United Church of Christ:* The staff of the Commission for Racial Justice continued to work on environmental racism throughout the 1990s. The UCC also maintained an ecological issues program and staff in the Office for Church in Society in Washington, DC, especially after the 1989 General Synod voted to make The Integrity of Creation, Justice, and Peace (ICJP) a priority for the church. The UCC Global Ministries program in New York hired staff to work on "integrity of creation" issues worldwide, and a national volunteer network, the Network for Environmental and Economic Responsibility (NEER), formed to do education and lobbying. However, the General

Synod eliminated ICJP as a priority in 1995, and the institutional focus has declined since.

- *The United Methodist Church:* The Department of Environmental Justice and Survival was expanded with new staff and renamed the Ministry of God's Creation. The Methodists also have staff who work partly on environmental issues in their Global Ministries and UN offices in New York. In addition, the Women's Division of the UMC created a separately funded and staffed Office of Environmental Justice in 1995, which brings women's perspectives into the UMC's environmental justice programs, educates women, and fosters more environmentally responsible institutional behavior.

The denominations continued to have constant contact with one another through the NCC's Eco-Justice Working Group. Starting in 1986, the Working Group provided the staff support for the Environmental Stewardship network of Interfaith IMPACT (until its dissolution in 1995), a group coordinating legislative advocacy in Washington, DC, by mainline groups. The Working Group also created a Public Policy Subcommittee in DC. This allowed them to divide up the work of staying on top of individual policy areas, allowing each denomination to put out statements and do advocacy on a range of environmental issues—they could take letters or action alerts written by other Working Group members and add language or doctrine from their own denominational policy statements. This coordinated policy advocacy also made it possible for the mainline to present a larger and more united public face on any particular environmental issue. The Eco-Justice Working Group also continued to publish educational and liturgical materials, often jointly written by Working Group members.[19]

A Major Ecumenical Initiative Seeks a Major Impact

As this program expansion occurred, some prominent religious leaders of many faiths were planning a major ecumenical program that would try to put faith-based environmentalism on the front page. This effort in turn provided a significant boost to mainline Protestant groups. Paul Gorman, an author, radio host, and staff member at the Episcopal Church's Cathedral of St. John the Divine, met Carl Sagan and then-Senator Al Gore at the Global Forum of Spiritual and Parliamentary Leaders in Moscow in January 1990. Gorman helped Sagan draft an "Open Letter to the Religious Community" from scientists, on the theme "Preserving and Cherishing the Earth." The letter, which was eventually signed by thirty-two leading scientists, including Stephen Jay Gould and E. O. Wilson, asserted that the environmental crisis "must be recognized from the outset as having a religious as well as a scientific dimension." Gorman set about encouraging an interfaith response from the religious community, and eventually 271 spiritual leaders from eighty-three nations signed a statement agreeing, "We believe the environmental crisis is intrinsically religious."

Inspired by this exchange, Gorman, with the help of Sagan, Gore, and others, spent the next two years raising money and gathering membership commitments for what came to be called the National Religious Partnership for the Environment (NRPE), announced officially in 1993 at the White House, with then–Vice President Gore presiding.[20] NRPE, with Gorman as director, is a partnership of four groups: the National Council of Churches of Christ USA, the Evangelical Environmental Network, the United States Catholic Conference, and the Coalition on the Environment and Jewish Life. With $4.5 million in foundation funding, NRPE set up staff in the national offices of each of these four groups, which for the Protestants meant that the NRPE began to provide funding for the staff and programs of the existing NCC Eco-Justice Working Group.

NRPE programs include developing or expanding a commitment to environmental goals in each faith group (including the explication of a theological rationale specific to each faith), bringing that message to seminaries and rabbinical colleges, providing materials and assistance to congregations, recognizing model congregations and promoting "covenant congregations," organizing regional trainings for clergy and lay people who want to start local projects, connecting religious leaders with environmental and scientific elites, and promoting the partnership's basic message publicly and broadly via a media campaign. But the ultimate goal of the NRPE, as Gorman said in our interview, is to "renew religious life itself." As they describe it on their website, "Care for creation must be integrated throughout religious life, must come to the heart of what it means to *be religious*. Once and for all."

The NRPE has been very effective at getting elite endorsement, media attention, and generous funding. They received more major funding in 1997 to work specifically on the connections of poverty and environmental problems, and have raised millions for other programs, which has definitely had a major impact on the NCC and mainline organizations. For example, NRPE allows mainline groups to send mass mailings to congregations to an extent that was not possible before this—for example, sending 70,000–80,000 study guides and worship plans to congregations for Earth Day every year. NRPE has also been effective at trumpeting a simple and consistent, but still substantive, message that has media appeal. In the beginning, for example, they sent a mailing to more than nine hundred publications and took out full-page ads in major newspapers proclaiming, "Environmentalism didn't start with Earth Day, it started in Genesis."

Finally, NRPE has clearly been effective at bringing elites from many fields together and maintaining contact with key governmental figures. The inaugural NRPE event in 1993 was a summit of black church leaders and secular environmentalists in Washington, DC, that addressed the problem of toxic waste risks in minority communities. NRPE also met with Secretary of the Interior Bruce Babbitt and others in 1995, which led to a "retreat" and consultation with senior administration leaders on spiritual and moral perspectives on the environment. Babbitt later began to talk frequently about personally coming to understand his own religious motivations for his environmental work, something that Gore also discussed in his book, *Earth in the Balance*. Gorman has also twice organized similar retreats for the leaders of major secular environmental organizations—the so-called Green Group coalition of twenty-eight national organizations. Most recently, the partnership organized a multiday "private summit" on global climate change issues that brought together people such as Monsanto chairman Robert Shapiro, AFL-CIO president John Sweeney, and Sheri Rowlands, the scientist who discovered the ozone hole.

Recent Campaigns and Issues—Mainline Protestants Seek a Major Impact

The promise of the newly expanded and officially sanctioned programs in the mainline denominations, combined with the momentum created by the National Religious Partnership for the Environment, has led mainline Protestants to seek a greater and more diverse public impact in recent years. They have sought to do this on specific national issue campaigns, as well as through increased network coordination and local grassroots contact.

One instance in which the mainline environmentalists appear to have successfully influenced a policy decision is their campaign to block proposed reforms in the Endangered Species Act (ESA) following the 1994 Republican Congressional victories. The 1994 elections brought in many of the proponents of the Contract with America who soon set about trying to eliminate or significantly curtail many national environmental regulations. Their first target was the ESA. Proposals for revising the ESA were introduced in 1995, and the debate over these intensified by early 1996 as the environmental movement mobilized to fight the changes. All sectors of the religious environmental community mobilized also. The mainline organizations developed their Earth Day mailing in 1995 on the theme of the Endangered Species Act, providing information for their members to hold worship and other meetings about the issue, and encouraging them to write letters to their Congresspersons and to lobby them on a local level. They also conducted training and mobilizing meetings in specific states in 1996, with funding from the NRPE and the National Environmental Trust. And the Washington office staff of the mainline groups met frequently with legislators and Hill staff.

The mainline's evangelical partners in the NRPE, the Evangelical Environmental Network, also launched a visible, million-dollar campaign to fight the proposed ESA rollback. The evangelicals focused in particular on making a biblical argument about the ESA as the "Noah's Ark of Our Day."[21] So there developed at the time somewhat unusual scenes of members of Congress asking aides to bring them their Bibles so they could have a theological debate with evangelical religious leaders over a scientifically based environmental law. The press took much note of this campaign. An ABC "World News Tonight" story mentioned that Newt Gingrich was getting letters from schoolchildren saying, "Dear Speaker Gingrich, I think people should protect the endangered animals because God made them."[22]

The ESA revisions were eventually tabled, to the delight of environmentalists, who acknowledged the key role mainline and evangelical groups played in the defeat (some Republicans acknowledged this also). The mainline staff I talked to firmly believe that their involvement was consequential, even though the evangelicals got most of the press coverage and were more public in their campaign. The mainliners feel they were perhaps more influential, but in a quieter way. For instance, the ABC news story on the evangelicals had mentioned that the schoolchildren's letters were the result of "educational kits" sent around the country; many if not most of these were sent by mainline organizations. Other mainline representatives believe their moderate voice was essential for getting many moderate legislators to oppose the ESA revisions. As Paz Artaza-Regan of the United Methodist Church explained in our interview,

> I felt pretty good after the Endangered Species work because we were told by the environmental community that it was the faith community's involvement that turned it around . . . because they [Congress] started hearing from a different constituency. It wasn't just what they called a lunatic fringe of an environmental movement calling for

a protecting of a species, but it was somebody who was calling saying, "Look, I'm a United Methodist. I'm a Presbyterian. I'm a Lutheran, and because of that, because of my faith understanding of creation and dominion and what we're here for, I cannot abide by you rolling back the Endangered Species Act."

The other major recent issue campaign of the mainline churches, on global warming, does not end with the same sort of overt evidence of success (or failure). But it does provide another good example of how the mainline community crafts a diverse campaign on a specific issue. Even though global warming, or "climate change," seems to be one of the more scientifically framed environmental problems—the "science of it" being the most common terrain for dispute—and even though it is controversial among many mainline congregation members (e.g., in coal-producing areas), religious environmental advocates have made this one of their primary issue areas.

The watershed event on the issue of global warming was a summit in Kyoto, Japan, in December 1997. The nations there, including the U.S. delegation led by Gore, designed the Kyoto Protocol that calls for greenhouse gas emission reductions in industrialized countries. As at Rio, an NGO summit was held concurrent with the Kyoto negotiations, and this included many religious leaders. The mainline contingent in Kyoto were very active in trying to persuade Gore to commit to the summit's goals, and as Jaydee Hansen of the United Methodist Church describes, they seemed to have an effect: "When we were in Kyoto at the climate conference, Gore told me, '[I]f it were not for the religious community pushing us, we would not be as far along in our position.' . . . And I don't think he was just being platitudinous." (Other interviewees doubted that Gore was influenced so much by the religious voice, in Kyoto or after.)

Since Kyoto, the U.S. mainline Protestant community has pushed for a more active U.S. response to the problem of global warming. Several members of the Eco-Justice Working Group sent a letter to Clinton in October, 1997. They sent action alerts to fifty thousand congregations to encourage letter-writing to pressure the administration, and they created a Climate Change Strategy Packet for organizers, which included a public service announcement video on religion and climate change narrated by Maya Angelou. In addition, the Working Group began a mobilization campaign targeting twelve key states that are major contributors to the emissions said to cause global warming, despite opposition from some local politicians and industry leaders.

Another way in which mainline Protestants have recently sought to make a greater public impact is through expanding their internal networks and encouraging action by individual congregations. As Richard Killmer, the director of environmental justice for the NCC, explained, they want to avoid just working on environmental policy in Washington and instead help eco-justice to "be plowed into the soil of church life." However, attempts to do this have not been as effective as leaders hoped.

The program expansions in each of the denominations, described earlier, included establishing networks of members who have an interest in environmental issues (the size of these networks ranges among the denominations from a few hundred to more than three thousand). Most denominations have also developed networks of designated coordinators at their regional or judicatory levels—for example, the Presbyterians' Restoring Creation Enablers, the Lutherans' Earthkeeping Network of Synods, and the Methodists' Environmental Justice Coordinators. With funding help from the NRPE, the NCC Eco-Justice Working Group created an Environmental Justice Covenant Congregation Program in which a congregation promises to promote certain "green" principles in its worship, teaching, and congregational operations. The Working Group also arranged special funding within the EPA's Energy Star program to support individual congregations that agree to make their operations more energy efficient—for example, by engaging in "environmental tithing," reducing a church's energy use and waste by 10 percent.

Current Programs

The basic structures of the current environmental advocacy programs in each mainline denomination are quite similar to one another. National program staff focus on "resourcing" congregations, producing materials on specific environmental issues, and building internal networks. Washington Office staff work closely with other Washington environmental groups to coordinate their advocacy efforts and lobby policymakers directly—for legal reasons they call this work "advocacy" rather than "lobbying." While there is great difference across denominations in the level of Washington staff commitment (half the denominations do not have environmental staff in Washington), there is more parity in the amount of national office staff.

Both of these levels of staff members work closely with their counterparts in other denominations via the NCC Eco-Justice Working Group or other interdenominational committees. However, *within* each denomination there is often little coordination between the national office staff and the Washington staff (except in those cases in which they are both located in Washington). As we saw, one way the staff people have dealt with this is to develop a number of different networks of members, but this can sometimes confuse or overburden the most interested members. However, even with these problems, the multilayered institutional (and inter-denominational) structure of the mainline groups is considered a primary source of strength for them.

Mainline environmental programs also have similar policy statements and issue emphases. The basic policy statements of all the denominations share similar (though not identical) language and theological arguments, and all the mainline denominations take similar positions on a wide variety of environmental issues.[23] The diversity of issues covered by each group is striking. For example, looking at an average issue (winter 1999) of the United Methodist Church's newsletter, *Environmental Justice News*, we find some coverage of the following issues or legislative concerns (this is a sample, not a complete list): consumption and lifestyle issues, ancient forests, clean air, clean water, endangered species, electric utility reform, climate change, Superfund, "right-to-know" laws, children's environmental health, urban sprawl, and "greening" hospitals.

ASSESSING THE IMPACT OF MAINLINE ENVIRONMENTAL ADVOCACY: HOW AND WHY

The rest of this chapter seeks deeper insight regarding how and why mainline Protestant organizations have (or have not) been influential on environmental issues. Judging the mainline's impact and effectiveness is tricky. Some instances described above reveal a clear impact—for example, the UCC's early leadership in the birth of the environmental justice movement, and the mainline groups' crucial role in blocking Endangered Species Act reforms. However, in most cases, the influence of mainline Protestant groups on environmental issues is more subtle or unclear. For example, it is difficult to measure the mainline's effectiveness in "raising awareness" of their members, or in convincing secular environmentalists to think of the environment as a religious issue. In the analysis here, I rely mostly on what the current mainline staff said in interviews about their distinctive impact.

"Quietly Influential" in Legislative and Policy Advocacy

Clear-cut legislative victories like the blockage of ESA reform are rare; in most cases the mainline groups have a more moderate and incremental influence on environmental legislation and other forms of policymaking.

In the words of current mainline Protestant staffers, they "can't march on Capitol Hill and say, 'This is what I want. Do it!' " but they can, in various ways, be "*quietly* influential." Mainline Protestant environmentalists feel their effectiveness on Capitol Hill or in agency offices depends on the legitimacy of their voice, legitimacy that they see as deriving from many different sources. First, the prophetic or moral authority of their religious message gives them legitimacy, allowing them to "affect the tone or the terms of legislative debate" as one person put it. Second, people listen to the mainline groups because they speak for (and can potentially mobilize or sway opinion among) the large groups of voters who sit in their pews.[24] In addition, the mainliners feel they have influence because they are seen as moderate voices for the environment compared to the secular environmental movement, and moderate voices on religion and values compared to the Religious Right. They are also more legitimate than other "special interests" like the industrial lobbyists against whom they often compete. Further, the fact that mainline groups are well-known, long-term fixtures in Washington gives them legitimacy. Politicians have been known to call mainline Washington offices to gauge potential "religious reaction" to an emerging environmental issue, and the UCC Commission for Racial Justice is consulted by regulatory agencies on environmental justice issues, because, as commission head Bernice Powell Jackson explains, "I don't think they have much choice but to seek out our voice . . . [b]ecause we've been seminal on environmental justice." Finally, mainline groups feel they gain legitimacy and potential power through the importance of certain elite members of their constituency whom they enlist to voice their message. Paz Artaza-Regan of the United Methodist Church describes their approach in a sample scenario: "The bishop is a good friend of a member of Congress? Well, perhaps a little chat with the bishop." She adds that this is a distinct advantage of mainline advocates: "This is the hierarchy that the evangelicals don't have." These multiple sources of legitimacy are not mutually exclusive, and the multiple sources are seen as a definite advantage.

While they often present their distinctively religious message on environmental issues, mainline environmental advocates do not just make this religious argument to legislators of their own faith. Like other advocates, they talk to whomever is strategically important. Still, they do often encourage their constituents to focus on the religious message primarily when contacting policymakers. Consider, for example, the instructions that Chris Walvoord of the Lutheran Office of Governmental Affairs gives to religious leaders from local congregations whom he brings in to lobby

Congress on global warming. He knows they might be challenged on the scientific questions, but says, "I always tell them, 'You are a religious leader first, and that's the argument you make first, that to whom much has been given, much will be required.' "[25]

The most time-honored currency for garnering legislative impact is, of course, a large number of voters—or, perhaps, a small number of very important voters. The mainline denominations are blessed with both large numbers and influential members, and they sometimes mention this in doing environmental advocacy. However, because of the nature of representation structures in the denominations, most mainline staff are quick to say they do not "represent" all members of the denomination, just the official positions of the church. But having a constituency is important, and mainline environmental leaders often use the tactic of mobilizing their constituency for direct advocacy, so that "*they* [constituents] become the advocates and *they* become the people [who] do the calls" or write the letters. The organizers believe this strategy worked well in the fight over the ESA, and even acknowledge that in pursuing this strategy they were trying to duplicate the direct constituency mobilization that worked so well for the Christian Coalition. Others have made this constituency approach a central principle of their advocacy for more than just strategic reasons. Pamela Sparr of the United Methodist Church's Women's Division says she sees her job as doing "advocacy *with*" rather than advocacy for people: "Our political position is that it's really important for affected people to speak for themselves when at all possible."

Raising Awareness and Having Local Impact

Given the history of debates over whether religion is good or bad for environmentalism, raising awareness on many levels—among the general public and media, among elites, among mainline Protestant members— has been a primary goal of faith-based environmental programs. The mainline Protestants lament that they are not as good at public relations and media solicitation as their Religious Right and evangelical counterparts. However, they have made some strides in this area recently, and they have also benefited from the media savvy and effectiveness of the ecumenical National Religious Partnership for the Environment. Also, both the NRPE and the mainline denominations specifically claim some success in influencing key elites, from politicians to secular environmentalists and major religious leaders who never thought of the environment as a religious issue before.

The mainline environmental advocates also seek, ultimately, "awareness" in a more ambitious sense: putting environmental concerns at the core of their denominations' social mission, and even transforming what it means to be religious. Environmental advocates in each denomination have succeeded in this to varying degrees during the program expansion years in the early 1990s, when their national assemblies made official commitments to environmental concerns. Gorman of the NRPE argues that most people are unaware of the potential for this environmental work to "renew religious life itself." He makes a bold prediction about the mainline Protestant environmentalists in particular: "When the history of twentieth-century mainline Protestant life is written, its prophetic recognition of environmental protection and care for creation as a fundamental religious mission will stand out as one of the hallmarks of the century's work."

The main element of this general task is to raise awareness at the level of lay members and congregations, and many interviewees felt they were good at this task.[26] They certainly produce and distribute thousands of educational guides and worship materials. Of course, there is little data on whether congregations actually use these materials, and so "success" in raising member awareness is hard to measure. We do get some useful data from the Presbyterian Panel survey conducted for this project, in which 27 percent of the sample of Presbyterian members reported having heard a sermon on environmental issues in the past twelve months, and 63 percent of clergy reported preaching one.[27] There is also plenty of anecdotal evidence of success in raising awareness. Pamela Sparr cites increased member awareness of local environmental problems: "A lot of our members . . . really are seeing the everyday impact of environmental problems in their lives, whether it's their landfill closing up, or somebody getting cancer, or kids that have asthma in part aggravated by air pollution. They're getting it."

Raising awareness at the local level is often cited as a key goal *because* those involved hope it will lead to local action. However, many interviewees confided that while they felt very effective at *educating* their congregations and members—and perhaps getting some individuals to contact their legislators or teach a Sunday School class on the environment—they were not very effective at this crucial next step of *mobilizing* congregations and stimulating sustained local action. As the NCC's Richard Killmer explains:

> We certainly are better able to do analysis of issues and write about
> issues because people who are in Washington have gotten very good at
> that. Getting that to be understood by the people in the pews and
> then getting the folks to do something about that is always a challenge.

. . . We all work at the question of making this real in congregations. But that's a continual struggle . . . and not a lot of people have written the Fred Astaire dance plan on that.

In short, mainline environmentalists feel they've been better at getting people to "think globally" than to "act locally."

Difficulty in achieving sustained "grassroots" impact is cited as the chief frustration by almost every mainline leader interviewed, even though many also designate this as their most important goal. They know what is going on at a local level—for example, congregations that have "adopted" local streams or organized opposition to proposed toxic dumps in their communities—and they do a good job at "resourcing people," but they constantly struggle with encouraging other congregations to start new programs. What makes this finding a bit surprising is that the extensive institutional structure and normalized channels of communication between national offices and local members are often identified as a distinctive advantage of the mainline Protestants, which would seem to encourage local action. However, there are many more organizational and cultural barriers to initiating and sustaining a local program than there are to distributing materials to a network of congregations, maintaining contact with existing programs, or encouraging the participation of the most interested members.

Of course, plenty of faith-based environmental activity already occurs at the local church level, so the problem for the national mainline organizations is often one of encouraging other churches to follow these good examples. In fact, Bill Knox of the Presbyterians for Restoring Creation network argues, "Most of the lay people are way ahead of the church. They're already involved in many other groups, like Sierra Club, Wildlife Federation, et cetera. . . . They can't understand why the church hasn't done more." To try to do more, many national staff people try to make use of these active local members, as a staff member of the Episcopal Church explains: "I believe there's a philosophy that what's happening at the congregation or the community level is where the expertise is. . . . The person sitting in the pew brings the passion to it. When somebody calls me and says, 'What is the Episcopal Church's position on sustainable agriculture?' I'll say, . . . 'If you want to know about the issue, let me refer you to Allison up in upstate New York, who's been working on this for the last twenty-five years.' " Nevertheless, as Owen Owens of the American Baptist Churches argues, the main problem is still generating interest where none currently exists. His response is to focus on what he's good at—education—and hope this serves as a "seed-planting ministry."

An additional hurdle to having local impact on these issues is that environmentalism is not always a popular agenda with some local members or congregations. The owners and employees of greenhouse-gas-producing factories are often also churchgoing Lutherans and Methodists. However, the national environmental staff people express surprisingly little concern over this conflict. In fact, many say they welcome it as a way to clarify the church's position, and perhaps even overcome some of the barriers to having more local impact—for example, by forcing them to have more in-depth meetings with local members. Still, many interviewees described getting angry letters and phone calls from their members, and they acknowledge that other members silently oppose the policies and just throw out the mailings they get on these issues.

The Benefits of Working Together and Having Structure

In the interviews, many mainline environmental leaders argued that a key reason for their effectiveness or influence was that they worked well together (ecumenically or interdenominationally), and they had an established institutional structure. In other words, they were often successful for exactly the same reasons that other organizers and environmental advocacy groups were successful—they built effective coalitions and set up solid organizational programs.

Many interviewees said working ecumenically or interdenominationally was *necessary*, given the scope and diversity of the environmental issues they want to address. By working together, they can divide up the labor somewhat—for example, one person in a coalition can "specialize" in biodiversity issues and another in clean water, and then they can share their expertise. What makes this cooperative work possible is that each denomination usually has no problem letting someone from another denomination, or even another faith, present the "religious perspective" on an issue in an advocacy forum like a congressional hearing. And presenting a united religious front can often have more impact.

Many environmental staff in the mainline organizations felt that each denomination's extensive institutional structure was also a benefit, even while acknowledging problems with this structure (noted earlier). For example, they felt they could mobilize members for a letter-writing campaign more effectively than most secular environmental organizations. However, even the denominations with the greatest number of national staff designated to work on environmental issues cited their lack of staff resources and internal funding as a major constraint on their work.

Relations with the Secular Environmental Movement

Environmental advocacy by the mainline community has certainly influenced the secular environmental movement in some specific ways (e.g., the UCC's role in starting the environmental justice submovement) but has also had more general influence. Paul Gorman of the NRPE sees the upsurge in religious environmental activity as having benefits for environmentalism as a whole: "A modest assessment is that I think that we helped really underscore in a certain sense, set in permanence, the *moral* consensus for environmental protection. . . . I think we helped move it [environmentalism] into the mainstream. I think we've helped contribute to the depth of it."

In many ways, the mainline Protestant environmental advocates are quite similar to their secular environmentalist counterparts. They focus on a wide range of similar issues, and they make many of the same arguments (e.g., sustainability, the inherent value of wilderness). Their organizational strengths and weaknesses are also similar—both secular (at least mainstream) and mainline Protestant environmentalists feel more adept at writing policy reports, distributing educational materials, and advocating in Washington than at mobilizing effectively at the grassroots level.[28] Still, the two communities have only recently begun cautiously to move from working together informally and individually to cooperating publicly and collectively.

Many mainline staff people mentioned specific ways that they were working closely with the environmental community, in Washington and in local communities. And they said some secular environmental groups—especially after recent legislative victories—now count religious environmentalists as strategic allies, even if they are still unsure how to "reach out" to religious groups. Doug Hunt of the UCC Network for Environmental and Economic Responsibility heralds the importance of this new relationship: "At critical times on critical issues, to have some of the major environmental groups come saying, 'We really need to have you on this because we don't think we can make it work without you.' That I consider a success story."

However, the two communities also keep their distance. Some secular environmentalists continue to blame strong Judeo-Christian beliefs for justifying human control of nature. On the other side, many people in the mainline denominations continue to think of environmentalism as too much worship of creation and not enough of Creator. Others wonder, as one interviewee quoted a constituent, "How come I never see any people on Sierra Club calendars?" When organizing NRPE, Paul Gorman encountered this hesitancy. But he also tried to *maintain* the distance because he wanted to highlight what the religious voice brings *to* environmentalism, and to avoid the perception that "the religious community was just kind of a constituency for rent, that they [environmentalists] were less interested in the teachings than the troops, the messages than the mailing lists."

Being a Prophetic Voice: Reframing Environmentalism as a Religious and a Justice Issue

What is perhaps most distinctive about mainline environmental advocates is their attempt to frame environmental issues in a religious way, their explicit desire to be a "prophetic" voice proclaiming the need to be good stewards of the earth because it is "God's creation." Rather than discussing these religious justifications only with other religious advocates, mainline environmentalists actively project this religious voice in various public arenas; and they believe it has been an effective advocacy approach at times. In addition, they have also tried to be prophetic in their efforts to reframe environmental concern as a justice issue.[29]

Framing environmental issues as religious issues is often done by simply taking a problem with how we are treating the earth and talking about it as a problem with how we treat "God's creation." For example, here's how one mainline newsletter on global warming described the preferred goal of a natural climate balance: "God created the world with a wonderful way of heating it."[30] At other times, the message is explicitly biblical. We find biblical references in congregational worship guides as well as in letters to politicians, such as one to President Clinton on global warming in which mainline leaders quote from Luke, "From everyone to whom much has been given, much will be required" (Luke 12:48) and urge the president, "We hope you will see climate change as a moral issue."[31] The specific biblical links made are very similar across denominations, such as references to passages in Genesis where creation was declared "good" (Genesis 1:31), and Christians are called to "keep" the earth (Genesis 2:15) and have a "covenant" with "every living creature" (Genesis 9:12).

The mainline advocates do not avoid making these religious or biblical arguments in secular political arenas; on the contrary, they feel this is often a way to be *more* effective at environmental policy advocacy. Job Ebenezer of the Evangelical Lutheran Church in America contends this was the case in the victory over ESA reform: "Many people actually were turned around by the biblical argument. I would say the Christian argument is much more powerful than the scientific one." Jaydee Hansen of the United Methodists thinks the religious argument often gets a politician's attention because that person is usually "motivated at some level by religious ideas."

Some mainline staffers suggest further that advocacy on environmental issues, *as compared* to other political issues, can be particularly enhanced by turning to religious arguments. Curtis Ramsey-Lucas, who deals with many different policy issues in the Baptists' Washington office, argues that the biblical connection is particularly important in environmental advocacy because it sets the religious voice apart *more* in that policy area than in others. And Richard Killmer of the NCC argues that, in environmental debates against large industries, showing that you are spiritually motivated and not concerned with your own self-interest means that you will always win any "public relations contest" because "the motivation's different."

Framing environmental issues as religious issues is also effective, mainline leaders claim, when trying to mobilize their membership on a local level. An organizer for the Episcopal Church says emphasizing religious arguments has strategic benefits in talking to members: "Once they see the connections with who they are as people of faith, then it's going to be a little bit easier to sell some of these specific issues. . . . I see it as an organizing strategy as much as anything." The other side of this coin is that these sorts of biblical arguments do not work in other arenas, especially when working with secular environmentalists. As Paz Artaza-Regan of the United Methodist Church says, "I don't think I would go to a secular group that's working on an environmental issue and start quoting the Bible. I don't think they would listen to me very long."

The other major way in which the mainline Protestant community seeks to be "prophetic" in environmental advocacy is in trying to frame environmental issues as fundamentally about justice. They identified "eco-justice" as their distinctive perspective on environmentalism early on, and they still see this as contributing to any influence they might have. Today, mainline Protestant environmentalists are still much more likely than their secular counterparts to talk about the justice connections. And they also still talk about "justice" in a very broad way. As Jaydee Hansen claims, what sets mainline environmentalists apart is, "We talk about *all* of our work being environmental justice work."

THE DISTINCTIVE CONTRIBUTION OF MAINLINE PROTESTANT ENVIRONMENTALISTS

This review and analysis of mainline Protestant environmental advocacy over the past three decades reveals the mainline's distinctive, if limited, influence on public debate, mobilization, and public policy. Mainline Protestant organizations have been much more active pro-environment advocates than previously acknowledged by scholars or most secular environmentalists. They have been "quietly influential" on a national scale, at times playing a key part in particular legislative decisions or specific mobilizations of the environmental community. They have made modest strides in raising awareness and in reframing environmental issues as religious issues and as issues of justice. However, they feel less successful in their ultimate goal of getting environmental concern "plowed into the soil of church life" on a local level.

Mainline Protestant environmental advocacy is, in one sense, very similar to secular environmental advocacy. Despite their religious orientation, mainliners have been just as strategic in their advocacy and organizing tactics as secular environmental groups. While they often speak with a religious voice, they have also made use of a similar range of other sources for legitimacy, emphasizing their large numbers or their lack of financial "special interest" taint. But in another sense, these faith-based environmental advocates have presented a distinctive case for environmental protection, and it is this distinctive perspective which might hold the most promise for their future influence on the environmental movement and policymaking.

The current state of environmentalism seems in need of a unifying substantive consensus or moral framework. The fights for local "environmental justice," and against "environmental racism," have fundamentally altered the landscape of issues addressed by environmental advocates, and have challenged the movement's traditional agenda as insufficiently focused on human and social injustice. The new challenges to free trade, corporate globalization, and traditional "development" programs for being environmentally destructive and bad for labor—exemplified in protests against the World Trade Organization—have prompted new attention to the overlap of economic justice problems with global ecological problems. Integrating and nurturing these energizing but independent new frontiers of environmentalism seems dependent on developing a broader justification and philosophical vision for the movement, one that will also allow environmentalism to partner more successfully with other progressive movements for justice.

As described in this chapter, mainline Protestant environmentalists have a long history of trying to develop such a broad, substantive moral framework for "eco-justice" work, to elaborate a philosophical (and theological) grounding for connecting environmental issues with social justice concerns. Though this broad conception of eco-justice has not been widely adopted, it could still become their major contribution to environmentalism in general. While an explicitly *religious* view of eco-justice might not be well received by secular environmentalists, an expansive philosophical and moral vision of eco-justice might now find a more receptive audience than it has in the past. Rather than feel frustrated over a lack of success at grassroots organizing—getting people to "act locally"—the mainline should consider embracing the "prophetic" role that they already feel is their relative strength—getting people to "think globally" about eco-justice.

NOTES

Thanks to Wendy Cadge, John Evans, Paul Lichterman, Robert Wuthnow, and two anonymous reviewers for terrific comments, and to the other contributors to this volume for their helpful suggestions. Also, thanks to the mainline staff who participated in the research, and especially those who passed on key materials or corrected confusing details.

1. Lynn White Jr., "The Historical Roots of Our Ecologic Crisis," *Science* 155 (March 1967): 1203–7.

2. Ibid., 1207.

3. According to religious environmentalists, Carl Pope, the executive director of the Sierra Club, recently apologized for this.

4. Interviews were conducted with sixteen individuals with between one and twenty-nine years' experience in mainline or other religious environmental work. Interviewees are designated here using their real names. Though given the option of being completely anonymous, all interviewees agreed instead to a modified "on-the-record" format in which they could designate specific comments as off-the-record and anonymous. Documents and materials from each organization included official statements and resolutions, lobbying letters, "action alerts," press releases, newsletters, and educational materials for congregations.

5. The approach of this study parallels other recent empirical analyses of environmental activists and how they understand and orient their work. See Paul Lichterman, *The Search for Political Community* (Cambridge: Cambridge University Press, 1996); and Nathan Teske, *Political Activists in America* (Cambridge: Cambridge University Press, 1997). This study also sees nonprofit organizations as strategic yet public-good-oriented players in public debate. See J. Craig Jenkins, "Nonprofit Organizations and Policy Advocacy," in *The Nonprofit Sector: A Research Handbook*, ed. Walter W. Powell (New Haven, CT: Yale University Press, 1987), 296–318; and Elizabeth Boris and Eugene Steuerle, eds., *Nonprofit and Gov-*

ernment: Collaboration and Conflict (Washington, DC: Urban Institute Press, 1998).

6. See René Dubos, *A God Within* (New York: Charles Scribner's Sons, 1972); E. F. Schumacher, *Small Is Beautiful: Economics as if People Mattered* (New York: Harper and Row, 1973); and Wendell Berry, *The Unsettling of America: Culture and Agriculture* (San Francisco: Sierra Club Books, 1977). I cannot deal here with the many issues in the "eco-theology" debate, except to list a few prominent voices that have emerged: Thomas Berry, Sallie McFague, Jay McDaniel, Dieter Hessel, James Nash, and Max Oelschlaeger. For a review, see Stephen Bede Scharper, *Redeeming the Time: A Political Theology of the Environment* (New York: Continuum, 1997). See also Dieter Hessel and Rosemary Radford Ruether, eds., *Christianity and Ecology: Seeking the Well-Being of Earth and Humans* (Cambridge, MA: Harvard University Press, 2000).

7. This period is reviewed in Roger Shinn, "Eco-Justice Themes in Christian Ethics Since the 1960s," in *For Creation's Sake: Preaching, Ecology, and Justice,* ed. Dieter Hessel (Philadelphia, PA: Geneva Press, 1985), 96–114.

8. Donella Meadows et al., *The Limits to Growth* (New York: Universe Books, 1972).

9. On eco-justice as a response to critiques by justice advocates, see Dieter Hessel, ed., *After Nature's Revolt: Eco-Justice and Theology* (Minneapolis, MN: Fortress, 1992).

10. Presbyterian Eco-Justice Task Force, *Keeping and Healing the Creation* (Louisville, KY: Committee on Social Witness Policy, Presbyterian Church [USA], 1989), 58–59.

11. For example, Mark Dowie's recent history of the environmental movement applauds Protestant organizing in the last few years and notes, "American Baptists . . . recently declared that ecology and justice are inseparable." In fact, they declared this in 1972; see Dowie, *Losing Ground: American Environmentalism at the Close of the Twentieth Century* (Cambridge, MA: MIT Press, 1995), 232.

12. The Washington offices of other denominations, like the UCC, also addressed environmental issues occasionally. See Paul J. Weber and W. Landis Jones, *U.S. Religious Interest Groups: Institutional Profiles* (Westport, CT: Greenwood Press, 1994).

13. For a recent collection of such sermons, see Jeffrey Golliher and William Bryant Logan, eds., *Crisis and the Renewal of Creation: Church and World in the Age of Ecology* (New York: Continuum and the Cathedral of St. John the Divine, 1996).

14. For descriptions of the movement, see Richard Hofrichter, ed., *Toxic Struggles: The Theory and Practice of Environmental Justice* (Philadelphia, PA: New Society Publishers, 1993); and Robert Bullard, *Dumping in Dixie: Race, Class, and Environmental Quality* (Boulder, CO: Westview Press, 1990).

15. Commission for Racial Justice, *Toxic Wastes and Race in the United States: A National Report on the Racial and Socioeconomic Characteristics of Communities with Hazardous Waste Sites* (New York: United Church of Christ, 1987).

16. While the UCC commission is still a major player, it is no longer the primary organizational locus, as it was in the beginning; there really is no such locus.

17. See Dowie, *Losing Ground;* and Philip Shabecoff, *A Fierce Green Fire: The American Environmental Movement* (New York: Hill and Wang, 1993).

18. A few American mainline representatives continue to participate in the NGO Steering Committee at the UN Commission on Sustainable Development,

and others are active in the Religious Working Group on the IMF and World Bank.

19. For one example, see Shantilal Bhagat, ed., *God's Earth Our Home* (New York: National Council of Churches of Christ in the USA, 1994).

20. Gorman also helped Gore with the spiritualism chapter in the book he was writing at the time; see Al Gore, *Earth in the Balance: Ecology and the Human Spirit* (Boston: Houghton Mifflin, 1992).

21. Bill Broadway, "Tending God's Garden: Evangelical Group Embraces Environment," *Washington Post*, February 17, 1996, C8.

22. American Broadcasting Companies, Inc., "Evangelical Environmentalists," ABC *World News Tonight*, January 31, 1996, Transcript #6022–5.

23. These mainline programs also draw information and guidance from a growing number of other religious environmental programs, such as the Black Church Environmental Justice Program and Theological Education to Meet the Environmental Challenge.

24. This finding seems to support both sides of a debate in the scholarly literature on religious lobbying. While Hertzke emphasizes that religious lobbyists get their legitimacy primarily from their representation of members, Hofrenning argues that religious lobbyists are influential as "prophetic" voices for moral positions. See Allen Herztke, *Representing God in Washington: The Role of Religious Lobbies in the American Polity* (Knoxville: University of Tennessee Press, 1988); and Daniel J. B. Hofrenning, *In Washington but Not of It: The Prophetic Politics of Religious Lobbyists* (Philadelphia, PA: Temple University Press, 1995).

25. This last phrase is clearly meant as a paraphrase of the famous passage from Luke 12:48, "From everyone to whom much has been given, much will be required."

26. Members appear to want the national offices to continue to focus on this function. Choosing from a list of fifteen possible tasks that the Presbyterian Church environmental program might be involved in, a sample of Presbyterian members, elders, and pastors all indicated "providing educational materials" was the most important; see Presbyterian Church (USA), "The Public Role of Presbyterians," *Presbyterian Panel Report* (August 1999): A-18.

27. Ibid., A-1.

28. On secular environmental groups, see Riley Dunlap and Angela Mertig, eds., *American Environmentalism: The U.S. Environmental Movement, 1970– 1990* (Washington, DC: Taylor and Francis, 1992). On the shift to this national "advocacy" focus among all groups in American civil society, see Jeffrey Berry, *The Interest Group Society*, 3rd ed. (New York: Addison Wesley Longman, 1996); and Theda Skocpol and Morris Fiorina, eds., *Civic Engagement in American Democracy* (Washington, DC: Brookings Institution Press, 1999).

29. Social movement scholars have recently focused more attention on this sort of strategic "framing" of movement messages. For a review, see James Jasper, *The Art of Moral Protest* (Chicago: University of Chicago Press, 1997).

30. Eco-Justice Working Group, "Climate Change," *Environmental Justice Notes* 2 (summer, 1997): 1.

31. Letter dated October 10, 1997.

10 Vital Conflicts
The Mainline Denominations
Debate Homosexuality
Wendy Cadge

INTRODUCTION

For the past thirty years, the mainline churches have been thinking about, talking about, and quite often arguing about homosexuality. In the past ten years, the debates have increased in intensity and been broadcast on the front pages of religious and secular newspapers across the country. The upswing in mainline churches' activities around homosexuality come at a time when Americans' attitudes toward homosexuality are gradually softening.[1] While 67 percent of people in 1976 believed sexual relations between people of the same sex were always wrong, only 56 percent of people in 1996 agreed, and aside from their opinions about the morality of homosexual behavior, increasing numbers of Americans support the civil rights of homosexual people.[2]

Homosexuality is a controversial issue for mainline members, ministers, and denominational leaders in part because it is a prism through which all of the denominations' central questions and issues can be seen to reflect and refract. For these reasons, participants see a lot at stake in these discussions and debates. Homosexuality is about Scripture: How is the Bible to be read, interpreted, and understood? It is about creation: How are the people that God creates intended to behave sexually? It is about families and reproduction: Who can be married? bear children? adopt children? raise children? What should those children be taught about sexual behavior? Homosexuality also raises important questions about who can serve the church and how those people and the church are to act in the world. In their struggles and debates around all of these questions, the mainline churches have added and continue to add a range of voices and perspectives to public dialogues about homosexuality occurring in society at large.

This chapter describes discussions and debates about homosexuality that have occurred since 1970 in the United Church of Christ, United Methodist Church, Presbyterian Church USA, Evangelical Lutheran Church in America, Episcopal Church, and American Baptist Church. This research is based primarily on the policies, reports, studies, and church court cases of the mainline churches and related special-interest groups as well as on interviews with relevant leaders. The issue of homosexuality has caused a great deal of pain for many people inside and outside of the mainline churches: gay and lesbian clergy have lost their jobs or not been ordained, congregations have divided, and countless hours have been spent in civil and not-so-civil debate. While I acknowledge the "dark," or conflictual, side of the homosexuality issue, I disagree with those who see the issue as a sign of mainline churches' weaknesses or who believe that the churches are spending an unnecessary amount of time on the subject. Rather, I argue in this chapter that the mainline churches have been successful in their struggles with homosexuality not in their resolution of the issue—it has by no means been resolved—but in their continued commitment to be in dialogue and debate about the topic. These ten- to thirty-year-old discussions are the marks of vital denominations comprised of people who are strongly committed to their churches and to ongoing, often difficult, conversations about homosexuality.

The first half of this chapter describes mainline churches' actions concerning homosexuality since they first addressed the issue in the early 1970s. In the second half, I argue that the mainline churches have added their voices to more public debates about homosexuality in two important ways. First, mainline churches have provided forums in congregations and in denominational meetings in which public discussions about homosexuality can occur. Indeed, the mainline churches are one of few places that Americans not actively involved with gay or ex-gay organizations can meet and talk about homosexuality. Second, by recognizing the issue, the mainline churches have opened up discussions about homosexuality to a broader range of the U.S. population and granted legitimacy to all sides of the debate. As sociologist Robert Bellah points out, the "public church" has almost never spoken with a single voice, but this has not diminished "its significance in our common life."[3] By speaking about homosexuality with a plurality of voices, the mainline churches have added substantially to public dialogue and conversation about the issue for the past thirty years.

HISTORY

Before 1970, leaders of mainline churches had started to talk about homosexuality, but no formal policies on the subject had been proposed or passed by national denominational bodies. The first religiously oriented group organized around homosexuality, the San Francisco Council on Religion and Homosexuality, was formed in 1964 to work for social justice for homosexuals. After their first event, a New Year's Eve dance for the gay community, the council ended up in court, protesting the arrest of four people at the dance and the intimidation tactics used by police at the event. This was a significant moment in gay history, historian John D'Emilio argues, because the clergy presence "provided a legitimacy to the charges of police harassment that the word of a homosexual lacked."[4] Additional chapters of the council were later started in Dallas, Los Angeles, Washington, and Seattle and held symposia that formed an important backdrop to the mainline churches' first discussions about homosexuality.

Mainline church activity increased after the watershed events at Stonewall in 1969. Stonewall, a gay bar in the heart of New York City's Greenwich Village, was raided often by police, but on June 27, 1969, gay patrons fought back. The resulting riots are typically considered to mark the beginning of the gay liberation movement in the United States. The United Church of Christ had actually begun to think about homosexuality several years before Stonewall and had devoted the December 1967 issue of a denominational magazine to the civil liberties of homosexuals.[5] In 1969, the United Church of Christ's Council for Christian Social Action passed the first formal statement from a mainline denomination on homosexuality. This policy opposed all laws that made private homosexual relations between consenting adults a crime and opposed "the total exclusion of homosexuals from public employment and from enlistment and induction into the armed forces."[6] The policy compared homosexuals to other minority groups to argue the "time is long overdue for our churches to be enlisted in the cause of justice and compassion for homosexual persons."[7]

Other mainline churches made their first statements about homosexuality in the early 1970s.[8] These statements largely condemned homosexual behaviors while supporting the civil rights of gay and lesbian people. The statements called homosexuality "biblically . . . a departure from the heterosexual structure of God's Creation," "a sin," and "incompatible with Christian teaching."[9] However, they simultaneously viewed the "sexual behavior of consenting adults" as "not an appropriate subject for legislation or police action."[10] National studies about homosexuality followed these initial statements that were designed to begin dialogue in the denominations and local congregations about the history and background of homosexuality. The Episcopal Church made its first statement about homosexuality in 1976.[11] Rather than focusing on homosexuality as the other denominations had, the General Convention of the Episcopal Church focused on homosexuals, calling them children of God. The General Convention also made a statement in support of the civil rights of homosexual people and developed a plan to study human sexuality broadly.

Discussion and debate about gay ordination also started in the early 1970s in mainline churches. Some denominations continued to ordain gay people, while others codified policies that forbid the ordination of homosexuals. Bill Johnson became the first openly gay man to be ordained in a mainline church in 1972 when he received his ordination credentials from the United Church of Christ. A known lesbian was ordained in the Episcopal Church in 1975, though two years later the Executive Council of the Episcopal Church released a strong statement against homosexual ordination.[12] In 1975, Bill Silver presented himself as the first openly gay Presbyterian candidate for ministry and was turned down. But in 1978, the Presbyterian task force that was charged in 1976 with studying homosexuality reported that homosexuality should not be a bar to ordination. Quickly contradicting the task force, the General Assembly of the Presbyterian Church concluded that "homosexuality is not God's wish for humanity and homosexual practice does not accord with requisites for ordination."[13] Mainline leaders who opposed gay ordination generally called on biblical references to the men of Sodom, the Levitical rule, and the creation accounts to claim that Scripture directly and obviously condemned homosexual behaviors. While not denying the presence of these texts, clergy and laity who supported gay ordination tended to argue for a different approach to Scripture.

As the debates about homosexuality got under way in the mainline churches' national bodies, activities around the issue started appearing at the grassroots. First on the scene were support groups for gay men and lesbians who belonged to mainline churches. United Church of Christ minister Bill Johnson started the UCC Gay Caucus in 1972 to provide support to gay and lesbian members of his denomination. In 1974, Rev. David Baily Sindt founded Presbyterians for Lesbian and Gay Concerns, and Louie Crew started a newsletter, *Integrity*, that by 1976 had evolved into a 1,200-member grassroots group for gay and lesbian Episcopalians by the same name. While these groups initially focused on supporting people at the grassroots, several began to lobby national denominational bodies to change their policies in the 1980s.

Also at the grassroots, Rev. Robert Davidson, a minister at West Park Presbyterian Church in New York City, wrote a statement of conscience in 1978 that was the first step toward a network of congregations that identified themselves as formally welcoming gay and lesbian people into their churches. Rev. Davidson's central idea was that congregations who disagreed with statements or actions their denominations made around homosexuality should say so, publicly, and welcome gay men and lesbians into their congregations. While the mainline churches have never suggested excluding homosexuals from their congregations, proponents of these "More Light," or homosexual welcoming, congregations argue that policies that call homosexuality incompatible with Christian teaching do effectively exclude homosexuals.

By the end of the 1970s, all of the mainline churches except the American Baptists had made a formal denominational statement about homosexuality. The Lutheran Church in America (a forerunner to the Evangelical Lutheran Church in America), Presbyterian, and United Methodist denominations opposed homosexual behaviors based on scriptural evidence but supported the civil rights of gay men and lesbians. The majority of Episcopal leaders also opposed homosexual behavior, though there were enough who did support it to draft a 1979 dissent statement. The United Church of Christ, on the other hand, did not oppose homosexual behavior and actively supported the ordination of gay men and lesbians. Grassroots activities in support of gay men and lesbians had started and gained momentum and membership throughout the decade.

Denominational studies on homosexuality and debates about gay ordination continued into the 1980s. The Episcopal Church called for three years of study and reflection about homosexuality in 1985, declared in 1988 that no dialogue had occurred, and called for another attempt at conversation, this time specifically with the gay and lesbian members of Integrity. The United Methodist General Conference and Evangelical Lutheran Church of America both initiated their first studies of homosexuality in 1988, and the Presbyterian General Assembly commissioned its second study of human sexuality in 1987. Episcopal bishops in certain dioceses continued to quietly ordain homosexual people throughout the 1980s, while the United Methodist Book of Discipline was amended in 1984 to outlaw gay ordination, and the Presbyterian General Assembly declared definitively in 1985 (by reaffirming their decision from 1978) that homosexual people could not be ordained as clergy.[14] At least partially because of the growth of "More Light" or "welcoming" congregations, mainline national church courts saw their first cases related to homosexuality in the mid-1980s.

In addition to addressing their internal issues, several mainline denominations made statements in their national meetings about secular gay and lesbian topics throughout the 1980s. The Episcopal General Convention reaffirmed its previous support for gay and lesbian civil rights in 1982 and expressed support for hate crime legislation at the General Convention in 1988.[15] The United Church of Christ approved resolutions in its national governing body that rejected "institutionalized homophobia" (1983), supported gay and lesbian families (1983), supported privacy (1987), and brought attention to violence against homosexuals in American society (1989).[16] The Presbyterian General Assembly supported the repeal of remaining sodomy laws.[17] The Presbyterian Church and the United Church of Christ's Office of Church and Society jointly filed an *amicus curiae*, or "friend of the court," brief in the 1985 Supreme Court case, *Bowers v. Hardwick*, in support of Mr. Hardwick, based on previous denominational statements that viewed private, consensual sexual behavior as an inappropriate subject for state legislation.[18]

Grassroots support for gay men and lesbians in mainline denominations increased significantly in the 1980s. Following the design of the Presbyterian More Light Churches network, congregational programs in support of gay men and lesbians were started in three other denominations: United Methodist Reconciling Congregation Program (1984), Evangelical Lutheran Reconciling in Christ Program (1984), and United Church of Christ Open and Affirming Congregation Program (1986). Mark Bowman, the founder of the United Methodist Reconciling Congregation program, explains that the programs' main emphases were to shift the focus of discussion in the mainline away from morality toward ministry. Morality questions focus on what the Bible says about homosexuality and about whether individuals can be both gay and Christian. Ministry questions emphasize the question, "Can you be a Christian and exclude people from your church?" This shift in emphasis has also personalized questions about homosexuality.[19]

Toward the end of the 1980s, a new focus emerged in certain quarters: that of forming support organizations for people known as ex-gays, or former homosexuals, people who previously understood themselves to be homosexual but now believe themselves to be heterosexual. This trend started in 1988 with the beginning of the Transforming Congregation program in the United Methodist Church. Born at a retreat held by the Evangelical Renewal Fellowship of the California-Nevada Annual Conference, this group was formed to provide "information, resources, and training to churches, districts, and annual conferences in understanding and involvement in a ministry of transformation of homosexuals."[20] By "transformation" this group means that it provides support, in congregations and small groups, for ex-gays. Some of these people say they have come to understand themselves as heterosexuals through the intervention of God's love, while others have come to the church after their struggles with homosexuality. Similar groups for former homosexuals, like Exodus International and Homosexuals Anonymous, exist in wider society. Interestingly, the Transforming Congregation program was modeled organizationally after gay-supporting, welcoming congregation programs.

Discussions about homosexuality in national denominational meetings and at the grassroots increased dramatically in the 1990s in every denomination as a result of changing public opinion on the issue and the extent of gay-related religious activities at the grassroots. The American Baptist Churches entered the fray for the first time with a formal denominational statement on the subject in 1992: "We affirm that the practice of homosexuality is incompatible with Christian teaching."[21] The General Board voted for dialogue and prayer on issues of human sexuality in 1993 and, after several American Baptist churches were disfellowshipped or kicked out of their regional denominational bodies for publicly welcoming homosexual people, the denomination began talking more vigorously about how to disagree.[22] The United Methodists and Presbyterians (1991) read and discussed their studies about homosexuality and human sexuality respectively in the early 1990s, and the United Methodists added a stronger principle of support for gay and lesbian people to their Social Principles (1992). The Evangelical Lutheran Church in America (ELCA) drafted a social statement about human sexuality in the 1990s. After receiving twenty thousand pieces of mail from church members across the country in response to their first draft, the denomination encouraged church members to deliberate about homosexuality while examining their own attitudes about human sexuality. In 1995 the ELCA started to develop materials about how to disagree about homosexuality as a denomination, and in 1996 they adopted a Social Message on sexuality that said very little about homosexuality.[23] More dialogue about homosexuality occurred in the Episcopal Church in the early 1990s. The General Convention amended the canons of the church in 1994 to ensure non-discrimination on the basis of sexual orientation in access to ordination, and a liturgical commission began to study what forms the blessings of lesbian and gay relationships could take. The General Convention formally apologized to gays and lesbians, inside and outside of the church, in 1997 for "years of rejection and maltreatment by the church."[24]

Dialogues and debates about gay ordination also heated up in each of the mainline denominations during the 1990s. By the end of the decade, homosexual people could be and were being ordained in the United Church of Christ and Episcopal denominations. In a widely publicized church court trial, retired Episcopal Bishop Walter Righter was brought to trial and acquitted on charges of ordaining a gay man who was living in a homosexual relationship.[25] The Presbyterians and Lutherans had no such firm position, and they vigorously debated, throughout the decade, whether gay men and lesbians should be ordained. After stating that ministers who are gay are expected to refrain from sexual activity (1990) and removing several gay pastors from the clerical roster (1994), the Lutherans decided definitively in 1997 that "homosexuals are precluded from the ordained ministry of the church."[26] The Presbyterians engaged in the most public discussion about gay ordination through public debate and voting on two amendments (amendment A and amendment B) in their local congregations and presbyteries. At the end of the decade, amendment B, which forbids gay ordination, remained in the constitution, and the General Assembly declared a sabbatical on the issue. The United Methodists' ban on gay ordination (from 1984) was upheld throughout the decade, in spite of sustained discussion and debate about the subject. Ordination in the American Baptist Churches occurs at the congregational level, making it difficult to generalize about their practices. While some gay American Baptists have been ordained in the past and a few were working through the ordination ranks in the 1990s, few were called to serve the American Baptist Churches during the decade.

Commitment ceremonies or marriages between people of the same sex were also the topic of much controversy in the mainline denominations in the 1990s. As they did with regard to questions about ordination, supporters of the ceremonies tended to argue that, through their position, they were rejecting selective use of the Scriptures and acting out God's Word in the world. They emphasized their commitments to their congregations and what those commitments required them to do to be faithful to their denominations. Opponents argued that homosexual behaviors are forbidden on scriptural grounds and that clergy who perform commitment ceremonies are defying the rules of their denominations. Commitment ceremonies were performed by some United Church of Christ clergy in church buildings throughout the decade. The United Church of Christ Board for Homeland Ministries supported equal marriage rights for same-gender couples in 1996 and declared in 1997 that fidelity and integrity in marriage were the standards for all people. The Episcopal General Convention recognized heterosexual marriage as well as "people living in other arrangements" in 1991, and in 1994 began to study the "theological foundations and pastoral considerations involved in the development of rites honoring love and commitment between persons of the same sex."[27] In 2000 the Episcopalians narrowly rejected a plan to develop rites recognizing same-sex couples but approved a resolution to minister to same-sex couples. Discussions about gay marriage in the Evangelical Lutheran Church of America started in some regions in the 1990s but were not addressed by the national body. The General Assembly of the Presbyterian Church stated in 1991 that gay marriage was not forbidden. This decision was justified in 1994 by the argument that decisions about marriage should remain with the regional presbytery rather than be the subject of national policy. In 2000, however, the Presbyterian General Assembly narrowly approved a ban on same-sex ceremonies that now must be ratified by the church's presbyteries or regional units in order to become church law.

Debates about gay marriage in the 1990s focused largely on the United Methodists because of ambiguity in denominational policy early in the decade and well-organized support for gays and lesbians at the grassroots. Denominational policy on the subject was clarified after Rev. Jimmy Creech was tried in church court in 1998 for marrying a lesbian couple inside his church building. Creech was found not guilty of violating denominational policy on a rather technical issue: the extent to which the policy was binding to local congregations (rather than intended simply to guide local churches) was ambiguous. The implications of the policy were quickly clarified, however, to affirm that the statement in the 1996 Discipline that "homosexual unions shall not be conducted by our ministers or in our churches" was church law and that those who violate this new church law are liable to be brought to church court.[28] Rev. Greg Dell was found guilty of violating this new, clear church law in March 1999 and lost his ministerial credentials for one year. In January 1999, 150 United Methodist clergy officiated jointly at a lesbian wedding in California to challenge this new denominational policy. Charges against 68 of these clergy were filed and then dropped on the grounds that the complaints brought against the clergy were not proper for trial.

Mainline denominations also took public positions about secular gay issues in the 1990s through denominational statements, the actions of their

Washington offices, and by signing *amicus curiae* briefs in state and federal court cases. With the exception of the American Baptists, each denomination had passed a resolution by the early 1990s in support of full civil rights for lesbians and gays. The Episcopal General Convention approved a resolution in 1991 that called on the denomination's Washington, DC, office to work in support of all gay- and lesbian-related legislation, especially in the areas of health, home, and work. The Episcopal Washington, DC, office did just that in 1996 and 1998, joining the Washington offices of the Evangelical Lutheran Church in America, the Presbyterian Church, the United Church of Christ, and the United Methodist Church in their support of the Employment Non-Discrimination Act, an (unsuccessful) federal attempt to add sexual orientation to the list of characteristics employers may not consider in decisions about hiring and firing. Each of the mainline denominations' Washington offices also supported hate crimes legislation in 1997 and 1998. The United Church of Christ Office for Church and Society also worked in support of gays in the military in 1993, and Rev. Paul Sherry, president of the United Church of Christ, testified before the Armed Services Committee in 1994 arguing that the ban on gays in the military should be lifted. The mainline denominations, most especially the Presbyterians, also filed several *amicus curiae* briefs during the 1990s on the gay-supportive side of federal and state court cases based on statements the national denominational body had previously made about homosexuality.[29]

Grassroots activities on all sides of the homosexuality issue continued to increase throughout the 1990s. Much of the dialogue in support of gay ordination and gay marriage that occurred at national denominational meetings was initiated, led, or supported by members of gay-supportive organizations at the grassroots. Welcoming congregation programs in all of the mainline denominations continued to grow throughout the decade and included more than eight hundred total congregations in forty-five states by the summer of 2000. An ecumenical welcoming congregation movement also developed in the 1990s, and members met at a series of national welcoming congregation meetings and conferences.[30] Additional grassroots organizations, such as That All May Freely Serve (PCUSA) and the Extraordinary Candidate program (ELCA), started to promote gay ordination in their denominations by trying to find ways homosexual people could be ordained.

In response to grassroots gains made in the 1980s by gay mainliners and their advocates, grassroots activities by people opposed to homosexual behavior developed in the 1990s. The United Methodist Transforming

Congregation program, which started in 1988, included seventy-six congregations by the summer of 2000. This program was joined in the early 1990s by a Presbyterian program, One by One. Rather than focusing on congregations, One by One focused primarily on individuals. In addition to distributing educational materials and participating in denominational discussions, this group ministered to victims of sexual abuse and people who felt their sexual orientation had changed from homosexual to heterosexual.[31] Support groups for those who identify as former homosexuals were also organized in the late 1990s by members of Episcopal and Lutheran congregations in some regions of the United States.

Despite the increase in grassroots activities and public debate during the 1990s, bear in mind that the majority of mainline members have not belonged and do not belong to groups on either side of the homosexuality issue. The majority of mainline members are probably in what is sometimes called the loyal middle. What this group believes about homosexuality is not clear. The point is that this middle group is hard to mobilize and tends not to take positions until the churches are in crisis. Once in crisis, as during the debates about homosexual ordination in the Presbyterian Church, the loyal middle tends toward conservative positions that favor the church "as it is" and do not provoke change.[32]

THE PUBLIC IMPACT

In the process of struggling with their internal issues over homosexuality since the early 1970s, the mainline churches have, directly and indirectly, contributed to wider public debates about homosexuality. The second half of this chapter argues that, while the process has been painful and difficult at times, the mainline churches have contributed to wider public debates about homosexuality by providing forums in which conversations about homosexuality could occur and by recognizing and legitimating positions on all sides of the issue. The effects or results of the mainline churches' direct and indirect participation in wider societal debates are considered in this chapter's conclusion.

First, we need to consider briefly what the mainline churches' discussions and debates about homosexuality indicate about the mainline denominations more generally. The groundswell of activity around homosexuality shows primarily that the denominations are not dead or deteriorating institutions but are vital organizations grappling with current issues. Rather than leaving the churches when this debate started, many people demonstrated the depth of their commitment to the churches and to the issue by digging in for the fight. While some people have undoubtedly left mainline churches because of this issue, many did stay and became vigorous participants in the debate.

The rapidity with which groups related to homosexuality and congregational networks supportive of gay and lesbian people developed at the grassroots level is the most convincing evidence for this argument. There are currently more than fifty such organizations in the mainline, most supported not by the denomination but through small grants, membership dues, and voluntary contributions from the members themselves. Some, but not all, of the people involved with these groups are gays and lesbians who, despite mainline churches' policies, have not left their institutional homes. The fact that many gay and lesbian people have decided to stay in mainline churches to work for change, rather than leave, is one reason some straight mainline advocates give for their commitment to gay-supportive grassroots groups and the broader cause.[33]

The public activities of some of these grassroots groups and of the many gay-supporting congregations further illustrate how energized many clergy and laity are around the homosexuality issue. In addition to the public positions some congregations have taken on homosexuality, congregations are active in other ways. Some congregations and grassroots groups march in local gay and lesbian pride parades or send contingents to national gay and lesbian gatherings. Some congregations show their support for gays and lesbians by putting rainbow flags in their sanctuaries or the emblem of their welcoming congregation program on their church bulletins. Others have hosted the "shower of stoles project," a collection of about four hundred liturgical stoles from lesbian, bisexual, transgender, and gay people of faith who have been barred from serving their churches or religious communities because of their sexual orientation.[34] Some congregations host secular gay and lesbian groups or AIDS organizations in their buildings, while others host support groups for ex-gays and their families.

Mainline actions around homosexuality also illustrate localism, that is, the extent to which geographic location and other factors influence a congregation's position about homosexuality. Rather than denominational policy influencing the behavior of all United Methodist congregations equally, for example, other local factors seem more likely predictors of how particular congregations will handle issues. Sociologist Robert Wuthnow has pointed out this division within mainline denominations, a division which is particularly evident in discussions about social issues.[35] Some mainline denominations, particularly the Episcopal, United Church of

Christ, and American Baptist, are organized in ways that encourage local-ism, designating individual congregations or regional bodies as the au-thorities on matters pertaining to ordination and other practices. Although localism is not supported or advocated by denominational rules or policies in the other three mainline denominations, it has been somewhat tolerated, largely as a technique for diffusing some of the tension and ambivalence around denominational policies related to homosexuality.

The Mainline Provides Forums for Discussion and Debate

Mainline churches have fostered debate about homosexuality in wider so-ciety by providing spaces in congregations and denominational meetings in which conversations about homosexuality could occur and by legiti-mating positions on all sides of the issue. As one of few public institutions where Americans might discuss homosexuality face to face with others, the public role of mainline churches around the issue is particularly sig-nificant.

Much of the public talk and action related to homosexuality has oc-curred in individual congregations. This talk and action occurs in a number of ways and is most significant because it draws mainline church members into conversations about homosexuality that they may not have engaged in otherwise. While national, state, and local governments have certainly discussed homosexuality and many Americans have participated, their in-volvement has most often been indirect, through their elected represen-tatives.[36] Mainliners have also participated in denominational discussion through their representatives to national denominational meetings, but they have also had local forums in which to converse. In a recent survey, for example, 20 percent of Presbyterian church members reported hearing a sermon about gay and lesbian issues in the past twelve months.[37] In a 1997–98 study of congregations, homosexuality was named in half of mainline congregations as a denominational issue that concerned the con-gregation. While some of these congregations had not discussed the topic in depth, many had devoted adult Sunday School classes, youth group sessions, and evening meetings to discussion of the issue. Mainline churches were distinct from Evangelical, Pentecostal, Catholic, and historic African American denominations in which the issue of homosexuality was almost never mentioned.[38] Homosexuality has also been studied exten-sively in most of the roughly 875 congregations across the country that have declared themselves gay-welcoming congregations or transforming congregations. While controversies in congregations often get a lot of press coverage, the quiet ways in which mainline church members are thinking and talking about homosexuality in their congregations have often gone largely unnoticed.

Some congregations choose to talk about homosexuality, while others find themselves unintentionally in the midst of such conversations. The First United Methodist Church in Germantown, Philadelphia, is a large urban congregation that decided, apart from any specific event, to address homosexuality. The senior pastor proposed the issue, and several members of the church's Social Concerns Committee considered the topic and how to address it. A special committee was formed, and a two-year process of study and reflection began shortly thereafter. At the end of this process, the congregation voted to declare themselves a gay-welcoming congregation.[39]

In a very different example, a United Methodist congregation in suburban Chicago began to discuss homosexuality more indirectly. The senior minister of the church supports holy union or commitment ceremonies for gay and lesbian United Methodists, and had supported United Methodist minister Greg Dell when he was on trial for performing a holy union ceremony for two gay men in his church. When the minister expressed support for Dell in the prayers of the people on Palm Sunday in March 1999, several members of the congregation walked out of the sanctuary. Hurt feelings and lack of trust got to such a point several months later that intervention was needed. Following Methodist process, the district superintendent was invited to hear the grievances of the congregation and the frustrations of the pastoral staff. While the issue has not been fully resolved, and some members have left to find other church homes, this congregation has had a thorough, if not completely intended, conversation about the subject.[40]

In addition to congregational gatherings, national denominational meetings have provided another comparatively unique forum for the discussion of homosexuality. As James Wood and Jon Block point out in reference to a national United Methodist denominational meeting, "diversity, orderly procedure, and common ground" provide the social structural base necessary for civil discourse about homosexuality that occurs at these meetings.[41] In a society in which it is all too easy for proponents and opponents of homosexuality to sling their arguments past each other without meeting, the face-to-face dialogue the mainline denominations have facilitated in their national meetings has been unique and significant. In addition to the face-to-face dialogue, the twenty thousand pieces of mail received by the Evangelical Lutheran Church in America in response to the draft of a denominational social statement on sexuality and the voting by clergy and church elders in the Presbyterian church in response to amendments A and B provide further evidence that denominational discussion of homosexuality has facilitated local and regional consideration of the issue.

In addition to providing forums in which discussions about homosexuality could occur, mainline churches legitimated positions on all sides of the issue. When the mainline denominations first addressed homosexuality in the early 1970s, events in Greenwich Village, New York, and other urban centers were marking the beginning of the gay liberation movement in the United States. Mainline churches contributed to this movement indirectly—and probably unintentionally—by recognizing and addressing homosexuality rather than treating it as a subject too obscure or taboo to name. While some would argue that most mainline denominations detracted from the developing gay rights movement by calling homosexuality incompatible with Christian teachings, the mainline churches did name and recognize the issue early on, and they overwhelmingly supported civil rights for homosexual people.

By first naming and addressing homosexuality and then showing that there is a plurality of religious opinion about the topic in mainline religious traditions in the United States, the mainline denominations granted greater legitimacy to those on *both* sides of the homosexuality issue by showing that there is diversity in mainline religious opinion about the subject. While a look at the denominations and some public opinion data alone suggests that many mainline members do not approve of homosexual behaviors, the activities of local congregations demonstrate clearly that mainline opinion is not homogenous and that churches are granting legitimacy to positions on both sides of the issue.[42]

The Mainline Disagrees without Dividing

Through their years of disagreements, the mainline churches have learned, at least thus far, how to disagree without dividing. They have done so by helping opponents focus on their commonalities, including their membership in a common faith tradition, rather than their differences. Most especially, the denominations have emphasized their commitment to gays' and lesbians' civil rights, a position opposed only by those with the most extreme positions. More generally, the mainline denominations have recently begun to focus on how to disagree and remain one denominational organization, especially by focusing on shared history and tradition. The Presbyterians' recent "Unity in the Midst of Diversity" campaign is one such example.

Certain groups, particularly gay-supporting groups, have suggested or advocated breaking off from the Presbyterian church and other mainline denominations to form their own denominations. In explaining why she stays when many think she and others who support gay people should leave the Presbyterian Church, Barbara Wheeler, the president of Auburn Theological Seminary, emphasizes what she shares with her opponents: "I am deeply enmeshed, not by my own choice but by God's sometimes puzzling providence" with "my opponents."[43] She goes on to argue that she and others who support full rights for gay and lesbian people in the church should stay put in the mainline denominations, being vocal and honest about their positions to encourage and continue the vigorous debate.

Conversations and debates about homosexuality in mainline churches contribute substantially to wider public conversation about homosexuality by bringing people on all sides of the issue into dialogue. In no other American social institution have proponents and opponents struggled for so long to resolve or find some compromise about the issue. Opponents' shared commitments to their churches draw them to return repeatedly to debate the issue. As Robert Bellah says in *The Good Society*, in religious communities, like those of the mainline denominations, concerned about the common good of our "nation," "all human beings," and "ultimate responsibility to a transcendent God," disagreement is inevitable.[44] As mainline leaders and church members have entered into discussion about homosexuality and our common life, it would be unrealistic, Bellah would argue, to expect them to agree. What is important is that they have begun and continued discussion and vigorous debate about the issues. Throughout the length and volume of the debate the mainline denominations have maintained a range of perspectives, sometimes tenuously, within their ranks. The plurality of opinion about homosexuality and the space given to continually debate the issue make mainline congregations and denominations vital components of American civic life.

EFFECTS

The direct and indirect public impact of all of this debate about homosexuality in the mainline has been difficult to gauge. Overall, it appears that there has been more indirect impact, though such impact by its nature is more difficult to substantiate. Nationally, lobbying by the Washington, DC, offices and the *amicus curiae* briefs filed by the denominations on gay-related cases may have had some impact on the decisions about bills and court decisions. The United Church of Christ and gay-supportive grassroots organizations in other denominations are increasingly involved with secular gay rights organizations like the National Gay and Lesbian Task Force through the Religious Leadership Roundtable.

The results of this debate in congregations are more visible, especially from those on the gay-supportive side of the issue. Public opinion data clearly demonstrate that religious background and the intensity of individuals' religious commitments influence their opinions about homosexuality, with those who are more religious expressing less support for gay civil rights and more negative feelings about homosexuality generally.[45] While longitudinal data that examine mainline members' opinions about homosexuality or their changing opinions in light of current debate are not available, limited qualitative evidence suggests that for some, change has occurred.[46] Doris Beadsley, a member of a United Methodist congregation that voted to become a Reconciling Congregation in 1984, thought gay men and lesbians were eccentric people. As she heard gay people speak at her church, she began to realize "that they are just people . . . healthy people raising children. . . . When you love people you want to be supportive of what they need and you learn."[47] The most direct effect of this debate appears to be how it has influenced changes in mainliners' hearts and minds. Of those whose minds have not changed or who remain undecided, many have at least grappled with the issue and learned more about homosexuality in the process.

RECOMMENDATIONS

The history, length, and vigor of the mainline denominations' debates over homosexuality show that there is no easy solution that will create a workable compromise or make the issue resolve itself. The mainline denominations' histories generally show the strategies that have been tried and what has and has not worked overall. Neither side's efforts to "win" or to change denominational policy clearly and unambiguously in one direction or the other have succeeded. Limited efforts to ignore the issue have failed, and efforts to postpone denominations' conversations on the topic have not been entirely successful. Little success has come from the mainline's continued attempts to work through the issue, as far as substantial results are concerned, partially because the churches have not capitulated to special-interest groups or attempted simplistic solutions.

Ideas or strategies about how the mainline might address homosexuality in the future depend largely on the aims of the person making the suggestions. Individuals who value denominational unity and fear schism have very different suggestions than do those who want the homosexuality issue to get worked out in the mainline churches regardless of the cost. Some suggestions that might appeal to everyone follow.

First, the mainline denominations should try to stop viewing controversy generally and the continuing controversy generated around homosexuality specifically as bad or threatening. While the issue does threaten denominations' internal unity, it is not going to go away, and the denominations might move on to think about how to deal with that fact. The Evangelical Lutheran Church in America and the American Baptist Churches have begun to think about how to disagree as denominations, and the Presbyterian General Assembly has launched a denominational program to that end. Other denominations might think about following suit. These and future programs might also emphasize that it is not homosexuality that has divided the denomination, as some mainline Protestants are inclined to argue. Rather, the historical and theological issues that underlie homosexuality are at the base of the debate. Homosexuality, like women's ordination before it, is the most recent lens or issue through which these disagreements have been made manifest. While this recognition will not change the division or the debate, it does take gays and lesbians off the hook as "the cause" of the current problems. The denominations might also look outside of themselves a bit more and recognize that numerous institutions in American society (most especially the military) have dealt just as unsuccessfully with the homosexuality issue as they have. The controversies that face the mainline face other organizations in American society today.

Second, the mainline denominations might ask themselves which denominations have had more controversy over homosexuality than others and why that is. While membership demographics are a likely part of the explanation, the organization of the denominations is a significant factor as well. The United Church of Christ, American Baptist Churches, and Episcopal Church have had less controversy overall than have the United Methodist Church, Presbyterian Church, and Evangelical Lutheran Church in America. This is partially because the first three denominations grant more authority to their congregations and regional bodies than do the others. Maybe asking all United Methodists to agree about issues related to homosexuality is simply not realistic. Perhaps granting local congregations or regional bodies in the latter three denominations more authority over issues related to homosexuality (such as ordination and marriage) would dispel some of the tension in denominational meetings and lead to more peaceable relations among mainline members with opposing opinions about homosexuality.

Third, the mainline denominations should continue and develop current practices of conversation and clergy education. Conversation might happen in organizations or informal sessions, perhaps organized regionally, devoted to talking about but not taking a position on homosexuality. Clergy and laity could both be invited to these meetings, relying on an agenda prepared in advance that clearly explains how supporters and opponents of homosexual behavior and homosexual people in the mainline articulate their arguments. Rather than focusing only on homosexuality, the presentation might emphasize the history of variation in denominational opinion around women's ordination, divorce, and other issues and begin to discuss the underlying reasons why such division occurs. The homosexuality issue will likely not be resolved without honest discussion and debate about what issues underlie it, how they have been addressed in the past, and why they are so controversial. All of the discussion, however, needs to be tempered with conversation about what participants, as members of a common denomination, share and with questions about whether these similarities continue to justify their common membership.

As most who have participated in their congregations' and denominations' debates over homosexuality agree, the people on either side of the issue sometimes appear to be speaking different languages. Whether they will split into their own denominations or whether translators will continue to emerge who can bridge the gap, is an issue that will be decided only with time.

NOTES

Thanks to Miguel Centeno, Erin Kelly, Katie Klingensmith, Laura R. Olson, Nina Paynter, Annika Lister Stroope, Bob Wuthnow, and the PROMP research group.

1. I use "homosexuals" and "gays and lesbians" interchangeably throughout this chapter. While I prefer "gays and lesbians," the denominations have used and continue to use both expressions, so I use both here. With the exception of the United Church of Christ, bisexual and transgender individuals have been overlooked—or at least not commented on specifically—by the mainline, and therefore, they are not addressed here. The UCC presently refers to gays, lesbians, bisexuals, and transgender people as one group and supports them all.

2. Alan Yang, "Trends: Attitudes toward Homosexuality," *Public Opinion Quarterly* 61, no. 3 (1997): 477–507. In recent surveys, 44 percent of people felt that homosexuality should be considered an acceptable alternative lifestyle, while 84 percent believed that gay men and lesbians should have equal rights in terms of job opportunities; see "Homosexuality/Gay Rights, November 21–24, 1996," CNN/*USA Today*/Gallup Poll Survey #GO11533, and "Homosexuality/Gay Marriages, March 15–17, 1996," CNN/*USA Today*/Gallup Poll Survey #GO106521.

3. Robert Bellah et al., *The Good Society* (New York: Vintage Press, 1991).

4. John D'Emilio, *Sexual Politics, Sexual Communities* (Chicago: University of Chicago Press, 1983), 194.

5. D'Emilio, *Sexual Politics*, 215.

6. "Resolution on Homosexuals and the Law," Council for Christian Social Action, April 12, 1969.

7. Ibid.

8. "Report of the Committee to Study Homosexuality of the General Council on Ministries on the United Methodist Church as Adopted by the 1992 General Conference," and "Recommendation," United Presbyterian Church, 182nd General Assembly. See also James Anderson, "The Lesbian and Gay Liberation Movement in the Presbyterian Church U.S.A., 1974–1996," *Journal of Homosexuality* 34, no. 2 (1997): 37–65.

9. "Sex, Marriage, and the Family," Lutheran Church in America, Fifth Biennial Convention Social Statement, 1970; "Sexuality and the Human Community," United Presbyterian Church, 182nd General Assembly, 1970: 468–470, 888; "Addition to Social Principles," United Methodist Church General Conference, 1972.

10. "Sex, Marriage, and the Family," Lutheran Church in America.

11. "Resolution 1976-A071, Support the Right of Homosexuals to Equal Protection of the Law," 65th Episcopal General Convention, 1976.

12. "Witness of the Church to Moral Issues," Executive Council of the Episcopal Church, April 1977.

13. "The Church and Homosexuality," United Presbyterian Church USA, 1978: 261–62.

14. United Methodist General Conference, 1984; Anderson, "Lesbian and Gay Liberation Movement in the Presbyterian Church U.S.A."

15. "Gay and Lesbian Persons' Civil Rights," Episcopal General Convention, 1982; "Condemn Violence against Homosexuals," Episcopal General Convention, 1988.

16. "Resolution on Institutionalized Homophobia within the United Church of Christ," 14th General Synod, June 1983; "Resolution in Response to the Concerns of Same-Gender Oriented Persons and Their Families within the United Church of Christ," 14th General Synod, June 1983; Resolution, "The Right to Privacy," 16th General Synod, June 1987; "Deploring Violence against Lesbian and Gay People," 17th General Synod, June 1989.

17. Overture 97–87 on "Elimination of laws governing private sexual behavior of consenting adults," Presbyterian General Assembly, 1987.

18. *Bowers v. Hardwick*, 478 U.S. 186 (1986), On Writ of Certiorari to the Eleventh Circuit Court of Appeals. Official denominational policies are the guidelines that General Counsels and church leaders use when they decide whether or not to file a brief.

19. Mark Bowman, telephone interview, December 9, 1998.

20. Bud Searcy, representative of Transforming Congregations program and New Creations Ministries, telephone interview, November 30, 1998. Also from a pamphlet titled "Transforming Congregations" (n.p., n.d.).

21. "Resolution on Homosexuality," American Baptist Churches, General Board, October 1992.

22. "An American Baptist Resolution Calling for Dialogue on Issues of Human Sexuality," General Board, March 1993.

23. "A Message on Sexuality: Some Common Convictions," Evangelical Lutheran Church in America, November 1996.

24. "Apology to Gays and Lesbians" Episcopal General Convention, 1997.

25. Walter Righter, *A Pilgrim's Way* (New York: Alfred Knopf, 1998).

26. "Vocation of Gay and Lesbian Lutherans," Evangelical Lutheran Church in America News Service, March 17, 1997.

27. "Prepare Report Considering Rites for Same-Sex Commitments," Episcopal General Convention, Resolution 1994-C042.

28. Judicial Council Special Session D-833, United Methodist Church, August 1998.

29. *Amicus curiae* briefs were filed by one or more of the mainline denominations on each of the following cases: *Bowers v. Hardwick; Romer v. Evans,* 517 U.S. 620 (1996); *Equality Foundation of Greater Cincinnati v. City of Cincinnati,* 116 S. Ct. 2519 (1996); *Commonwealth of Kentucky v. Wasson,* 842 SW 2d 487 (Ky. 1992); *State of Texas v. Morales, Doyal, Cramer, Taft, and Thomas,* 826 SW 2d 201 (Tex. App.–Austin 1992).

30. An ecumenical welcoming congregation program began in 1990 when nine leaders of welcoming congregation programs in the mainline denominations met. It grew through the joint publication of a journal for welcoming congregations, *Open Hands,* and continued meeting throughout the decade; see <http://www.rcp.org/history>.

31. Theresa Lantini, interview, November 3, 1998.

32. William Weston, "The Presbyterian Fidelity and Chastity Competition as a Loyalist Victory," *Review of Religious Research* 41 (1999): 207–22.

33. Barbara Wheeler, "The Confession: A Presbyterian Dissenter Thinks about the Church," speech delivered at a meeting of the Covenant Network, Atlanta, GA, November 5, 1999; James Creech, "Letter to Supporters," December 2, 1999.

34. For additional information see <http://www.umaffirm.org/cornews/letroy.html>.

35. Robert Wuthnow, *The Restructuring of American Religion: Society and Faith since World War II* (Princeton, NJ: Princeton University Press, 1988), especially chap. 7.

36. Americans have also participated indirectly in conversations about homosexuality via radio and TV talk shows. Schools and places of employment have tended to skirt the issue, and a large proportion of the American public has not been involved with the special-interest groups that address homosexuality. Churches are among the few public institutions in American society where people may talk about homosexuality directly.

37. "Public Role of Presbyterians," Presbyterian Panel, August 1999.

38. "Organizing Religious Work," project of the Hartford Institute for Religion Research, Nancy Ammerman, principal investigator; see <http://www.hirr.hartsem.edu> for more information.

39. Wendy Cadge, "God's Rainbow Families of Faith: Reconciling Congregations Bridging Gay and Straight Communities," honors thesis, Swarthmore College, Department of Sociology and Anthropology, 1997.

40. Annika Lister Stroope, sermon prepared for The Task of Preaching course, McCormick Theological Seminary, Chicago, IL, December 1, 1999.

41. James Wood and Jon P. Block, "The Role of Church Assemblies in Building a Civil Society: The Case of the United Methodist General Conference on Homosexuality," *Sociology of Religion* 56, no. 2 (1995): 121–36.

42. Presbyterian panel entitled, "Human Sexuality" (June 1989); Presbyterian panel entitled, "Current Issues in PCUSA" (February 1996).

43. Wheeler, "The Confession."

44. Bellah et al., *Good Society,* 182.

45. John Cochran and Leonard Beeghley, "The Influence of Religion on Atti-

tudes toward Nonmarital Sexuality: A Preliminary Assessment of Reference Group Theory," *Journal for the Scientific Study of Religion* 30, no. 1 (1991): 45–62; Nathan Wright, "Religion and Tolerance of Homosexuality," paper delivered at the annual meeting of the American Sociological Association, Washington, DC, August 2000.

46. Cadge, "God's Rainbow Families of Faith," 156–66.

47. Ibid., 160.

11   For the Sake of the Children?

Family-Related Discourse
and Practice in the Mainline

W. Bradford Wilcox

The dramatic demographic shifts that have marked the last three decades have occasioned sustained public interest in the nature, health, and prospects of the family. This chapter, which focuses on the relationship between mainline Protestantism and the family from 1950 up to the present, suggests that this interest is well deserved: changes in the American family have proven enormously consequential for the well-being of children, the commonweal, and, indeed, for the church.

Recent developments in family scholarship confirm the important influence that demographic changes have had upon children, as well as upon the civic and religious life of the United States. A mounting body of research indicates that children have suffered as a consequence of dramatic increases in divorce and out-of-wedlock births since the 1960s. For instance, sociologists Sara McLanahan and Gary Sandefur, in their award-winning book, *Growing Up with a Single Parent* (1994), found that a range of negative consequences—teenage pregnancy, dropping out of high school, and unemployment in early adulthood—were associated with growing up in a family affected by divorce or out-of-wedlock birth, even after controlling for a range of socioeconomic factors. They also found that remarriage did not help children, noting that biological parents generally have stronger ties with their children and are significantly less likely to physically and sexually abuse them.[1] These demographic changes also bear on the nation's commonweal: recent changes in family structure are tied to significant increases in public expenditures and child poverty, higher crime rates, and lower levels of civic engagement.[2]

Moreover, demographic trends and family practices have had a marked impact on the fortunes of American religion. Demographic trends—rates and timing of births, marriages, divorces, and mortality—are closely linked to church membership and practice. In the words of one recent study of church attendance, "As the fortunes of that family/household type [two parents with children] rise and fall, so will the fortunes of mainstream organized Protestantism."[3] Likewise, the internal dynamics of family life— the extent of parental religious devotion, the character of parental affect and discipline, and marital quality—shape the religious practice of adults and children in families. Thus, insofar as the mainline's influence on public life is linked to its institutional size and vitality, the changing fortunes of the American family have an indirect, negative influence on the mainline's capacity to command public attention.

Of course, the relationship between religion and the family is reciprocal: religious belief and practice also influence the fortunes of the family. For much of the nation's history, religious institutions have supplied generic and family-related moral discourse to families and the society at large; they have also offered families social support and control, and a framework of meaning to make sense of the joys, stresses, and transitions that accompany family life. This influence continues up to the present. Religious attendance, for instance, is a strong predictor of marital quality and duration; moreover, the family-related discourse of religious conservatives has played a formative role in shaping recent public discussions about the family.[4]

Thus, it is surprising that a leading mainline Protestant scholar recently charged mainline Protestant churches with a "failure" to develop a compelling family ministry and public family ethic.[5] Nevertheless, Don Browning, director of the Religion, Culture, and Family Project of the Lilly Endowment and professor at the University of Chicago Divinity School, has argued that the mainline, since the sixties, has largely turned its attention away from the family to focus on more "public" issues like racial justice, peace, and poverty. Moreover, he has contended that, to the limited extent that it has addressed family-related issues, the mainline has focused on issues related to sexuality and abortion, to the exclusion of matters related more directly to marriage, parenting, and child welfare.[6]

This chapter seeks to evaluate the legitimacy of Browning's critique and to show how changes in American family life have influenced mainline Protestantism. It suggests that Browning's assessment catches an important dimension of the relationship between the mainline and the family in the recent past and the contemporary period. Since the 1960s, the cultural logic of *expressive liberation*, loosely linked to mainline seminaries, national church bureaucracies, women's organizations, social justice groups, and a large minority of liberal churches, has dominated the political pronouncements of the mainline and important facets of its pastoral life. Drawing on prophetic strands in Christianity and the left, this logic has focused on an evolving series of social justice issues—from racial justice to equal rights for women—and stressed state action as the primary vehicle for social change. To the extent that it focuses on family-related matters, expressive liberation is associated with a therapeutic ethic of care and self-fulfillment, and an ethic of tolerance for a range of family configurations and sexual practices. This logic is especially apparent in the political and pastoral discourse issuing from mainline bureaucracies and, to a lesser extent, congregations.

However, Browning's argument misses the cultural logic of *progressive familism*—grounded in suburban churches, a small cadre of mainline elites, and parachurch family ministries—that has emerged in the last decade and plays a significant role in the pastoral life of mainline churches. Combining elements of egalitarian feminism and 1950s familism, this logic has championed a pastoral focus on families—especially egalitarian married couples with children—and a public ethic that seeks to promote social justice and family stability through a mix of state and civic action. The existence of this familist impulse in the mainline is but one indication of a deeper strand of implicit familism—discourse and practices centered around family life—that has shaped and, as this chapter shows, continues to shape life in mainline Protestant churches. The logic of progressive familism is particularly visible in the many child-centered pastoral practices of mainline congregations.

Although there are important differences between the liberationist and familist camps in the mainline, the cultural and social sources of their approaches to religious life have a great deal in common. Both logics reflect conventional values found in the white middle- and upper-class culture that still dominates the mainline. In fact, this chapter shows how the conventional character of mainline Protestant religion has wedded the health of the mainline to the shifting fortunes of the family in the United States. Thus, insofar as the public presence of the mainline depends upon its own institutional vitality, that presence is tied, indirectly, to the health of the American family. But this chapter also suggests that the mainline's own response to the shifting demographic currents in American society over the last fifty years has had an independent effect on its own destiny and, indeed, that of the American family.

FIFTIES FAMILISM

By almost any demographic measure, the 1950s were an exceptional decade in twentieth-century American family life: the birth rate peaked at a century high in 1957, age at first marriage declined to its century low, and an almost century-long rise in divorce halted for virtually the entire decade.[7] These demographic trends reflected a turn toward bourgeois domesticity in which marriage, a gendered division of labor, and childrearing were exalted as integral and achievable components of the American Dream. This 1950s-style familism was predicated on economic and political developments—the postwar economic boom, the GI Bill, and federal financing of single-family homes—that lifted millions of adults out of the working class and into the middle-class suburbs springing up throughout the country. As historian Elaine Tyler May has observed, 1950s familism linked the prospect of individual fulfillment to adherence to a particular kind of social convention: "[T]hese men and women were hopeful that family life in the postwar era would be secure and liberated from the hardships of the [recent] past. They believed that affluence, consumer goods, satisfying sex, and children would strengthen their families. . . . In pursuing their quest for the 'good life,' they adhered to traditional gender roles and prized marital stability; few of them divorced."[8]

The mainline Protestant churches were the biggest beneficiaries of this specifically suburban style of familism, as mainline Protestant church membership grew by more than 20 percent in this family-centered decade.[9] Most of the men and women forming families in the suburbs were Protestants. Spurred in part by strong cultural conventions that linked family life to religion (such as the slogan "The family that prays together, stays together"), they sought out churches that would provide religious and moral education for their children, as well as opportunities to join in church-related activities—from Boy Scouts to potlucks and square dances—with the families filling new homes around them. One study found, for instance, that the 1950s surpassed the 1940s in the incidence of "the family going to church together, the reading of the Bible at home, and saying grace at meals."[10] The link between family and churchgoing was also manifest in the way that women, who focused on the expressive and domestic work of family life in this period, took the lead in church attendance, Sunday School teaching, and church-related activities like United Methodist Women.[11]

The churches responded to this interest with a host of family-related programs that catered to the domestic orientation of the decade. The

United Presbyterian Church's efforts to provide a range of child-centered programs in this decade are emblematic of broader patterns in mainline churches. Paul Calvin Payne, head of the church's Board of Christian Education from 1940 to 1957, launched a new curriculum, *Christian Faith and Life*, and increased his staff more than fivefold to over one hundred to focus the church on a children's education program with an annual budget of four million dollars.[12] What made Payne's approach particularly noteworthy is that he sought to extend the Christian education of children beyond the Sunday School and into the home with magazines, books, and devotional Bible reading.[13] The rationale for this approach was articulated in a 1955 United Presbyterian Church General Assembly meeting: "Educators are pointing to the home, long neglected, as the most critical and decisive educational experience of life."

The pastoral discourse that mainline families encountered in their churches held up a vision of fulfillment and freedom, but both these ideals were closely tied to conventional piety and behavior.[14] For example, premarital pastoral care, influenced by the growth of pastoral psychology in the decade, began to focus less on the institutional dimensions of family life—social roles, childrearing, and religious life—and more on the emotional dynamics of an increasingly egalitarian married life. In the words of pastoral theologians John Patton and Brian H. Childs, "Premarriage ministry was to help a couple achieve an intense interpersonal involvement and exchange through an open and free communication of feelings."[15] Still, this advice was given and received with the assumption that this expressive focus would lead to marital success and stability. In other words, mainline Protestant churches hewed closely to the decade's insistence that individual fulfillment could be found in the religiously sanctioned observance of social convention.

Much of the public discourse issuing from mainline Protestantism on family-related topics was in keeping with this familism. For example, in 1956, the Methodist General Conference declared, "The family is traditionally the bulwark of the Christian faith," affirmed the primacy of God's love in families, and pointed to hopeful signs of a family renaissance: higher birth rates, more family togetherness, and increased parental devotion to children.[16] The conference also expressed concerns about working mothers, decried divorce, and for the first time taught the legitimacy of planned parenthood "in Christian conscience."[17] Even the almost universal embrace of contraception among mainline churches in the latter half of the decade was tied to its general approach to family life. Mainline church leaders like Episcopal Bishop James Pike, head of Planned Parenthood's clergy advisory committee, argued that contraception promoted responsible parenthood and allowed married couples to reap the emotional benefits of sex without fear of an unintended pregnancy.[18] The mainline's embrace of contraception was primarily designed to protect the economic and, more important, emotional well-being of the intensely expressive, nuclear family that had emerged in the American suburbs.

But the mainline's embrace of contraception might also be interpreted as one sign that the ties that had grown between mainline Protestantism and a child-centered, conventional culture were coming undone. Toward the end of the decade, there were more signs. Religious intellectuals—like the Episcopal priest Gibson Winter, who launched his first broadside, "The Church in Suburban Captivity," in the *Christian Century* in 1955—began publicly attacking American religion's privatized focus on suburban status quo living and its blindness to more public questions of social justice.[19] In fact, more than 40 percent of the articles published by the *Christian Century* in 1955 urged the mainline to tackle social justice issues like poverty and racial segregation (see figure 11.1).[20] Many of these same intellectuals also began championing a compassionate pastoral ethic that deliberately set itself against "legalistic," traditional Christian moral teaching. This emphasis on compassion helps explain why, by 1958, the Episcopal, Presbyterian, and Lutheran Churches had liberalized their divorce policies to allow for remarriage in virtually any case, overturning the traditional Protestant understanding that remarriage ought to be available only to "innocent" victims of adultery or abandonment.[21]

SOCIAL JUSTICE AND PERSONAL LIBERATION

Although the mainline played an integral role in the cultural and political upheavals associated with the 1960s and 1970s—especially the civil rights and antiwar movements—the cultural and demographic shifts ushered in by the 1960s and 1970s were not good for the institutional health of the mainline. From 1965 to 1990, the mainline experienced dramatic declines in membership and attendance, with some denominations losing a third or more of their members. Overall, mainline Protestantism lost 6.4 million members in this period and saw its share of active churchgoers fall behind that of conservative Protestantism and Roman Catholicism.[22] The decline of the mainline has occasioned a voluminous and complex scholarly literature, but most studies now agree that declines in the number of young mainline families with children and difficulties in retaining the religious

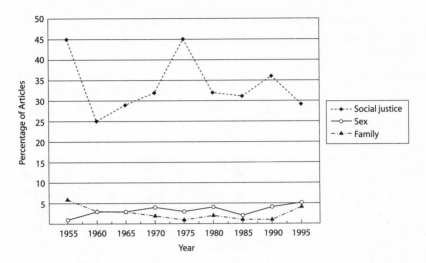

Figure 11.1. The Topical Focus of *Christian Century*

loyalty of the men and women who came of age in the tumultuous 1960s and 1970s played critical roles in this decline.[23] In other words, demographic and devotional trends associated with the "boomers" were closely tied to the destiny of the mainline during this period.

The mainline's failure to retain the religious loyalty and involvement of a substantial sector of its boomer youth in the sixties and seventies— two studies found only 39 percent of boomers reared in the mainline were active in the tradition in the early 1990s—can be understood partly as a consequence of the larger cultural currents that swept the entire nation.[24] The protest movements and youth culture of the era raised serious questions about the legitimacy of American institutions like the church, questions that led many boomers to give up on "organized religion."

This decline was also tied to patterns of childrearing and childbearing that affected the whole society but, once again, were particularly consequential for the mainline. Many American parents had sought out mainline churches in the 1950s not because they had strong Christian convictions but because they wanted to provide their children with religious and moral training. These parents adhered to what one study called "lay liberalism"—a combination of vague religious beliefs, cultural tolerance, and a belief that religion's primary function is to support good behavior (e.g., the Golden Rule). This lay liberalism meant that many mainline parents didn't have a strong religious identity to pass on to their children: the boomers of the 1960s and 1970s. Thus, when conventional norms on behalf of churchgoing were questioned, many young adults from the mainline decided that they had no need for the church.[25]

Moreover, this tendency to drop out and stay out was profoundly augmented by changing demographic patterns. Five interrelated phenomena—the "contraceptive revolution" of the 1960s, the sexual revolution occasioned by this revolution, the anti-institutional tenor of the era, the dramatic increase in women's educational and employment status, and the preoccupation with personal fulfillment—all combined to dislodge the familial patterns of the 1950s. From 1957 to 1973, the fertility rate fell from 3.8 to 1.9 children, the divorce rate almost doubled, and the number of young women who remained unmarried increased by a third. Accordingly, the men and women who came of age in this period were much less likely to marry and have children at an early age.[26] Wuthnow observes that these trends were of "enormous religious significance" because they increased the chances that boomers would not return quickly and as often to church to give children the religious and moral education their parents had given them.[27] Moreover, the surge in cohabitation and divorce in this period also caused boomers to leave or stay away from religious institutions that did not support their lifestyle choices.[28]

The mainline was struck particularly hard by these trends, partly because its middle- and upper-class members were more likely to be affected by the cultural break with fifties familism.[29] But the discourse issuing from mainline clergy and intellectuals also accommodated and perhaps augmented this shift. While most mainline clergy in the early 1960s would probably have agreed with the Methodist bishop Gerald Kennedy of Los Angeles, who decried the rising tide of "promiscuity" in a 1964 *Time* article on the "sexual revolution," mainline churches had made their support for birth control and planned parenthood exceedingly clear.[30] For example, my survey of the mainline literary flagship, the *Christian Century*, reveals that news and editorial comment on Protestant support for birth control was the leading topic of family-related articles in 1960.

But more important, by the end of the 1960s much of the intellectual and pastoral discourse issuing from the mainline explicitly or implicitly sanctioned the expressive individualism that marked the era, as well as its attacks on fifties familism. Following a path forged earlier by mainline intellectuals like pastoral theologian Seward Hiltner and theologian Paul Tillich, an increasing number of clergy, church leaders, and seminary faculty were adapting a pastorally oriented ethic of love. This ethic, which was closely connected to the growing popularity of humanistic psychology in the wider culture and the rise of pastoral counseling in the mainline, defined love in terms of interpersonal authenticity and the pursuit of personal fulfillment for oneself and others, even if that meant dispensing with the "legalism" associated with much of traditional Christian morality. It was also associated with a revolt against moralizing in pastoral care—for instance, Hiltner urged "understanding" and "clarification" in place of "moral judgements."[31]

The institutional ascendancy of this love ethic in family matters is exemplified in pastoral discourse regarding divorce from the period. For instance, in a 1977 issue of the *Christian Century*, Methodist pastor Robert Sinks gave voice to the therapeutic ethic sweeping through the mainline: "Sometimes divorce may be little other than an escape from the intolerable. On other occasions it may be a clear and creative movement toward fulfillment through which persons recognize that their present relationship no longer gives hope to the growing potentialities of either partner."[32] Thus, by the end of the 1970s, the mainline's earlier effort to link fulfillment to the adherence to social convention had been overtaken, at least in many quarters, by an effort to seek fulfillment directly, even if that meant the rejection of family-oriented social convention.

The move away from the familial ethic at the pastoral level was paralleled at the level of the national leadership of the denominations in this period. Many mainline church leaders, moved both by the intellectual critique of the churches' "suburban captivity" and the endemic racism and poverty in America, focused the voice and resources of the mainline on a series of "public" issues—first on civil rights and then on a succession of progressive causes. Figures 11.2 through 11.4 indicate that social-justice-related topics—especially poverty, civil rights, the Vietnam War, and gender equality—garnered significantly more attention in the 1960s and 1970s in two of the three denominations that I surveyed. Specifically, the percentage of pages that mentioned social justice issues in the denominational journals of the national meetings for the Methodist and Presbyterian churches rose more than 40 percent from 1955 to 1976. Only Episcopal Church discourse on social justice remained essentially constant.[33]

Church resources—staff, clergy, and millions of dollars—were also poured into efforts devoted to foster justice and create social change. By 1972, for instance, the Episcopal and Methodist churches had spent more than $10 million in grants on "minority group empowerment."[34] Meanwhile, the institutional churches' ministry to the "private" realm—family ministry, children's and youth religious education, and family conferences—took a back seat. For example, the percentage of the national budget

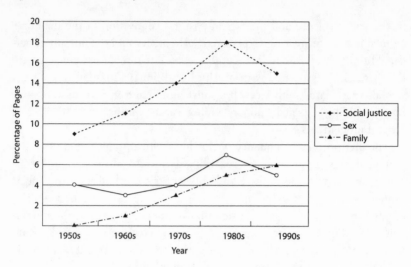

Figure 11.2. The Topical Focus of *Methodist General Conference Journal*

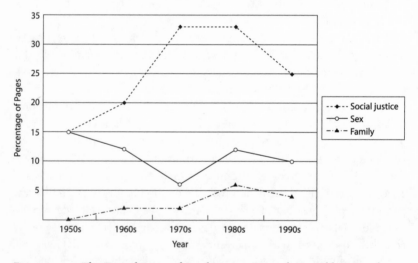

Figure 11.3. The Topical Focus of *Presbyterian General Assembly Journal*

of the Methodist Church devoted to evangelism and education, which also included family-related ministries, fell more than 40 percent, from 5.08 percent in 1950 to 2.88 percent in 1975.[35] Mainline discourse directed to the family also declined, at least at the national level. Figures 11.1 through 11.4 indicate that the amount of family-related discourse—on topics like

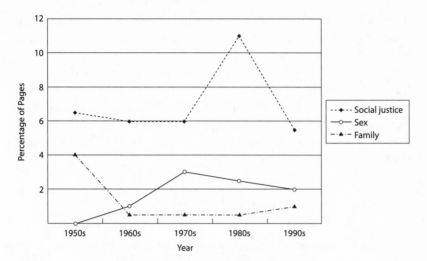

Figure 11.4. The Topical Focus of *Episcopalian General Convention Journal*

youth ministry, marriage, divorce, and parenting—declined by more than 55 percent in the *Christian Century* and the journals of the United Presbyterian Church and the Episcopal Church.

To the extent that family-related topics were addressed, they were generally viewed through the social justice lens that had provided the leadership focus of the churches in this period. Not only were the optics of this lens shaped by the mainline's long-standing concern with socioeconomic injustice, they were also strongly influenced by the rise of the women's movement of the 1970s. Spurred by feminist critiques of the fifties-style family, dramatic increases in women's status, and the sexual revolution, women's groups in mainline churches pressed for gender equality in the family and the church; they also argued that the decline of the "traditional" fifties-style family—through, say, divorce or female employment—would liberate women from the burdens of stultifying marriages and male dominance.[36]

The mainline's commitment to social justice and personal liberation was in full view as it weighed in on the controversies surrounding the White House Conference on Families (1980). Rev. Eileen Lindner, a National Council of Churches (NCC) staff member, told a congressional committee that the mainline supported family policies that would "remove the onus of responsibility for systematic injustice from its victims [i.e., families]."[37] At the conference, the NCC, the United Methodist Church (UMC), and the United Church of Christ called for measures like full employment, universal health and childcare, and universal access to family planning and abortion. They also expressed their affirmation of family pluralism—what the UMC's Board of Church and Society called "a wider range of options than that of the two generational unit of parents and children (nuclear family)."[38] Thus, the mainline's participation in the White House Conference exemplified its emerging public discourse about families, a discourse that highlighted, in the political sphere, expanded welfare state measures for families and, in the pastoral sphere, a therapeutic ethic that legitimated dramatic shifts in family structure and practice.

RESTRUCTURING, EXPRESSIVE LIBERATION, AND PROGRESSIVE FAMILISM

Although the impact of the 1960s and 1970s significantly restructured the political and pastoral orientation of the mainline to the family, this restructuring should not be exaggerated. The familial orientation and functions of American religion, including mainline Protestantism, remained deeply entrenched even through this period of upheaval. Indeed, many of the most dramatic shifts in the mainline family-related discourse and practice that took place in this era were concentrated in the mainline's elite institutions—its national church bureaucracies and seminaries—and among its boomers, especially high-status members of this generation. At the congregational level, considerable evidence indicates that most mainline churches continued to center much of their ordinary religious life around family-centered activities like children's Sunday School, perhaps after spending five or ten years focusing intensely on social justice sometime in the 1960s and 1970s.[39] Thus, by the 1980s, the mainline combined elements of 1950s-familism and 1960s-liberationism.

The conservative political, cultural, and religious currents of the 1980s, as well as dramatic declines in mainline membership and financial resources, put the mainline on the defensive during the Reagan-Bush era. This defensive posture was signaled by a decline in significant institutional and cultural innovation in the mainline during this period. Accordingly, for much of the last two decades of the twentieth century, the mainline's approach to the family has continued to incorporate strands of familism and expressive liberation drawn from, respectively, the 1950s and the 1960s/1970s.

The logic of expressive liberation, which is indebted to the therapeutic and social justice currents of the 1960s and 1970s, has been described by sociologist Benton Johnson as an "ethic of personal autonomy and moral relativism in private life and an ethic of moral absolutism in public affairs."[40] With respect to the family, the logic of expressive liberation stresses tolerance and affirmation of family pluralism, and affirms the importance of gender equality and an ethic of care in a range of marital and nonmarital relationships. This approach is grounded in the assumption that family pluralism is a social reality that must be accepted, and that families need to be judged on the quality of their care rather than the marital status of adult partners. This ethic is captured in *Christian Marriage and Family* (1988) by pastoral theologians John Patton and Brian Childs: "There is no ideal form for the Christian family toward which we strive. There is, however, a normative function: care."[41] In pastoral practice, this approach stresses adult-centered programs designed to reach out to the divorced, single parents, and homosexuals, and fosters grassroots advocacy on behalf of the marginalized—including poor children.

The orientation of expressive liberationism in the political sphere, on the other hand, is both prophetic and absolutistic. This logic is indebted to the more radical political currents of the 1960s and 1970s, as well as to liberation theology, which accentuates the emphasis on public justice in the Old and New Testaments. Oriented toward the poor, the marginalized, and the oppressed, the public face of expressive liberation seeks to remove all limitations on individual expression—be they economic, racial, or sexual. An expansive welfare state is seen as the primary instrument of justice. Although the family per se does not receive a lot of attention, expressive liberationism accords central importance to the interests of women and children. "Without identifying children and families as a top priority," says Mary Anderson Cooper, associate director of the National Council of Churches' Washington, DC, office, "when we choose our [legislative] priorities it's always with a view to how they affect racial and ethnic minority groups and children, families, women—anybody who has traditionally been at a disadvantage in this society."[42]

The logic of progressive familism seeks to chart a middle way between expressive liberationism and the family program of the Religious Right. Theologically, progressive familism recovers and refashions classical Protestant understandings of marriage as a covenant, as well as traditional understandings of human sin and divine grace. Lifelong marriage is seen as normative for most persons—a divinely sanctioned covenant ordained by God to protect the well-being of adults and the children who often follow from heterosexual coupling.[43] However, progressive familism departs from the classical tradition in its insistence that marriage must be based on an egalitarian ethic of mutuality between men and women.[44]

Moreover, progressive familism's emphasis on human sinfulness is linked to a spirit of graceful tolerance for departures from the intact family norm. Finally, in terms of pastoral practice, the logic of progressive familism is associated with a strong pastoral emphasis on family-related ministries— from marriage preparation to religious education programs for children to divorce support groups.

In terms of its policy orientation, progressive familism also embraces a strong state role in the promotion of public justice. However, its view of the state is chastened by a Niebuhrian emphasis on human sinfulness that suggests that the state can become overweening—crowding out civic, familial, and religious organizations—and that poorly crafted public policy can endanger the health of the family. "[B]oth civil society and individual persons (particularly children) are damaged when the state programmatically and directly tries to assume or control the historical roles of the family: production, reproduction, consumption, and nurture," writes social ethicist Max Stackhouse, adding, "The state better serves humanity when it protects and supports the nongovernmental institutions that do these things well."[45] Accordingly, progressive familism supports civic efforts like community marriage policies, where congregations from different religious traditions work together to establish common norms and supports for married and engaged couples, and state measures that promote the health and stability of the intact family—measures like expanding the Earned Income Tax Credit for lower-income couples.[46]

THE FAMILY AND MAINLINE CONGREGATIONS

At the congregational level, the family-oriented practices that had such power in the 1950s have, to a large degree, maintained their presence in the mainline. Indeed, data taken from the 1998 National Congregation Survey (NCS), which surveyed more than 1,200 congregations, indicate that the mainline continues to offer what sociologist Penny Edgell Becker calls the "standard package" of family ministries aimed at married couples with children that were institutionalized earlier in the century.[47] Virtually all mainline congregations (70.9%) offer Christian education classes to children (Sunday School), and a significant minority (22.1%) offer other formal, "standard" family programming like Marriage Encounter or parenting classes (see table 11.1).[48] What's striking about the survey results is that, despite the Religious Right's strong symbolic emphasis on the "traditional" family, mainline congregations are just as likely to have formal programming that targets married couples with children as are con-

Table 11.1. Presence of Family Ministries in Mainline versus Conservative Protestant Congregations

Ministry	Mainline Protestants with Specified Ministry (%)	Conservative Protestants with Specified Ministry (%)
Traditional		
Marriage/family/parenting[a]	22.1	20.4
Children's worship[a]	70.9	39.5
Daycare[b]	55.0	42.0
Nontraditional		
Support groups for single parents, the divorced, and/or single adults[a]	4.5	11.4

[a]Data taken from the National Congregation Survey (1998).
[b]Data taken from the Religion and Politics Survey (2000).

servative Protestant churches. Thus, much of the mainline's family-related pastoral practice remains in line with the basic thrust of 1950s familism.

However, mainline churches have added two distinctively progressive elements to their pastoral ministry to families. First, they are significantly more likely to offer opportunities for children's worship than any other religious tradition—indeed, they are almost twice as likely to have such programming as conservative Protestant churches (see table 11.1). For instance, many churches offer a "children's sermon" geared to children right before the primary sermon. This effort to integrate children into the worshiping life of congregations is indebted to insights from developmental psychology and a new inclusive theological emphasis in mainline churches on the importance of including all the baptized in worship.[49] In the words of Christian educators David Ng and Virginia Thomas, "God's Kingdom is for all, and God's love draws all together. . . . [C]hildren and adults worshiping together make the statement of faith."[50] This emphasis on child-centered worship is also in keeping with the egalitarian, child-centered ideology that appeals to middle- and upper-class American parents, who are disproportionately represented in the mainline.

Second, mainline congregations have also made a concerted effort to offer daycare to their members. More than half of mainline Protestants (55 percent) attend congregations where daycare is provided; in fact, mainline churches are significantly more likely to provide daycare to their members than are conservative Protestants (42 percent) (see table 11.1). This commitment to daycare signals the mainline's normative commitment to gender equality, reflected, for instance, in the current Methodist teaching that women and men are "equal in every aspect of their common life" and that "every effort [should] be made to eliminate sex-role stereotypes . . . in all aspects of voluntary and compensatory participation in the Church and society."[51] Thus, at the level of pastoral practice, mainline Protestant churches are significant producers of "standard" and innovative services for families—especially child-centered services. In other words, the family-related pastoral practice of mainline churches is largely structured by the logic of progressive familism.

In some ways, the family-related culture found in mainline congregations also reflects the logic of progressive familism. The laity still hear about the family from the pulpit. One recent survey found that 79 percent of mainline Presbyterians mentioned that family issues had come up in the last year—more than any other social or political issue.[52] Extensive ethnographic work led by sociologist Nancy Ammerman suggests that many mainline churches foster a "Golden Rule Christianity"—loosely tied to the spirit of the New Testament—that stresses an ethic of care for self and others, especially one's children.[53] Finally, on the question of family structure, the vast majority of mainline clergy and members appear to believe that the intact, two-parent family is best for children. A survey of Presbyterians found that more than 90 percent of laity and clergy agreed that "[i]t is best for children to grow up in an intact two-parent family."[54]

In many ways, however, the content of family culture in many mainline churches typifies the uncritical acceptance of family pluralism and self-realization characteristic of expressive liberation. Many churches seek to create an atmosphere of acceptance for family pluralism that is based on an ethic of tolerance and a desire to minister to persons in a way that validates their sense of self. They are convinced, in the words of Patton and Childs, that "[t]he stress on the structure of the nuclear family . . . also contributes to the ignoring of others in less traditional family structures."[55]

This ethic of tolerant acceptance stands in tension with the mainline's commitment to the intact family. For instance, while the vast majority of Presbyterian pastors support the intact, two-parent family in theory, 73 percent of these pastors also think that the church should be "tolerant of family changes (divorce, remarriage, same-sex couples) now taking place."[56] The mainline faith in tolerance leaves many clergy unable or unwilling to articulate theological and moral concerns about divorce, even when children are involved. For instance, mainline clergy involved in full-time pastoral care of families are more accepting of divorce than secular therapists. One survey of pastoral care counselors—62 percent of whom are mainline clergy—found that only 50 percent of pastoral counselors are more cautious about divorce when children are involved. This is especially striking because 74 percent of secularly trained family psychiatrists indicated that they would be more cautious in this situation.[57] Here, pastoral care's commitment to tolerance and individual fulfillment appears to trump concerns about family stability for children.

This ethic of tolerant acceptance can also contribute to an inability to articulate a broader, normative vision of family life. The commitment that many mainline clergy have to this ethic as well as their distaste for the Religious Right's approach to the whole issue of "family values" have left many churches unable to present a clear vision of what families should aspire to beyond a vague ethic of love for family members, and a stress on including all types of families.[58] One prominent Presbyterian church in Chicago offers a theologically grounded discourse that critiques the Religious Right's family values by talking about Jesus Christ's ministry of inclusion. This is a church, in the view of Christian ethicist Lois Livezey, that favors "conversation" rather than "definitive guidance" in its approach to family issues.[59] Becker's survey of mainline pastors in upstate New York found that more than 85 percent believed that "God approves of all families" and almost half rejected the phrase "family ministry" as an exclusionary term; by contrast, no conservative Protestant pastors thought God approved of all families, and only 13 percent thought that family ministry was an exclusive term.[60]

One ironic consequence of this tendency appears to be that mainline churches actually do less in the way of formal programmatic support for nontraditional families than do conservative Protestant churches. As Don Browning and his colleagues argue, churches that have articulated a normative theology of the family *and* tempered that vision with a strong emphasis on human fallibility—including a significant number of innovative conservative Protestant megachurches—are often better equipped to speak frankly about departures from their ideals, and to offer services to members who have fallen short of these ideals.[61] For example, the National Congregation Survey revealed that 11.4 percent of conservative Protestant congregations, versus 4.5 percent of mainline Protestant congregations, offered nontraditional family ministries, like support groups for the divorced and single adults. Conservative Protestant churches are more than twice as likely as mainline Protestant churches to offer these ministries (see table 11.1).

The mainline mix of familistic practice and discursive cultural liberalism is apparently attractive to many young and middle-aged married couples with children, who made up 34 percent of the active adult attendees of mainline churches in the 1990s, a clear majority of active attendees age sixty and under (see figure 11.5).[62] The mainline's share of married couples with children approximates patterns found in the general population—where 34 percent of adults age 60 and under were also married with children.

Figure 11.5 also reveals that mainline churches were significantly less likely to have single parents age forty and under, as well as young, single adults and married couples without children, compared to the population at large. Somewhat surprisingly, mainline churches also drew smaller shares of young, single parents in their congregations (4 percent) than did conservative Protestant churches (7 percent). Mainline churches also had smaller shares of young single and married adults without children (12 percent) than conservative Protestant churches (14 percent).

Given their symbolic stress on inclusion, it is striking that mainline Protestant churches are less likely to have young adults in nontraditional family households than conservative Protestant churches. Apparently, the inclusive family ethic articulated in mainline congregations functions more as an identity marker than as a guide to congregational practice. The discourse of expressive liberation allows mainline churches to signal their adherence to the canons of cultural liberalism and to erect symbolic boundaries against fundamentalism. At the same time, however, the pastoral practice of mainline churches is child-centered in ways that reproduce the long-standing ties between mainline Protestant religion and the two-parent family. Thus, the family paradox of mainline Protestantism—at least at the congregational level—is that the discourse of expressive liberation coexists with the practice of familism, albeit progressive familism.

This paradox makes sense in light of contemporary patterns of conventional life in middle- and upper-class America. Many middle- and upper-class adults raised in the mainline, or disillusioned with their upbringing in Catholic or conservative Protestant churches, only start attending a mainline congregation once they have reached the stage in life when they are married with children. They want to give their children the religious and moral formation they received as children, they are looking for a place to meet other young families, and they tend to connect their new social

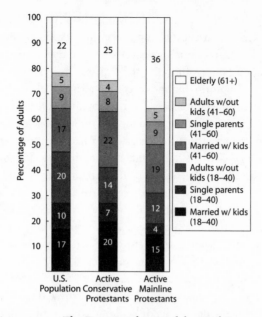

Figure 11.5.   The Demographic Breakdown of Conservative and Mainline Protestants versus the General U.S. Population. SOURCE: Data are from the General Social Surveys.

status as parents and community stakeholders with churchgoing. At the same time, they are looking for a Golden Rule Christianity that does not violate middle- and upper-class cultural conventions such as tolerance of moral and religious pluralism, gender equality, and a therapeutic ethic of self-realization. Thus, they end up in churches that, in the words of sociologist Wade Clark Roof, "are open theologically to family diversity yet on the whole are bastions of familism."[63]

PASTORAL MINISTRY AND POLITICAL WITNESS AT THE NATIONAL LEVEL

At the national level, the pastoral ministry and political witness of the mainline generally tilts toward the logic of expressive liberation. From an organizational perspective, family ministry generally garners little institutional support compared to that given to social justice. My survey of the Methodist, Presbyterian, and Episcopal churches revealed that the latter two churches have no full-time staff working on family ministry. This is particularly striking since the Presbyterian and Episcopal churches each have about nine staffers working in social justice ministries and their

Washington policy offices. Even the Methodist Church, which recently made progress in this area by hiring two employees in 1996 to focus full-time on family ministry, employs approximately twenty men and women in its Washington policy office and social justice ministries.

My survey of mainline public discourse also reveals that the national leadership of mainline churches, as well as its intellectuals, have been pre-occupied with questions of social justice at the expense of family-related matters. From 1980 to 1995, for instance, 32 percent of the articles in the *Christian Century*—which can be taken as a fairly good barometer of the concerns of mainline intellectuals—dealt with questions of public justice—from poverty to racism and sexism (see figure 11.1). In this same period, only 5 percent of articles dealt with family- and sex-related topics. Although the differentials between social justice and family-related discourse are not as dramatic at national meetings of the Methodist, Presbyterian, and Episcopal churches in the 1980s and 1990s, they exhibit similar patterns. Over these two decades, approximately 17 percent of the pages in the journals recording the national meetings of these three churches mentioned social justice issues, while only about 10 percent of the pages mentioned family- or sex-related topics. Moreover, more than 40 percent of the family- and sex-related topics in these journals, and in the *Christian Century*, focused on matters like human sexuality and child welfare that could as easily fall under the framework of social justice. Accordingly, I turn now to outline the basic approach that mainline Protestant national bureaucracies have adopted in regard to these two topics.

Human sexuality has been a central pastoral preoccupation of the main-line since the 1970s. In fact, the churches have generated more study papers on sexual relationships, homosexuality, and abortion in this period than at any comparable period in their history (as figures 11.1 through 11.4 suggest).[64] Much of this institutional discourse on human sexuality tends toward the logic of expressive liberation. Influenced by the feminist and gay rights movements of the 1970s and 1980s, this discourse emphasizes a relational ethic of fulfillment and interpersonal authenticity, critiques the family as inherently patriarchal, and celebrates sexuality as a divine gift to be enjoyed in a wide range of consensual relationships. Thus, it explicitly breaks with the classical Protestant idea that sexual intimacy should be grounded in the covenantal institution of lifelong, heterosexual marriage.

The most prominent example of this tendency in mainline discourse is the 1991 Presbyterian report *Keeping Body and Soul Together*. In the name of "justice-love" and "inclusive wholeness," this report suggests that a wide range of relationships—from cohabitation to nonsexual friendships and marriage—might embody the kind of sexual and emotional intimacy, equality, and respect that would qualify them as theologically and morally legitimate.[65] The report did not articulate a robust ethic of commitment in its discussions of relationships centered around justice-love, nor did it address the potential impact of these adult relationships on children. To the extent that it focused on marriage, *Keeping Body and Soul Together* decried the "distorted power dynamics" of patriarchal marriages and instead offered a vision of married life centered around a therapeutic ethic of justice-love: "[A]uthentic marriages enhance individual identity in the midst of deepening intimacy and interpersonal encounter."[66] Due in part to its endorsement of homosexual relationships, this report, like a similar report issued three years later in the Evangelical Lutheran Church, was rejected by a church-wide assembly that included a more representative sample of clergy and laity. Nonetheless, the report's stress on inclusion and therapeutic self-realization suggests how the logic of expressive liberation has come to guide the thinking of many influential mainline elites.

The other family-related issue that has recently captured the attention of national mainline leaders is the well-being of children. Children conjure up biblical images of dependence and vulnerability, as well as more modern notions of innocence and entitlement. The millions of American children who grow up in desperately poor and dangerous neighborhoods are particularly salient symbols of the "least among us" championed by Jesus. They also serve as popular beneficiaries of public welfare measures in an American political climate that is exceedingly suspicious of "big government." For all these reasons, the mainline has increasingly framed its political advocacy of social justice around the needs of "children and their families."

In the past decade, all three denominations that I studied for this project issued major statements on children—from the Episcopal Church's *A Children's Charter for the Church* (1997) to the Methodist Church's *Putting Children and Their Families First* (1996).[67] These statements typically underline a host of hazards confronting children—from gun violence to child poverty—and then call for generous welfare policies. Also stressed is the churches' responsibility to advocate on behalf of children at the federal, state, and local levels. Simultaneously, denominational offices and social justice groups have worked to raise the profile of children's issues in the mainline.

The mainline's primary partner in its political advocacy on behalf of children and families is the Children's Defense Fund (CDF). Since 1982, when the CDF established an office of religious affairs, it has worked closely with virtually all of the mainline offices in Washington, as well as with many mainline leaders in denominational headquarters and grass-roots social justice networks around the country.[68] The two most prominent examples of this mutual relationship on behalf of children are the 1996 CDF-sponsored rally, Stand for Children, and the annual Children's Sabbaths that are designed to focus congregations on the plight of children, especially disadvantaged children. On June 1, 1996, more than two hundred thousand people gathered at the Lincoln Memorial in Washington to demonstrate their commitment to "protecting and improving the quality of life for all children," in the words of CDF president Marian Wright Edelman. Although extensive media coverage of the event generally did not highlight the event's religious dimension, Stand for Children was, in some ways, the mainline equivalent of the Promise Keeper rally, Stand in the Gap, that was held on the Mall a year later. Mainline congregations, social justice networks, and national organizations like United Methodist Women sponsored approximately fifty thousand attendees.[69]

Edelman's address conjured up images of Martin Luther King's "I Have a Dream" speech. It was laced with scores of religious allusions, such as "God's sacred covenant with every child." Edelman touched on the importance of parental responsibility, national spiritual revival, and cultural renewal. Nevertheless, the bulk of her speech was dedicated to underlining the social forces, from racism to poverty, putting millions of children at risk and the imperative of relying on public policies, from publicly financed childcare to gun control laws, to help them. She made no mention of the dramatic rises in divorce and out-of-wedlock births that have also affected children.[70]

Similar themes emerge in the Children's Sabbaths program started by the CDF in 1992. The program, which occurs on the third weekend of each October, is designed to promote child-centered worship, advocacy, and educational initiatives around particular annual themes—from health care to early child education. The CDF produces a volume containing a model worship service for Protestant, Catholic, and Jewish congregations, as well as a series of activity modules for children and adults of all ages. It reaches more than thirty-five thousand congregations across America, with the lion's share of packets going to mainline churches. Although the program does place some emphasis on the necessity of a "moral start"—that is, spiritual and moral guidance from parents and congregations—most of the Children's Sabbaths revolve around public advocacy or programmatic activity on behalf of children. A Protestant sermon in the 1999 volume suggests that "works of faith" should result in "programs, laws, and policies that support children and their families," that "labors of love" ought to be focused on activities like mentoring teenagers and advocating for universal childcare, and that Christians are called to "hope" that God will supply adequate food, shelter, health care, and education to all children.[71]

All this is in keeping with the liberationist tenor of mainline discourse on the plight of "children and their families." While the mainline has a great deal to say about the social-structural evils that afflict children, it sidesteps the impact of family breakdown on child well-being and has very little to say about the responsibilities that individual parents have to their own children. For the most part, the ethic of responsibility is pushed upwards into the arenas of civic and particularly governmental action. Thus, at the national level, to the limited extent that the mainline has articulated a public ethic on family-related matters, that ethic largely follows the canons of the logic of expressive liberation that emerged out of the tumult of the 1960s and 1970s.

THE DESTINY OF THE MAINLINE AND THE FAMILY

This chapter has demonstrated that the fortunes of the mainline in the last half of the century have been closely tied to the destiny of the family, particularly the intact, two-parent family. Indeed, Figure 11.6 shows that trends in active mainline adult membership for the last three decades have closely paralleled the percentage of married adults age forty and under with children.[72] Moreover, Figure 11.6 also suggests that the mainline has been more dependent on the prevalence of this household type than has conservative Protestantism, which has managed to expand its share of active adherents in the United States population even though the intact, two-parent family championed by conservative Protestantism is less prevalent than it used to be in the population at large. Perhaps surprisingly, the mainline continues to function as a key bulwark of familism, offering an array of family-oriented services to its members, especially services targeted at children.

Of course, the irony of the relationship between the mainline and the family is that much of its political discourse, and even a significant portion of its pastoral discourse, has paid virtually no attention to the health and stability of the intact, two-parent family. Indeed, in some cases, the mainline has been allied with cultural forces contributing to the decline of the intact, two-parent family. For instance, in its devotion to the ethic of expressive liberation, the mainline liberalized its divorce policies well ahead

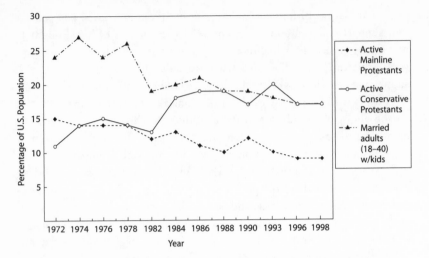

Figure 11.6.   Demographic and Religious Trends among Mainline and Conservative Protestants in the United States. SOURCE: General Social Surveys.

of state legislatures and has had virtually nothing to say about the role of marriage in its more recent, and commendable, public campaign on behalf of children. In addition, the institutional and intellectual resources of the mainline have often been devoted to questions of public justice—including battles over homosexuality and abortion—at the expense of crafting a theologically grounded family ethic for the twenty-first century.

The mainline's predicament is particularly delicate because demographic trends and the elite conventional wisdom about the family appear to be moving in different directions. On the demographic side, divorce and illegitimacy rates have soared to, respectively, 40 and 30 percent, even as the European-American birth rate has dipped below the replacement rate of 2.11 children per woman, and the percentage of unmarried 30–34-year-olds has risen to a twentieth-century high of more than 20 percent.[73] This means that more adults are living outside of a child-centered, intact, two-parent family than ever before in the nation's postwar history.

At the same time, the intellectual and political climate has begun to turn against some of these trends, as evidenced by the emergence of a national marriage movement led by a range of religious *and* secular leaders, where the mainline's absence is conspicuous. Figures like Isabel Sawhill, a senior fellow at the Brookings Institution, University of Chicago sociologist Linda Waite, and political philosopher William Galston, a former domestic policy advisor to President Bill Clinton, have come out in favor of a range of cultural, civic, and political measures designed to bring divorce and illegitimacy rates down. And civic and religious organizations like the National Fatherhood Initiative, the National Marriage Project, and Marriage Savers have successfully pushed a range of national, state, and local marriage initiatives.

The shifting demographic currents of American life suggest that, in some ways, the logic of expressive liberation holds the most promise for the long-term survival of mainline Protestant churches. This approach, which is represented—to a degree—in the United Churches of Christ and the Episcopal Church, entails a very pronounced rhetoric of tolerance and inclusion and a programmatic focus on adult-centered pastoral activities. The peril of this strategy is that there may be a limited market for this kind of religious approach, given that unmarried, divorced, and/or childless American adults are more likely to pursue spirituality outside the confines of "organized religion." Moreover, the ethic of personal liberation entailed in this kind of approach stands in tension with the mainline's commitment to children, as well as its commitment to public justice for the poor and marginalized. Proponents of the logic of expressive liberation have not yet come to terms with the social scientific evidence that children do not do well in a world that is indifferent to adult commitments to marriage.

A rather different mix of challenges and opportunities faces the small cadre of mainline leaders and intellectuals, like the aforementioned Don Browning and Max Stackhouse, who would like to push the mainline in the direction of affirming a pro-marriage, progressive familism. They can take advantage of the increasing elite political and intellectual consensus that marriage is good for children to push for ministries and policies that promote marital stability and quality. They can also turn to the rich Protestant heritage of covenantal theology to make the case for a renewed mainline commitment to the institution of marriage. Finally, if the mainline does champion marriage, the prospects for the success of the burgeoning marriage movement will be greatly increased—given the substantial legitimacy the mainline has in the public sphere.

At the same time, proponents of progressive familism will have to work hard to show that their approach can foster a marriage ethic without endangering the mainline's contemporary commitment to tolerance, personal fulfillment, and gender equality. Their calls, for instance, for reforms in state laws *and* church practices regarding divorce and remarriage could fall on deaf ears in mainline churches that have accommodated contemporary divorce trends for more than twenty-five years. Moreover, they will have to provide models of family ministry that promote marriage *and* attract the increasing number of adults who live outside the bounds of the intact, two-parent family with children. This may be impossible, given the demographic trends outlined above.

Still, the success that conservative Protestant churches have achieved in combining a clear vision of family life with innovative family programming for nontraditional families suggests that the mainline could attempt something similar. Of course, a successful mainline approach to family ministry and discourse would be distinguished by its emphasis on a *progressive* approach that favors egalitarian gender roles and—given the egalitarian trajectory of mainline churches—eventually incorporates gay marriage. The destiny of the mainline and the well-being of countless "children and families" will depend on the pastoral and public strategy that mainline churches take in responding to the new demographic climate now facing the contemporary United States.

NOTES

I thank Sarah Curran and Niall Fagan for their invaluable research assistance in surveying the *Christian Century*, as well as the national meetings of the Episcopal, United Methodist, and Presbyterian (USA) churches. I am also deeply indebted to the denominational officials, clergy, and seminary professors who were interviewed for this project. Finally, I also benefited from comments from Nancy Ammerman, Penny Becker, Benton Jonson, Lynn Robinson, and Brad Wigger.

1. See Sara McLanahan and Gary Sandefur, *Growing Up with a Single Parent* (Cambridge, MA: Harvard University Press, 1994), 1, 38.

2. For a discussion of child poverty and public costs, see Isabel V. Sawhill, "Families at Risk," in Henry Aaron and Robert Reischauer, eds., *Setting National Priorities: The 2000 Election and Beyond* (Washington, DC: Brookings Institution Press, 1999), 97–135. On the link between family breakdown and crime, and for evidence of family structure effects on civic engagement, see Robert J. Sampson, "Crime in Cities: The Effects of Formal and Informal Social Control," in Albert J. Reiss Jr. and Michael Tonry, eds., *Communities and Crime* (Chicago: University of Chicago Press, 1987), 271–307.

3. Mark Chaves, "Family Structure and Protestant Church Attendance: The Sociological Basis of Cohort and Age Effects," *Journal for the Scientific Study of Religion* 30 (1991): 512.

4. See Kevin J. Christiano, "Religion and the Family in Modern American Culture," in Sharon Houseknecht and Jerry Pankhurst, eds., *Family, Religion, and Social Change in Diverse Societies* (New York: Oxford University Press, 2000), 49–68.

5. Don S. Browning, "Religion and Family Ethics: A New Strategy for the Church," in Nancy Ammerman and Wade Clark Roof, eds., *Work, Family, and Religion in Contemporary Society* (New York: Routledge, 1995), 158.

6. Ibid., 157–76.

7. See Andrew J. Cherlin, *Marriage, Divorce, Remarriage* (Cambridge, MA: Harvard University Press, 1992), 6–27, 34–43.

8. Elaine Tyler May, *Homeward Bound: American Families in the Cold War Era* (New York: Basic Books, 1988), 12.

9. James Hudnut-Beumler, *Looking for God in the Suburbs* (New Brunswick, NJ: Rutgers University Press, 1994), 32–36. See also R. Stephen Warner, *New Wine in Old Wineskins: Evangelicals and Liberals in a Small-Town Church* (Berkeley: University of California Press, 1988), 24–25, for figures used to calculate growth rates for Episcopal and Presbyterian churches.

10. Fairchild and Wynn, cited in Penny Long Marler, "Lost in the 1950s: The Changing Family and the Nostalgic Church," in Ammerman and Roof, eds., *Work Family, and Religion,* 33.

11. Robert Wuthnow, *After Heaven: Spirituality in America since the 1950s* (Berkeley: University of California Press, 1998), 36.

12. Richard W. Reifsnyder, "Transformations in Administrative Leadership in the United Presbyterian Church in the U.S.A., 1920–1983," in Milton Coalter, John Mulder, and Louis Weeks, eds., *The Pluralistic Vision: Presbyterians and Mainstream Protestant Education and Leadership* (Louisville, KY: Westminster/John Knox Press, 1996), 259–61.

13. Craig Dykstra and J. Bradley Wigger, "A Brief History of a Genre Problem: Presbyterian Educational Resource Materials," in Coalter, Mulder, and Weeks, eds., *Pluralistic Vision,* 180–204.

14. Robert Wuthnow, *The Restructuring of American Religion* (Princeton, NJ: Princeton University Press, 1988), 55.

15. John Patton and Brian H. Childs, *Christian Marriage and the Family: Caring for Our Generations* (Nashville, TN: Abingdon Press, 1988), 75.

16. *Journal of the 1956 General Conference of the Methodist Church* (Nashville, TN: Board of Publications of the Methodist Church, 1957), 205–6.

17. Ibid.; and Jean Miller Schmidt and Gail E. Murphy-Geiss, "Methodist: 'Tis Grace Will Lead Us Home," in Phyllis D. Airhart and Margaret Lamberts Bendroth, eds., *Faith Traditions and the Family* (Louisville, KY: Westminster/John Knox Press, 1996), 89.

18. See May, *Homeward Bound,* 150–52.

19. Hudnut-Beumler, *Looking for God in the Suburbs,* 131–45.

20. With the assistance of Sarah Curran and Niall Fagan, I surveyed the *Christian Century* from 1955 to 1995 at five-year intervals. All articles dealing with race/civil rights, poverty, the Vietnam War, the peace movement, sexism, and gender-inclusive language were coded as *social justice* articles. All articles dealing with sexual practices and ethics (e.g., family planning, premarital sex), abortion, and homosexuality were coded as *sex-related* articles. Articles addressing marriage, parenting, divorce, day care, gender roles in the family, family/work balance, domestic violence, youth groups, Sunday School, and children's issues were coded as *family-related* articles.

21. The Episcopal, United Presbyterian, and United Lutheran churches liberalized their divorce policies in, respectively, 1958, 1953, and 1956. See James G. Emerson, *Divorce, the Church, and Remarriage* (Philadelphia, PA: Westminster Press, 1961), 111–29.

22. My analysis of the General Social Survey indicates that Catholics and conservative Protestants surpassed mainline Protestants in active churchgoing—defined as attending church at least once a month—in the 1970s.

23. See, for instance, Dean R. Hoge, Benton Johnson, and Donald A. Luidens, *Vanishing Boundaries: The Religion of Mainline Protestant Baby Boomers* (Louisville, KY: Westminster/John Knox Press, 1994) 175–202.

24. See Hoge, Johnson, and Luidens, *Vanishing Boundaries,* 72; and Wade

Clark Roof, *A Generation of Seekers: The Spiritual Journeys of the Baby Boom Generation* (New York: HarperCollins, 1993), 178.

25. See Hoge, Johnson, and Luidens, *Vanishing Boundaries,* 197–200.

26. For discussions of the demographic patterns, see Cherlin, *Marriage, Divorce, Remarriage,* 43–57; and Wuthnow, *After Heaven,* 68.

27. Wuthnow, *After Heaven,* 67.

28. See Ross M. Stolzenberg, Mary Blair-Loy, and Linda J. Waite, "Religious Participation in Early Adulthood: Age and Family Life Cycle Effects on Church Membership," *American Sociological Review* 60 (1995): 84–103.

29. See Michael Hout, Andrew Greeley, and Melissa J. Wilde, "The Decline of the Mainline: Demography, Doctrine, and Attachment" (unpublished ms., Survey Research Center, University of California at Berkeley, 1999).

30. See Donald T. Critchlow, *Intended Consequences: Birth Control, Abortion, and the Federal Government in Modern America* (New York; Oxford University Press, 1999), 57.

31. Hiltner, cited in E. Brooks Hollifield, *A History of Pastoral Care in America: From Salvation to Self-Realization* (Nashville, TN: Abingdon Press, 1983), 281; see pp. 259–356 for a wide-ranging discussion of this therapeutic turn.

32. Robert F. Sinks, "A Theology of Divorce," *Christian Century,* April 20, 1977, 379.

33. My research team surveyed the journals of national meetings for the Episcopal Church, the Presbyterian Church, and the Methodist Church in one year from each decade in the last fifty years. Specifically, they surveyed the following years/denominations: the 1955, 1967, 1976, 1985, and 1997 journals of the General Convention of the (Protestant) Episcopal Church; the 1955, 1965, and 1975 journals of the General Assembly of the United Presbyterian Church (USA), and the 1985 and 1995 journals of its successor, the Presbyterian Church (USA); and the 1956, 1968, 1976, 1988, and 1996 journals of the General Conference of the Methodist Church (which became the United Methodist Church in 1968). Using the topical guides noted in note 20, the team then read each journal to estimate the percentage of pages in each journal that mentioned social justice issues, sex-related issues, and family-related issues.

34. Thomas C. Reeves, *The Empty Church: The Suicide of Liberal Christianity* (New York: Free Press, 1997), 140.

35. *Journal of the 1976 General Conference of the United Methodist Church* (Nashville, TN: Board of Publications of the Methodist Church, 1977), 2062–64.

36. See, for instance, Schmidt and Murphy-Geiss, "Methodist," 91–94.

37. United States Senate, *White House Conference on Families, 1978,* Joint Hearings before the Subcommittee on Child and Human Development of the Senate Human Resources Committee and the Subcommittee on Select Education of the House Committee on Education and Labor, 95th Cong., 2d sess. (Washington, DC: GPO, 1978), 90.

38. White House Conference on Families, *Listening to America's Families: Action for the 80's [sic],* Report to the President, Congress, and Families of the Nation (Washington, DC: GPO, 1980).

39. See, for instance, Warner, *New Wine in Old Wineskins.*

40. Benton Johnson, "Liberal Protestantism: End of the Road?" *Annals of the American Academy of Political and Social Science* 480 (1985): 49.

41. Patton and Childs, *Christian Marriage and Family,* 12.

42. Mary Cooper, interview, May 10, 1999.

43. Max L. Stackhouse, *Covenant and Commitments: Faith, Family, and Economic Life* (Louisville, KY: Westminster/John Knox Press, 1997), 136–60.

44. Don S. Browning, Bonnie J. Miller-McLemore, Pamela D. Couture, K. Brynolf Lyon, and Robert M. Franklin, *From Culture Wars to Common Ground* (Louisville, KY: Westminster/John Knox Press, 1997), 2.

45. Stackhouse, *Covenant and Commitments*, 108.

46. Browning et al., *From Culture Wars to Common Ground*, 307–13.

47. Penny Edgell Becker, "The Family Orientation of Local Congregations" (unpublished ms., Department of Sociology, Cornell University, 2000).

48. All NCS data are taken from W. Bradford Wilcox and Mark Chaves, "Focused on the Family? Religious Traditions, Family Discourse, and Pastoral Practice" (unpublished ms., Department of Sociology, Princeton University, 2000).

49. Robert L. Browning and Roy A. Reed, "Families and Worship," in Herbert Anderson, Don Browning, Ian Evison, and Mary Stewart Van Leeuwen, eds., *The Family Handbook* (Louisville, KY: Westminster/John Knox Press, 1998), 258–63.

50. Ng and Thomas, cited in Browning and Reed, "Families and Worship," 261.

51. *The Book of Discipline of the United Methodist Church* (Nashville, TN: Cokesbury Publishing, 1996), paragraph 66F.

52. "Public Role of Presbyterians," Presbyterian Panel, August 1999.

53. Nancy Ammerman, "Golden Rule Christianity," in David Hall, ed., *Lived Religion in America: Toward a History of Practice* (Princeton, NJ: Princeton University Press, 1997), 204.

54. "Public Role of Presbyterians," Presbyterian Panel, August 1999.

55. Patton and Childs, *Christian Marriage and Family*, 154.

56. "Public Role of Presbyterians," Presbyterian Panel, August 1999.

57. The percentage of mainline clergy involved in pastoral care is calculated from a membership list of the American Association of Pastoral Counselors (Fairfax, VA, 2000). The survey of family counselors can be found in Browning et al., *From Culture Wars to Common Ground*, 201–2, 358.

58. See Laura R. Olson, *Filled with Spirit and Power: Protestant Clergy in Politics* (Albany, NY: State University of New York Press, 2000), 114–19, and Ammerman, "Golden Rule Christianity," 199–203.

59. Lois Livezey, "The Fourth Presbyterian Church of Chicago," in Brynolf Lyon and Archie Smith, eds., *Tending the Flock: Congregations and Family Ministry* (Louisville, KY: Westminster/John Knox Press, 1998), 119–44.

60. Becker, "Family Orientation of Local Congregations," 20.

61. Browning et al., *From Culture Wars to Common Ground*, 319.

62. Figure 11.5 is calculated using General Social Survey data. Only active churchgoers—that is, adults attending once a month or more—are counted in the conservative Protestant and mainline Protestant categories.

63. Wade Clark Roof, *Spiritual Marketplace: Baby Boomers and the Remaking of American Religion* (Princeton, NJ: Princeton University Press, 1999), 251.

64. Stackhouse, *Covenant and Commitments*, 13.

65. Special Committee on Human Sexuality, *Keeping Body and Soul Together: Sexuality, Spirituality, and Social Justice* (Baltimore, MD: Presbyterian Church [USA], 1991), 13–18.

66. Ibid., 53, 52.

67. *Where the Children's Charter for the Church Comes From* (New York: Episcopal Church, Office of Children's Ministries, 1997); and Laura Dean Ford Friedrich, *Putting Children and Their Families First: A Planning Handbook for Congregations* (New York: General Board of Global Ministries, United Methodist Church, 1998), 61–64.

68. Interview with Anna Rhee, director of religious affairs, Children's Defense Fund, June 3, 1999.

69. Interview with Shannon Daley-Harris, former director of religious affairs, Children's Defense Fund, March 20, 2000.

70. See <www.childrensdefense.org/stand96_mwe.html>.

71. Shannon Daley-Harris, ed., *National Observance of Children's Sabbaths* (Washington, DC: Children's Defense Fund, 1999), 44.

72. Figure 11.6 is derived from data taken from the General Social Survey. Active church attendance is defined as attending church once a month or more.

73. See Daphne Spain and Suzanne M. Bianchi, *Balancing Act: Motherhood, Marriage, and Employment among American Women* (New York: Russell Sage Foundation), 5.

12 From Engagement to Retrenchment

An Examination of First Amendment Activism by America's Mainline Churches, 1980–2000

Derek H. Davis

On 16 February 1984, President Ronald Reagan sent a letter to approximately five hundred American religious leaders extolling the progress being made in the U.S. Congress toward the passage of a voluntary school prayer amendment. One can only imagine the president's astonishment when, just two weeks later, twenty-three prominent American clergymen, including representatives from each of the mainline Protestant denominations, submitted a jointly drafted letter to members of the U.S. Senate in which they voiced respect for the "power and importance of prayer" but concurrently announced their "vigorous opposition to proposed constitutional amendments . . . which would effectively return state-sponsored prayer, oral or silent, to America's public schools."[1] President Reagan had contended that "most of us would agree that God should never have been expelled from our children's classrooms" (in obvious reference to the Supreme Court's *Engel v. Vitale* decision of 1962),[2] but the religious leaders retorted that "[n]o Supreme Court decision has ever removed God or religion from the public schools."[3]

The kind of solidarity that was influential in the subsequent defeat of the Reagan-backed school prayer amendment was the exception and not the rule of religious involvement in the First Amendment debates of the final two decades of the twentieth century.[4] A growing perception that Congress and the Supreme Court are eroding the wall of separation between church and state in America raises the question of who is "minding the store" respecting constitutional protections of religious liberty. Traditionally, mainline Protestantism has been a vocal supporter of church-state separation and an enthusiastic defender of religious freedom. However, the mainline's limited degree of activism in recent legislative and judicial deliberations on First Amendment issues raises the question of whether it has abdicated its historic role as the champion of the First Amendment.

If such an abdication has occurred, it bodes ill for the preservation of First Amendment freedoms at a critical time in the nation's history. Indeed, the years between 1980 and 2000 witnessed a continuous and furious debate over constitutional protections of religious liberty that revealed a nation suspended between an expanding religious pluralism that guarantees free exercise privileges to all and a more monolithic Christian identity that treats nontraditional faiths as threats to social solidarity. The polemics have been such that conservative religious leaders have demonized the public schools and generally condemned the moral degradation of secular culture, while liberal religious leaders have often been portrayed as identifying so closely with left-wing politics as to be indistinguishable from "secular liberals." The growing influence of exclusionary politics within the sphere of American Christianity has contributed to a divisiveness that arguably is threatening religious liberty as a basic freedom guaranteed to all Americans. As a traditional defender of this most important constitutional pillar, mainline Protestantism is a pivotal institution in the maintenance of the American experiment.

Church-state politics in the final two decades of the twentieth century were characterized by a succession of quite colorful—though often disturbing—political and judicial events that have culminated in decisions viewed as extreme from both sides of the debate. Most persistent throughout this period were the various attempts of congressional representatives (with the assistance of Roman Catholics, evangelicals, and even some mainline Protestants) to construct some form of voucher system that would enable public funds to be channeled to private—mostly religious—schools. Other First Amendment debates similarly focused on the nation's education system. Congressman Ernest Istook attempted to inject prayer into public school classrooms via constitutional amendment, and a 1998 resolution by the U.S. House of Representatives called for the posting of the Ten Commandments in U.S. courtrooms, public school classrooms, and government buildings. The Equal Access Act of 1984, which established the rules by which student groups may make use of public school facilities for religious meetings, arguably was the most intriguing piece of church-state legislation of the past two decades, attracting both accommodationist and traditional separationist supporters.

Additionally, a robust undercurrent of events and shifting attitudes enlivened First Amendment debates from 1980 to 2000 and, though less visible than direct constitutional challenges, they were quite influential in altering the balance of power between separationist and accommodationist camps. Among mainline Protestants, the increasing emphasis on ecumenical movements and coalition politics served to restructure religious institutions amid charges that within these churches the gulf is widening politically, and perhaps even theologically, between the more liberal clergy and an increasingly conservative laity. In the 1980s, the popularity and perceived success of the Reagan administration in "returning the nation to its roots" undoubtedly alienated some mainline congregations from the perceived liberal political policies of their respective churches. In addition to President Reagan's insistence on the return of God to the classroom in the form of school prayer, his designation of 1983 as the "Year of the Bible," and his appointment of an ambassador to the Vatican were seen as antagonistic acts by traditional defenders of First Amendment rights.[5] The 1980s also witnessed the rise of a formidable political foe for the mainline in the informal alliance between evangelical Protestants and Roman Catholics over the issues of school vouchers and school prayer. These two groups put aside theological differences and joined forces in an effort to gain official acceptance of their views. These newly majoritarian attitudes of traditional religious minorities are a challenge to decades of cultural dominance by mainline Protestantism.

This chapter focuses on the role of mainline denominations in First Amendment debates during the 1980s and 1990s, analyzing specifically the nature and level of activism of the churches, the consistency of their respective positions on First Amendment issues, and the strength of each denomination's commitment to religious liberty vis-à-vis other social and political priorities. I examine the activities of the government affairs offices of the respective denominations and analyze their influence on recent decisions that have transformed church-state relations in America. As one commentator has observed, there has always been some "slipperyness around the edges" in defining the term *mainline*.[6] Therefore, to make this analysis more manageable, the denominations included under the mainline umbrella are limited to the United Methodist Church, the Evangelical Lutheran Church of America, the Presbyterian Church (USA), the Episcopal Church, the American Baptist Churches, and the United Church of Christ. However, coalitions in which these churches participate and ecumenical organizations that represent them in lobbying activities also will be addressed.

I raise certain fundamental questions in order to ascertain the contemporary disposition of mainline churches regarding the First Amendment. Specifically, what have been the methods of the mainline churches in their

First Amendment activism, and have these methods been successful? Is the perceived diminution of mainline activism in recent Supreme Court cases and First Amendment legislation accurate, and, if so, does it reflect a de-emphasis of First Amendment issues in the politics of mainline churches? Have the social policy agendas of mainline denominations deflected attention and/or resources from their traditional advocacy of religious liberty? Are mainline leaders still experiencing political backlash for their support of past decisions (e.g., *Engel v. Vitale*, 1962, the decision that "took God out of the classroom") that have become increasingly unpopular with their own constituencies and with the nation as a whole? Also, has the drain on mainline membership and the corresponding loss of political and financial resources so limited the mainline churches that they are simply no longer able to be significant players in the First Amendment debate?

Finally, in consideration of these questions, I argue that traditional policies and practices of the mainline churches have been rendered less effective by a steadily evolving political climate to which the mainline leadership has been largely unresponsive. The modern defense of religious liberty guaranteed by the First Amendment is taking place in an American culture dramatically different from the one that existed during the mid-century heyday of mainline Protestantism. Consequently, methods and approaches must be revisited and, in some cases, reformulated to account for those differences.

THE BACKGROUND OF MAINLINE POLITICAL ACTIVISM

Before assessing the role of the mainline churches in late-twentieth-century First Amendment engagements, we need to recognize the critical function of two additional diverse and highly influential religious organizations. The National Council of the Churches of Christ in the U.S.A. (NCC) and the Baptist Joint Committee on Public Affairs (BJC), although not tied exclusively to the mainline churches, are key organizations in unraveling the mainline Protestant contribution to First Amendment activism. In fact, the NCC represents thirty-five different Anglican, Orthodox, and Protestant member communions with an aggregate membership of more than 53 million. Although the mainline churches identified as the subject of this chapter are all members of the NCC, they vary as to their consistency of agreement with NCC policy directives, legal briefs, and congressional testimony on First Amendment issues. The Baptist Joint Committee represents only one of the mainline groups covered here (the American Baptist Churches in the U.S.A.) along with eleven other Baptist denominations. However, the BJC's leadership and influence, along with its greater legal resources, establish it as something of a *de facto* representative body for the mainline on certain issues.

The importance of these two organizations to mainline Protestant groups arises from the constitutional expertise and legal resources of the NCC and BJC, on which the mainline churches (and other religious organizations) rely heavily. The NCC and BJC often perform administrative and coordinative functions for many of the coalitions that form around First Amendment issues and that generally include mainline Protestant representatives. They facilitate the establishment of committees that are given specific functional responsibilities in advocating a particular coalition's position. Also, the NCC and BJC serve as repositories for critical information, maintaining documents such as "whip lists" that track how various congressmen are "leaning" with regard to specific pieces of legislation, and designating members of a particular coalition to lobby those House or Senate members.[7]

Mainline Methods of Engagement

The activities of the mainline national staff organizations in the advocacy of various First Amendment issues include legal activism, legislative lobbying, participation in coalitions, and the publication of statements/directives. Independent legal activism by mainline denominations often has been exaggerated, most likely because of its high profile relative to the other forms. Mainline representatives from the national offices admit readily that few legal resources are at their disposal and that such activities are best left to the NCC and BJC, as well as to coalitions, ecumenical groups, and secular legal organizations such as the American Civil Liberties Union (ACLU) and Americans United for the Separation of Church and State (AU).[8] Still, when legal cases affect a particular church's institutional structure or conflict with its fundamental understanding of the church-state relationship, mainline representatives do take independent action. In some cases a church or its parent denomination will enter into a suit directly. More often, however, legal activity takes the form of filing an *amicus curiae* (friend-of-the-court) brief in a particular case in which the church wishes to express its position.

Table 12.1 provides an idea of the extent of legal activism of the mainline denominations on church-state issues relative to that of the NCC. It is not asserted that the table represents every First Amendment case in which these denominations were involved, but rather represents a compilation by the NCC of cases from 1980 through 1995 in which the NCC

Table 12.1. *Amicus Curiae* Briefs Filed by the NCC and Mainline
Denominations, 1980–1995

	1980–1989	1990–1995	Total
American Baptist Churches[a]	10	0	10
Episcopal Church	0	1	1
Evangelical Lutheran Church in America	5	2	7
National Council of Churches	68	28	96
Presbyterian Church (USA)	13	4	17
United Church of Christ	9	0	9
United Methodist Church	8	1	9

SOURCE: These figures were tabulated from a spreadsheet obtained from the NCC archives (Washington Office), 16 December 1999.

[a]Filings by the Baptist Joint Committee were not included in the total given for the American Baptist Churches.

filed friend-of-the-court briefs and the mainline churches shown here also filed.

This table shows that all of the mainline denominations under examination sometimes participated independently in the litigation of church-state cases from 1980 to 1995, but also that they more often relied heavily on the NCC in representing their interests. But participation in court cases does not present the totality of activism by these groups. Mainline activism in the aftermath of the 1990 *Oregon v. Smith* decision, which substantially altered the "compelling state interest" test for measuring violations of the Free Exercise clause, ranged, for example, from simple affirmation of previous policy statements on free exercise to highly charged testimony by church representatives at Senate committee hearings. The *Smith* case held that states must no longer show a compelling interest in denying a religious liberty claim, but must show only that a contested law infringing religious liberty is "neutrally" applied against all persons and groups. The decision was widely unpopular among religious freedom advocates because it left religious freedom at the mercy of state legislators. Perhaps most significant in this particular case was the formation of the Coalition for the Free Exercise of Religion, whose membership included sixty-eight incredibly diverse religious organizations. The coalition's crowning achievement was pushing through Congress the Religious Freedom Restoration Act (1993), which sought to correct the harmful effects of the *Smith* decision.

Nevertheless, we should note that, of the seven committee chairs within the Coalition for the Free Exercise of Religion, none was occupied by a mainline Protestant.[9] This coalition was so diverse and so specialized in its formation and focus as to be the archetype of politically expedient, special-interest politics. The dependence of the mainline denominations on ecumenical organizations and coalitions is part of a goal that mainline denominations have traditionally pursued, but it also reflects a widely perceived decline in mainline political influence. That decline undoubtedly is conditioned by a very real drop in membership of constituent churches and a corresponding decrease in funding for their national offices. In 1993, for example, funding cuts forced the Episcopal Church to eliminate approximately 20 percent of its national headquarters' staff.[10] And by 1992, benevolence giving in the American Baptist Churches in the U.S.A. had declined more than 25 percent from its 1970 level.[11]

Moreover, the members who remain in mainline Protestant pews appear increasingly detached from their Washington offices and the positions for which they lobby. The Evangelical Lutheran Church has more than five million members, yet it sends its *Legislative Update* to only around five thousand, presumably those who are most politically active. As Daniel Hofrenning observes, this detachment of the Lutheran national staff from its membership "is repeated in other mainline Protestant bodies. Most members of denominations are unaware that they have a lobbying office in Washington."[12] This detachment often results in an ideological disconnect between church leaders and their respective laities on critical issues. For example, a survey taken in 1980 revealed that 75 percent of United Methodist membership favored school prayer as opposed to just 29 percent of the staff at national headquarters.[13]

A 1992 study produced some surprising results that may also shed light on the ideological separation between national church leaders and their constituencies. Attempting to categorize the separationist/accommodationist leanings of certain segments of the U.S. population, this study found, predictably, that "academic elites" overwhelmingly favored a strong separationist attitude toward church-state relations in this country, with 86 percent choosing the "no help/high wall" category as a statement of principle. By contrast, only 36 percent of the "mass public" chose "no help/high wall"; and, as might be expected, a mere 25 percent of Catholic priests selected the most separationist category. Perhaps most surprising in the study, however, was the finding that less than 50 percent of Protestant ministers selected "no help/high wall" as their personal statement of principle concerning church-state relations in America.[14] Unfortunately, the study did not separate mainline from evangelical ministers in its categorization of Protestant clergy, and conservative evangelicals undoubtedly tilted the balance of this category more in the accommodationist direction. Still, the statistic reflects what officials of the mainline government affairs offices described in interviews conducted to gather information for this chapter—that the clergy of their respective denominations are increasingly unwilling to assist in First Amendment defenses. According to mainline national staff members, many local clergymen are backing off positions concerning school prayer, school vouchers, and other issues on which their denominations have traditionally held separationist views.[15]

Beyond legal activism, coalition participation, and congressional testimony, mainline organizations often publish their First Amendment positions in newsletters or post them on their respective websites. The Lutheran Office for Governmental Affairs crafted an eloquent appeal to the Lutheran membership in its *Legislative Backgrounder* that explained the reasons behind the formation of the Coalition for Free Exercise and urged church members to aid in the fight to restore the compelling-interest test that *Smith* obliterated.[16] An attached document offered support for amendments to the American Indian Religious Freedom Act, identifying the *Smith* decision as a particularly egregious infringement on the religious liberty of Native Americans.[17] These statements were well-crafted and unequivocal in their common message that the *Smith* decision had placed the First Amendment rights of Americans in jeopardy. Of course, statements of position are less expensive than the resources required to aid in the legal defense of religious minorities or to file briefs of *amicus curiae* in First Amendment cases. Such statements are also less controversial than appearing before Congress or actively attempting to rally support for a First Amendment cause from within the membership.

The Washington offices of the mainline churches are understaffed, underfunded, and vastly overwhelmed with issues as diverse as supporting AIDS Awareness Week, encouraging the U.S. government to grant debt relief to third-world countries as a part of Jubilee 2000, and promoting greater access to health care for the poor. When pressed as to the priority given to First Amendment issues vis-à-vis other political issues, the leaders of the respective denominations' governmental affairs offices are quite candid in acknowledging that First Amendment items fall low on the list. Jay Lintner of the United Church of Christ stated that "church/state is about our tenth or fifteenth highest priority, and not where we are exerting leadership."[18]

Still, the Washington offices of the mainline churches have maintained generally strong separationist voices, despite growing skepticism from within their respective denominations and the temptation to post rather than promote their views. We now turn to an examination of specific mainline activism regarding the major First Amendment issues of the past two decades in the face of increasing internal dissension and the formation of accommodationist alliances that served to challenge liberal Protestant influence.

ADDRESSING THE ISSUES

Defending the Free Exercise of Religion

Even a few days prior to the start of the 1980s, a significant legal case involving the Cherokee Indians would foreshadow future First Amendment cases (including the watershed *Oregon v. Smith* decision) that challenged the religious practices of several minority religions. On 19 November 1979, the American Baptist Churches in the U.S.A., the Presbyterian Church (USA), and the National Council of Churches announced the filing, along with other organizations, of an *amicus curiae* brief in the case of *Sequoyah v. TVA*.[19] This case involved the use of the Energy and Water Development Appropriation Act, signed into law by President Carter on 25 September 1979, to build a dam on the Little Tennessee River that would cause the flooding of Cherokee burial lands.[20] In the petition to file, the group had observed that the Sixth Circuit Court, in dismissing the suit brought by the Cherokees, had failed even to mention the compelling-interest test, a test that had been, since 1963, the prevailing Supreme Court doctrine for determining violations of the Free Exercise Clause. That test protected a religious practice unless the government could prove that it had a "compelling interest" in proscribing the practice.

In contrast, a highly controversial Supreme Court case in 1983 directly employed the compelling-interest test. *Bob Jones University v. United States* (1983) involved a fundamentalist Christian university in South Carolina that implemented student policies many considered racially discriminatory, including the prohibition of interracial dating within the student body. The IRS acted to revoke Bob Jones University's status as a tax-exempt institution on the grounds that it must not only meet the basic criteria for charitable institutions but also that it "must not be contrary to established public policy."[21] The Supreme Court upheld the constitutionality of the IRS policy and agreed with the appellate court's finding against the school. Justice Burger issued the opinion for the Court, stating that even "sincerely held religious beliefs" could not overcome a compelling state interest which "substantially outweighs whatever burden denial of tax benefits places on petitioners' exercise of their religious beliefs."[22]

This case put mainline Protestant leadership in the awkward position of having to choose between the right to free exercise—even if it meant supporting a racially discriminatory religious institution—and its traditional commitment to civil rights. The facts of the case severely divided mainline Protestants, both interdenominationally and within their respective congregational bodies. In *amicus curiae* filings, the American Baptist Churches in the U.S.A. continued their tradition of staunchly defending free exercise by favoring reversal of the lower court decision. However, Earle K. Moore wrote a brief for the United Church of Christ urging affirmation of the lower court decision.[23] One Presbyterian leader stated that "black Presbyterians were themselves divided" on the issue, and the Stated Clerk of the General Assembly ultimately decided to join the American Baptists in their brief favoring reversal.[24] The 1983 General Assembly of the PCUSA had clearly done its homework before arriving at this decision, soliciting the expertise of constitutional heavyweights Douglas Laycock and Derrick Bell, and consulting with Gayraud Wilmore, then Dean of the Center for Black Church Studies at Colgate Rochester.[25] Still, the clamor caused by the *Bob Jones* case within the PCUSA led certain presbyteries to challenge the Stated Clerk's authority in the filing of legal briefs.

However, the *Oregon v. Smith* case in 1990 was clearly the defining moment in the constitutional battle over the free exercise of religion in America during the past two decades. Even after observing the omission of the compelling-interest test in *Sequoyah v. TVA*, mainline organizations appeared to have been caught "off-guard" by the *Smith* decision,[26] which targeted ritual peyote use in Native American ceremonies. The *Smith* Court abandoned the compelling-interest test in favor of a "neutral law" standard. Consequently, two Native Americans' ritual use of peyote had little protection from state proscription. The State of Oregon only had to show that its law proscribing use of peyote applied "neutrally" to all citizens; it no longer had to demonstrate a compelling interest in restricting the religious use of peyote. The case sent shock waves through much of the religious community, since the new standard threatened many religious minorities whose practices might be made illegal by simple passage of a "neutral" law.

No mainline organization or coalition in which the majority of mainline churches were members contributed briefs in the *Smith* case,[27] though all the mainline denominations became involved in the subsequent lobbying campaign that led to the passage of the Religious Freedom Restoration Act

(RFRA) in 1993, which attempted to resurrect the compelling-interest test that was rejected in the *Smith* decision. The activity of this broad-based coalition (the Coalition for the Free Exercise of Religion) was temporarily successful in restoring "compelling interest" as a standard in the determination of government intrusions on the free exercise of religion. However, in 1997, the Supreme Court ruled in *Boerne v. Flores* that Congress, in passing the RFRA, had acted outside its sphere of power and responsibilities and placed an undue burden on the states. The compelling-interest test had once again been lost.

By the late 1990s, mainline denominational organizations were well-alerted to the damage done by *Smith* and the overturning of the RFRA, and these groups initially provided considerable support to the proposed Religious Liberty Protection Act (RLPA). The RLPA, like the RFRA, was designed to resurrect the compelling-interest standard. In testimony in support of the RLPA before the House Judiciary Committee in July of 1998, the Reverend Elenora Giddings Ivory, director of the Washington Office of the Presbyterian Church (USA), identified some specific government restrictions on free exercise drawn from within her own denomination. One case involved a coalition of local churches in Richmond, Virginia, that initiated a "meal ministry" to serve the poor. This program became a victim of its own success, for as it grew, it came into conflict with a city zoning ordinance that limited feeding and housing programs for the homeless provided by churches to "no more than 30 homeless individuals for up to seven days between the months of April and October."[28] The ordinance clearly targeted religious organizations, yet the parish had to challenge the ordinance in civil court in order to defend its First Amendment rights. Reverend Giddings Ivory made it clear that the existence of the Religious Freedom Restoration Act in 1996 (prior to the Supreme Court's declaring it unconstitutional) saved the program from elimination.

Oliver Thomas, special counsel for the NCC, also provided testimony before the House Subcommittee on the Constitution in support of the RLPA. Thomas retraced the various attempts to restore the religious liberty safety net lost in the *Smith* decision. His testimony on 12 May 1999 also served as a preemptive defense, alerting committee members to RLPA opposition from the right and left. On the left, ironically, a traditional ally of mainline Protestants in religious liberty cases, the American Civil Liberties Union (ACLU), came out against the RLPA because of fears that it threatened gay rights.[29] However, not even five months after his testimony before the Constitution Subcommittee, Thomas penned a letter to senators he had lobbied, announcing the decision of the NCC to withdraw support from the bill for reasons not of "principle" but of "strategy." In the letter, Thomas expressed his view that RLPA would inevitably be overturned by the Supreme Court, offering as evidence the "trend by the Court to curtail Congress's power to regulate the activities of state and local governments," which the RLPA expressly did.[30] Thomas's concern was that the over-turning of the RLPA would further "delay efforts to restore legal protections to those most seriously damaged by *Smith*."[31] However, the fraying of the traditional coalition must have influenced the NCC's decision as well. By October of 1999, at least a dozen members of the Coalition for the Free Exercise of Religion had withdrawn their support, and the effort was effectively doomed.[32]

Keeping God Out of the Classroom

As noted earlier, many leaders of mainline denominations have accurately observed that no Supreme Court decision has ever removed God or religion from the public schools. Yet several of the major First Amendment debates of the 1980s and 1990s concerned the place of religion in the American public school system. Of particular significance to this chapter, the *Engel v. Vitale* (1962) and *Abington School District v. Schempp* (1963) decisions, respectively, ruled that "official" prayer and formal Bible reading in the public schools were unconstitutional. These rulings were consistent with the First Amendment views of a majority of the mainline Protestant leadership, and most mainline denominations released statements following these decisions to explain their concurrence with the Supreme Court rulings.

But the school prayer controversy has continued since the *Engel* decision, and it repeatedly surfaced over the past two decades as perhaps the most contentious and emotionally charged of all First Amendment issues. In the 1980s, it was Senator Jesse Helms of North Carolina who led the charge to return God to American classrooms in the form of officially sanctioned prayer. Helms attempted a back-door subversion of the constitutional system by constructing an amendment that would have placed legislation on school prayer beyond judicial review. The controversy spawned by the Helms Amendment led to several attempts at less coercive and less constitutionally confrontational legislation.[33]

With strong support from mainline Protestants, the Helms Amendment was defeated. The Senate did vote in favor of the constitutional amendment (56 to 44); however, that was some 11 votes short of the two-thirds majority required for passage. Each of the mainline denominations of interest here opposed the amendment.[34]

In the summer of 1995, however, another challenge emerged in a school prayer amendment offered by Representatives Sam Johnson (R-TX) and James Duncan (R-TN), which proposed to deny all Department of Education funds to any local or state education agency "which effectively prevents participation in constitutionally protected prayer in public schools by individuals on a voluntary basis."[35] The NCC joined with People for the American Way (PFAW) in a lobbying campaign to prevent passage of the amendment. The lobbying campaign was directed at all House members—"minus about 100 hardcore conservatives"—and it requested that rather than new legislation, a measure contributed by Nancy Kassebaum (R-KS) to the previously adopted Improving America's Schools Act be given time to work before enacting other measures.[36] PFAW and the NCC preferred the Kassebaum measure because it required "willful" misconduct by education agencies before penalties could be assessed, whereas the Johnson/Duncan bill implied that "negligent" behavior could trigger the denial of funds.

In her testimony before the House Committee on the Judiciary's Subcommittee on the Constitution on 23 July 1996, Reverend Elenora Giddings Ivory of the Presbyterian Church (USA) projected some of the potentially damaging effects of the Legislation to Further Protect Religious Freedom and reiterated the lack of necessity for such legislation, noting that "students already have the right to pray in student-led Bible study groups under the Free Access Law."[37] Reverend Giddings Ivory avoided much of the constitutional issue to focus instead on the potential abuses of such authority by school employees largely untrained in religion and theology. And she addressed the obvious, though often overlooked, question of how, presuming such legislation should pass, the state could possibly craft a meaningful prayer that is satisfactory to the various religious groups represented in the public schools. Rev. Giddings Ivory noted that "we Christians do not even agree on how to pray together, let alone mix us in with Jews, Moslems and Hindus."[38]

Rep. Ernest Istook (R-OK) once again raised the issue of school prayer in 1997 in the House of Representatives in the form of a proposed constitutional amendment. Debate on the proposal was heated. Representative Chet Edwards of Texas, who played a key role in opposing the Istook Amendment in the House, was accused by Pat Robertson's organization of "religious bigotry" and of displaying "attitudes [that] have no place in Texas or anywhere in America."[39] Congressman Edwards defended the Christian Coalition's right to advocate legislation that it deemed desirable, but lamented the McCarthy-like tactics and the sad state of affairs in the politics of the Religious Right, where it is "now anti-American to defend the Bill of Rights."[40]

Ultimately, the Istook Amendment failed by a vote of 224 in favor to 203 against, some 61 votes shy of becoming the law of the land.[41] While representatives from the mainline churches fought vigorously to see that the Istook Amendment was defeated, it had a sturdy opponent in an emerging coalition of evangelicals, Catholics, and others who wanted to see a greater accommodation of religion by government. Indeed, the drive to institute official prayer in the public school system appears to be growing even among more "liberal" segments of American society.[42] Therefore, the first order of business for the national staffs of the mainline churches has become convincing their respective laities of the perils of injecting government-sanctioned prayer into the classroom. Rearticulating previous statements of policy is no longer sufficient. The movement to bring government-sanctioned prayer into the nation's public schools will be impossible to stave off without an energized mainline community that fully understands the dangers of such action. Mainline organizations will face an uphill battle on this issue. School prayer is forced to compete with myriad other agenda items that often swamp their governmental affairs offices.

Public Funds for Parochial Schools

Another public school issue that continually resurfaced during the 1980s and 1990s concerned the proposed distribution of public funds to private, including religious, schools. In 1981, Senators Daniel Patrick Moynihan (D-NY) and Robert Packwood (R-OR) introduced a tuition reimbursement bill designed to provide tax credits to parents of parochial school children. Providing vigorous support for the bill, the U.S. Catholic Conference held nine meetings in major cities throughout the country to drum up political momentum for "parochiad."[43] Secular opposition to the bill came from diverse sources, including major newspapers like the *Chicago Tribune* and academicians, including Donald Kennedy, the president of Stanford University.[44] Among mainline groups, the BJC took the initiative, with executive director James Dunn publicly predicting that the bill would have taxpayers "paying a premium with tax dollars for withdrawing children from the public schools."[45] The NCC reiterated its policy statement against school vouchers that had been developed in the early 1960s, speaking for all its constituent organizations. The statement opposed the use of public funds for grant, tuition, or scholarship programs for "private or church-related elementary or secondary schools."[46]

By the late 1980s a few chinks in the mainline armor had begun to appear concerning school vouchers. The Ford-Durenberger Amendment, authored by the "pro-voucher" U.S. Catholic Conference, was designed to expand "choice" by enabling parents to use vouchers for parochial day-care centers. The Protestant Church lobbies opposed the bill along with the ACLU and NEA on grounds that it would forge an excessive entanglement between church and state. However, education associations from within the Lutheran and Episcopal Churches came out in favor of the bill, contravening their own Washington lobbying organizations and sending a mixed message to Congress on the position of mainline Protestantism.[47]

In the early 1990s, another case involving public aid to parochial schools tested the waters of "educational flexibility" and, consequently, mainline solidarity regarding the wall of church-state separation. *Zobrest v. Catalina Foothills School District* involved the constitutionality of the government provision of an interpreter for a deaf student at an Arizona Catholic high school. This case caused a significant rift in the traditional separationist stance of mainline Protestantism. The NCC, staunchly separationist in past filings as a representative of the mainline Protestant and other organizations, sided with the accommodationist camp in a joint *amicus* filing with groups like the Christian Life Commission and Catholic League for Religious and Civil Rights.[48] What was surprising about the NCC's willingness to join this coalition in filing was the brief's strong condemnation of the "*Lemon* test." In the 1971 case of *Lemon v. Kurtzman*, the Supreme Court had established a strongly separationist, three-pronged test to aid in the determination of such parochial cases. However, the brief in which the NCC participated characterized the *Lemon* test as "deeply flawed" and stated that the test "produces unnecessary and destructive conflicts between the principles of free exercise and nonestablishment."[49] The BJC also filed a brief (jointly with the American Jewish Congress and the Union of American Hebrew Congregations) favoring the Zobrests' attempt to obtain a publicly funded interpreter. However, the legal foundation of this brief differed dramatically from the one in which the NCC participated. It held that it was unnecessary for the Supreme Court to amend the *Lemon* test in order to accommodate the Zobrests, which would, thereby, preserve the prevailing standard for Court decisions in cases involving government aid to religious schools.[50]

In polls taken from among the general population, opposition to vouchers was revealed to be thin and eroding. It was reported in a Phi Delta/Gallup survey that the percentage of Americans favoring some form of private-school voucher had grown significantly from 24 to 36 percent between 1993 and 1996.[51] And the prospects for private-school vouchers undoubtedly will increase into the twenty-first century since the new president, George W. Bush, is a declared supporter of school vouchers.

Opportunities for More Positive Activism: Equal Access and Charitable Choice

Two First Amendment issues in particular emerged near the end of the millennium that provided opportunities for greater conciliation between the national staffs of the mainline churches and their constituencies. These two issues, known commonly as Equal Access and Charitable Choice, offered less constitutionally controversial means by which institutions of church and state might cooperate, ostensibly in advancing the public good.

The Equal Access Act emerged as a political compromise offered by those who opposed school prayer amendments but desired some accommodation of religion by public schools. This legislation, introduced by Senator Jeremiah Denton of Alabama, applied to secondary public schools and called for "equal access and opportunity to public school students who wish to meet voluntarily for religious purposes."[52] Senator Denton's bill also utilized the coercive force of denying federal funds to school districts that denied "students or faculty or groups of students or faculty" the ability to "seek to engage in voluntary prayer, religious discussion or silent meditation on school premises during non-instructional periods."[53] The Equal Access Act became law in 1984.

One mainline official noted that Equal Access legislation was popular among politicians who are opposed to school prayer because it gave them "the chance to demonstrate that they favor truly voluntary religious expression by students."[54] The issue was similarly popular among national staff members of the mainline churches. Though ardent separationist groups opposed the measure, several mainline political organizations recognized Equal Access as a touchstone issue of potential common ground between themselves, their respective clergies, and their seemingly more accommodationist laities. Once the concept took on an air of inevitability, Equal Access became an issue of positive activism, energizing the Washington offices of most mainline churches. Several mainline groups participated in cooperative efforts to develop guidelines for the aid of school administrators and others in the implementation of Equal Access, and traditional adversaries came together in support of it. The BJC published a detailed set of guidelines in "question/answer" form intended to clarify the wording of the law.[55] The BJC, along with the NCC, contributed to a similar document (along with groups like the American Jewish Congress, the National Association of Evangelicals, and the National Education Association) that provided details about the Equal Access Act. In addition, Dean Kelley testified before the House Committee on Education and Labor on 28 March 1984 that if public institutions provided limited forums for "voluntary extracurricular student activities, [these] could not exclude religious speech."[56] The Lutheran Council in the U.S.A. was one of the few mainline groups to come out strongly against the Equal Access Act on the basis that religious groups that more aggressively proselytize would use the law to their advantage in converting those of other faiths.[57] Still, Equal Access must be seen as one of the least contentious First Amendment issues of the past twenty years.

Another less contentious First Amendment issue resulted from the welfare reform law of 1996 that enabled state governments to enter into contracts with various religious groups to provide social services—the so-called Charitable Choice law.[58] Under this arrangement, religious organizations are provided funds from the public till to compensate them for the services provided. Traditionally, such a relationship would have been viewed as an overt breach of church-state separation. However, faced with mounting pressures from within the memberships to help right the moral course of the country, some mainline organizations have become more receptive to the idea of Charitable Choice.

In fact, the Lutheran Church via its Lutheran Social Services organization had been receiving public dollars for the provision of services for many years prior to the enactment of the law. The Lutheran Office for Governmental Affairs published a document promoting Charitable Choice as "an opportunity for congregations to expand their social ministry." The document did cite the caveat that "congregations accepting public funds would be subject to scrutiny by federal auditors," and it advised groups pursuing Charitable Choice "to keep a separate set of books for these funds."[59] However, as to specific guidelines for implementation, the document recommended contacting the state, county, or municipal department of social services.

The Presbyterian Church (USA) also provided a document to constituent organizations detailing fourteen specific guidelines for the implementation of Charitable Choice.[60] A supplemental newsletter, "Questions about Charitable Choice," acknowledged that "many local congregations are excited about this possibility," but the document also raised some serious questions that the allure of federal money might tend to overshadow, such as, "Will a congregation be obliged to check the immigration status of the people it serves?"[61] The two documents are well-balanced in acknowledging the new federal law as a statutory reality that poses a real danger of church-state entanglement, while offering substantive guidelines for minimizing this risk.

Charitable Choice, like Equal Access, has provided the mainline Protestant churches with a First Amendment issue that allows them to promote their constitutional expertise without becoming confrontational with member congregations. The majority of mainline government affairs offices, while leery of potential church-state entanglement in these two areas, are providing guidelines to advise their local congregations rather than warning them against involvement. Only the BJC joined a coalition called "The Working Group for Religious Freedom in Social Services," which sought to provide an alternative voice to Charitable Choice proponents.[62] The gray areas of Equal Access and Charitable Choice are enticing to the mainline churches, which have been characterized as experiencing a collective identity crisis, because they appeal to mainline Protestantism's traditional identity, which is grounded in community involvement and social activism. Promises to maintain arms-length relationships with government in the use of government facilities and the subcontracting of social services will be difficult at best.

Mainline Protestantism and the Abortion Controversy

The mainline Protestant churches were rocked by a Supreme Court decision in the 1970s that threatened the delicate truce between the leadership of these denominations and an increasingly uneasy and conservative segment of the mainline membership. *Roe v. Wade* (1973), the incendiary decision that legalized abortion, resulted in an ideological divide within the mainline that, in many respects, contributed to the loss of status of the national staff organizations of these churches that has persisted to the present day.

Only a year after the abortion decision, the United Methodist General Board of Church and Society formed the Religious Coalition for Abortion Rights (RCAR). RCAR would evolve its "Statement of Purpose" to eventually ground its support for abortion rights in the "constitutional guarantees of privacy and religious freedom," arguing that government had no right to restrict any woman's freedom of conscience.[63] The Board of Homeland Ministries and Center for Social Action of the United Church of Christ, another mainline member of RCAR, recommended the "repeal of all legal prohibitions of physician performed abortions."[64] Other mainline Protestant RCAR members detailed the specific conditions under which abortion could be a morally acceptable alternative. The General Executive

Board of the Presbyterian Church (USA), for example, established valid socioeconomic criteria for abortion, while the Division of Social Ministries of the American Baptist Churches declared a "virtually unqualified" right to choose in the first trimester of pregnancy.[65] Similarly, the Episcopal Church, while disavowing support of "abortion for convenience," stated its opposition to legal restrictions on abortion in a statement released by its General Convention in 1979.[66]

Mainline Protestantism continued its rather liberal stance toward abortion into the decade of the 1980s. In its "Covenant and Creation: Theological Reflections on Contraception and Abortion (1983)," the Presbyterian Church (USA) issued the following statements: "The decision to terminate a pregnancy is a question of one's covenant responsibility to accept the limits of human resources. . . . When someone can discern that it would not be good for a child to be born as the result of a particular pregnancy, she has a responsibility to take her human limitations seriously and to act accordingly."[67] The Episcopal Church took a somewhat more stringent line on abortion in a resolution created by its Sixty-ninth General Convention, which said abortion should be an option only in "extreme situations," and announced its opposition to abortion for purposes of "birth control, family planning, sex selection, or any reason of mere convenience." Yet the same resolution also stated that legislation is not the answer and that "individual conscience is respected."[68] Likewise, the ELCA in its "Resolution on Abortion (1990)," urged "those dealing with problem pregnancies to avail themselves of competent Christian guidance to help them explore the entire issue, including long-range effects and options other than abortions."[69] Indeed, none of the mainline churches discussed in this chapter called for legal prohibitions, even with qualifications, on abortion rights in the United States during this period. And, while several have reconsidered their positions since the 1980s, their general support for abortion rights remains. The importance of the abortion debates of the 1970s and 1980s is not found in the largely pro-choice positions taken by the mainline churches during this period, however. Rather, it is that these churches located the right to abortion in the religion clauses of the First Amendment, causing an ideological divide between the mainline leadership and a large segment of the membership that opposes abortion. The trauma inflicted by the association of what many conservative Protestants consider a moral evil with that most noble of secular documents, the United States Constitution, has never abated. Although several of the mainline organizations have since revisited their positions on abortion, the perception of many who left mainline churches in this period, and even of many members who remain, is that the constitutional right to religious freedom has been used to support the killing of innocents.[70] This perception undoubtedly contributed to a decline of influence of the mainline churches' national staff organizations with their respective memberships.

CONCLUSION

The decline of mainline Protestant influence in First Amendment debates and the concurrent rise in influence of the informal coalition of Roman Catholics, conservative evangelicals, and other accommodationist factions have led to increasingly majoritarian attitudes within the American polity. In addition, viewed from the perspective of traditional mainline advocacy, the recomposition of the Supreme Court along conservative lines already has contributed to decisions that have eroded First Amendment rights. The mainline churches have always served as an effective counter to these forces, but that counter is weakening and might continue to weaken if certain corrective measures are not instituted.

The mainline churches lost a tireless and powerful voice for religious freedom with the death of Dean Kelley in 1998. Likewise, the departure of Kelley's successor Oliver Thomas from the NCC in 1999 created a void in First Amendment activism that will be difficult to fill. The impassioned personalities that have so eloquently crafted the defense of church-state separation perhaps have masked underlying weaknesses in institutional structure.[71] The well-chronicled dissipation of resources from mainline organizations is quite evident in the lack of staff and equipment at their national offices. Cuts in funding have taken a considerable toll on the ability of these organizations to perform their jobs effectively. This situation must change. Consistent levels of funding and the abolishment of "litmus test" issues often used by constituent congregations for the determination of funding are essential to the future success of mainline lobbies in the promotion of religious liberty.[72]

Realistically, however, resources will not be forthcoming until the national organizations find ways to reenergize their respective memberships on the importance of issues like the defense of religious liberty. This effort will require that national staff members get out of Washington and into the pews and pulpits of their constituent churches. Lay members of the mainline denominations must not only encourage their national staff members in their important work, but also create a more effective voice for defense of the First Amendment through greater personal involvement. If the clergy and laity of the mainline churches are indifferent, or worse, antagonistic toward church-state separation and its importance to the nation, the cause could be lost regardless of the level of advocacy of the Washington offices.

The condition of modern political discourse in America dictates that the defense of religious liberty will require vigilance, resources, and commitment. Mainline lobbies must do a better job of keeping their constituents informed so that they will provide more vocal and financial support. National staffers also must be more cognizant of the need to ground their political positions in the teachings of their respective churches, working more closely with theologians and ministers. Concurrently, all mainline organizations must be more willing to distance themselves from the platform of any particular party or political faction. Unless the national organizations of the mainline churches are able to reenergize their memberships on the importance of this cause, the battle to preserve Americans' First Amendment liberties might be lost by default!

NOTES

1. Letter from twenty-three American clergymen dated 1 March 1984 to members of the U.S. Senate; obtained from vertical files, J. M. Dawson Institute of Church-State Studies, Baylor University, Waco, TX.

2. The White House Office of Media Relations and Planning, "Text of a Letter by the President Sent in Response to Approximately 500 Religious Leaders Across the Country on His School Prayer Amendment," 16 February 1984; obtained from vertical files, J. M. Dawson Institute of Church-State Studies, Baylor University, Waco, TX.

3. Ibid.

4. In fact, however, a similar letter from clergymen and other interested parties appeared in 1991 addressed to President George Bush, whose administration was advocating the abolishment of the traditional "*Lemon* test" used by courts to determine violations of the Establishment Clause. Yet the point here is that true solidarity in the fight for religious freedom requires constancy and diligence in the active promotion of First Amendment liberties rather than reactive and highly sporadic statements against specific threats. See "A Letter to the White House," *Church & State* 44, no. 11 (December 1991): 251.

5. Allen Hertzke has observed that Reagan foreign policy initiatives actually "galvanized the liberal religious community, whose greatest successes lay in checking the administration's more unpopular policies. In this curious way, the Reagan Administration helped the liberal Protestants retain some relevance." See Allen D. Hertzke, "An Assessment of the Mainline Churches since 1945," in *The Role of Religion in the Making of Public Policy*, ed. James E. Wood Jr. and Derek Davis (Waco, TX: J. M. Dawson Institute of Church-State Studies, Baylor University, 1991), 55.

6. Ibid., 45.

7. A "Religious Liberty Whip List," for example, was located at the NCC Washington office; it is organized by House of Representatives member name (separated by political party) and contains representatives from various participant groups

who have agreed or been assigned to lobby each representative. List dated 28 April 1998; obtained from NCC archives (Washington office), 17 December 1999.

8. Eleizer Valentin-Castanon of the United Methodist Board of Church and Society (UMBCS) stated that the attitude toward church-state legal issues among many staff members of the mainline churches is to "leave it to the Baptists—that's what they do best," referring principally to the Baptist Joint Committee on Public Affairs; Eleizer Valentin-Castanon, UMBCS, interview with author, Washington, DC, 16 December 1999.

9. Committee chairpersons came from two secular groups in addition to the Church of Jesus Christ of Latter-day Saints, the American Jewish Committee, the American Jewish Congress, the Anti-Defamation League, and Christian Legal Society; "Coalition for the Free Exercise of Religion Task Force Assignments," fax memorandum from J. Brent Walker to coalition members, 9 July 1997; obtained from NCC archives (Washington office), 17 December 1999.

10. Revenue shortfalls in the Presbyterian Church (USA) and Evangelical Lutheran Church in America (ELCA) forced similar reductions. See Ronald E. Vallet and Charles E. Zech, *The Mainline Church's Funding Crisis: Issues and Possibilities* (Grand Rapids, MI: William B. Eerdmans, 1995), 12.

11. Ibid., 22.

12. Daniel J. B. Hofrenning, *In Washington but Not of It: The Prophetic Politics of Religious Lobbyists* (Philadelphia, PA: Temple University Press, 1995), 87.

13. A. James Reichley, *Religion in American Public Life* (Washington, DC: Brookings Institution, 1985), 269–74; cited in Hofrenning, *In Washington but Not of It,* 150.

14. Clyde Wilcox, et al., "Public Attitudes toward Church-State Issues: Elite-Mass Differences," *Journal of Church and State* 34 (spring 1992): 271.

15. Comments taken from interviews conducted with Eleizer Valentin-Castanon of the United Methodist Board of Church and Society (UMBCS), the Rev. Elenora Giddings Ivory, director of the Washington Office of the PCUSA, and Tom Hart, director of the Episcopal Church Office of Government Relations (Washington, DC, 16–17 December 1999).

16. Kay Bengston, "The Religious Freedom Restoration Act (RFRA)," *Legislative Backgrounder,* 23 October 1992, 1–2. Current issues of the Lutheran Office for Governmental Affairs' *Legislative Updates* are available via the internet at <www.loga.org/LOGALUs.htm>.

17. Mia Baumgartner, "Amendments to the American Indian Religious Freedom Act," *Legislative Backgrounder,* 23 October 1992, 3.

18. Jay Lintner, personal e-mail, 15 December 1999.

19. The other organizations filing with the Protestant organizations were the American Civil Liberties Union and the Center for Constitutional Rights; see "Press Release from ACLU," contact Trudi Schutz, 19 November 1979; obtained from NCC archives (Washington office), 17 December 1999.

20. *Sequoyah v. TVA,* 437 U.S. 105 (1979). The proposed dam would flood the burial sites of Cherokees—including that of their great leader Sequoyah—some of which dated back 10,000 years; see ibid.

21. *Bob Jones University v. United States,* 461 U.S. 574, 586 (1983).

22. *Bob Jones University v. United States,* 574, 604.

23. On 3 March 2000, Bob Jones University announced that it was dropping its policy disallowing interracial dating in the aftermath of controversy that arose from visits by Republican presidential candidates George W. Bush and Alan Keyes.

24. Dean Lewis noted how painful the decision was for him personally in the strained relationships caused by his recommendation to William P. Thompson,

Stated Clerk of the General Assembly, that the PCUSA join in the filing of the brief opposing the government's position. After the decision was made, the influential Presbytery of Louisville Union strongly requested withdrawal from the brief, stating that while Bob Jones University was protected in its beliefs under the First Amendment, it had no justification to "thereby seek tax-exempt status to support operations that would be contrary to established public policy" ("Presbyterian Experience in the Bob Jones Case 1982–83," fax memorandum received from Dean Lewis, 22 March 2000).

25. The consultation papers and reports by both the Advisory Council on Church and Society and the Council on Church and Race were distributed to each PCUSA congregation as an explanation of the decision to file; see ibid.

26. *Oregon v. Smith*, 494 U.S. 872 (1990). The opinions rendered in *Lyng v. Northwest Indian Cemetery Protective Association*, 485 U.S. 439 (1988); *Bowen v. Roy*, 476 U.S. 693 (1986); and *Jimmy Swaggart Ministries v. California Board of Equalization*, 493 U.S. 378 (1990) all provided indications of the Supreme Court's drift away from the compelling-interest test and foreshadowed the *Smith* decision.

27. *Amicus curiae* briefs supporting *Smith* were filed for the American Civil Liberties Union et al. by Steven R. Shapiro and John A. Powell; for the American Jewish Congress by Amy Adelson, Lois C. Waldman, and Marc D. Stern; for the Association on American Indian Affairs et al. by Steven C. Moore and Jack Trope; and for the Council on Religious Freedom by Lee Boothby and Robert W. Nixon; see *Oregon v. Smith*, 874; briefs obtained at <supreme.findlaw.com/Supreme_Court/briefs/index.html>; accessed 20 March 2000.

28. Elenora Giddings Ivory, "Testimony on Religious Liberty Protection Act," before the U.S. House of Representatives Committee on the Judiciary, Washington, DC, 14 July 1998; accessed at <www.pcusa.org/wo/features/liberty.htm> on 1 October 1999.

29. Arguments were raised during debates on the RLPA that, for example, landlords could use this proposed law to deny leases to prospective gay tenants if a landlord's religious beliefs held that homosexuality was immoral. Thomas attempted to alleviate such criticism in his testimony before Congress. See National Council of Churches of Christ in the U.S.A., "Testimony of Oliver S. Thomas before the Subcommittee on the Constitution," 12 May 1999.

30. "Letter" from Oliver Thomas, special counsel for religious and civil liberties, National Council of Churches of Christ in the USA, to U.S. Senators, 28 September 1999; obtained from the NCC archives (Washington office), 17 December 1999.

31. Ibid.

32. The NCC, People for the American Way, Americans United for Separation of Church and State, the United Church of Christ, and the Anti-Defamation League had all withdrawn their support by this time; see "Liberty Coalition Is Fraying," *Christian Century*, 13 October 1999, 957.

33. Senator Orrin Hatch of Utah offered his own "compromise" school prayer amendment in 1983. The critical clauses were as follows: "Nothing in this Constitution shall be construed to prohibit individual or group prayer or other public institutions. No person shall be required by the United States or any state to participate in prayer. Nor shall the United States or any state compose the words of any prayer to be said in public schools." The problem here, as with other such proposals, was that the wording of this amendment was entirely consistent with that of Supreme Court decisions on public school prayer, making the amendment an unnecessary, purely symbolic gesture. See "Double Trouble: Senate Judiciary

Committee Reports Two School Prayer Amendments," *Church & State* 36, no. 9 (July/August 1983): 153.

34. "Senate Record Vote Analysis," 98th Congress, 2nd sess., 20 March 1984, p. s-2901 (Temp. Record), vote no. 34; accessed via internet at <www.senate.gov/ rpc/rva/982/98234.htm> on 15 September 1999.

35. Letter from Jim Halpert, PFAW, to members of the House of Representatives on 1 August 1995; obtained from NCC archives (Washington office), 17 December 1999.

36. Ibid.

37. Elenora Giddings Ivory, director, Washington Office, Presbyterian Church (USA), "Testimony on State-Sponsored Prayer," before House Committee on the Judiciary, Subcommittee on the Constitution, 23 July 1996.

38. Ibid. Oliver Thomas, special counsel for religious and civil liberties at the NCC, also provided testimony on "Schools and Religion" before the United States Commission on Civil Rights on 20 May 1998. In that testimony, Thomas traced the failure of past approaches to the dilemma of how to include religion in the public schools. He observed the institution of the "*sacred* public school" early in American history, a quasi-establishment of nonsectarian Protestantism. Thomas cited the "Bible Wars" that occurred in Cincinnati and Philadelphia as evidence of the conflict generated by the "sacred school" concept. The second approach to religion in the public schools that Thomas observed was the "religion-free zone" approach, in which government attempts at strict neutrality "drove every vestige of religion out of the curriculum and out of the classroom." This too has been a failed approach that has engendered social divisions. Finally, Thomas offered the middle-of-the-road approach offered in the First Amendment handbook *Finding Common Ground*, edited by Thomas and Charles C. Haynes and published by Vanderbilt University's Freedom Forum First Amendment Center, as an alternative to the failed extremes of the "sacred public school" and "religion-free zones." His observation that groups from the American Center for Law and Justice to the Anti-Defamation League had endorsed the general approach found in this handbook was evidence that a moderate third approach is indeed possible. See Oliver Thomas, "Schools and Religion," testimony before the United States Commission on Civil Rights, 20 May 1998; obtained from NCC archives (Washington Office), 17 December 1999.

39. Rob Boston, "Istook Amendment Defeated!" *Church & State* 51, no. 8 (July/August 1998): 152.

40. Ibid.

41. The Istook Amendment was reintroduced in the U.S. House of Representatives in 1999 to be undertaken once again in 2000. For a history and critique of proposed "religion" amendments from 1995 to 1996, see Derek H. Davis, "Assessing the Proposed Religious Equality Amendment," *Journal of Church and State* 37 (summer 1995): 453–508; and "A Commentary on the Proposed 'Religious Equality/Liberties' Amendment," *Journal of Church and State* 38 (winter 1996): 5–24.

42. A Gallup/CNN/*USA Today* poll taken 25–27 June 1999 revealed that "seven out of ten Americans favor allowing daily spoken prayers in the nation's classrooms, and a somewhat greater percentage—74%—support a proposal allowing schools to display the Ten Commandments." Interestingly, a majority (58 percent) of persons describing themselves as "liberal" support school prayer according to this study. See "Most Americans Support Prayer in Public Schools," Princeton, NJ: Gallup Organization, 9 July 1999, 1; accessed at <www.gallup.com/poll/ surveys/index.asp> on 31 March 2000.

43. "Packwood-Moynihan Parochiad Bill Introduced," *Church & State* 34, no. 3 (April 1981): 75.

44. Ibid., 79.

45. Ibid.

46. George R. LaNoue, *Public Funds for Parochial Schools? A Resource Document* (New York: National Council of Churches of Christ in the U.S.A., 1963), 2.

47. Allen Hertzke, "An Assessment of the Mainline Churches," 68–69.

48. *Zobrest v. Catalina Foothills School District*, 509 U.S. 1 (1993). Rob Boston, "Hearing Problem," *Church & State* 46, no. 6 (February 1993): 30.

49. Ibid. The *Lemon* test stated that government aid to religious schools must have a secular purpose, must not have the principal effect of promoting religion, and must not lead to an excessive entanglement between church and state; see *Lemon v. Kurtzman*, 403 U.S. 602 (1971).

50. Boston, "Hearing Problem," 32.

51. Ibid., 31.

52. Ibid., 34.

53. Ibid.

54. Jim Buie, "A Season of Prayer," *Church & State* 37 (May 1984): 6.

55. "The Equal Access Act: Public Law 98–377 Guidelines," reprinted from the *Congressional Record*, 98th Congress, 2d sess., by the Baptist Joint Committee on Public Affairs, Washington, DC, October, 1984.

56. "Testimony of the Rev. Dean M. Kelley" on behalf of the National Council of Churches of Christ in the U.S.A. before the House Subcommittee on Elementary, Secondary, and Vocational Education, Washington, DC, 28 March 1984.

57. Ibid., 6.

58. See section 104, "Services Provided by Charitable, Religious, or Private Organizations," Public Law 104–193, enacted 22 August 1996; available at http://cpjusticeorg/CGuide/Guide.html. For a balanced treatment of Charitable Choice, see Derek Davis and Barry Hankins, eds., *Welfare Reform and Faith-Based Organizations* (Waco, TX: J. M. Dawson Institute of Church-State Studies, Baylor University, 1999).

59. "Charitable Choice Offers Social Ministry Opportunity," ELCA, Lutheran Office for Governmental Affairs (September 1998), accessed at <www.loga.org> on 5 March 1999.

60. The guidelines recommended for every denomination the establishment of "a specialized board or committee" to deal with the complexity of the Charitable Choice arrangement; see "Implementation of Charitable Choice" (Washington, DC: PCUSA Washington Office, 13 January 1998).

61. Another question left unaddressed by the general guidelines for the implementation of Charitable Choice is whether staff positions within church-affiliated organizations receiving these federal funds will "be open to anyone who may apply." See Elenora Giddings Ivory, "Questions about Charitable Choice," supplement to "Implementation of Charitable Choice" (Washington, DC: Presbyterian Church [USA], Washington Office, rev. ed., 13 January 1998).

62. The coalition includes representatives from Americans United for Separation of Church and State, the ACLU, the American Jewish Committee, the American Jewish Congress, the Anti-Defamation League, People for the American Way, and a few other staunchly separationist organizations. See Rob Boston, "The 'Charitable Choice' Charade," *Church & State* 51, no. 7 (February 1998): 31.

63. "Statement of Purpose," in *Religious Coalition for Abortion Rights, An-*

nual Report, 1986 (Washington, DC: RCAR, 100 Maryland Avenue, N.E. Suite 307, 1987), 2.

64. Samuel A. Mills, "Abortion and Religious Freedom: The Religious Coalition for Abortion Rights," *Journal of Church and State* 33 (summer 1991): 571.

65. Samuel A. Mills, *The Religious Coalition for Abortion Rights (RCAR): An Analysis of Its Role in the Pro-Choice Movement, 1973–1989*, Master of Arts thesis (Baylor University, Waco, TX, 1990), 24; referenced in Hollie Nading, "The Religious Coalition for Abortion Rights (RCAR): A Case Study," in *Religion and the Body Politic Seminar Papers* (Waco, TX: J. M. Dawson Institute of Church-State Studies, Baylor University, 1990), 5.

66. "Mainline Churches Reassess Pro-Choice Stand on Abortion," *Christian Century*, 14 December 1984, 72.

67. Presbyterian Church (USA), "Covenant and Creation: Theological Reflections on Contraception and Abortion (1983)," in J. Gordon Melton, *The Churches Speak On: Abortion* (Detroit, MI: Gale Research, 1989), 93.

68. Episcopal Church, "Resolution on Abortion (1988)," in ibid., 49.

69. Evangelical Lutheran Church in America, "Resolution on Abortion (1990)," in ibid., 52.

70. See "Mainline Churches Reassess Pro-choice Stand on Abortion," 72.

71. Increasingly, the contemporary First Amendment debate is being "secularized" in the sense of a loss of influence of the mainline churches on the separationist side and a concurrent repositioning of the accommodationist camps in favor of groups like Focus on the Family, Family Research Council, Christian Coalition, and so forth.

72. Recent signs are not encouraging. The largest denominational member of the NCC, the United Methodist Church, suspended payments to the Council in October of 1999, alleging financial mismanagement and noting the absence of a financial plan. Other members cite the NCC's liberal stance on issues like universal health care, gun control, and affirmative action as being out of step with their membership and a valid reason to withhold funding. Some have even called for the NCC to disband. The national organizations of the independent mainline churches face similar pressures. See Richard N. Ostling, "Church Group's Cash Woes a Faith Test," *Waco Tribune-Herald*, 7 November 1999, section B, p. 9.

13   Doing Good and Doing Well

Shareholder Activism,
Responsible Investment,
and Mainline Protestantism

Lynn D. Robinson

> For the love of money is the root of all evils; it is
> through this craving that some have wandered away
> from the faith and pierced their hearts with many
> pangs.
>   1 Timothy 6:10

The Interfaith Center on Corporate Responsibility and the mainline churches, as institutional investors and advocates, are slowly changing the way a significant percentage of American dollars are invested. Through shareholder activism at the annual meetings of major corporations, lay members and clergy demand changes in corporate policy on many issues, from the degradation of the environment to the use and sale of genetically modified foods, with sometimes remarkable results. Few Americans recognize the economic role played by mainline Protestantism over the years, unless they have been attentive each year to the business press during the season in which shareholders inform companies of resolutions that they want other shareholders to consider for corporate annual meetings.

This chapter delineates the successes of denominations and the Interfaith Center on Corporate Responsibility in changing the practices of publicly held firms and the investment practices of many Americans through information gathering, socially responsible investment strategies, and shareholder activism. The sections of this chapter include a background for understanding socially responsible investment practices and shareholder activism, a history of the mainline Protestant denominations and their involvement, an analysis of the effectiveness of these efforts, and finally some thoughts about the future for mainline Protestant participation in the socially responsible investment movement.

THE SOCIALLY RESPONSIBLE INVESTMENT (SRI) MOVEMENT

Socially responsible investment includes concerns about investment practices and managing a securities portfolio through the buying and selling of these investments. Shareholder activism describes the actions of investors who use their stocks to exercise governance over a company. Shareholders own a small amount of a company, so they can introduce policy changes in the company through resolutions at the annual shareholders meeting, within parameters set by the federal government's Securities and Exchange Commission (SEC).

The SRI movement works on the following principles: invest in companies whose policies and practices match the values of the investor, avoid investment in companies whose policies and practices the investor finds objectionable, divest from companies that initiate new, objectionable policies and practices, and find vehicles to promote community investment. The mutual funds, institutional investors, individual investors, and organizations that compose the SRI movement exercise considerable influence on corporate policies and practices when threatening to screen out the stock of particular companies.[1]

In the 1960s, shifts in thinking about civil rights, the Vietnam War, environmental pollution, and investment in South Africa attracted many Americans to think about the commercial ventures in which they had their money invested. For example, in 1968 a synagogue in Boston asked an investment firm to create a "peace portfolio" in response to discontent with companies manufacturing weapons used in the Vietnam War. The investment firm placed a small advertisement in the New York Times, and approximately six hundred readers responded with interest in having their investment portfolios screened by this firm.[2] From 1969 onward, the SRI movement gained new attention and support from many investors.

But the SRI movement has a deeper history than this. Some churches, even in the nineteenth century, chose to avoid stockholdings in companies that produced tobacco products or liquor. In the 1960s, the mainline Protestant denominations received calls from clergy and lay members to assess where church money was invested. These pressures permitted the denominations to move toward socially responsible investing without significant challenge to the fiduciary soundness of such a move, particularly with regard to pension funds.[3]

Shareholder activism came somewhat later. Before the enactment of the Securities Exchange Act of 1934, publicly held companies regularly manipulated the voting of their shareholders. After 1934, such practices were challenged, and shareholders received greater power to exercise discretionary control over their property. In 1942, the SEC elaborated on the existing law with an administrative rule that required companies to include shareholder resolutions in their proxy statements if the resolutions were matters of concern to all those who owned company stock and not matters of "daily business concern." For many years, this discretionary power meant that concerns about the kinds of individuals appointed to the board of directors and other matters of governance within the corporation could be driven by financially astute shareholders.

In the 1960s, many new concerns, demanding social and political change, came to the foreground in shareholder activism. One event, receiving a particular remark from an experienced shareholder activist, was the Freedom, Integration, God, Honor—Today (FIGHT) campaign led by Saul Alinsky against alleged discriminatory employment practices at Eastman Kodak in Rochester, New York.[4] As the battle between FIGHT and Eastman Kodak escalated, Alinsky proposed to take the grievances to the shareholders of the company through shareholder resolutions. FIGHT purchased the necessary number of shares to participate in the annual shareholder meeting and recruited sympathetic institutional shareholders to join them at the meeting. Alinsky anticipated the future and wrote in *Rules for Radicals*, "I couldn't help noting the irony that churches, having sold their spiritual birthright in exchange for donations of stock, could now go straight again by giving their proxies to the poor."[5] While the outcome of the FIGHT campaign was quickly forgotten, the strategy of using the rights of stockholders to compel senior management to respond to demands for social responsibility at corporate meetings resonated with social activists, particularly mainline Protestants and Roman Catholics.[6] Unlike the social screening of stock that was used by both politically conservative and liberal investors, shareholder resolutions provoked activity primarily among liberals until the 1990s.[7]

EARLY MAINLINE CONCERN FOR CORPORATE SOCIAL RESPONSIBILITY

While pundits may make too much of the 1960s, those years were a period of change in American life, particularly within the life of mainline Protestantism.[8] The precursors of change in socially responsible investment were visible in 1952 within the United Methodist Church (UMC) when it reviewed existing investment policies to bring them into compliance with sound Christian and economic principles.[9] The experiences of students and seminarians who entered positions within the denominations during the 1960s changed the mainline denominational and ecumenical structures quite dramatically. The radicalized World Christian Student Fellowship and the participation of mainline Protestants in the civil rights and peace movements pressured the mainline Protestant denominations to become more active in social change.[10]

With a new generation of radicalized seminarians and students entering positions of influence, the denominations and National Council of Churches (NCC) spoke in more emphatic tones in their policy statements. The NCC in 1963 stated that denominations should review their investments and sell any holdings in companies with continuing histories of racial discrimination. Similar demands were made in Methodist documents and those of other denominations. The General Board of the NCC also asserted that firms should be accountable for their actions and the effects of those actions on society more broadly.[11]

In addition to investigating the strategy proposed by Saul Alinsky, the denominations articulated a means for evaluating investments—in an effort to balance justice and financial yield.[12] In 1968, the United Presbyterian Church created an independent corporation, the Presbyterian Economic Development Corporation, to manage a portion of the church's funds, which were to be spent in higher-risk, lower-return ventures for the good of society. Also in 1968, the UMC Board of Missions pulled investments worth approximately $10 million from First National City Bank (now known as Citibank), because this bank, along with Chase Manhattan Bank, were the two largest lenders to the South African government.[13] During the World Council of Churches (WCC) assembly in the same year, the activities of the World Christian Student Fellowship, the WCC, NCC, and mainline Protestant denominations highlighted the connections between investment practices and the capital necessary for the racist policies of the South African government to persist.[14]

Robert Massie, writing in the *Christian Century*, clearly described the first religiously inspired shareholder resolution:

> Twenty years ago, on May 21, 1971, at the annual meeting of the General Motors Corporation in Cobo Hall in Detroit, the presiding bishop of the Episcopal Church, John Hines, resplendent in his purple clerical shirt, appeared at the microphone during the time reserved for questions. In a speech that would mark the beginning [of] a new era in corporate governance, Hines asked the board of directors of the nation's largest auto company to support a shareholder resolution filed by his church asking the firm to withdraw from South Africa.

He argued that the Episcopal Church, which possessed 12,574 shares of General Motors stock, had the right to make such a request because the church was an owner of the corporation.[15]

And according to the *Corporate Examiner*, later in 1971, religious investors submitted resolutions to IBM, Mobil, Gulf Oil, and Goodyear regarding each company's cooperation with the apartheid government in South Africa.[16]

In 1972, the Lutheran Church in America (LCA—a predecessor of the Evangelical Lutheran Church in America [ELCA]) joined the fray by making its first policy statement on socially responsible investment. Fiduciary responsibility, justice in the United States and abroad, the public good, the relationship between nation-states, the witness of the church, and prudence with regard to the complex interplay between these criteria were the norms given to Lutherans to be considered when making investment decisions. Research and shareholder activism were listed as possible tools for use in shaping the behavior of publicly held firms.[17]

In 1972, the Corporate Information Center (CIC) issued a study, *Church Investments, Technological Warfare, and the Military-Industrial Complex*, that embarrassed the leadership in all the denominations and even the NCC itself. The information in this report revealed which corporations had the largest contracts with the various branches of the military and the Defense Department. More important, the report indicated how much stock in these companies was held by each of the denominations through endowments and pension funds. The report stated the mission of the SRI movement succinctly in the foreword:

> The private or institutional investor is both a seeker of profit and/or financial security and a citizen. In the past most investors considered only economic speculation or security in investment decisions. Today as we become increasingly aware of the awesome power of business to affect the lives of all human beings and to influence our own and other governments, the role and responsibility of the investor must be seen in a new light. The social impact of the policies of the company in which he invests must be taken very seriously. Investment decisions now more than ever are deeply significant moral and social acts. If the investor chooses not to consider social criteria in his investment decisions thereby abdicating his responsibility, he places himself in complicity with an irresponsible or immoral or socially injurious act of the corporation in which he has invested.[18]

While this portion of the report's foreword caused little embarrassment and sounds rather prophetic, the remainder of the foreword called the mainline Protestant denominations and the NCC itself to task for investing directly in the production of military hardware. The report's conclusion stated the following:

> Some of the churches and agencies included in this report have taken strong stands against the growing militarism in America, against national priorities that divert vital resources into implements of war and away from the tools of peace, and against the rationale for and conduct of the war in South East Asia.
>
> To date these ethical and moral concerns have not been expressed through the investment policies and responsibilities of the church. The moral and social economic power and leverage of the church have not been used as appropriate and practical ways for the church to affect the military-industrial complex.
>
> Instead, like other investors, the church has placed itself in a position of complicity with the irresponsible, immoral and socially injurious acts of the corporations represented here. Instead, the churches are providing an important amount of economic support for the military-industrial complex, and the war in South East Asia. Instead, they are assisting in the manufacture and use of weapons of mass human and environmental destruction.[19]

In response to these demands, the American Baptists sold their twenty-one thousand shares in United Aircraft after the company refused to discuss conversion to nonmilitary production in 1973. In New York City, Union Theological Seminary students and faculty feuded with the seminary's board of trustees over selling off IBM shares because of the company's involvement in the production of military hardware.[20]

Despite the successes and possibilities of this approach to bring publicly held companies to a position of social responsibility, there were numerous critics from both ends of the political spectrum. Pro-business pundits wanted corporate activism to end because it distracted companies from more important matters, namely, profitability. Left-leaning critics hoped to overturn a legal system based upon property rights and replace it with a mixed-socialist or fully socialist economy. Even with these criticisms, the vigorous SRI movement continued to grow.

Until this time, the denominations failed to coordinate action and did not have a central clearinghouse for information. New possibilities for cooperative efforts among mainline Protestants necessitated a unifying organization to coordinate their activities. During 1971 the Interfaith Committee on Social Responsibility in Investments (ICSRI—the shareholder activists) and the CIC (the information-gathering mechanism), working together at the NCC headquarters in New York City, began to coordinate the efforts of the denominations.

THE COORDINATION OF ACTIVISM

Under the leadership of Timothy Smith, a Methodist layman who worked in the United Church of Christ's Council for Social Action, the two NCC entities, the ICSRI and the CIC, merged to form the Interfaith Center on Corporate Responsibility (ICCR) in 1974. This merger drew together a wide array of groups with an interest in shareholder activism and socially responsible investment, and has eventually come to oversee $90 billion of investments.[21] The ICCR's central role in the battle against companies invested in South Africa from 1972 through 1993, its advocacy on behalf of public health in the United States and abroad, its resources for socially responsible mutual funds, and its advocacy of shareholder rights during SEC hearings deserve extensive consideration and continue to fire the moral imagination of key actors in the mainline Protestant denominations.[22]

Originally all the member organizations of the ICCR were Protestant, and included all six of the major denominations under consideration here. But in 1973, the National Catholic Coalition for Responsible Investment (NCCRI) was formed in response to economic and investment concerns similar to those of Protestants, and in 1974 it gained formal representation on the board of the ICCR. Catholic member organizations were religious orders, select dioceses, and Catholic hospitals.[23] Representatives from the member organizations met together to create an agenda that included the prioritization of social issues, firms to target, and the delegation of responsibilities for action. The small ICCR staff in New York gathered, assembled, and distributed information through their network of member organizations, creating an effective way to keep abreast of matters nationwide. In addition to the member organizations, some seminary libraries, universities, colleges, and firms under frequent scrutiny subscribed to the ICCR's *Corporate Examiner,* a publication packed with detailed information on shareholder resolutions and interactions with corporations. ICCR publications emphasized factual information and evidence, avoiding unsubstantiated statements that might spark litigation for misrepresentation. From the beginning, the ICCR focused on particular issues: multinational corporations that exercise influence across the borders of nation-states, equal employment opportunity for minorities and women, the production and sale of military hardware, and a cluster of environmental issues, including agriculture and energy production.[24]

THE BATTLE AGAINST SOUTH AFRICAN APARTHEID

As mentioned already, investment in South Africa was a matter of concern in the late 1950s and early 1960s for mainline Protestants and continued to cast a long shadow on the many other activities of the ICCR throughout the 1970s and 1980s. In 1976, religious organizations and denominations began fully divesting of stock in companies operating in South Africa. There was evidence that the ICCR and mainline Protestants had influence beyond the walls of the NCC headquarters in New York.

In the 1980s, the ICCR started to cultivate relationships with large pension funds that wanted to use screens to invest their money only in socially responsible companies. One person at the ICCR told me how the pension funds were tools of state and local governments during the years of both Reagan administrations. When Federal regulatory mechanisms no longer protected equal-opportunity employment or the environment in the manner desired by local and state governments, many enlisted the resources of pension funds to pressure companies to comply voluntarily with standards for employment and environmental protection. For example, while Jerry Brown was governor of California, he used CALPERS, the California state pension fund, to force companies to enact progressive policies. The executives of other states and municipalities did the same. These institutional investors required good and reliable sources of information for screening their investments, and they relied heavily upon the ICCR as one of those sources.[25] One of the matters taken up by these pension funds was South Africa. During the 1980s, pension funds threatened companies with the withdrawal of close to $200 billion worth of investments, bringing incredible pressure to bear upon corporate management.[26]

Meanwhile, the ICCR continued to broaden the base of opposition to apartheid in South Africa using various economic tools to put pressure on businesses that remained in South Africa (or in some way supported the economic stability of the South African government). With information from the ICCR, the Southern Christian Leadership Conference called a boycott of Winn Dixie Stores over the presence of South African products on the store shelves in 1986. After a fifteen-week boycott, Winn Dixie removed the products. The threat of a similar boycott caused Coca-Cola to sell its South African operations to a business group composed of black

South Africans. General Motors and IBM, after years of resistance, sold their operations in South Africa to former company managers, though maintaining some ties with these operations. The ICCR continued to place pressure on these companies to cut all ties with their former operations there.[27]

With years of activism, anti-apartheid shareholder activism began to yield returns like the 1987 closure of Citibank's South African subsidiary, the only American-owned bank operating in South Africa. In 1989, Mobil Corporation, an aggressive opponent of withdrawal from Africa, announced plans to remove all personnel and resources from South Africa. And in 1990, the South African government released Nelson Mandela and repealed the ban on anti-apartheid organizations like the African National Congress (ANC) and the more radical Pan-African Congress (PAC). The ICCR, in consultation with representatives from the South African Council of Churches (SACC), advocated a continuation of economic and military sanctions until the apartheid system was fully dismantled.[28]

In 1993, the SACC proposed a "Code of Conduct for Businesses Operating in South Africa" with the full support of the ICCR. With the announcement of inclusive elections and a transitional government, the anti-apartheid movement and the international community lifted existing boycotts and embargoes, and encouraged renewed investment in South Africa. In 1994, ICCR affiliates used shareholder resolutions to bring companies returning to South Africa into compliance with the SACC's Code of Conduct. Immediately, twelve companies agreed to abide by the principles elaborated in this code. Additionally, the ICCR organized a meeting between a delegation from four major U.S. banks, ICCR affiliates, the South Shore Bank of Chicago, and other organizations involved in the anti-apartheid movement. Together, they created the South African Community Reinvestment Program. This program provided resources and training for community leaders in South Africa to help develop economic capacity among black South Africans.[29]

The symbolism of this victory remained for those involved with shareholder activism and socially responsible investment in the mainline Protestant denominations. The peaceful transition in South Africa and the visit to New York by South African anti-apartheid leaders provoked an emotional response. One activist remembered Archbishop Desmond Tutu and Nelson Mandela thanking the NCC and mainline Protestants for their support and advocacy for an inclusive South Africa.[30] The ICCR's victory was clearly based in economics: between 1983 and 1985 alone, the American dollars invested in South Africa dropped to $1.3 billion from $2.8

billion, primarily because of pressure placed on companies by activist investors and consumer boycotts.[31]

WARNING AMERICANS ABOUT HEALTH RISKS

Another memorable and significant series of events for those demanding socially responsible commerce involved the marketing of infant formula. Many public health advocates and mainline Protestants working in developing countries found that the marketing practices of a number of corporations, including Abbott Laboratories, American Home Products, Borden, Bristol-Myers, Carnation, and Nestle, were leading to poorer infant health. In the 1970s, these companies marketed infant formula as a good substitute for breast milk. As many sources of data indicated, the infant formula, a mixture of vegetable fat, milk, sugar, vitamins, and minerals, was nutritious when used properly. But medical researchers demonstrated that the substitution of infant formula, especially in places with impure water, inadequate sanitation, and few resources to purchase adequate amounts of formula led to greater childhood illness, brain damage, and sometimes death when poor parents used contaminated water or diluted the formula too much in an effort to conserve this expensive resource. The producers of the infant formula failed to respond when these studies of their products were made public, and various groups demanded that they stop marketing their products in developing countries. The companies continued widespread advertising campaigns in developing countries, provided free samples to consumers, and encouraged doctors and medical personnel to promote infant formula with various kinds of incentive programs.[32]

In 1975, religious investors began to introduce shareholder resolutions to educate the public about the marketing practices of corporations selling infant formula in developing countries. In 1976, the Sisters of the Precious Blood sued Bristol-Myers, one of the makers of infant formula, because the company changed the language of a shareholder resolution introduced by the religious order. The company settled the suit out of court, correcting the statements in proxy forms and permitting Sisters of the Precious Blood and other ICCR members to address the company's board of directors directly.[33] During this period, the UCC, the United Presbyterian Church in the U.S.A. (to become PCUSA), and the UMC sponsored shareholder resolutions at Bristol-Myers and American Home Products meetings.[34]

In 1977, the Newman Center at the University of Minnesota announced a movement to boycott Nestle products with the goal of stopping what many believed to be Nestle's unethical marketing of infant formula.[35] Shareholder resolutions were ineffective for companies that were not publicly held within the United States; and Nestle, a Swiss company, thus existed beyond the reach of shareholder activism. A boycott was then the only financial tool at the disposal of activists wanting to change Nestle's policies. Within a year of the boycott announcement, both mainline Presbyterian denominations (to become the PCUSA), the Lutheran Church in America (to become the ELCA), the NCC, and the UCC joined the boycott.[36] Additionally, these denominations started organizing demonstrations at Stauffer's restaurants (owned by Nestle) across the United States.

The business press criticized the boycott, describing the participants as suburbanites and church members with good intentions but with little knowledge of economics and economic development. For example, in its 1 November 1979 issue, the *Wall Street Journal* carried an editorial entitled "The Nestle Boycott Kills Babies."[37] Similarly, *Fortune* printed an article that attacked the political identity of staff members of ICCR, who were orchestrating the Nestle boycott:

> For student radicals of the 1960s, one way to turn the "struggle" into a steady job is to join the issues staff of organizations like the Interfaith Center on Corporate Responsibility, where they have come to occupy some key positions and coordinate and orchestrate those shareholders' resolutions that almost every chief executive of a large American corporation is familiar with by now. To generalize, the resolutions seem designed less to uplift the world's less fortunate people than to indict the business establishment. . . . For the radicals, the alliance with church groups has many other tangible advantages. It provides a way of conducting political programs behind the shield of tax exemption, and access to a large organizational network. The church activists can gather information from missionaries throughout the world and disseminate propaganda to the memberships of participating churches.[38]

As these two examples suggest, the business community found the ICCR, with its shareholder activism and boycotts, to be annoying and inconvenient for executives and other upper-level management. Viewed differently, however, these articles and others like them indicate that the ICCR was effective in getting its message across.

In the midst of the Nestle boycott and aggressive work against apartheid in South Africa, the ICCR and its members began a campaign against tobacco products sold in both the United States and abroad. In 1981, the ICCR coordinated its first shareholder resolution at Philip Morris's annual meeting, raising questions about the company's marketing strategy in de-

veloping countries. Then, during 1982 and 1983, the ICCR targeted both
Philip Morris and R. J. Reynolds.[39]

In 1984, Nestle executives agreed to and signed the guidelines created
by the World Health Organization and endorsed by the ICCR and other
allies in the Nestle boycott, effectively suspending the boycott of Nestle
products in the United States. This concession by Nestle placed considerable pressure on other companies producing infant formula to also accept
the "Code of Marketing for Breastmilk Substitutes" as well.

In 1990, the ICCR, through member organizations, submitted resolutions to Philip Morris, American Brands, and Loews calling on them to
stop the production of all tobacco products. Over time, the pressure that
began with religious investors and activists expanded to include various
institutional investors, particularly pension funds. Their new resolutions
proposed labeling, changes in advertising, and changes in manufacturing.[40]

Through the 1990s, the ICCR and other religious investors continued
campaigning against tobacco companies. In 1995, the ICCR headlined the
"Kleen Tobacco Out of Kimberly Clark" campaign to stop the company
from selling tobacco-related products (like filters, paper, and reconstituted
tobacco). This marked the beginning of the ICCR's expansion of the tobacco campaign to companies that supported tobacco companies. Knight-
Ridder adopted a set of guidelines offered by the ICCR for considering and
placing tobacco advertising in its newspapers. The guidelines prohibited
advertisements for free tobacco samples and tobacco-related products. In
1996, the American Medical Association allied with the ICCR in calling
for divestment from tobacco in all investment portfolios. Minnesota Mining and Manufacturing (3M) agreed to no longer accept advertisements
from tobacco companies on any of its billboards, based upon pressure from
the ICCR.[41] President Clinton publicly recognized the sizable role of the
ICCR in his administration's campaign against tobacco products: "And you
may have heard that just last week, the 3M Company and the Interfaith
Center on Corporate Responsibility reached an agreement that 3M would
no longer accept tobacco advertising for its billboards, and good for them.
This is the first major national media company to take this step. I want to
commend Livio DeSimone, the chairman and CEO of 3M, and Reverend
Michael Crosby of the Interfaith Center for this remarkable accomplishment."[42]

In the following years, the efforts of the ICCR and the rest of the SRI
movement received significantly less attention than the discussion of the
tobacco industry through class-action lawsuits, state-level litigation, and
Congressional action.[43] Nevertheless, the ICCR fought for greater public

consciousness on matters of health and safety, including the dangers of improperly used infant formula and tobacco as a carcinogen. These issues were the two most visible public issues in which the ICCR and the mainline Protestant denominations played a significant role. Many other issues were covered as well. The ICCR's activism against irradiated food and bovine growth hormones began in the 1980s, and it continues to work to keep genetically modified foods off the market in the United States. Additionally, the ICCR has recently been in discussion with pharmaceutical companies about the pricing of products and their availability to poor members of society.[44]

SOCIALLY RESPONSIBLE MUTUAL FUNDS

As neoconservative criticisms of socially responsible investment and shareholder activism began to taper off, the SRI movement continued to institutionalize through the creation of socially responsible mutual funds and other investment instruments. By the 1990s, the ICCR was one of the primary information sources for these funds, gathering considerable grassroots information from its member organizations, such as the Texas Coalition for Responsible Investment and the UMC.[45] In 1998, the resources handled by various organizations within the SRI movement were valued at approximately $1.185 trillion, accounting for approximately one out of every ten U.S. dollars invested. The concept of "doing good while doing well" took off with portfolio management firms like Franklin Research and Development. Calvert and Working Assets advertisements became familiar to anyone picking up a copy of the *Utne Reader* or the *Nation* in the 1990s.[46] A nonprofit membership organization, the Social Investment Forum, claimed more than four hundred investment practitioners and institutional investors as members by 1998.[47]

While firms were becoming more global in their orientation, the ICCR was adapting to the demands of the global marketplace by joining in coalition with its British and Canadian equivalents.[48] In 1998, the ICCR, the Ecumenical Council for Corporate Responsibility in Britain, and the Taskforce on the Churches and Corporate Responsibility in Canada released an eighty-page document, *Principles for Global Corporate Responsibility*. This document set down guidelines for shareholder activism and the behavior that these three organizations expected of publicly held corporations.[49]

Although advocacy through shareholder resolutions has been their primary task in recent years, a staff member at the ICCR claimed that the organization was not blind to the leverage that investors can gain by using the ICCR's materials for investment decisions. Beginning in the 1990s, the ICCR's staff members wrote a number of documents useful to the average investor. In 1999 and 2000 alone, ICCR published the following resources: a guide to faith-based community development investment funds to promote investment in local communities frequently overlooked by commercial lenders; a guide to socially responsible mutual funds and other investment services; and a guide to international socially responsible investing for pension fund managers and others.[50]

The ICCR and other participants in the SRI movement have frequently been involved in negotiations with the SEC over the rules which structure how investors can influence corporations. Other interest groups, particularly those affiliated with business firms, lobbied for a curtailment in the number of shareholder resolutions by whatever means necessary. The demands for social responsibility by corporate activists and the demands for profitability by some corporate raiders caught executives in a tough bind, forcing them to be responsive to both social concerns and profitability.[51]

Conflict began with shareholder resolutions filed with Wal-Mart Stores, Inc. and Cracker Barrel Old Country Stores, Inc., in 1991 and 1992. These two resolutions, written for religious groups and others, questioned the equal employment practices of these two companies. In an appeal to the SEC, both Wal-Mart and Cracker Barrel received approval from the SEC to omit these resolutions. Accepting the reasoning that these resolutions were about "ordinary business," the SEC deemed equal employment concerns out of reach to shareholder activists under the current rules. Though these were only two decisions among many, they signaled a shift in the SEC's approach to shareholder resolutions, placing concerns about minority hiring and possible discriminatory policies out of the realm of shareholder discussion.[52]

During the following years, the SEC tried to raise the percentage of votes necessary to reintroduce a proxy resolution the following year from 3 percent, 6 percent, and 10 percent to 6 percent, 15 percent, and 30 percent for the first, second, and subsequent years, respectively. These measures were clearly an attempt to eliminate many of the rights guaranteed to shareholders.[53] In May 1998, with memories of corporate discrimination at Texaco and Denny's Restaurants still fresh in public memory, the SEC reversed itself, keeping the existing thresholds for shareholder resolutions and repealing its decision on matters of employment policy as "ordinary business" in the cases of Wal-Mart and Cracker Barrel. The SRI thus claimed an important victory over the SEC's attempts to pursue tighter restrictions on shareholder activism. The apparent turning point was in December 1997, when the Social Investment Forum (the Washington association of SRI members) released a study on the impact of SRI on corporate practices and publicized a joint letter signed by more than three hundred organizations supporting the existing interpretation of the rules on owner input. The study demonstrated that only 20 percent of the shareholder resolutions currently allowable under the existing standards were going to be allowable under the proposed SEC standards.[54] Again, the ICCR, a critical component of the SRI movement, helped to maintain and strengthen the position of shareholders.

EFFECTIVENESS OF SRI AND SHAREHOLDER ACTIVISM

In the cases outlined above, the ICCR and its constituent mainline Protestant denominations, as founding members of the now burgeoning SRI and shareholder activist movements, demonstrated considerable effectiveness in providing an ideologically broad-based approach to social regulation of the marketplace. Their campaigns achieved their intended goals in many instances. By the turn of the millennium, socially responsible investment and shareholder activism appeared to be successful by that most basic of market standards: profitability.

The Domini 400 Index, a socially responsible stock index, regularly outperformed the Standard & Poor (S&P) 500, a standard index of stocks. Overall, the socially responsible forms of investment did not perform worse than investment instruments without socially responsible screens, because the number of companies that were screened out was not large enough to diminish the diversity of stocks in any one portfolio.[55]

While the ICCR, as a program of the NCC, received constant criticism for its "leftist" and "Marxist" leanings in the 1980s by neoconservative critics,[56] it used the tools at hand pragmatically to regulate business through legal rights rather than through direct government regulation. Of course, libertarians and conservatives objected to the goals and politics of the ICCR, but the mechanisms were fundamentally sound from these intellectual perspectives. In other words, the methods of the ICCR were politically and philosophically acceptable across the political spectrum. Unfortunately this point was never made, though it could have proved effective in promoting the strategy to a wider range of mainline Protestants.[57]

On at least three indicators, the ICCR and mainline Protestant denominations were successful in their approach to socially responsible investing and shareholder activism. They utilized a method that was broadly acceptable upon ideological grounds, their method was effective at getting companies to change their practices, and socially responsible investment did not diminish financial returns. In the grand tradition of mainline Protestantism, denominational social teachings were honored while the growth of the economy was supported.

PROPOSALS FOR THE FUTURE

What is perhaps most fascinating about the story of the ICCR and socially responsible investment in the mainline Protestant denominations is the paucity of commentary it has received. A Presbyterian Panel Study Summary in 1995 reported that only 20 percent of lay Presbyterians and only 44 percent of Presbyterian clergy were very familiar with socially responsible investment. Nearly a third (32 percent) of lay Presbyterians had no familiarity with socially responsible investment. Even fewer lay members were aware that the PCUSA used socially responsible investment practices. Though unfamiliar with these concepts, a majority of lay members indicated that they approved of avoiding investments in the companies screened out by most socially responsible investors (makers of tobacco, alcohol, armaments, and weapons, abusers of human rights abroad, polluters of air and water).

Clearly, more lay education is necessary. Subscribing to the ICCR's *Corporate Examiner* is one way to provide investors in the congregation with a great deal of specific information on both potential mutual funds and the practices of companies in which lay members have already invested. Such exposure might create animosity toward the ICCR and their denominations' choices of issues; currently the organization receives significant buffering by being relatively unknown by the laity. But the ICCR's potential growth from increased shareholder resources suggests that the gamble of outreach may be worthwhile.

At a different level within mainline Protestantism, clergy are getting their standard church and society, or social ethics, courses at seminary, but few are reading the *Corporate Examiner*. Approximately a third of ABC-USA, ECUSA, ELCA, PCUSA, UCC, and UMC seminary libraries subscribe to this publication, but some of those holdings are no longer current. In all likelihood, very few clergy are familiar with the ICCR's materials or the material from their denomination on corporate responsibility, shareholder activism, or socially responsible investment. Greater attention to these matters within the course of seminary education could provide a better connection between social ethics, practical theology, and ministry.

Like Gary Dorrien, an Episcopal theologian, I think that socially responsible mutual funds are a means to increase the number of people exercising ownership over capital and that shareholder activism is a tool to create a discussion between the owners and management of American companies about social responsibility.[58] Max L. Stackhouse, who has contributed to the ICCR's *Corporate Examiner,* and Dennis McCann suggest that we can think about corporations as a form of community that, like any other structure of creation, can be corrupted and sinful, yet worthy of redemption:

> If public theology can help us overcome our contempt for corporations as mere money machines, then Christians can begin to articulate what we expect of these institutions. We can even learn to love them as we have learned to love our churches, neighborhoods, nations, schools and hospitals—although we must not be tempted to seek from them the loves that are proper to other relationships. . . .
>
> While rejecting as both false and unjust the view of the corporation as an inhuman piece of organizational machinery, public theology also must be aware of the limits of this form of covenantal community. Corporations become idols when we become married to firms, when our loyalty is to them only, when we bend all politics to their service, when their distinctive modes of operation get confused with the ideals that must govern health care, education and culture. Corporations become idols, in short, when we think that they can bring salvation to human life. . . .
>
> While affirming the corporation as a covenantal community, a public theology fully resonant with our emerging world will have to collaborate in developing new systems of public accountability to ensure that corporations respect God's gift of creation.[59]

Although much of the discussion at ICCR meetings is about setting priorities, these matters concern the churches more broadly, and their input should be solicited. More deliberation in seminaries and congregations about what it means to be socially responsible is vital for sustaining this movement and creating a form of market economy filled with producers, providers, consumers, managers, owners, and workers who have the religious vocabulary to articulate what is acceptable and unacceptable economic behavior. Without these resources, discussion slips easily back into questions of efficiency or government regulation—on both the political left and right.[60]

Most important, the ICCR, denominational pension funds, and endowments must continue their practice of socially responsible investment. Although other religious and secular groups practice socially responsible investing, the kind of shareholder activism that mainline Protestants
continue to practice and promote makes corporate managers and executives
accountable to the public for their actions and brings new issues to the
foreground that have previously been neglected. Although many groups
do the former, few are willing to place significant resources behind new
issues. This is a vital act of public conscience. We should hope that mainline
Protestants will continue to do good and do well, and bring more of their
members, both lay and clergy, into discussion and activism.

NOTES

1. Severyn T. Bruyn, *The Field of Social Investment* (New York: Cambridge
University Press, 1987), 2–15. See also the Council on Economic Priorities and
Myra Alperson, Alice Tepper Marlin, Jonathan Schorsch, and Rosalyn Will, *The
Better World Investment Guide* (New York: Prentice Hall, 1991); Amy Domini
and Peter Kinder, *Ethical Investing* (Boston: Addison-Wesley, 1984).

2. The Council on Economic Priorities et al., *Better World Investment Guide*, 3.

3. See Bruyn, *Field of Social Investment*.

4. Interview at the Interfaith Center on Corporate Responsibility, 30 March
2000.

5. Saul Alinsky, *Rules for Radicals* (New York: Vintage, 1971), 173.

6. Lauren Talner, *The Origins of Shareholder Activism* (Washington, DC: Investor Responsibility Research Center, 1983), 28–32.

7. See Gregory E. David, "Resolutions of Conscience" *Financial World* 162,
no. 16 (1993); Manuel Schiffres, "Ethical Investing the Right Way," *Kiplinger's
Personal Finance Magazine* 50, no. 4 (1996).

8. See Wade Clark Roof and William McKinney, *American Mainline Religion:
Its Changing Shape and Future* (New Brunswick, NJ: Rutgers University Press,
1987); Robert Wuthnow, *The Restructuring of American Religion: Society and
Faith since World War II* (Princeton, NJ: Princeton University Press, 1988).

9. Thomas C. Oden, *Conscience and Dividends: Churches and the Multina-
tionals* (Washington, DC: Ethics and Public Policy Center, 1985), 22.

10. See Risto Lehtonen, *Story of a Storm: The Ecumenical Student Movement in the Turmoil of Revolution* (Grand Rapids, MI: Eerdmans, 1998), chap. 15;
Ronald H. Preston, *Confusions in Christian Social Ethics* (London: SCM Press,
1994).

11. Oden, *Conscience and Dividends*, 22–23.

12. Ibid., 24–25; United Church of Christ, *Minutes of the Sixth General Synod*
(New York: United Church of Christ, 1967).

13. Council on Economic Priorities et al., *Better World Investment Guide*, 4.

14. Oden, *Conscience and Dividends*, 25.

15. Robert K. Massie Jr., "Corporate Democracy and the Legacy of Divestment," *Christian Century*, 24–31 July 1991, 716.

16. "Twenty-Five Years of Leadership," *Corporate Examiner* 25, no. 5 (1996),
1–24.

17. The Evangelical Lutheran Church in America (ELCA), formed in the 1980s, was active from its inception in the SRI movement. In 1988, the ELCA took the statements of the LCA as historical documents, not binding policy. See Christa R. Klein and Christian D. von Dehsen, *Politics and Policy: The Genesis and Theology of Social Statements in the Lutheran Church in America* (Minneapolis, MN: Fortress Press, 1989), 127–28; Oden, *Conscience and Dividends*.

18. Corporate Information Center, *Church Investments, Technological Warfare, and the Military-Industrial Complex* (New York: Friendship Press, 1972), i–ii.

19. Ibid., 13–14.

20. See Oden, *Conscience and Dividends*; Roy W. Morano, *The Protestant Challenge to Corporate America: Issues of Social Responsibility* (Ann Arbor, MI: UMI Research Press, 1984).

21. Interview at the Interfaith Center on Corporate Responsibility, 30 March 2000. See Council on Economic Priorities et al., *Better World Investment Guide*, 7; Massie, "Corporate Democracy."

22. This chronology reflects some of the contours of the organization's history as described to me during an interview at the Interfaith Center on Corporate Responsibility, 30 March 2000.

23. The Council on Economic Priorities et al., *Better World Investment Guide*, 6–7; Oden, *Conscience and Dividends*, chap. 1, passim.

24. Interview at the Interfaith Center on Corporate Responsibility, 30 March 2000.

25. Interview at the Interfaith Center on Corporate Responsibility, 30 March 2000. See Council on Economic Priorities et al., *Better World Investment Guide*, 9–12, passim.

26. See Donald R. Culverson, "The Politics of the Anti-Apartheid Movement in the United States, 1969–1986," *Political Science Quarterly* 111, no. 1 (1996), 127–49.

27. Ibid., 146.

28. Interfaith Center on Corporate Responsibility, "Freedom and Democracy in Southern Africa," *Corporate Examiner* 25, no. 5 (1996): 9.

29. Ibid., 9.

30. Interview at the Interfaith Center on Corporate Responsibility, 30 March 2000.

31. David E. Provost, "Corporate Responsibility," *Christian Century* 110, no. 11 (1993), 356–58.

32. Oden, *Conscience and Dividends*, 91–95; Morano, *Protestant Challenge to Corporate America*, 55–56.

33. Interfaith Center on Corporate Responsibility, "Promoting International Health," *Corporate Examiner* 25, no. 5 (1996): 18; Interview at the Interfaith Center on Corporate Responsibility, 30 March 2000.

34. Morano, *Protestant Challenge to Corporate America*, 56.

35. Interfaith Center on Corporate Responsibility, "Promoting International Health," 18.

36. Morano, *Protestant Challenge to Corporate America*, 110–11.

37. Ibid., 112; "The Nestle Boycott Kills Babies," *Wall Street Journal*, 1 November 1979, 28.

38. Oden, *Conscience and Dividends*, 87–88. Interestingly, the *Washington Post* investigated Herman Nickel, the author of the *Fortune* article, only to find that he was being underwritten by money from Abbot Laboratories, American Home Products, and Nestle; see Interfaith Center on Corporate Responsibility, "Corporate Social Responsibility," *Corporate Examiner* 25, no. 5 (1996): 5.

39. Ibid., 18.

40. Interfaith Center on Corporate Responsibility, "Promoting International Health," 19.

41. Ibid., 19.

42. William J. Clinton, "Remarks on Kick Butts Day in Woodbridge," *Weekly Compilation of Presidential Documents* 32, no. 19 (1996), 791–833.

43. James M. Wall, "Tackling Tobacco," *Christian Century* 113, no. 36 (1996): 1219; Interfaith Center on Corporate Responsibility, *The Proxy Resolutions Book: January 2000* (New York: Interfaith Center on Corporate Responsibility, 2000): 65–72. In 2000, there were sixteen resolutions to six companies about tobacco-related issues. Interestingly, religious conservatives and liberals agree on the screening of stock portfolios for tobacco and tobacco-related stocks.

44. Ibid., 17–19; interview at the Interfaith Center on Corporate Responsibility, 30 March 2000. The ICCR is currently filing resolutions with nineteen companies involved in some way with genetically modified foods, from production to delivery to consumers. See also Toby Becker, "Stockholder Resolutions Target Genetic Engineering," *National Catholic Reporter* 36, no. 13 (2000): 12–13; "Corporate Responsibility Groups Target Genetic Tweaking of Food," *America* 182, no. 4 (2000): 5.

45. Council on Economic Priorities et al., *Better World Investment Guide*, 9–12.

46. R. Bruce Hutton, Louis D'Antonio, and Tommi Johnsen, "Socially Responsible Investing: Growing Issues and New Opportunities," *Business and Society* 37, no. 3 (1998): 281–82.

47. Steve Fahrer, "Socially Responsible Investing Comes of Age," *Dollars & Sense*, July/August 1998, 32.

48. Robert B. Reich, *The Work of Nations: Preparing Ourselves for 21st-Century Capitalism* (New York: Vintage, 1992).

49. "Global Guidelines for Business," *Christian Century* 115, no. 20 (1998): 671–72; *Principles for Global Corporate Responsibility: Bench Marks for Measuring Business Performance* (New York: Interfaith Center on Corporate Responsibility, 1998).

50. Interview at the Interfaith Center on Corporate Responsibility, 30 March 2000. See also Interfaith Center on Corporate Responsibility, *2000 Guide to Religious Community Development Investment Funds* (New York: Interfaith Center on Corporate Responsibility, 2000); Dana Burch, *International Socially Responsible Investing: Portfolios and Mutual Funds* (New York: Interfaith Center on Corporate Responsibility, 1999), and *The Conscientious Investor's Guide to Socially Responsible Mutual Funds and Investment Services* (New York: Interfaith Center on Corporate Responsibility, 1999).

51. Massie, "Corporate Democracy," 718–20. See the negative view of shareholder resolutions taken by some in the business press who wanted the SEC to gag shareholder activists: Thomas G. Donlan, "Resolved: Fewer Resolutions," *Barron's* 77, no. 46 (1997), 70.

52. Provost, "Corporate Responsibility," passim.

53. Mark Dowie, "Stockholders Sold Short," *Nation* 265, no. 18 (1997): 6–7.

54. "Social Investment Forum Statement on SEC Action Today Rejecting Curbs on Shareholder Rights," *PR Newswire*, 20 May 1998; "SEC Adopts Modest Changes for Votes on Shareholder Resolutions," *Dow Jones Online News*, 20 May 1998; "Shareholders and Corporate Hiring," *New York Times*, 23 May 1998, A14; "Corporate Democracy—Not Such a Radical Idea," *San Francisco Chronicle*, 24 July 1998, A25.

55. Hutton, D'Antonio, and Johnsen, "Socially Responsible Investing," passim.

56. See K. L. Billingsley, *From Mainline to Sideline* (Washington, DC: Ethics and Public Policy Center, 1990), chaps. 14–15, passim; Oden, *Conscience and Dividends*, chaps. 4–5, passim.

57. See "Religious Leaders Call for Sudan Disinvestment," *Christian Century* 117, no. 6 (2000): 203.

58. Gary Dorrien, *Soul in Society: The Making and Renewal of Social Christianity* (Minneapolis, MN: Fortress Press, 1995), 293–308, passim.

59. Max L. Stackhouse and Dennis P. McCann, "A Post-Communist Manifesto: Public Theology after the Collapse of Socialism," *Christian Century*, 16 January 1991, 44–47.

60. See also Rebecca M. Blank, *Do Justice: Linking Christian Faith and Modern Economic Life* (Cleveland, OH: United Church Press, 1992).

14 Love Your Enemies?

Protestants and United States Foreign Policy

Lester Kurtz and Kelly Goran Fulton

> . . . but I say, love your enemies and pray for those
> who persecute you.
>
> Matthew 5:44

The teachings of Jesus—who insisted that his followers love their enemies—raise serious questions today, as they did in the early church, about war, human rights, and economic justice in a nation's foreign policy. These questions may be rarely discussed in Congress or the news media, but they are the focus of considerable activity on the part of religious institutions, individuals, and this investigation. Although people from a variety of faith traditions are involved in attempting to influence U.S. foreign policy, we focus here on the impact of the mainline Protestant denominations.

AN INSTITUTIONAL INFRASTRUCTURE FOR DISSENT

Mainline Protestantism provides an institutional infrastructure for dissent that has no rival on the contemporary American political scene. Certainly peace and justice movements, universities, labor unions, and occasionally political parties provide a forum for dissenting opinions regarding U.S. foreign policy. It is primarily in the churches, however, that persistent voices of dissent are found, and it is from the churches that the resources flow that facilitate these voices' being heard. The mainline churches have been so effective in expressing dissent largely because they have historically been the U.S. political mainstream and are thus viewed as insiders.[1] Allen Hertzke contends that "if domestic social policy constitutes the major priority and the principal success of the fundamentalist groups, foreign policy is a major focus of the liberal groups and represents their greatest effectiveness in galvanizing constituents into action."[2]

In the pages that follow we explore the impact of mainline Protestant church positions on U.S. foreign policy from the mid-1970s to the present.

We examine the ideological and institutional bases for dissent provided by the churches, provide concrete examples of their actions, and discuss their possible impact. We will, moreover, try to evaluate the strategies used by those institutions and their members in addressing U.S. policies in three major areas: war and peace, human rights, and economic justice.

A Culture of Moral Resistance

Protestantism is the bedrock of American culture but also the major source of ethical teachings that challenge fundamental assumptions of U.S. foreign policy. Our discussion is limited to the last quarter of the twentieth century, but the relationship between churches and foreign policies has a complicated, two-thousand-year history. The church's position on war is an illuminating example. Christians have swung back and forth between two poles: the warrior and the pacifist; the resources of the church have been used both to promote and to oppose warfare. Ecclesiastical leaders have lobbied, cajoled, and threatened thousands of heads of state over the years and publicly supported or opposed their policies.

Although the early Christian church was a pacifist community in which it was unethical to use violence even in self defense,[3] this quickly changed. The ambivalence of the church's history provided the foundation for the dilemmas of contemporary mainline Protestants. On the one hand, Protestant Christianity is a central pillar of modern American culture and a fundamental advocate of the system. On the other hand, it plays a prophetic role that evaluates U.S. foreign policy by a standard that deviates markedly from the dominant *Realpolitik* political culture.

That tension between the poles of advocacy and criticism is at the core of mainline involvement in U.S. foreign policy. Despite pervasive nationalism in the American churches, the biblical tradition and denominational structures provide the most significant and broadly based challenge to U.S. foreign policy. "Just War" and Crusade traditions have shaped much of the attitude of Christians to their governments' respective foreign policies, but the pacifist tradition runs deep under the dominant position, and occasionally has a profound impact.

CASE STUDIES AND SELECTED ISSUES

We cannot pretend to be comprehensive in this brief treatment; instead, we focus on some major topics addressed by mainline Protestants during the past quarter-century. We begin by examining the central issues of war and peace—especially the issue of U.S. military involvement in Central

America. Second, we explore church involvement in U.S. policies regarding various human rights movements, emphasizing the anti-apartheid struggle in South Africa. Finally, we examine efforts to influence international economic policies, notably the Jubilee 2000 movement to forgive foreign debt.

Central America

To many, mainline involvement in protesting U.S. policies in Central America hearkened back to earlier civil rights and antiwar activism. During the late 1970s and throughout most of the 1980s, the Protestant opposition to U.S. policies in Central America was predominant and was well documented in newspaper headlines.[4] Nicaragua, El Salvador, and Guatemala were three major arenas of involvement.

During the 1980s, the U.S. waged what was only a partially covert war against the socialist government of Nicaragua. Earlier, a group consisting of the National Council of Churches (NCC), Roman Catholics, and the American Friends Service Committee had called for the U.S. to help remove Nicaraguan dictator Anastasio Somoza. They called for decisive action, including the removal of military assistance, the enforcement of an economic blockade, the cessation of U.S. training of military personnel, and the refusal to recognize Somoza and his system of government. They believed that these actions would help Nicaragua make a shift from dictatorship to a stable electoral democracy. A year later, the Sandinistas rose to power and implemented a Marxist regime.

The United States subsequently backed the rebel Contras, an action that the NCC and mainline officials consistently criticized. Critics of the NCC accused the council of ignoring human rights abuses by the Sandinistas, especially toward the Miskito Indians, and of supporting the Sandinistas through contributions to Sandinista Defense Committees, which they said were networks of government informers who helped keep the populace in line. The NCC called for a cessation of activities by the U.S. intended to destabilize the governments of Central America and was critical of the mining of Nicaraguan harbors (an action later found illegal by the World Court). The NCC also called for an end to the embargo against Nicaragua.[5]

The situation in El Salvador also mobilized people in U.S. churches. In 1980 the NCC called for an end to military aid to El Salvador, and a year later it advocated temporary refugee status for those fleeing the civil war. This status had previously been given to refugees from Vietnam, Laos, Uganda, and Nicaragua, but the United States claimed that the refugees from El Salvador were economic, rather than political, refugees. The NCC and other Protestant groups contended that the U.S. policy was a denial that its ally was repressive. In 1981, Protestant leaders took to the streets in Washington, DC, to protest military aid to El Salvador, in part because the Reagan administration had refused to discuss Central American policy with them.[6] It was the affront to church authority that also stimulated ecclesiastical action regarding El Salvador.

In Guatemala the Lutheran Church and the NCC actively tried to facilitate the peace process. Members of the Lutheran Church in 1993 helped organize discussions among the Guatemalan factions of the civil war, all of whom welcomed UN involvement in negotiations. While the Lutheran Church generally felt it outside proper bounds to take a partisan position, providing a forum in which people could discuss their differences was considered appropriate. They did state, however, that in this case they were not neutral, but took the side of the poor and oppressed, giving them a chance to speak where possible and speaking for them when they might not have access. Three years later, the process came to fruition, and the NCC facilitated official negotiations, pushing for greater indigenous participation in the peace process. The NCC was instrumental in the formation of a Civil Society Assembly that included Indian organizations, church groups, trade unions, representatives of the university, and other groups. The role of this assembly was to provide a "third voice" in the debate.

Witness for Peace   More than seven thousand people, many of them from mainline churches, have gone to Central America, Cuba, Mexico (Chiapas), and Haiti since 1983 as part of a faith-based program called Witness for Peace.[7] The program's goal was to reduce the fighting by having church people and others from the United States living and working in the war zones where U.S.-backed Contras were fighting the Sandinista government. Military activity may have been occasionally thwarted by the presence of U.S. citizens, but the most important consequence of the action was that many church members were seeing evidence that contradicted the official U.S. government definition of the situation. They returned to their churches and communities, offered a perspective that often directly contradicted press releases from the White House and the Pentagon, and facilitated a groundswell of opposition. Witness for Peace thus dramatically increased awareness and a passion for involvement in the peace process and protests against U.S. policies.[8]

At one point a group of United Methodist bishops took out a full-page ad in the *New York Times* declaring "Stop the Lies! Stop the Killing!" Finally, in what may have been the first time in history that a war was ended through democratic politics, and with pressure from church leaders and people of faith across the country, the U.S. Congress voted to cut off funding for the Contras in August of 1984.

The Sanctuary Movement   The March 1980 assassination of Salvadoran Archbishop Oscar Romero while he was serving communion and the subsequent murder of four religious women from the United States, allegedly by the Salvadoran National Guard, caught the attention of church people the world over.[9] The atrocity stimulated a network of people sheltering Salvadoran refugees called the Sanctuary Movement, based on the ancient Judeo-Christian-Islamic tradition of providing sanctuary for refugees.

At first the movement was primarily a grassroots affair initiated by local clergy and laity. Because it involved acts of civil disobedience that were a direct violation of U.S. law, some church officials may have been reluctant to take up the cause even if they were sympathetic. After U.S. Immigration and Naturalization Service (INS) investigators entered the apartment of Darlene Nicgorski, a Catholic nun in Phoenix, Arizona, and arrested a Salvadoran woman staying there, church officials began to protest. In the wake of the INS action, the government was condemned and the movement supported by the governing bodies of the American Lutheran Church, the Presbyterian Church (USA), the United Methodist Church, the United Church of Christ, and the American Baptist Church, among others.

In an official statement in 1984, the NCC urged a moratorium on the deportation of aliens to Central America and asked the government to cease harassing and prosecuting the Sanctuary Movement. Six months later, another NCC resolution urged leaders of member churches to provide guidance to members contemplating nonviolent resistance to U.S. policy in Central America. It recommended serious consideration of the Sanctuary Movement as an expression of Christian duty to the suffering stranger, but noted the real risks of prosecution and possible jail time.

Critics of the movement such as Richard Neuhaus (an influential Lutheran theologian) contended that its participants merely wanted to "score points" against the Reagan administration rather than to shelter people,[10] an allegation hotly denied by those involved. Moreover, the movement persisted well beyond the Reagan administration. In the 1990s, for example, the INS improved its asylum procedures and accepted the reopening of 150,000 cases of Salvadorans and Guatemalans, in part because it was facing a suit filed by the American Baptist Church.[11]

One reason for high-level mainline involvement was that the churches themselves were frequent targets of oppressive South American regimes and later the U.S. government. One telling example is what happened when Anglicans were arrested by the government of El Salvador. The presiding bishop of the Episcopal Church went to the State Department and met with the assistant secretary for Latin America. One outcome of the visit was that the Episcopalians organized a meeting in 1990 between religious leaders and President Christiani of El Salvador. Episcopal staff member the Rev. Canon Brian Grieves claimed that the meeting was very important for developments in El Salvador because it "gave religious community access to people in high levels for the first time." Later, Grieves recalls,

> The FMLN approached [Bishop] Ed Browning and asked if he'd deliver a proposal for a peace process to the State Department, which he did. He pushed the administration to consider the proposal and to end its military posture there. Shortly after that the process was all moved over to the UN and there was a lot of appreciation expressed by James Baker to the church for promoting that. We had disagreements with the Bush administration around that issue and the Middle East. But when they signed the Oslo agreement—our presiding bishop went to the signing with Arafat and the others. James Baker said, "Well, we've had our disagreements, but now here we are working together on something very important."[12]

Human Rights

The last decades of the twentieth century saw a remarkable growth in human rights movements around the world, a development that constituted another major focus of the U.S. religious community's foreign policy efforts. Drawing upon Gandhian tactics of nonviolence from the Indian Freedom Movement and United Nations–sponsored human rights activity, nongovernmental organizations and movements struggled against abuses in every corner of the globe.

The churches were at the core of that development. Indeed, as Lowell Livezey puts it in his analysis, "[I]n the expansion of the nongovernmental human rights movement in the United States since the Vietnam War, nothing has been more important than the increasing role of the U.S. religious community." Among the Protestants, that effort was dominated by the mainline churches associated with the NCC. Many human rights activists came out of an antiwar perspective from the Vietnam era, and they coalesced to some extent in the creation of the NCC's Human Rights Office in 1977. The work of that office "represented a new direction in the international role of liberal Protestantism adopted in light of the experience of Vietnam, Watergate, and [the] civil rights movement."[13]

The human rights community is very diverse, of course, and goes far beyond the religious community to include such organizations as Amnesty International, the International League for Human Rights, and various UN agencies and Human Rights Watch committees. Religious organizations and people in the faith communities, including the mainline Protestant churches, are active in the human rights movement. Not only do the denominations and peace fellowships do human rights work, but the leaders of many secular organizations are active in various faith communities.

Dimensions of Mainline Involvement with Human Rights   Although he does not focus on mainline Protestants, Livezey's analysis suggests a number of ways in which religious bodies work in the field of human rights. In this section we examine the work of the mainline churches in South Africa. It is helpful, however, to look at the broader picture, especially since the mainline churches carried out so much of their human rights work cooperatively with other organizations, such as the NCC.

First, much of the churches' human rights activity involves direct humanitarian services. Service agencies (e.g., Church World Service) often promoted human rights causes while informing congregations about abuses as part of their education about the reasons for services such as free publicity to victims, legal services, refugee support, disaster relief, hunger and development programs, and so forth.[14] Second, religious bodies sometimes lobby the political process by either promoting or opposing specific legislation. Washington offices of the denominations (what is often called the "Washington religious lobby") as well as individual members are urged to contact their congressional representatives.[15] It is difficult to assess the actual impact of such activity on the legislative process because of the diversity of opinions on foreign policy within the mainline Protestant churches and the lack of systematic data.

Third, and perhaps most important, religious institutions promote human rights by engaging in broad education on the issues. As Livezey puts it,

> The great strength of religious organizations in the United States is
> their capacity to disseminate ideas. For all the money devoted to their
> service activities, and for all the controversy generated by their
> lobbying efforts, the dominant current of their work consists of the
> tremendous complex of activities by which ideas are articulated,
> examined, celebrated, inculcated, and promoted. The U.S. Sunday

school is surely one of the greatest propaganda machines running today. While it is not primarily devoted to human rights, its lessons are replete with interpretations of political values . . . that have a bearing on human rights.[16]

The most visible aspect of the mainline work on human rights has been carried out by the NCC Human Rights Office, which operates within the mainstream United Nations tradition on human rights and is guided by the International Bill of Rights and the international human rights treaties.[17] Livezey suggests that it is difficult to summarize the NCC's complicated position, although it does have some central features. First, its main focus is on defending "people against violations of civil and political rights, especially violations involving violence or the danger of violence," that is, those involving the "security of the person." This emphasis is often found in the U.S. government's advocacy of human rights, as opposed to other kinds of rights, such as social and economic rights, that are not emphasized by official U.S. positions.[18]

A second major human rights concern of the NCC has been religious freedom, especially the suppression of work by religious institutions "in social and political affairs—work with the poor in El Salvador; holding political discussions in South Korean churches; aiding political prisoners—rather than for apolitical forms of religious practice." Livezey notes, however, that the NCC is not always consistent in its position; for example, a spokesperson for Church World Service defended the Vietnamese government's decision to close church hospitals and schools as part of its nation-building efforts after the war.[19] The NCC has also been concerned with the issue of self-determination, as in the cases of Namibia and the Palestinian people. In these cases, as elsewhere, the NCC almost always defines human rights as freedom from political repression and seldom affirms other human rights such as "subsistence rights."[20]

The NCC has supported a number of strategies to promote human rights, from the effort to implement legislation tying U.S. foreign assistance to human rights practices to the mobilization of economic pressure through divestment and stockholder resolutions. It has also sought to influence the vast membership of its constituent denominations by producing pamphlets and books through its own publishing house, Friendship Press.[21]

The Anti-Apartheid Case   One of the most significant Protestant human rights cases was the struggle against the apartheid regime in South Africa.

Of particular importance was the mainline's role in mobilizing worldwide opposition to put pressure on the white regime and provide support for opposition forces.

The first significant round of opposition from the mainline churches came in the form of a shareholder resolution that eventually led to a massive campaign to get foreign firms to divest their business in apartheid-ruled South Africa. In 1971 the Episcopal Church filed an unprecedented shareholder resolution with General Motors that signaled the beginning of the movement. The presiding Episcopal bishop, John Hines, acted swiftly after the church's General Convention resolution asking its Executive Council to pressure General Motors to withdraw from South Africa. Bishop Hines wrote a letter to GM's chairman of the board on 1 February 1971 and went to the annual shareholders meeting to present a resolution personally.[22] At the meeting, Baptist pastor Leon Sullivan, who became a prominent leader in the divestment campaign, gave a rousing speech to the stockholders, challenging the corporation's policies at its annual meeting for the first time.

The process initiated by the Episcopalians eventually resulted in the consortium called the NCC-affiliated Interfaith Center for Corporate Responsibility, which monitors American companies in the United States and abroad. Much of the ecclesiastical battle against apartheid was carried out by the NCC, which consistently challenged its member denominations, and the United States as a whole, to evaluate their investment practices. The Episcopalian shareholder action demonstrates how the mainline churches can be disproportionately effective. At the time of the anti-apartheid action, the Episcopal Church constituted only about 1.2 percent of the American population, but about 15 percent of the U.S. Congress and, according to one study, 21 percent of all chief executive officers. The CEO of GM, James M. Roche, a devout Roman Catholic, was reportedly infuriated at the invasion of the church in corporate affairs and informed the Executive Club of Chicago that a "radical crusade" was threatening to "all but destroy free enterprise as we know it."[23]

Economics and Foreign Policy

As with human rights issues, much of the activity of the denominations with regard to economics and U.S. foreign policy was carried out collectively through the NCC. The NCC has been broadly concerned with economic issues since its inception, many on the domestic scene. Since these are covered in other chapters, we focus our attention on issues that relate to the international arena. The NCC participated in the Nestle boycott, joining with others in the United States and Europe who had concerns about sanitation problems and the cost, especially for a product deemed not to be as good as breast milk. An investigation of the Gulf & Western sugar operation in the Dominican Republic for allegations of union busting and paying substandard wages occurred in 1976. The NCC also supported Guatemalan efforts to unionize against Coca-Cola in 1980. In the late 1980s the NCC's emphasis on corporate responsibility also incorporated environmental concerns. During the aftermath of the 1986 Union Carbide spill in Bhopal, India, the NCC vigorously fought on behalf of the Indians for the trial to occur in the United States, where the multinational corporation would be the defendant. In 1989, the NCC set a corporate code on environmental conduct and in 1991 joined a coalition concerned with the environment and corporate responsibility. Economic sanctions are another issue about which the NCC has been outspoken, particularly in opposition to the Cuban embargo and sanctions against Iraq.

Jubilee 2000   The most significant recent development was the emergence of wide participation of Protestants in Jubilee 2000, a movement that calls for a "one-time cancellation by the year 2000 of the unpayable debt owned by the World's poorest countries under a fair and transparent process."[24] In 1996, the International Monetary Fund and the World Bank wrote the Heavily Indebted Poor Countries (HIPC) initiative to address the consequences of debt burdens. Poor countries are forced to divert vast amounts of tax revenue into debt payments, which compromises investment in infrastructure, education, health services, and programs to reduce poverty and hunger. U.S. participation is crucial for the HIPC initiative to become reality. Several bills have been introduced in the Senate and House of Representatives that propose specific action to achieve debt relief. Testimony before a U.S. House of Representatives committee submitted by Faith Action for People-Centered Development Policy (consisting of Catholic and Protestant groups, Bread for the World, and the NCC) notes that in terms of gross national product, the United States spends less on international assistance than any other of the twenty-one wealthiest nations. In part, it is this backdrop of U.S. reluctance to fund foreign aid that makes the Jubilee 2000 story quite remarkable: until it emerged, debt relief was not even on the "radar scope."[25]

The Jubilee 2000 campaign was initiated in the United Kingdom by Bill Peters and Martin Dent, two Christians who had lived in West Africa and came up with the idea of linking the nearing millennium with the biblical idea of jubilee.[26] The movement spread, and when Bill Peters first came to the United States to gain contacts for the cause, he met first with Walter Owensby at the Washington Office of the Presbyterian Church (USA). Although Owensby had previously been focused on debt relief issues, he wanted Bill Peters to meet with Marie Dennis, a Maryknoll sister more on the forefront of debt relief at the time. Out of this meeting came the launching of Jubilee 2000 U.S.A. by the Religious Working Group, Marie Dennis's conglomerate group of organizations that included several mainline Protestant churches.[27]

A papal call for debt relief, support by such celebrities as Bono of the rock group U2, and the unique millennial timing set the stage for global participation in Jubilee 2000. Through a combination of "good lobbying and good luck," a bipartisan committee sponsored a bill, and debt relief became a dynamic, "real" issue.[28] Jubilee 2000 provides an example of the participation in the two spheres that Olson notes in her earlier chapter—the Washington offices and the grassroots.

Some of the crucial participation by the mainline Protestant churches involved the writing of the legislation for Jubilee 2000, bringing attention to those aspects of the debt-relief question that required U.S. participation. The Debt Roundtable, a group that split off from the Jubilee 2000 steering committee, was instrumental in drafting this legislation. The informal split was prompted by a division between the more "pragmatic" and more "prophetic" groups within the movement, which is not always unified on how best to achieve its goal of complete debt reduction. For example, certain organizations in the coalition want to see complete debt relief and do not support measures that appear to be "half a loaf." Other organizations, including several mainline Protestant denominations, take a different tack. Because the majority of the denominational representatives on the Jubilee 2000 steering committee are from the Washington offices, they are oriented toward pragmatic policy, which entails compromise. The Presbyterian and Episcopal staff have been instrumental in helping draft bipartisan legislation for debt relief that is not complete, but is a start. As it is, the current legislation is "quite a jump" for some members of Congress; pushing for more, the pragmatists claim, would jeopardize progress. The consensus among the group working on the legislation is that, while they are not content with "half a loaf" measures, such measures are better than holding out for total debt relief, which may be unattainable in one fell swoop.[29]

Another example of involvement is the lead taken by Lutheran Washington Office's Mark Brown in assisting in the organization and coordination of one of the main Jubilee 2000 U.S.A. rally and lobby days in Washington, DC. Scheduled for a week before the IMF and World Bank meetings, the event was designed to draw attention to debt relief. Because of the top priority status given to debt relief by the ELCA, Brown was able to take the time to head up the weekly meetings to plan the April 9–10 events.[30]

It is difficult to tease out the distinctive contributions of the mainline Protestant churches to the Jubilee 2000 campaign. First, it is impossible to arrive at a quantitative measure of the pressure or influence of the mainline churches. Melanie Hardison, the coordinator of Jubilee 2000 activities for the Presbyterian Church (USA) notes that although the denomination determined specific goals for the campaign, such as writing a certain number of letters to Congress, or holding so many educational activities in the various presbyteries, it is difficult to track these numbers.[31] Despite these difficulties, those who work in the Washington offices are quick to point out the importance of the grassroots efforts of the mainline Protestants. Walter Owensby, of the PCUSA's Washington office, noted that the Washington office representatives are not that influential on their own. Members of Congress are skeptical because "everybody represents others, or say they do—so it always depends on being able to show that people across the country are involved in the issue, and care about the issue."[32] Most of the mainline Protestant churches have various educational resources available for their members.[33] The Presbyterian Church (USA) is unique in that they have a staff member at the national headquarters in Louisville, Kentucky, devoted full time to Jubilee 2000. She disseminates information about Jubilee 2000 to congregational contacts, participates in monthly steering committee meetings in Washington, DC, and writes and compiles educational materials, as well as suggesting ways for churches to get involved in the campaign. She makes use of the established networks that have affinities with Jubilee 2000, such as the hunger, peace, and women's advocacy groups, and utilizes resources from other advocacy groups with more experience in direct mobilization, such as Bread for the World's Offering of Letters kit, which facilitates direct contact with congressional representatives.[34]

Another important aspect of mainline Protestant participation in the movement is its impact in creating "social ambiance" that supports debt relief. Rallies and educational events sponsored by churches capture local media coverage, which contributes to the notion of popular support and lends a sense of "normalcy" to the debt relief movement. Support from the mainline might be perceived by congressional representatives as support by "ordinary people."[35] It is interesting to note that, as one example, more than 10 percent of Senate members maintain a United Methodist affiliation.[36] Although shared affiliation may not result in shared values or legislative priorities, the denominational affiliation and moral legitimacy of the mainline churches offer them access to Congress that many social movements simply do not have.

THE POLITICS OF ECCLESIASTICAL INTERVENTION

Mainline Protestantism plays a special role in foreign policy debates, both because of its transnational character and because of its position in American society. Mainline denominations have strong links to institutions outside of the United States that often give them a different perspective from those who move in national circles and represent national interests. The church was the most significant institution bridging the peoples of the two major superpowers during the Cold War; it rivals powerful multinational corporations in its scope and influence on a global basis. Perhaps most important, a faith perspective on foreign policy can diverge dramatically from the point of view developed in the halls of power. Different frames for examining security issues are constructed from varying positions within the decision-making structure of a society. Mainline Protestantism consists of a broad range of voices, including a critical one; it is also in a position to be heard because of the moral authority the Protestant church has in American society and because of the social status of many of its members.[37]

Whereas more radical criticism of U.S. foreign policy might come from the historic peace churches such as the Religious Society of Friends (Quakers) , the Mennonites, and the Church of the Brethren, it is the mainline Protestants who bring a critical perspective into the mainstream. There are more local United Methodist congregations in the United States than there are post offices; clearly the institutional reach of mainline Protestantism is vast and deep. Even if members of local congregations do not agree with their pastors or their denomination's more progressive positions, they are more likely to listen to voices of dissent in the pulpit than to those in the streets.

It is difficult, of course, to evaluate the actual impact of mainline Protestantism on U.S. foreign policy, especially without a parallel world in which the same political events unfold without church intervention. What is clear, however, is that a considerable amount of individual energy and institutional resources was expended in the effort to shape foreign policy decisions and inform the broader public of a particular point of view. The most direct influence the churches have on foreign policy is that deliberately crafted and disseminated through the official bodies responsible for political and social concerns and their lobbies in Washington, DC discussed elsewhere in this volume.

Most important, the mainline churches provide people with differing points of view access at higher levels, which might not otherwise be available to them. Whereas most voices of dissent have difficulty getting the attention of even low-level officials, mainline leaders can reach the highest levels. As Episcopal staff member Brian Grieves puts it, "The church has access to government when it wants to. It certainly changes from administration to administration and certainly the Reagan years were not good years for the mainline churches. The Christian coalition had a lot of access and they were there every day. When George Bush came in, things changed; he was an Episcopalian and he was receptive; there were disagreements, but he listened to us."[38] Because of church connections and offices in Washington, Grieves suggests, "One of the things we do there is we have a face and they can see us and know us and we can know them as real people and not just people from the media." He contends that "that's very important—for addressing both members of Congress and the administration."[39]

In addition to, and sometimes as part of, the Washington lobbies, the churches also influence public policy by providing a platform for voices not usually heard. Because of their contacts on the ground around the world, church officials often have sources of information about what is happening in hot spots that are not accessible to U.S. government officials and who often present points of view that can influence policymakers. Indeed, according to Grieves, the information coming from church "partners" in other countries "pushes a lot of our work" in the Washington office. The Washington office may either take the information to officials, bring back people from the area to speak for themselves, and/or disseminate the information among congregations in the United States.

Rituals of Moral Resistance

In the final analysis the mainline churches may affect foreign policy most when they are doing what they do best: carrying out the business of the church—worshipping, praying, and educating its members. Such actions may be less dramatic than public protest or Jessie Jackson–style peace missions,[40] and they will probably not appear in the local newspaper, let alone the *New York Times*. They may, however, have a long-term impact on the way in which Americans think about foreign policies and the manner in which their leaders conceptualize them.

Not only do the churches regularly sponsor rituals that undercut nationalist sentiments and build bridges across political barriers, they have numerous ritual and educational events that provide alternatives to mainstream thinking about foreign policy. Messages of peace from the pulpit and an emphasis on Jesus as the Prince of Peace in the annual cycles of the liturgy are supplemented by prayers for peace at home and in the church.

A network of educational structures is often one of the few alternatives to the perspectives on foreign policy issues put forth by the government and disseminated daily by the media. From women's societies to Sunday School classes and publishing houses, the mainline churches often challenge mainstream views on foreign policy either overtly or subtly. Sometimes they do so simply by positing an ideal of a peaceful world desired by God that is seldom propagated by heads of state except on religious holidays, such as at the annual lighting of the Christmas tree on the White House lawn.

Sometimes pastors use their pulpits to represent others or even to allow them to speak. Antiwar protests are planned and sometimes carried out at church facilities. Sunday School classes offer middle-class Americans a place to hear protesters who might otherwise be seen simply as strangers on the streets. The publications of church presses, from religious education curricula to congregational newspapers, often provide information on perspectives that do not appear on the nightly news or in local newspapers.

The infrastructure of the mainline churches, with local congregations in every corner of the country and well-organized grassroots campaigns as well as national offices, presents one of the few spaces in American politics where dissident voices can be widely heard. Although thousands of NGOs across the United States and around the world may be more focused on foreign policy issues, it is, ironically, partly the churches' lack of focus on peace and justice issues that makes them so powerful. Most mainline congregants do not go to church to learn about or affect U.S. foreign policy. They go to worship God, to get married and buried, to baptize their children and babies, and to be part of a religious community. When they walk in the door, however, they step into a space in which a dissident voice regarding U.S. foreign policy may be heard, a voice that many of them might not hear anywhere else.

NOTES

1. See James Kurth, "The Protestant Deformation and American Foreign Policy," *Orbis* 42 (1998): 221–39.

2. Allen Hertzke, *Representing God in Washington* (Knoxville: University of Tennessee Press, 1988), 129.

3. See Roland Bainton, *Christian Teaching on War and Peace* (Nashville, TN: Abingdon Press, 1960).

4. Hertzke, *Representing God in Washington*, 129.

5. See K. L. Billingsley, *From Mainline to Sideline: The Social Witness of the National Council of Churches* (Washington, DC: Ethics and Public Policy Center, 1990). Also see Marjorie Hyer, "Church Council Criticizes Latin American Policy; Nonviolent Resistance to U.S. Military Action Supported," *Washington Post*, final ed., 18 May 1985, Religion sec., B6.

6. Marjorie Hyer, "Protestant Leaders March, Protest Aid to El Salvador," *Washington Post*, final ed., 18 April 1981, sec. 1, A9.

7. Website: http://www.witnessforpeace.org/deleg.html, 6 October 2000.

8. See http://www.witnessforpeace.org.

9. See Susan Bibler Coutin, *The Culture of Protest: Religious Activism and the U.S. Sanctuary Movement* (Boulder, CO: Westview Press, 1993); Hilary Cunningham, *God and Caesar at the Rio Grande: Sanctuary and the Politics of Religion* (Minneapolis: University of Minnesota Press, 1995); Robin Lorentzen, *Women in the Sanctuary Movement* (Philadelphia, PA: Temple University Press, 1991); and Ann Crittenden, *Sanctuary: A Story of American Conscience and the Law in Collision* (New York: Weidenfeld and Nicolson, 1988).

10. Ari L. Goldman, "U.S. Clerics Debating Ethics of Giving Sanctuary to Aliens," *New York Times*, 23 August 1985, A1.

11. Coutin, *Culture of Protest*, 223.

12. Telephone interview, 4 October 2000.

13. Lowell W. Livezey, "U.S. Religious Organizations and the International Human Rights Movement," *Human Rights Quarterly* 11 (1989): 14, 19; see also Lowell W. Livezey, *Nongovernmental Organizations and the Ideas of Human Rights* (Princeton, NJ: Center of International Studies).

14. Livezey, "U.S. Religious Organizations," 16; cf. J. Bruce Nichols, *The Uneasy Alliance: Religion, Refugee Work, and U.S. Foreign Policy* (New York: Oxford University Press, 1988).

15. Livezey, "U.S. Religious Organizations," 17; cf. Hertzke, *Representing God in Washington*.

16. Livezey, "U.S. Religious Organizations," 17.

17. Ibid., 22; cf. U.S. Congress, Senate Committee on Foreign Relations, *Hearing on the International Human Rights Treaties*, 96th Cong., 1st sess., 19 November 1976.

18. Livezey, "U.S. Religious Organizations," 23.

19. Livezey, "U.S. Religious Organizations," 23; cf. David Little, "Religion and Global Affairs: Religion and U.S. Foreign Policy," *SAIS Review* 18 (1998): 25–31.

20. One exception noted by Livezey is the "Right to Food Resolution" debated by Congress in 1976 (Livezey, "U.S. Religious Organizations," 26).

21. Ibid., 26–27.

22. Telephone interview with the Rev. Canon Brian Grieves, 4 October 2000; for a full account of the developments, see Robert Massie, *Loosing the Bonds: The United States and South Africa in the Apartheid Years* (New York: Nan A. Talese/Doubleday, 1997), 274 ff.

23. Quoted in Massie, *Loosing the Bonds*, 278.

24. The Jubilee 2000 Campaign, Church World Service home page: http://www.churchworldservice.org/cwsj2000.htm.

25. Telephone interview with Kathy Pomroy, director of organizing, Bread for the World, 26 September 2000.

26. See Martin Wroe's description of the beginnings of the Jubilee 2000 UK movement in the May–June 2000 issue of *Sojourners* magazine: "An Irresistible Force." Online address: http://www.sojourners.com/sojo005/000510.html.

27. Telephone interview with Walter Owensby, 26 September 2000.

28. Telephone interview with Tom Hart, 12 September 2000.

29. Telephone interview with Tom Hart, 12 September 2000; Walter Owensby, 26 September 2000; and Kathy Pomroy, 26 September 2000.

30. See www.elca.org/dcs/advocacyplan.

31. Telephone interview with Melanie Hardison, 21 September 2000.

32. Telephone interview with Walter Owensby, former PCUSA Washington Office staff member, 26 September 2000.

33. For example, with the exception of the American Baptists, the other five denominational web pages have information and links to sources about Jubilee 2000.

34. Telephone interview with Kathy Pomroy, 26 September 2000; and with Melanie Hardison, 21 September 2000.

35. Telephone interview with Kathy Pomroy, about the distinct contribution of the mainline to the Jubilee 2000 efforts, 26 September 2000. Her view is that mainline support is "ordinary" in contrast with others who may be perceived as "extreme" or "on the fringe."

36. As of the 106th Congress, 1999–2000, twelve senators and forty-seven representatives are United Methodists. See www.umc-gbcs.org/wfw2-1.htm.

37. See James D. Davidson, "Religion among America's Elite: Persistence and Change in the Protestant Establishment," *Sociology of Religion* 55 (1994): 419–40.

38. Telephone interview with Brian Grieves, 4 October 2000.

39. Ibid.

40. Note the visits of Jesse Jackson to Syria in 1983 and his visit to Serbia in 1999, to request the release of U.S. servicemen.

15 Beyond Quiet Influence?

Possibilities for the Protestant Mainline

Robert Wuthnow

Judging from newspaper headlines and television advertising, the American public is preoccupied with shallow materialistic pursuits—eating at gourmet restaurants, shopping and trading stock on the Internet, and splurging on cruise vacations and sports utility vehicles. On the rare occasion when religion becomes newsworthy, its message appears to be preoccupied with such controversial topics as abortion, prayer in public schools, and displaying the Ten Commandments in classrooms and police stations. Insofar as religion touches the public life of our nation, it appears to do so by challenging individuals to think about restraining the impulses of young people and those who do not show up regularly at church.

Not surprisingly, political candidates take their cues from these media-driven messages about what religious people presumably value. Candidates who choose to express their religious values do so by reminiscing about moments of personal salvation or by making appearances with religious groups defending the right to life or the right to pray in public schools. Pollsters follow their lead, asking voters in exit polls whether or not they sympathize with the Religious Right and, if so, how these sympathies influenced their vote.

Since the late 1970s, referring to someone as a liberal has become one of the surest ways of branding a political candidate as hopelessly idealistic if not downright un-American. To be sure, there are good reasons for this pejorative connotation: the excesses of the campus protests of the 1960s, the nation's slow coming-to-terms with its sense of having abandoned veterans of the Vietnam War (sometimes attributed to liberals' opposition to the United States's involvement in Vietnam), and deep-seated misgivings about affirmative action, feminism, or the unrest associated with the civil rights movement. Some forays into "L-territory" have been made under the guise of rescuing an earlier term *(progressivism)*, but these expeditions have seldom proven attractive to the wider public.

Thus it is easy to assume that the American public holds little interest in such liberal (or progressive) issues as combating racism and gender discrimination or helping the poor. Not that Americans are necessarily callous racists, sexists, and hard-hearted elitists. But such issues are likely to seem vaguely passé. Surely, some argue, these crusades were waged in an earlier era and were successfully accomplished: tolerance, respect, and equality for racial minorities, women, and the poor have been achieved. Or, as others would claim, such crusades may not have been successful, but foundered on their own idealism. Their time has passed. Feminism has largely been accepted or rejected, racial equality has gone about as far as it can go, and the poor (if not always with us) will at least always remain securely segregated in their own communities. It is time to move on, leaving such causes to historians.

For many clergy and religious leaders in mainline churches, this sense of a shift in public mood is a beguiling message. It is easy, if one is committed to progressive issues, to characterize oneself as a voice in the wilderness calling "Repent!" to a world uninterested in listening. It is just as easy, if one's own interests are mixed or preoccupied with the more pressing business of the day, to conclude that one's time is better spent working quietly in one's own garden, perhaps withdrawing from the messy business of American politics altogether.

But is the perception that American religion only mobilizes people around conservative causes accurate? What does the public actually think? Are some of the causes that mainline leaders have promoted, at least through their Washington offices, of such minor interest to the public that only meager successes can be expected? Is it better, in the face of massive disinterest, perhaps even opposition, to work quietly behind the scenes rather than attempt to enlist broader support? Or is there enough interest in the general public, not to mention among church members themselves, to work on a broader scale?

Certainly there is evidence that mainline members are active in their own communities and that mainline churches provide social services for the needy as well as opportunities for the faithful to worship. But has the public mood shifted entirely toward service activities at the local level? Or is the public still interested in such issues as social justice, poverty, discrimination, and human rights—issues that may require advocacy as well as service?

Because the agendas of most surveys dealing with religion and politics have been shaped by interest in the Religious Right, these questions have been difficult to answer. To rectify that imbalance, the Public Role of Mainline Protestantism Project conducted a national survey that posed questions about a different set of issues and about different ways in which churches and church leaders might be (or become) involved in social, political, and other public activities.[1]

INTEREST IN PUBLIC ISSUES

We carefully selected eleven issues that varied in terms of how much they had come up in earlier phases of our research. Mainline leaders had told us that all of them were important, but some were issues in which mainline leaders had been engaged in significant ways over an extended period, while others, they thought, may have received less attention within the churches themselves. The two issues that engage the interest of the largest proportion of the public are social policies that would help the poor and legislation to protect the environment. Six in ten Americans say they are quite interested in these issues, and nine in ten say they are at least fairly interested (see table 15.1). The extent of this interest is notable. Although mainline churches have long advocated efforts to combat poverty and economic injustice, their involvement in environmental issues is more recent. In both areas, specific strategies and programs continue to be debated. But it is significant that neither question refers to activities performed entirely on a voluntary basis (such as giving handouts to poor neighbors or recycling); both pertain to social policies.

Three other issues are of interest to a large majority of the public: overcoming discrimination against women, government policies to promote international peace, and achieving greater equality for racial and ethnic minorities. Almost six in ten Americans say they are quite interested in each of these issues, and nearly nine in ten say they are at least fairly interested. Mainline churches have actively promoted these issues over the past half century, and in each area enough success has been achieved that one might have supposed public interest had waned. Yet these data suggest that public interest is still strong.

The data also show that international human rights issues, the social responsibilities of corporations, and maintaining strict separation between church and state are of interest to large numbers of Americans. Approximately four in ten Americans say they are quite interested in each of these

Table 15.1. General Interest in Selected Social Issues

Social Issue	Respondents Who Are Quite Interested (%)	Respondents Who Are at Least Fairly Interested (%)
Social policies that would help the poor	60	90
Legislation to protect the environment	60	90
Overcoming discrimination against women in our society	58	87
Government policies to promote international peace	57	88
Achieving greater equality for racial and ethnic minorities in our society	54	86
International human rights issues	44	81
The social responsibilities of corporations	40	76
Maintaining strict separation between church and state	39	67
Campaign finance reform	29	58
Relief and development programs for people in Third World countries	27	68
Reducing intolerance toward homosexuals	27	53

issues, and at least two-thirds of the public reports being at least fairly interested. This level of interest is sufficient to suggest that church programs oriented toward these issues are capable of attracting widespread support.

The remaining issues in table 15.1 drew interest from a smaller share of the public. Campaign finance reform, despite the attention it received during the 2000 presidential campaign, is of prominent interest to less than a third of the public, as are relief and development programs for people in Third World countries and reducing intolerance toward homosexuals. Still, more than half the public claims to be at least fairly interested in these issues. These data suggest that church leaders need not apologize for the stands they have taken, nor should they worry that nobody else cares about these issues. What may be contested are specific programs or strategies for advancing some of these issues, not the fact that the issues themselves are important.

WHAT RELIGIOUS GROUPS SHOULD DO

Previous studies show that Americans are leery of religious leaders becoming too involved in certain kinds of political activities.[2] Such involvement apparently raises concerns about separation of church and state. Yet research also shows that most Americans trust the clergy, at least more than they trust leaders of government and industry, and recognize the churches' potential for helping to solve social problems.[3]

The results (shown in table 15.2) indicate that the public overwhelmingly supports the involvement of religious groups in civic activities.[4] Almost nine people in ten would like religious groups to be more active in encouraging people to do volunteer work. About the same number want churches to be more active in promoting a greater sense of community responsibility. Nearly as many—at least eight in ten—want religious groups to be more active in giving poor people a voice in public affairs and in raising awareness about racial discrimination. And about three-quarters of the public want religious groups to be more active in protecting the environment and in making Americans more aware of hunger and poverty in other countries.

It is worth acknowledging that a small minority of the public wants religious groups to be less active in each of these areas. These are people who think churches already have too much influence or who think religious groups should stick to spiritual matters instead of getting involved in the wider community. But most Americans think religious groups should be trying to make a difference in the larger society. And the ways of doing this that are identified in these questions apparently seem fairly innocuous to most people. Volunteering and community responsibility, according to other studies, are widely valued; indeed, they have come to be marks of good citizenship in the public's mind.[5] Similarly, giving poor people a voice and raising awareness about racial discrimination can be understood as ameliorative, educational activities that are appropriate for religious organizations, whereas engaging more directly in partisan politics might arouse more concern.

In comparison with these activities, which a large majority of the public support, fewer than half of the public want religious groups (or mainline Protestant churches) to be more active in bringing religious values to bear on public policy, and an even smaller number want religious groups to be more active in addressing concerns about genetic engineering. On both items, about four people in ten actually want the churches to be less active.

Notably, the items in table 15.2 that gain the most support can be per-

Table 15.2. Public Support for the Civic Activities of Religious Groups

	Respondents Asked about Religious Groups (%)	Respondents Asked Specifically about Mainline Protestants (%)
Should religious groups be more or less active in the following		
Encouraging people to do volunteer work		
More active	89	87
Less active	6	6
Promoting a greater sense of community responsibility		
More active	88	82
Less active	8	8
Giving poor people a voice in public affairs		
More active	81	78
Less active	12	11
Raising awareness about racial discrimination		
More active	81	77
Less active	12	13
Protecting the environment		
More active	78	75
Less active	16	15
Making Americans more aware of hunger and poverty in other countries		
More active	74	70
Less active	18	18
Bringing religious values to bear on public policy		
More active	49	48
Less active	40	38
Addressing concerns about genetic engineering		
More active	45	45
Less active	40	38

formed at the local level, especially encouraging volunteer work and promoting community responsibility. In contrast, bringing religious values to bear on public policy may sound distant and thus garner less support because people are unsure who is exercising influence, for what reason, and on whom.

For this reason, we asked people to say whether they favor or oppose religious congregations "in your community" doing various things, such as working with government agencies, making statements to public officials, and inviting public officials to meetings (see table 15.3). Almost nine out of ten people favor local congregations working with government agencies to provide better services for low-income families. About three-quarters of the public favor local congregations receiving government funds to help provide services to the poor—a possibility that has become more likely as a result of the Charitable Choice provision of the 1996 welfare reform legislation and President Bush's emphasis on faith-based service initiatives. An equally large proportion favors local congregations making statements to public officials on topics of concern to the community. About seven in ten favor local congregations sponsoring meetings to which public officials are invited. And almost seven in ten favor local congregations forming alliances among different religions, such as Christians, Jews, and Muslims.

These responses suggest that most Americans feel it appropriate for religious organizations in their own communities to have extensive interaction with the political arena, even to the point of receiving government funds or inviting public officials to church meetings. Certainly little evidence suggests that Americans believe in a strict wall of separation between church and state—a wall that excludes any kind of interaction or cooperation at all. Indeed, when asked if the leaders of religious organizations should keep silent on social and political issues or express their views on these issues, the public opts for religious leaders expressing their views by a huge margin (76 percent, compared with 18 percent who think religious leaders should keep silent).

Still, the public does recognize the importance of restricting such interaction to appropriate times and places. For instance, when asked, "Do you think it is ever right for clergy to discuss political issues from the pulpit?" only 37 percent say yes, while 57 percent say no (and 16 percent are undecided). In other words, the Sunday worship service appears to be regarded as a sacrosanct activity that can be corrupted or sullied by bringing in the mundane concerns of elections and public policy. Accordingly, it is more acceptable for clergy to preach on broad social and moral issues that can be related to biblical themes than to speak directly about politics. Yet the responses to questions about making statements to public officials and inviting them to meetings suggest that church members recognize other ways in which their interests can be expressed. (It is also instructive that most Americans think it is okay for politicians to bring religion into

Table 15.3. General Attitudes toward Congregations' Public Activities

	Favor (%)	Oppose (%)
Do you favor or oppose religious congregations in your community doing each of the following		
Working with government agencies to provide better services for low-income families	87	11
Receiving government funds to help provide services to the poor	74	22
Making statements to public officials on topics of community concern	77	18
Sponsoring meetings to which public officials are invited	71	23
Forming alliances among different religions, such as Christians, Jews, and Muslims	69	23

the political arena: 75 percent say it is okay for political candidates to talk publicly about their religious views; 22 percent say it is not okay.)

WHAT RELIGIOUS GROUPS ARE DOING

If there is widespread public support for religious groups (especially at the local level) engaging in social, political, and other civic activities, what are religious groups actually doing? Quite a lot, at least judging from the official reports given by clergy and other church leaders in the studies conducted by Mark Chaves, Helen Giesel, William Tsitsos, Nancy Ammerman, and others.[6] Those activities range from sponsoring volunteer programs to hosting self-help groups, and forging alliances with nonprofit social service agencies. But what about average church members? What kinds of activities are they aware of? How many church members are somehow exposed to the discussions of social issues that take place in their congregations? Do such activities reach a large number of church members? Or are they run by clergy or a few lay leaders with perhaps limited involvement or awareness on the part of the wider congregation?

For this part of our discussion, it will be helpful to compare people who are members of the various religious traditions. The Religion and Politics Survey makes comparisons possible among the following: members of evangelical Protestant churches, members of mainline Protestant denominations, members of black Protestant denominations, Catholics, Jews, and those associated with other faiths (unaffiliated persons are disregarded in this analysis). The six groups are identified using a scheme developed for other data and adapted to the present survey.[7] Respondents were asked first to identify themselves in terms of broad traditions (such as Protestants, Catholics, Jews, and others) and then, in the case of Protestants, to answer several questions designed to gain an accurate answer about their current denominational preference.

Table 15.4 (top half) shows how many of the members of various religious traditions in the United States say their congregations have helped to sponsor social programs of one kind or another during the past year. The percentages are based on responses from people who say they are members at their current place of worship and who attend religious services at least once a month (we would not expect those who attend only once or twice a year to give knowledgeable responses about their congregations). Nearly two-thirds of the members of the various traditions claim to be aware that their congregation operates a food pantry or soup kitchen. At least a third of members say their congregation helps to sponsor a day care center, and about the same proportion say this about a homeless shelter. Almost this many say their congregation sponsors a tutoring program, whereas fewer (about one member in six, on average) say their congregation sponsors voter registration drives. In comparison, as many as three or four in ten say their congregation is part of some interfaith program that involves other religions than their own (such as Christians, Jews, and Muslims). These results run parallel to those in other studies. Members of mainline Protestant churches are often the most likely of any of the Christian traditions to say their congregation sponsors these kinds of social programs. For instance, 70 percent of mainline members report that their congregation sponsors a soup kitchen, compared with 62 percent of evangelical members, 65 percent of members of African American denominations, and 63 percent of Catholics. Mainline members are also more likely than members of these other Christian traditions to say their congregation helps sponsor a day care center, a homeless shelter, and interfaith programs.

The bottom half of table 15.4 shows members' responses to a series of questions asking about topics they may have heard discussed at their congregations in the past year through sermons, lectures, or group discussions. Nearly half of the members in every tradition say they have heard discussions about improving the relationships between blacks and whites (a proportion that rises to nearly two-thirds in African American churches). Between three and four in ten people say they have heard sermons, lectures, or group discussions at their congregations about protect-

Table 15.4. Congregations' Public Activities, by Religious Tradition

	Evangelical (%)	Mainline (%)	African American Protestant (%)	Catholic (%)	Jewish (%)	Other (%)
Respondent's congregation has sponsored the following in the past year						
Soup kitchen	62	70	65	63	61	60
Day care center	33	45	33	36	45	35
Homeless shelter	36	48	40	43	34	40
Tutoring program	29	30	46	38	53	40
Voter registration	17	14	41	17	22	18
Interfaith program	29	40	35	39	63	35
At least one of these	73	78	76	70	81	74
Respondent has heard sermon or group discussion about the following in the past year						
Government policies toward the poor	28	30	42	33	45	27
Protecting the environment	29	40	42	32	55	34
Being more supportive of homosexuals	9	15	12	13	29	10
The widening gap between rich and poor people	24	26	38	30	42	31
Improving black-white relations	46	46	64	43	52	45
Social responsibilities of corporations	14	16	30	18	42	16
At least one of these topics	59	64	70	59	64	62

NOTE: Based on the responses of members who attend services at least once a month.

ing the environment. Almost this many have heard such discussions about government policies toward the poor or about the widening gap between rich people and poor people. About one member in six has heard discussions about the social responsibilities of corporations. And, despite the fact that many congregations have resisted or avoided talking about homosexuality, between a tenth and a sixth of members (more among Jews) say they have heard discussions about being more supportive of homosexuals. Overall, the results suggest that congregations are indeed significant places where public discussions of social and political issues occur: at least six in ten members, on average, report hearing discussions of at least one of these issues at their congregations in the past year.

Mainline members are sometimes more likely than other Christians to have been exposed to such discussions (especially about protecting the environment), but on the whole there are relatively small differences among evangelical Protestants, mainline Protestants, African American Protestants, and Catholics, while Jews are more likely to have heard discussions of most of these issues than Christians. Within the mainline itself, such discussions are more common in large congregations than in small churches, and they are much more common in churches with active social ministries (shelters, day care programs, tutoring programs, and the like) than in less active congregations.[8]

Caution is always necessary in determining the extent to which such exposure at one's church or synagogue affects how people think or behave in other times and places. Yet studies do suggest that people who hear sermons on other topics (for example, about stewardship or loving one's neighbor) do behave somewhat differently than people who do not hear such sermons.[9] What is interesting here is that members of congregations where social issues are discussed are significantly more likely to express interest in some of the issues mentioned earlier in this chapter than are members of congregations where social issues are not discussed. For instance, the former are 16 percentage points more likely than the latter to be quite interested in social policies that would help the poor, 15 points more likely to be quite interested in overcoming discrimination toward women, 14 points more likely to be quite interested in reducing racial inequality, and 13 points more likely to be quite interested in legislation to protect the environment. Perhaps people who are already interested in these issues are just more likely to have attended (or remember attending) discussions at their churches. But the discussions also seem likely to reinforce members' attention to important social issues.

WHAT RELIGIOUS PEOPLE ARE DOING

Table 15.5 shows the responses of members who attend services at least monthly at evangelical Protestant, mainline Protestant, black Protestant, Catholic, Jewish, and other congregations to questions about their civic activities within the past twelve months. On average, about one member in three has contacted an elected official about an issue that was of concern, nearly a fifth of members have attended a class or lecture about social or

Table 15.5. Congregants' Civic Activities, by Religious Tradition

	Evangelical (%)	Mainline (%)	African American Protestant (%)	Catholic (%)	Jewish (%)	Other (%)
Respondent performed the following activity in the past year						
Contacted an elected official	30	32	22	27	67	27
Gave money to a political candidate or party	14	18	13	12	22	12
Attended political rally or meeting	12	16	18	12	28	16
Attended class/lecture about social/political issues	18	23	23	20	52	25
Work for political campaign or voter registration drive	7	7	10	6	25	7
Volunteer work at a place of worship	72	71	64	57	67	72
Other volunteer work	44	55	39	48	72	52
Read about social or political issues on the Internet	29	35	22	26	41	33
Belonged to a service club	8	14	8	11	18	12

NOTE: Based on the responses of members who attend services at least once a month.

political issues, at least an eighth have attended a political rally or given money to a candidate or political party, and about one in fourteen has worked for a political campaign or voter registration drive. Members of religious organizations are more likely to have been involved in all of these activities during the past year than people who do not belong to religious organizations. Overall, mainline Protestants are the most likely among Christians to have engaged in at least one of these political activities in the past year (Jews score highest). Fifty-five percent of mainline members have participated in at least one of these activities, compared with 45 percent of evangelical Protestants, 46 percent of black Protestants, and 43 percent of Catholics.

But political activities are not the only ways in which church members become involved in their communities. For many, the church itself is the favored avenue of participation. In the survey, nearly three-quarters of mainline and evangelical Protestants said they had done volunteer work at their place of worship in the past year, as did more than half of black Protestants, Catholics, and Jews. Sizable proportions also do volunteer work at organizations other than a church or place of worship; this kind of activity is significantly more common among mainline Protestants than evangelical Protestants, black Protestants, or Catholics—a result that corresponds with other research showing that mainline Protestants are more likely to develop connections with other organizations in their communities, rather than performing all their voluntary effort at their churches.[10] The table also shows the percentages of each group who have read about social or political issues on the Internet during the past year and who have belonged to service clubs, such as Rotary or League of Women Voters. Overall, about a third of members have read about issues on the Internet, while fewer than half this number have been members of service organizations; in both cases, mainline members are more likely to have participated in these ways than members of other Christian traditions.

WHY MAINLINERS PREFER TO WORK QUIETLY

These results suggest that Americans in general are more interested in the kinds of issues that mainline leaders have been trying to promote in recent years than we might have imagined, and that mainline members belong to congregations that usually sponsor social programs in their communities, expose them to lectures and discussions about social issues, and encourage them to take an active part in such civic activities as contacting elected officials or volunteering. But the question remains: Do mainliners prefer to work quietly behind the scenes, supporting congregational ministries and engaging in good works as individuals, or are they interested in their denominations and leaders taking a more active, visible role in shaping public policy?

Our research among denominational leaders, clergy, and lay activists suggests that much of what mainline Protestants have been able to accomplish has been done by the few rather than the many. These leaders characteristically put the best face on their work, but typically acknowledge that they feel as if they are on their own, trying to make a difference without the direct support or involvement of members in the tens of thousands of congregations that make up their denominations. Is this perception true? And, if it is, what are the reasons behind mainline members' reluctance to become more actively involved beyond their own churches and communities?

To answer these questions, we compare mainline Protestants with evangelical Protestants (additional comparisons with black Protestants, Catholics, and Jews, while interesting, are beyond the scope of the present discussion). Evangelical Protestants are in many ways like mainline Protestants, sharing the same commitment to Christianity practiced in the style of the Reformation and often drawing members from similar, largely white segments of the middle class; yet evangelical Protestants have become known in recent decades for their aggressive support of religious leaders who run for public office or launch political movements and for their activism in the national arena on behalf of issues they hold dear.

The first three items in table 15.6 show some of the similarities between the two groups: both are about equally likely to have members who say they follow what's going on in government and public affairs most of the time; the overwhelming majority of both think the things religious groups do affect the nation a lot or some; and nearly everyone in both groups thinks the influence of religious groups on the nation is positive. In short, the more activist political style of evangelicals and the quieter style of mainline Protestants cannot be attributed to one group simply being more interested in politics or having a greater sense that religion can and does make a positive difference to the nation.

But the other items in table 15.6 reveal sharp differences between evangelical and mainline Protestants. Whereas half of evangelical Protestants say they would like to see their denomination doing more to influence public policy in Washington, this figure is only a third among mainline Protestants (and the difference might be even greater were it not true that a sizable minority of evangelicals belong to churches that are unaffiliated or only weakly affiliated with denominations). Similarly, about six in ten evangelicals would like to see their denomination doing more to influence public policy in their state, compared with only about four in ten mainline Protestants. It is also revealing to observe how the two groups respond to questions about religious leaders engaging in highly visible or activist forms of political activity. Evangelicals are more likely than mainline Protestants to say they would like to see *more* of each of the following: religious leaders appearing on television talk shows, religious leaders running for public office, and religious leaders forming political movements (there is a small but insignificant difference in responses to religious leaders criticizing public officials). And, while it is true that both groups are divided about the desirability of religious leaders engaging in such activities, a

Table 15.6. The Level of Political Involvement among Evangelical and Mainline Protestants

	Evangelical Congregants (%)	Mainline Congregants (%)
Follow what's going on in government and public affairs most of the time	44	49
Think religious groups affect this country a lot or some	79	82
Think religious groups have a positive effect on the country	88	88
Would like to see their denomination doing more to influence public policy in Washington	48	33
Would like to see their denomination doing more to influence public policy in their state	58	43
Would like to see more of each in the next few years:		
Religious leaders appearing on television talk shows	50	38
Religious leaders criticizing our elected officials	26	24
Religious leaders running for public office	58	39
Religious leaders forming political movements	42	28
Would like to see the following have more influence in shaping public opinion on important social issues:		
Evangelical Christians	60	38
Mainline Protestants	57	52

NOTE: Based on the responses of members who attend services at least once a month.

majority of evangelicals support some of these activities, while only a minority of mainline Protestants favor such activities. Finally, the table shows how the two groups respond when asked if they would like to see evangelical Christians have more influence in shaping public opinion on important social issues and how they respond when asked the same question about mainline Protestants. A majority of evangelicals would like to see their own group have more influence, and a majority of mainline Protestants feel the same about their group. But more evangelicals want to see their group have influence, compared with the proportion of mainliners who want their group to have influence. Indeed, the percentage of evangelicals who want *mainline Protestants* to have more influence is higher than the percentage of mainliners who want mainline Protestants to have more influence.

These questions tap into some different ways in which religious groups may move beyond individual and congregational activities to play a larger role in the national arena. One is through denominational efforts at the national or state level. Another is for religious leaders to run for office or form political movements. A third is for evangelicals or mainliners in some collective but unspecified way to shape public opinion on social issues (this might include denominational activities or the work of individual leaders but also might be carried out through coalitions, faith-based nonprofits, and special advocacy organizations such as those that have been formed to address poverty, racism, and environmental concerns). It will be helpful to examine some of the factors that may explain why evangelicals tend to be more supportive of these efforts than mainline Protestants.[11]

The first possibility is that support for various forms of political influence may be rooted in demographic factors—that is, social characteristics that happen to be associated with membership in one religious group or another but are not intrinsic to the beliefs and practices of that group. The data suggest that four demographic characteristics play an important role in shaping the political styles of evangelical and mainline Protestants. One is level of education. The higher a person's level of education (e.g., if someone has graduated from college), the less likely that person is to support most of these ways of bringing the influence of religion to bear on public policy. This is true among both mainline and evangelical Protestants. But the fact that a third (34 percent) of active mainline Protestants have graduated from college, compared to only a fifth (20 percent) of active evangelical Protestants means that higher education dampens enthusiasm for these forms of religious influence among mainliners more than it does among evangelicals. The reasons why higher education has this effect cannot be determined directly from the data, but probably can be understood in terms of other research that shows higher levels of education to be associated with a greater sense of political efficacy: people with college degrees are more likely to feel that they are part of the system, that the system basically works for them, and that the best means of exercising influence may be the specialized knowledge of scientists, policymakers, and other experts, rather than religious organizations or religious leaders.

Gender is an important factor in the preferred political styles of mainline and evangelical Protestants as well, and its role is related to differences in higher education. In general, mainline and evangelical women are more supportive of religious groups exercising political influence in the ways we have been considering than men are; but the effects of gender are stronger and more consistent among mainline members than among evangelicals. Why might this be the case? Closer inspection of the data offers two clues: mainline men are the least likely of any group to support these forms of political influence (i.e., mainline women resemble evangelical men and evangelical women), and mainline men tend to be significantly better educated than any of the other groups. Thus, differences in political efficacy may again be part of the story. Mainline men have perhaps felt that they could exercise influence through other means, whereas evangelical men have felt less enfranchised; women in both traditions are relatively more active in their churches, more oriented toward spirituality in their personal lives, and apparently more likely to feel that religion is an appropriate vehicle for exercising political influence.

Age differences play at least some role in shaping the political styles of mainliners and evangelicals. Younger members are more likely than older ones to support these interventionist forms of political influence, and these effects are stronger in the mainline than among evangelicals. Moreover, mainliners are about four years older on average than evangelicals, so some of the quieter political style of mainliners can be attributed to the disproportionate number of older people in these churches. Why older people are reluctant to support more nationally visible forms of political activity by religious leaders is a matter for speculation, but one possibility may be that younger people have been reared in an era when political protest movements, big government, and cable news coverage have made them more aware of political activity on a national scale. Another possibility may be that older people, perhaps especially in mainline churches, are comfortable with the settled ways in which local churches have always exercised influence.

The other demographic factor that shapes the different political styles of mainliners and evangelicals is region. A majority of the members of evangelical denominations are located in the South, whereas mainline members are more evenly distributed throughout the United States. On most of the questions, southern evangelicals are significantly more likely than non-southern evangelicals to register support for active religious intervention in politics, whereas this is not the case in comparing southern and non-southern mainliners. The reason for this difference may be denominational (southern evangelicals are likely to be Southern Baptists), but it may also reflect the fact that evangelicals are the majority religion in the South and thus may feel that their religious leaders deserve to have more power than they presently do.

Religious factors also play a role in accounting for the differences in political style between mainline and evangelical Protestants. These factors do not include the sheer frequency with which the two groups attend religious services. Although evangelicals attend somewhat more often than mainliners, attendance either has no effect on people's answers to the questions about political influence or (taking account of other factors) is associated with somewhat *lower* chances of supporting these kinds of political influence. Nor do the data support the possibility that evangelicals somehow channel their personal political involvement through their churches to a greater extent than mainline members do and for this reason support a more active role for religious leaders in national politics. While different, the extent of personal political participation among mainline and evangelical Protestants is unrelated to their views on questions about wider forms of religious influence in public affairs.

What does seem to matter, at least in the case of evangelicals, is associating themselves with the label "evangelical" or identifying themselves as religious conservatives. The sociologist Christian Smith has argued that evangelicals have adopted a kind of oppositional identity to mainstream American culture, which gives them a sense of being special, of having certain rights that need to be protected, and of needing to be vocal about their views in American politics.[12] One might suppose that this label applies equally to all members of evangelical denominations, but this is not the case. Some members of denominations considered evangelical prefer labels other than evangelical, such as mainline or liberal, or labels stemming from distinctive traditions (such as Reformed or Wesleyan); similarly, some members of mainline churches think of themselves as fundamentalists or evangelicals, rather than as mainliners or liberals. Moreover, identifying oneself as a religious conservative may or may not be the same thing as identifying oneself as a fundamentalist or evangelical. Thus, it becomes possible to examine the effects of these various labels on people's attitudes toward religion in politics. Although the results are mixed, they show that identifying oneself as an evangelical (or fundamentalist) often heightens the odds of favoring interventionist forms of political activity; also, these effects are stronger or more consistent in evangelical denominations than in mainline denominations, and they are stronger or more consistent than the effects of simply identifying oneself as a religious conservative. In short, evangelicals seem to have developed a label that gives them a kind of religiopolitical identity and encourages them to support visible forms of political activism, whereas mainline members do not for the most part have a distinct identity of this kind.

Two other religious factors make a difference, and these are particularly worth considering because they (to a greater extent than most of the factors considered thus far) suggest ways in which denominations and congregations can actually affect how their members think about public influence. One of these is whether or not members are aware that their denomination has an office in the nation's capital. Relatively few members (only about one in five) know that their denomination does (as all mainline churches do) maintain such an office. And those who know are significantly more likely than other members to favor exercising certain kinds of political influence. They do not want religious leaders running for office or starting political movements, but they do want their denominations to have more influence in Washington and in their own state. And, because these differences are present with other factors taken into account, the most likely explanation is not that some people just happen to be more politically knowledgeable and interested (i.e., the statistics are already adjusted to account for the different political participation rates of respondents). Instead, at least some of the explanation must be that people realize their denomination cares about making a difference beyond the local level and is doing some things in Washington that actually are making a difference. The other factor is how much is happening within congregations themselves to encourage people to think about public issues. People who belong to these activist congregations, if they may be called that, are more likely to support other ways in which religious groups might influence politics than people in less active congregations.[13] Yet this effect is largely limited to evangelicals, rather than including mainline members. Evangelical congregations apparently are more likely than mainline congregations to make the connection between discussions of social issues at the local level and political influence in larger arenas.

POSSIBILITIES FOR THE FUTURE

These results suggest that several common perceptions of mainline members are wrong. One is that mainline members do not support their leaders or denominations taking a more active role in public affairs simply because they hold shallower or more relativistic convictions than evangelicals. That argument falters in face of the evidence that many of the differences in preferred political styles between mainline and evangelical Protestants reflect demographic differences in the composition of their memberships. Another misperception is that mainline members withhold support for greater public influence because they disagree with their denominations' official positions (e.g., regarding them as too heavily oriented toward progressive issues) or are too internally divided to speak with one voice. The data provide no evidence to support that argument.

The data suggest that some of the factors inhibiting members' interest in their denominations playing a larger role in public affairs are beyond the control of church leaders. For instance, mainline memberships are not likely to include higher proportions of people with *lower* levels of education anytime soon. If the number of mainline members who thought of themselves as evangelicals increased, that might strengthen support for greater religious involvement in public life, but it might also result in these members leaving the mainline and joining evangelical denominations. The fact that younger members are more supportive of more visible public involvement may be encouraging, but these members' enthusiasm for such involvement may diminish as they grow older.

Mainline leaders may be able to benefit from what these data suggest about Washington offices, however. Members who become familiar with the work of these offices (or even of their existence) may realize that they promote some of the issues about which members are concerned (such as racial justice or legislation to protect the environment). This realization may in turn encourage them to think that their denomination should have greater influence in Washington (and elsewhere) than it presently does. Rather than thinking abstractly about influence that may seem like an ineffective expenditure of energy or even an infringement of the separation of church and state, they may discover ways to benefit from and support their Washington offices.

Raising members' awareness of their Washington offices would clearly take more of an investment on the part of denominational leaders than has been made in recent years. But this reluctance to support the Washington offices more visibly may diminish if leaders recognize that members are not opposed to the issues these offices have been charged with promoting. Greater visibility would probably heighten support rather than diminish it.

Denominational officials, clergy, and lay leaders should also ponder the implications of these data for discussions of social issues in congregations. In evangelical churches these discussions seem to encourage members to favor all kinds of wider influence in public life, ranging from denominational work in Washington to religious leaders running for public office. In mainline churches discussions of social issues seem not to result in that connection. But this is surprising. Local discussions could easily refer to what the denomination is doing at the national or regional level. To be sure, these discussions may not be inspired, as they are in some evangelical churches, by religious leaders having appeared on talk shows or having founded social movements. Yet local leaders could do more to link these discussions with activities being promoted on a larger scale by the denomination.

These are practical steps that church leaders can take if they want to develop a higher profile in public affairs. But is this desirable? After all, a majority of mainline members do not want their denominations to have a stronger voice in Washington and are uneasy with the talk show appearances, office seeking, and social movements that have become associated in recent years with fundamentalist and evangelical leaders. Many members prefer to work more quietly at the local level, especially by doing volunteer work in their communities, attending lectures about social issues, taking part in campaign politics, and supporting such congregational activities as soup kitchens and day care centers.

This quieter influence works reasonably well. Mainline members do not draw high walls between themselves and the rest of society, preferring instead to participate fully in the workplace, in higher education, in discussions of scientific and technological developments, and in the activities of community organizations. Because they occupy relatively privileged places in their communities, mainline members can be politically and socially efficacious in these ways, rather than having to support distinctly religious movements in order to be heard.

The problem is that full participation in the wider society also exposes people to cultural messages that instill complacency—messages about material success, comfortable lifestyles, and self-interest. Yet many of the issues in which mainline members (and a majority of all Americans) claim to be interested run counter to these messages: overcoming racism and intolerance, helping the poor, protecting the environment, and working for peace and justice. These issues are not likely to be pursued actively and aggressively unless mainline members and their leaders develop a clear oppositional stance toward certain aspects of the wider culture. A stance of this kind is likely to be encouraged by a growing appreciation of the church's own gospel message.

NOTES

1. The Religion and Politics Survey was conducted by SRBI Associates for Princeton University between January 6 and March 31, 2000. A total of 5,603 adults age eighteen or over who reside in the forty-eight continental states were interviewed by telephone. The survey has a statistical margin of error of plus or

minus 1.42 percentage points at the 95 percent confidence level. Households were selected randomly through a random-digit dialing procedure (RDD) that excludes nonresidential numbers, and individuals within households were selected through a randomizing procedure. Minor statistical weighting was used to ensure that the samples reflect national demographic patterns.

2. Andrew Kohut, *Religion and Politics Survey, 1996* (Washington, DC: Pew Center for the People and the Press, 1996).

3. George Gallup Jr. and D. Michael Lindsay, *Surveying the Religious Landscape: Trends in U.S. Beliefs* (Harrisburg, PA: Morehouse, 1999).

4. Half of the respondents were asked if they would like "religious groups" to take a more or less active role; the other half were asked, "Think now about mainline Protestant denominations, such as Presbyterians, Methodists and Lutherans, would you like these religious groups to take a more active role or a less active role?"

5. Robert Wuthnow, *Loose Connections: Joining Together in America's Fragmented Communities* (Cambridge, MA: Harvard University Press, 1998), chap. 7.

6. See chapters 4 and 5 in this volume.

7. Brian Steensland, Jerry Z. Park, Mark D. Regnerus, Lynn D. Robinson, W. Bradford Wilcox, and Robert D. Woodberry, "The Measure of American Religion: Toward Improving the State-of-the-Art," *Social Forces* 79 (2000): 291–318. The largest number of mainline Protestants are members of the six denominations on which the present volume focuses: United Methodist, Evangelical Lutheran Church in America, Presbyterian Church (USA), Episcopal Church, United Church of Christ, and American Baptist Churches in the USA; the largest numbers of evangelical Protestants are Southern Baptists, independent Baptists, nondenominational, Pentecostal, Assemblies of God, Lutheran Church Missouri Synod, Church of Christ, and Presbyterian Church in America; and among black Protestants, the largest groups are African Methodist Episcopal, African Methodist Episcopal Zion, National Baptist Church, National Progressive Baptist Church, and Churches of God in Christ.

8. Forty-seven percent of mainline members reported having heard discussions of poverty, environment, race, or corporate responsibility in the past year; this figure fell to 37 percent among members of congregations with fewer than one hundred members and rose to 60 percent among members of congregations with more than a thousand members; it rose to 65 percent in congregations with a homeless shelter and fell to 30 percent in congregations without a shelter; in congregations that had all six of the social ministries listed in the top half of Table 15.4, the figure rose to 95 percent; it fell to 2 percent in congregations that had none of these six social ministries.

9. Robert Wuthnow, *God and Mammon in America* (New York: Free Press, 1994).

10. Robert Wuthnow, "Mobilizing Civic Engagement: The Changing Impact of Religious Involvement," in *Civic Engagement in American Democracy*, ed. Theda Skocpol and Morris P. Fiorina (Washington, DC, and New York: Brookings Institution Press and Russell Sage Foundation, 1999), 331–68.

11. The results summarized here are from logistic regression equations.

12. Christian Smith, *American Evangelicalism: Embattled and Thriving* (Chicago: University of Chicago Press, 1998).

13. Activist congregations are defined as ones in which members have heard a sermon, lecture, or group discussion during the past year about government pol-

icies toward the poor, protecting the environment, being more supportive of homosexuals, the widening gap between rich and poor, improving black-white relations, or the social responsibilities of corporations; as noted earlier, these discussions also seem to occur more often in congregations that have social ministries than in congregations that do not.

Contributors

NANCY T. AMMERMAN is professor of sociology of religion at Hartford Seminary, where she has been since 1995, after eleven years on the faculty of Emory University. She is co-principal investigator on the Organizing Religious Work project that is examining the emerging forms of connection and cooperation that allow congregations, denominations, and other organizations to do their work. Her 1990 book, *Baptist Battles: Social Change and Religious Conflict in the Southern Baptist Convention*, won the Distinguished Book Award from the Society for the Scientific Study of Religion. She is also the author of *Congregation and Community* and *Bible Believers: Fundamentalists in the Modern World*.

CLEM BROOKS is associate professor of sociology at Indiana University, Bloomington. His research investigates electoral politics, public opinion, and the interrelationship of stratification and voter alignments. He has done research on political change, policy preferences, and U.S. social cleavages, and he is currently working on studies of partisanship and public attitudes toward family change. With Catherine Bolzendahl he is investigating sources of change in gender attitudes since the 1960s, and with Jeff Manza he is continuing collaborative work on the social bases of political inequality and policy preferences in the United States.

WENDY CADGE is a Ph.D. candidate in sociology at Princeton University. Her research about mainline Protestant denominations and homosexuality has focused both on policy debates from 1970 to the present and on the growth and development of "welcoming congregation" programs. In addition to the present chapter, she has published a paper with Laura R. Olson entitled, "Talking About Homosexuality: The Views of Mainline Protestant Clergy" in the *Journal for the Scientific Study of Religion*. She is currently working on a dissertation about Theravada Buddhism in America.

MARK CHAVES is professor of sociology at the University of Arizona. Much of his work spans the boundary between the sociology of religion and the sociology of organizations. Currently, he is principal investigator for the National Congregations Study, a survey of a nationally representative sample of religious congregations. Recent publications include "Religious Congregations and Welfare Reform: Who Will Take Advantage of 'Charitable Choice'?" (*American Sociological Review* 64 [December 1999]: 836–46) and, with Philip S. Gorski, "Religious Pluralism and Religious Participation" (*Annual Review of Sociology* 27 [2001]: 261–81).

DEREK H. DAVIS (B.A., M.A., J.D., Baylor University; Ph.D., University of Texas at Dallas) is director of the J. M. Dawson Institute of Church-State Studies, Baylor University, and editor of the award-winning *Journal of Church and State*. He is the author of *Original Intent: Chief Justice Rehnquist and the Course of American Church-State Relations* (1991); *Religion and the Continental Congress, 1774–1789: Contributions to Original Intent* (2000); and editor or coeditor of eleven other books, including the *Legal Deskbook for Administrators of Independent Colleges and Universities* and *The Role of Religion in the Making of Public Policy*. He serves numerous organizations given to the protection of religious freedom in international contexts, and is a frequent speaker on church-state relations, religious freedom, human rights, and the role of religion in society.

JOHN H. EVANS is assistant professor of sociology at the University of California, San Diego. He is the author of *Playing God? Human Genetic Engineering and the Rationalization of Public Bioethical Debate* (2002). In addition to his work on public debates and religion, he has also published a number of articles on attitude polarization. His most recent in this series is "Polarization in Abortion Attitudes in U.S. Religious Traditions, 1972–1998," forthcoming in *Sociological Forum*.

KELLY GORAN FULTON is a doctoral candidate in sociology at the University of Texas at Austin. Her interests include religion, family, and education.

HELEN M. GIESEL is a graduate student in sociology at the University of Arizona. Her interests include the sociology of religion, education, and culture. She is currently working on a master's thesis focusing on the world's dog breeds and their social origins.

R. MARIE GRIFFITH is the associate director of the Center for the Study of Religion at Princeton University, where she also teaches in the Department of Religion. A historian of American religion, she is the author of *God's Daughters: Evangelical Women and the Power of Submission* (1997) and numerous articles about gender and American religion. She is now working on a project about bodily disciplines in twentieth-century American Christianity. Additionally, she is directing a project on Women and Religion in the African Diaspora, funded by the Ford Foundation.

LESTER KURTZ is professor of sociology and Asian studies at the University of Texas at Austin and past chair of the Peace Studies Association and the Peace and War section of the American Sociological Association. He has written books and articles on the sociology of religion, peace and conflict, and social change, including *The Web of Violence* (edited with Jennifer Turpin; 1997); *Nonviolent Social Movements* (edited with Stephen Zunes and Sarah Asher; 1999); *The Nuclear Cage* (1988); *Third World Peace Perspectives* (edited with Shu-Ju Ada Cheng, a special issue of *Peace Review*) and *The Politics of Heresy* (1986). He is currently writing a book called *Fighting with Gandhi: The Paradox of India's Nonviolence.*

JEFF MANZA is associate professor of sociology and faculty fellow at the Institute for Policy Research at Northwestern University. He is a political sociologist who has done work on social cleavages (including religion) and postwar voting behavior in the United States, and is the coauthor (with Clem Brooks) of *Social Cleavages and Political Change: Voter Alignments and U.S. Party Coalitions* (1999). He is currently working (with Christopher Uggen) on a study of the political consequences of felon disfranchisement in the United States and is doing further research (with Clem Brooks) on the social bases of political inequality and policy preferences in the United States.

MICHAEL MOODY is assistant professor of sociology at Boston University. His recent work focuses on how nonprofit groups advocate their interests and visions of the public good, and what this reveals about political culture and pragmatic advocacy as an essential practice in civil society. He is working on a book about groups promoting competing solutions to water disputes in California. He has also written about charitable giving and the philanthropic tradition, the theory of reciprocity, the cultural meanings of success, public spaces in American suburbs, and the history of community service.

LAURA R. OLSON is associate professor of political science at Clemson University. She is formerly a visiting research fellow at Princeton University's Center for the Study of Religion. She is the author, coauthor, or editor of four books on religion in American politics, including *Filled with Spirit and Power: Protestant Clergy in Politics* (2000) and *Christian Clergy in American Politics* (2001), as well as several articles and book chapters. From 1999 to 2001, she served as chair of the American Political Science Association's section on religion and politics.

LYNN D. ROBINSON is a graduate student in the Department of Sociology at Princeton University.

BRIAN STEENSLAND is assistant professor of sociology at Indiana University, Bloomington. He received his Ph.D. from Princeton University, where he wrote a dissertation on the rise and fall of guaranteed income strategies to reform the American welfare system in the 1960s and 1970s. Together with Paul DiMaggio he is working on a project that examines cultural conflict in the United States during the 1980s and 1990s. His interests include politics, culture, and religion, particularly in relation to how societies struggle to define their collective values.

PETER J. THUESEN is assistant professor of the history of Christianity and American religious history in the Department of Comparative Religion at Tufts University. He is the author of *In Discordance with the Scriptures: American Protestant Battles over Translating the Bible* (1999).

WILLIAM TSITSOS is a graduate student in sociology at the University of Arizona. His interests are in the areas of religion and culture.

BRADFORD VERTER is visiting assistant professor of Religion and Culture at Williams College.

W. BRADFORD WILCOX's academic research focuses on religion and the family. A nonresidential fellow at the Center for Advanced Study of Religion at Yale University in 2001–2002, Wilcox will join the faculty of the Department of Sociology at the University of Virginia in 2002. He has published in a range of academic and popular journals, including the *American Sociological Review* and the *Responsive Community*.

ROBERT WUTHNOW is the Gerhard R. Andlinger professor of sociology and director of the Center for the Study of Religion at Princeton University. The author of numerous books and articles on American religion and culture, his publications include *The Restructuring of American Religion: Society and Faith Since World War II* (1988); *After Heaven: Spirituality in America since the 1950s* (1998); and *Creative Spirituality: The Way of the Artist* (2001). Besides directing the Public Role of Mainline Protestantism Project, he is engaged in research on religious formation and the arts.

Index

Abington School District v. Schempp, 328

abortion, 1, 288, 306, 310, 334–36; biblical interpretation, 46; mainline vs. conservative stances on, 17, 168, 169, 171; pro-choice and pro-life constituencies, 21; *Roe v. Wade*, 1, 334

Act for Better Childcare bill, 91

Act for Regulating Abuses and Correcting Disorders in Ecclesiastical Affairs (1742), 31

Adam, Karl, 43

affirmative action programs, 46, 184, 189, 191, 194, 195, 208n7, 381

African American churches, 17, 20, 130; burning and reconstruction of church buildings, 196; leaders' views of racial justice issues, 200–202; public activities of, 390, 391, 392; and outside organizations, involvement with, 133, 138, 139–40, 142, 145, 152, 154, 157n12

African American Male Project, 195

African Americans, 174, 191; Black Manifesto, 185, 187, 190; Black Panthers, 189; Black power, 187; civil rights, 167, 168, 169, 170; clergy, 192; demands for racial justice, 200; as heads of racial justice boards, 186–87; as mainline church leaders, 197, 198; National Committee of Negro Churchmen, 187;

paternalism toward, 183–84, 188, 192, 197, 205; poverty rates among, 220; racism and, 182–83, 203–4; voting trends until 1896, 161

African National Congress, 351

Age of Reason (Paine), 33

Aid to Families with Dependent Children, 215, 220, 223

Alcoholics Anonymous (AA), 142, 143, 146

Alinsky, Saul, 345, 346

Allport, Gordon, 201

American Anti-Slavery Society, 37

American Baptist Churches, 32, 37, 163, 189; abortion controversy and, 335; Asian, Black, and Hispanic ministries, 190; Board of National Ministries, 189, 190, 239; Division of Missions, 190; ethnic caucuses, 190; First Amendment issues and, 320, 322, 323, 325–26; General Board Executive Committee (GBEC), 190; homosexuality and homosexuals, stance on, 269, 271, 272, 282; investment practices of, 348; Baptist Joint Committee on Public Affairs (BJC), 320–21, 330–32, 334; membership, 4, 5, 6; National Ministries Program on Eco-Justice, 241, 245; Office of Government Relations, 62; and poverty, approaches to, 229; protest of U.S. policy in Central America, 368

education *(continued)*
13, 396, 397; parochial schools,
120, 330–32; religious freedom
and, 317–48; school voucher system, 318, 330–32; support for religious influence on public policy
and, 396; *Zobrest v. Catalina Foothills School District*, 331. *See also*
children; religious education; school
voucher system
Edwards, Chet, 329
Edwards, Jonathan, 30–31, 34, 43
Eisenhower, Dwight D., 159
El Salvador, 366, 368
Emerson, Michael O., 204
Employment Non-Discrimination
Act, 274
employment practices, 345, 350, 356–
57
Endangered Species Act, 238, 248,
249–50, 252, 254, 260
Energy and Water Development Appropriation Act, 325
Engel v. Vitale, 320, 328
Enlightenment period, 27, 30, 33
environmental advocacy, 17, 21, 196,
237–64, 373; awareness of, raising, 254–57; by evangelicals, 249;
churches' moral authority and, 253;
Earth Day, 239, 244; faith-based organizations for, 238, 244, 246, 254;
interfaith cooperation for, 257–58;
Judeo-Christian attitudes toward,
237–38, 258–59, 262n3; Kyoto Protocol, 250; and mainline Protestant
efforts, impact of, 252–60; public
interest in, 383, 384; as a religious
issue, 259–60. *See also* eco-justice;
socially responsible investment
environmental hazards, 241, 242, 373;
Exxon Valdez oil spill, 244; global
warming, 250, 254, 259; greenhouse gases, 250; Love Canal, 241,
243
environmental networks, 251
Environmental Protection Agency
(EPA), 251

environmental racism. *See* eco-
justice
Episcopal Church (ECUSA), 188, 191–
92, 194, 197; abortion controversy
and, 335; African American leadership, 191–92; Committee on the
Status of Women in the Episcopal
Church, 93; debt relief activism,
374; and El Salvador, involvement
in, 369; Environmental Stewardship Team, 244; family issues, 295,
297, 305, 307, 311; financial resources, 14, 23nn16,18; First
Amendment issues and, 322, 335;
homosexuality and homosexuals,
views on, 268–74, 276, 282; Jubilee
Ministries for Justice, Peace, and
the Integrity of Creation, 245;
membership, 4, 5, 6; Office of Gov-
ernment Relations, 62; shareholder
activism, 346–47, 372; Standing
Committee on Lay Ministry, 84–85;
Task Force on Energy and Environ-
ment, 242; United Thank Offering
Committee, 84; Urban Caucus, 192.
See also Anglicans
Episcopal Church Women (ECW), 80–
81, 83–85, 87, 92–93, 100, 103
*Episcopalian General Convention
Journal*, 296–97
Episcopalians, 74, 161, 163. *See also*
Episcopal Church (ECUSA)
Episcopal Society for Cultural and
Racial Unity (ESCRU), 186, 188
Episcopal Urban Caucus, 192
Equal Access Act (1984), 318, 332–34
Equal Employment Opportunity, 190,
194
Equal Rights Amendment, 83
ethnic groups. *See names of specific
ethnicities*
ethnicity: of mainline Protestants, 11,
12; race vs., 199–200
Evangelical Alliance, 35
Evangelical Environmental Network,
247, 249
evangelicalism, 31–33, 36

Compositor: Binghamton Valley Composition, LLC
Text: 10/13 Aldus
Display: Aldus
Printer and Binder: Haddon Craftsmen
Indexer: Beaver Wood Associates